Knowledge Networks:
Innovation Through
Communities of Practice

Paul M. Hildreth, K-Now International, United Kingdom

Chris Kimble, University of York, United Kingdom

IDEA GROUP PUBLISHING
Hershey • London • Melbourne • Singapore

Acquisitions Editor: Mehdi Khosrow-Pour
Senior Managing Editor: Jan Travers
Managing Editor: Amanda Appicello
Development Editor: Michele Rossi
Copy Editor: Ingrid Widitz
Typesetter: Sara Reed
Cover Design: Lisa Tosheff
Printed at: Yurchak Printing Inc.

Published in the United States of America by
        Idea Group Publishing (an imprint of Idea Group Inc.)
        701 E. Chocolate Avenue, Suite 200
        Hershey PA 17033
        Tel: 717-533-8845
        Fax: 717-533-8661
        E-mail: cust@idea-group.com
        Web site: http://www.idea-group.com

and in the United Kingdom by
        Idea Group Publishing (an imprint of Idea Group Inc.)
        3 Henrietta Street
        Covent Garden
        London WC2E 8LU
        Tel: 44 20 7240 0856
        Fax: 44 20 7379 3313
        Web site: http://www.eurospan.co.uk

Library of Congress Cataloging-in-Publication Data

Knowledge networks : innovation through communities of practice / Paul
Hildreth, editor, Chris Kimble, editor.
        p. cm.
 ISBN 1-59140-200-X (hardcover) — ISBN 1-59140-270-0 (softcover) —
ISBN 1-59140-201-8 (ebook)
 1. Knowledge management. 2. Organizational learning. I. Hildreth,
Paul M., 1959- II. Kimble, Chris.
  HD30.2.K6654 2004
  658.4'038—dc22
                                                    2003022608

British Cataloguing in Publication Data
A Cataloguing in Publication record for this book is available from the British Library.

Knowledge Networks:
Innovation Through Communities of Practice

Table of Contents

Preface viii

SECTION I: COMMUNITIES OF PRACTICE

Chapter I
Understanding the Benefits and Impact of Communities of Practice 1
Michael A. Fontaine, IBM Institute for Business Value, USA
David R. Millen, IBM Research Collaborative User Experience
Group, USA

Chapter II
Overcoming Knowledge Barriers with Communities of Practice:
Lessons Learned Through Practical Experience 14
Eric L. Lesser, IBM Institute for Business Value, USA
Michael A. Fontaine, IBM Institute for Business Value, USA

Chapter III
Cultivating a Community of Practice Between Business and IT 24
Valerie A. Martin, Brunel University, United Kingdom
Tally Hatzakis, Brunel University, United Kingdom
Mark Lycett, Brunel University, United Kingdom

Chapter IV
The Paradox of Communities of Practice: Knowledge Sharing
Between Communities 36
 Donald Hislop, University of Sheffield, United Kingdom

  SECTION II: COMMUNITIES OF PRACTICE AND KNOWLEDGE MANAGEMENT

Chapter V
Investigating the Influence that Media Richness has on Learning in
a Community of Practice: A Case Study at Øresund Bridge.................47
 Andrew Schenkel, Stockholm School of Economics, Sweden

Chapter VI
CoPs for Cops: Managing and Creating Knowledge through
Networked Expertise...58
 Maarten de Laat, University of Nijmegen and Utrecht University,
  The Netherlands
 Wim Broer, Police Education and Knowledge Centre,
  The Netherlands

Chapter VII
Communities of Practice in the Royal National Lifeboat Institution 70
 Roger Kolbotn, Directorate for Civil Protection and Emergency
  Planning, Norway

Chapter VIII
Innoversity in Communities of Practice...79
 Susanne Justesen, Innoversity Network, Denmark

Chapter IX
User Networks as Sources of Innovation 96
 Anders Lundkvist, Stockholm University School of Business,
  Sweden

Chapter X
Building Customer Communities of Practice for Business Value:
Success Factors Profiled from Saba Software and Other Case
Studies 106
 Brook Manville, Saba Software, USA

SECTION III: COMMUNITY OF PRACTICE DEVELOPMENT

Chapter XI
Creating a Multi-Company Community of Practice for Chief Information Officers 125
John Moran, Global Gateways, Inc., USA
Lee Weimer, Weimer Collaborative, USA

Chapter XII
Viable Communities within Organizational Contexts: Creating and Sustaining Viability in Communities of Practice at Siemens AG 133
Benjamin Frost, Siemens AG, Germany
Stefan Schoen, Siemens AG, Germany

Chapter XIII
Best Practices: Developing Communities that Provide Business Value 142
Wesley C. Vestal, American Productivity & Quality Center, USA
Kimberly Lopez, American Productivity & Quality Center, USA

Chapter XIV
Building Sustainable Communities of Practice 150
Bronwyn Stuckey, The University of Wollongong, Australia
John D. Smith, Learning Alliances, USA

Chapter XV
How Information Technologies Can Help Build and Sustain an Organization's CoP: Spanning the Socio-Technical Divide? 165
Laurence Lock Lee, Computer Sciences Corporation, Australia
Mark Neff, Computer Sciences Corporation, USA

Chapter XVI
Building a Community of Practice: Technological and Social Implications for a Distributed Team 184
Pete Bradshaw, Anglia Polytechnic University, United Kingdom
Stephen Powell, Anglia Polytechnic University, United Kingdom
Ian Terrell, Anglia Polytechnic University, United Kingdom

Chapter XVII
Facilitator Toolkit for Building and Sustaining Virtual Communities
of Practice 202
    Lisa Kimball, Group Jazz, USA
    Amy Ladd, Group Jazz, USA

Chapter XVIII
The Use of Intranets: The Missing Link Between Communities of
Practice and Networks of Practice? 216
    Emmanuelle Vaast, Long Island University, USA

SECTION IV: MOVING CoPs FORWARD

Chapter XIX
Extending Richness with Reach: Participation and Knowledge
Exchange in Electronic Networks of Practice 230
    Robin Teigland, Stockholm School of Economics, Sweden
    Molly McLure Wasko, Florida State University, USA

Chapter XX
Trusting the Knowledge of Large Online Communities: Strategies
for Leading from Behind 243
    John S. Storck, Boston University School of Management, USA
    Lauren E. Storck, Boston University, USA

Chapter XXI
Double Agents: Visible and Invisible Work in an Online Community
of Practice 256
    Elisabeth Davenport, Napier University, United Kingdom

Chapter XXII
Cultivating a Public Sector Knowledge Management Community of
Practice 267
    Shawn Callahan, IBM Cynefin Centre for Organizational
       Complexity, Australia

Chapter XXIII
Click Connect and Coalesce for NGOs: Exploring the Intersection
Between Online Networks, CoPs, and Events 282
    Nancy White, Full Circle Associates, USA

Chapter XXIV
Where Did That Community Go? Communities of Practice That
"Disappear" 295
    Patricia Gongla, IBM Global Services, USA
    Christine R. Rizzuto, NY Software Industry Association and
        Project Management Institute, USA

Glossary 308

About the Editors 315

About the Authors 317

Index 328

Preface

Communities of Practice are currently attracting much interest among academics, consultants and in commercial organisations. Academic researchers are undertaking research into how CoPs can be supported, the relationships within them and how this can help support the generation of new knowledge. Similarly, consultants in the field are developing tools and techniques for supporting, coaching and facilitating CoPs, advising organisations as to how they can identify and nurture CoPs and seeking to demonstrate how organisations can benefit from them.

Meanwhile, outside the Universities and Consultancies, Communities and Networks of Practice continue to grow and spread: both online through e-mail, bulletin boards and newsgroups and offline through meetings, lunches and workshops.

The network of relationships that develop in a CoP, the inner motivation that drives them and the knowledge they produce, lead to the creation of an environment that is rich in creativity and innovation. CoPs can help in finding and sharing best practices and serve as engines for the development of social capital. Many organisations now regard CoPs as a vital component in their KM strategy. We hope that this book will help the reader to unlock the secrets of CoPs in his or her own organisation.

There have been a large number of academic papers about Communities of Practice but, so far, only a few books. Most of the books have, by necessity, taken a rather theoretical approach. This book, however, will examine CoPs from a practical viewpoint; it is directed at the general reader rather than a specialist audience. Our aim is to draw on the experience of people who have researched and worked with CoPs in the real world and to present their views in a form that is accessible to a broad audience.

In this book you will find a blend of the best of current academic research in the field of Communities of Practice, observations from groundbreaking consultancy in the field of Knowledge Management and the accumulated wisdom of practitioners working at the cutting edge of Knowledge Networks. It is presented in a series of chapters, each of which seeks to offer pertinent and practical guidance for those involved with building or managing knowledge networks in their day to day work.

OVERVIEW

The current environment for organisations is one that is characterised by uncertainty and continuous change. This rapid and dynamic pace of change is forcing organisations that were accustomed to structure and routine to become ones that must improvise solutions quickly and correctly. To respond to this changed environment, organisations are moving away from the structures of the past that are based on hierarchies, discrete groups and teams and moving towards those based on more fluid and emergent organisational forms such as networks and communities. In addition to the pace of change, globalisation is another pressure that is brought to bear on modern organisations. Although some argue that the increased internationalisation should bring about an increased need for knowledge sharing (Kimble, Li & Barlow, 2000), many organisations have responded to this development by restructuring through outsourcing and downsizing, which paradoxically can result in a loss of knowledge as staff leave the organisation.

In the mid-1990s, a new approach called Knowledge Management (KM) began to emerge (Ponzi & Koenig, 2002). KM was seen as a new and innovative solution to many of these problems; however, in practice, much of what was called Knowledge Management was often little more than Information Management re-badged and simply dealt with structured data using a capture, codify and store approach (Wilson, 2002). More recently, there has been recognition of the importance of more subtle, softer types of knowledge that need to be shared. This raises the question as to how this sort of knowledge might be 'managed'. A certain type of community, the Community of Practice (CoP), has been identified as being a group where such types of knowledge are nurtured, shared and sustained (Hildreth & Kimble, 2002).

COMMUNITIES OF PRACTICE: A HISTORICAL VIEW

Communities of Practice (CoPs) as a phenomenon have been around for many years but the term itself was not coined until 1991 when Jean Lave and Etienne Wenger used it in their exploration of Situated Learning (Lave & Wenger,

1991). Situated learning is learning that takes place through working practices; for example, an apprenticeship where an employee learns skills 'on the job'. The five examples that Lave and Wenger looked at in their book were Vai and Goa tailors, meat cutters, non-drinking alcoholics, Yucatan midwives and US Navy quartermasters. However, although all their examples were based around an apprenticeship model, they emphasised that CoPs are not restricted to apprenticeships.

Lave and Wenger (1991) saw the acquisition of knowledge as a social process where people can participate in communal learning at different levels depending on their level of authority or seniority in the group, i.e., whether they are a newcomer to the group or have been a member for a long time. Central to their notion of a CoP as a means of acquiring knowledge is the process by which a newcomer learns from the group; they term this process Legitimate Peripheral Participation (LPP).

LPP is both complex and composite and although Lave and Wenger saw LPP as an inseparable whole, it is helpful to consider the three aspects—legitimation, peripherality and participation—separately. Legitimation refers to the power and the authority relations in the community. Peripherality refers to the individual's social rather than physical peripherality in relation to the community. This in turn is dependent on their history of participation in the group and the expectation of their future participation in and interaction with the community.

Thus, a new member of the community moves from peripheral to full participation in the community. Initially their activities may be restricted to simply gathering domain knowledge. Later the newcomer may become involved with gaining knowledge associated with the specific work practices of the community; for example, in the case of tailors, it might be cutting basic shapes out of cloth. Gradually, as the newcomer learns, the tasks will become more complicated and the newcomer becomes an old-timer and is recognised as a source of authority by its members.

COMMUNITIES OF PRACTICE TODAY

Lave and Wenger's (1991) CoPs attracted a lot of attention and gradually other researchers and practitioners extended the notion of a CoP and applied it in a Knowledge Management (KM) context in commercial settings. Since then much work has been undertaken to observe CoPs, how they work and what sort of defining characteristics there are. Many definitions have been put forward—indeed, in this book you will find a number of definitions in the chapters.

In this Introduction, we do not intend to try to create a single definition that will cover the whole book. Rather we prefer to note some of the characteristics that might be found in a CoP:

What Is It About?

This represents the particular area around which the CoP has organised itself. It is a joint enterprise in as much as it is understood and continually renegotiated by its members (Wenger, 1998).

How Does It Function?

People become members of a CoP through shared practices; they are linked to each other through their involvement in certain common activities. It is mutual engagement that binds members of a CoP together as a social entity (Wenger, 1998).

What Has It Produced?

The members of a CoP build up an agreed set of communal resources over time. This "shared repertoire" of resources represents the material traces of the community. Written files can constitute a more explicit aspect of this common repository, although more intangible aspects such as procedures, policies, rituals and specific idioms may also be included (Wenger, 1998).

Common Ground

The term Common Ground is taken from the work of Clark and Brennan (1991). For communication to take place, certain information must be shared; this information is called common ground. Similarly, for a CoP to function the members need to be sympathetic to the ideas around which the group is based and will probably have a common background or share common a common interest.

Common Purpose/Motivation

The CoP members will have some sort of common goal or common purpose and it is often the case that the CoP is internally motivated, i.e., driven by the members themselves as opposed to some external driver.

Evolution

There is often some sort of evolution in a CoP. It may be that the CoP has developed because of a common interest of a group of people. On the other hand, it may be that the CoP was a formally constituted group that has evolved into a CoP because of the relationships that have developed amongst the members.

Relationships

This is a key part of a CoP and is what makes it possible for a team to become a CoP—as the informal relationships develop, the source of legitimation in the group shifts in emphasis. These relationships are key to the issues of trust and identity in a CoP.

Narration

Narration (story telling) is very useful in both knowledge sharing and knowledge generation. In Lave and Wenger (1991), stories featured heavily. In particular, a central part of the journey undertaken by the non-drinking alcoholics involved the telling of the story. The quality of the story became the mark of an old timer and therefore the source of the legitimation in the community.

Formal or Informal?

In many cases, a CoP is not a formally constituted group and membership is entirely voluntary. In some cases, the organisation might not even be aware of its existence. In Lave and Wenger (1991), legitimacy was gained by being accepted and gaining informal authority through consensus within the group. This notion often sits uncomfortably with the more formal view of a CoP where simple domain knowledge or rank due to organisational hierarchy is seen as a source of authority.

BEYOND COPS

CoPs are now attracting an immense amount of interest. The growing internationalisation of business means that many organisations now work in a geographically and temporally distributed international environment. This raises the question: Can CoPs continue to operate in such an environment (Kimble, Hildreth & Wright, 2000)? Can a CoP be virtual? For example, can stories be exchanged over the Internet? Similarly, how might LPP translate to a geographically distributed environment when LPP is situated, as some of the knowledge is created during problem solving? If co-location is necessary simply because members need to share resources then it should be easy. However, if the learning is situated because the face-to-face meetings are essential then "going virtual" will have more impact.

As the debate about the nature of "virtual" CoPs got under way, the rapid diffusion of Internet-based networking technologies was accelerating the development of new forms of community. The Internet and Intranets provide a single convenient and flexible platform to support groups and networks of groups within larger communities. Because the underlying Internet standards are open and public, organisations can seamlessly connect their Intranet with those of clients and partners. However, while the pervasiveness of Internet technologies has enabled the creation of networked communities, they have also made it increasingly difficult for people to know the scope and range of their "virtual" social networks.

In exploring these wider networks, Brown and Duguid (2000) examine the role of documents—from newspapers to mailing lists—and their ability to generate a common language or practice.

"The 25,000 reps at Xerox theoretically make up, in theory such a network. They could in principle by linked through such things as ... 'an advice database or corporate newsletters aimed at reps.' Their common practice makes these links viable, allowing them to assimilate these communications in more less similar ways" *(Brown and Duguid, 2000).*

The strength of the Network of Practice (NoP) model is that these networks can extend beyond the organisation where the individual is situated. Brown and Duguid (2000) propose that the network of reps could be extended to include technicians in other companies, though they suggest that these links may be weaker, with less ground for common understanding. These links reflect the flow of knowledge that exists through the surrounding knowledge ecology (Brown & Duguid, 2000).

Wenger (1998) proposes a view of the organisation not as a single social community but as a constellation of interrelated CoPs. This reflects how membership of CoPs overlaps with each other within organisations and allows the transfer of knowledge and the facilitation of learning through a social link. This combines the strength of Brown and Duguid's Networks of Practice (NoPs) as a model for fast knowledge diffusion and assimilation over a wide network and the CoP model for the creation of new knowledge and meaning. The CoP model also provides a home for the identities of the members through the engagement in the combination of new types of knowledge and the maintenance of a stored body of collective knowledge.

ORGANISATION OF THE BOOK

This book is organised into four sections and contains 24 individual chapters. A brief description of each section and each chapter follows.

Section I: Communities of Practice

This section consists of four chapters and forms an introductory section to the book that looks at the importance of CoPs from the perspective of business and commerce.

In Chapter 1, *Understanding the Benefits and Impact of Communities of Practice,* Michael A. Fontaine and David R. Millen write from a consultant's perspective. They argue that organisations provide CoPs with resources in order to improve the flow of knowledge within the organisation. However, as with any investment, managers are interested in the impact on the bottom line.

Michael and David present a cost benefits analysis based on the results of their work with thirteen CoPs. They argue that the greatest impact that communities have is on time use in knowledge work activities. The general focus of the chapter is on organisations in the private sector, and in particular, it highlights how managers can collect useful data through "serious anecdotes". The chapter concludes with a set of recommendations for assessing the benefits and impact of a CoP.

Chapter 2, *Overcoming Knowledge Barriers with Communities of Practice: Lessons Learned Through Practical Experience,* by Eric L. Lesser and Michael Fontaine looks at a specific benefit of CoPs: overcoming knowledge barriers. Its general focus is on organisations in the private sector and its specific focus is on KM. It considers communities and groups that are virtual and formal. From their work with knowledge-based organisations, the authors identify four main barriers that prevent two parties from coming together and sharing knowledge: awareness, access, application and perception. Based on their research and experience as consultants, they describe how CoPs can be an important vehicle for breaking through each of these barriers and enabling knowledge to flow more effectively within organisations. The chapter concludes with a set of guidelines for overcoming the barriers.

Continuing the theme of using CoPs to overcome barriers, Valerie A. Martin, Tally Hatzakis and Mark Lycett present Chapter 3, *Cultivating a Community of Practice Between Business and IT.* Writing from more of an academic perspective, this chapter describes the efforts that were made to bridge the perceived gap between the "IT" and the "Business" wings of a large financial services company through the establishment of a Relationship Management Community of Practice. Arguing against what they describe as the dominant, tool-driven, IT-based paradigm of Knowledge Management, the chapter illustrates how cultivating a Community of Practice can provide a holistic way of managing the dynamics of knowledge sharing across the different communities that exist within an organisation. The chapter concludes with some guidelines on cultivating a CoP through relationship management.

Following on from the previous chapter, Donald Hislop continues the theme of cross community relations in Chapter 4, *The Paradox of Communities of Practice: Knowledge Sharing Between Communities.* Donald explores knowledge sharing between, as opposed to within, communities. The general focus of the chapter is on organisations in the private sector and it considers communities and groups that are distributed, global and formal. This chapter is also written from an academic perspective and suggests that knowledge sharing between communities is likely to prove more complex than knowledge sharing within them. Three brief case studies are presented to illustrate the arguments made. Two main conclusions are drawn from the case studies. Firstly, inter-community knowledge sharing requires social relationship and trust between the communities. Secondly, organisations need to balance their efforts at building CoPs with supporting inter-community interactions.

Section II: Communities of Practice and Knowledge Management

The chapters in Section 2 illustrate the importance of CoPs in the field of Knowledge Management (KM). The chapters in this section fall into two broad categories. Chapters 5, 6 and 7 look at the role that CoPs play in learning in organisations and Chapters 8, 9 and 10 concentrate on CoPs as sources of new ideas and innovation.

In Chapter 5, *Investigating the Influence that Media Richness has on Learning in a Community of Practice: A Case Study at Øresund Bridge,* Andrew Schenkel also writes from an academic perspective and considers formal communities and groups that are both co-located and distributed. Through a case study, Andrew explores the influence that rich media have on learning in a CoP at a large multi-billion dollar infrastructure project, the bridge between Sweden and Denmark. He argues that rich media are essential for effective learning in CoPs. Andrew hopes that the understanding of how communication influences learning will assist managers through providing an understanding of the central role that communication has on learning and researchers, and through introducing the concept of equivocality and media richness into the domain of CoPs.

Chapter 6, *CoPs for Cops: Managing and Creating Knowledge through Networked Expertise,* is written by Maarten de Laat and Wim Broer who write from an academic and a practitioner perspective, respectively. Presenting a wide-ranging case study from a public sector organisation—the Dutch Police Force—they consider both formal and informal communities that are both co-located and distributed. In the chapter, Maarten and Wim discuss how KM within the Dutch police is an integral part of the organisation and how explicit and tacit knowledge is shared to create new corporate knowledge. They present examples of how CoPs within the Dutch police play a role in both sustaining and developing their own practice and how these communities are crucial to the learning organisation.

Chapter 7, *Communities of Practice in the Royal National Lifeboat Institution,* by Roger Kolbotn, is also written from an academic perspective. It focuses on the role of volunteers in the public sector through a case study of the Royal National Lifeboat Institution. It looks at communities and groups that are both co-located and informal and concentrates on CoPs in the relationship between the managers and the volunteers in the organisation. Altruism and trust are vital elements for sharing and creating knowledge among volunteers in the organisation. Roger argues that overlapping CoPs are needed to deal with unstructured practices at sea and that managers should learn to foster CoPs among the volunteers. He hopes this chapter will provide a practical under-standing of CoPs and that the discussion of a volunteer organisation will bring some new insights into the concept of CoPs.

Chapter 8, *Innoversity in Communities of Practice,* is an introduction to Innovation in CoPs. Susanne Justesen writes from a consultant's perspective and focuses on organisations in the private sector, considering communities and groups that are co-located and formal. Susanne introduces the term innoversity (hence the title of the chapter: Innoversity in Communities of Practice), which describes the role of diversity in fostering innovation. In this chapter, she sets out to discuss when and under what circumstances of innovative practice di-versity should be encouraged, as opposed to similarity. She explores three specific questions: 1) What is innovation? 2) How does innovation take place in CoPs? 3) Why is diversity in CoPs important in fostering innovative practice? The chapter concludes with some guidelines about how to foster innovation within and among CoPs.

In Chapter 9, *User Networks as Sources of Innovation,* Anders Lundkvist continues the theme of innovation. Writing from an academic's perspective, he considers communities and groups that are both virtual and informal. In this chapter, Anders observes that it is not uncommon for users to become involved in problem solving and sharing of experiences, not only as the customers of a company but also as member of a group of users. He suggests that user groups could be useful as a source of innovation as well as for solving specific prob-lems. The case study that he presents is based around the Cisco newsgroup and this indicates that user networks are vital sites of innovation. The chapter concludes that such communities are powerful tools for creating an understanding of how innovation, work and learning are interrelated.

Continuing the theme from Anders Lundkvist, Brook Manville, in Chapter 10, *Building Customer Communities of Practice for Business Value: Suc-cess Factors Profiled from Saba Software and Other Case Studies,* writes from a practitioner's perspective and explores how CoPs can bring benefits for both organisations and customers. Brook points out that CoPs can be applied across the entire value chain of an organisation - including the company's cus-tomers. He explores the strategic value of building Customer Communities of Practice (CCoPs): learning networks of customers whose win-win value propo-sition is that customers gain valuable insights from peers while the sponsoring company gains new ideas, loyalty and a deeper insight into the markets they serve. He concludes the discussion with several lessons learned and practical guidelines for building successful CCoPs in any industry.

Section III: Community of Practice Development

This section is intended to be of practical help to CoP practitioners and covers two areas. Chapters 11, 12, 13 and 14 examine the problems of building and sustaining a CoP, while Chapters 15, 16, 17 and 18 look at the issues of IT support for CoPs.

Chapter 11, *Creating a Multi-Company Community of Practice for Chief Information Officers,* is written by John Moran and Lee Weimer from a practitioner's perspective. It is a first-hand account of the creation and evolution of a fee-based, multi-company CoP for Chief Information Officers in Silicon Valley. In the chapter, they describe how the community has grown over a six-year period and outline the principles, processes and practices needed to build and maintain a trust-based, face-to face, learning community where members can share their accumulated knowledge. In addition, the chapter outlines some of the benefits to individuals and the Information Technology industry in general that have resulted from participation in the community. John and Lee hope that this chapter will foster the same sense of excitement for would-be practitioners that they still clearly feel.

In Chapter 12, *Viable Communities within Organizational Contexts: Creating and Sustaining Viability in Communities of Practice at Siemens AG,* Benjamin Frost and Stefan Schoen also write from a practitioner's perspective of their experiences with CoPs in Siemens. The focus is clearly on CoPs in the private sector. Stefan and Benjamin highlight five factors that they argue are necessary for a CoP to be viable, that is, active, alive and creating benefit in an organisation. They introduce and explain each of the five factors in turn and claim that together they represent an approach that can be used to analyse and improve CoPs. The chapter also serves as a set of guidelines for CoP members and moderators to maintain viability in their own CoPs.

Another set of guidelines with a strong practical orientation can be found in Chapter 13, *Best Practices: Developing Communities that Provide Business Value,* by Wesley C. Vestal and Kimberley Lopez. Writing from a perspective that is one of both a practitioner and a consultant, Kimberley and Wesley consider a range of communities and groups selected from several best-practice organisations. The chapter examines the key factors involved in cultivating CoPs: the selection of a community, gaining support and establishing resources, roles and development, ongoing facilitation and technology support. The chapter concludes with a list of nine critical success factors that can help community leaders, central support groups, KM practitioners and management to build functioning, strategic CoPs.

Bronwyn Stuckey and John D. Smith, in Chapter 14, *Building Sustainable Communities of Practice,* explore the importance of stories in CoPs. They write from a practitioner perspective and present seven case studies that illustrate the range and diversity of the CoPs they have been involved with. The chapter covers both co-located and virtual groups, as well as formal and informal groups. Bronwyn and John argue that stories play a crucial role in motivation and learning in a community. Within communities, the swapping of stories is a means by which local theories of cause and effect are developed and contextualised. These stories provide powerful ways of invoking context, of framing choices and actions and of constructing identity. The chapter concludes with four key lessons learnt about effective strategies for community building.

Having looked at developing and sustaining CoPs, we now turn to how Information Technology can be used to support the work of a CoP.

In Chapter 15, *How Information Technologies Can Help Build and Sustain an Organization's CoP: Spanning the Socio-Technical Divide?*, Laurence Lock Lee and Mark Neff write as consultants and practitioners and use detailed case studies of two large, but quite different, global private sector organisations to explore the role of Information Technology (IT) in supporting CoPs activities. In this case, both organisations could be considered to be early adopters of the CoP concept and this chapter tracks their evolution and highlights the lessons that were learned along the way. The chapter concludes with the identification of five common themes and challenges for organisations of a global nature with a commitment to using CoPs as a primary vehicle for knowledge sharing across their operations.

This is followed by Pete Bradshaw, Stephen Powell and Ian Terrell, who, in Chapter 16, *Building a Community of Practice: Technological and Social Implications for a Distributed Team,* provide a set of guidelines for building commitment, ownership, engagement and focus in a distributed CoP. In their chapter, they focus on the way in which a remote and distributed team can be transformed into a CoP. This, they argue, is a process that takes time and can be aided by the use of appropriate media and platforms. They look at the work of a team of approximately 20 remote workers and examine how they gradually developed into a CoP. They explore the roles that technology and communication methods had on the formation and development of the community and conclude with a detailed set of guidelines.

In Chapter 17, *Facilitator Toolkit for Building and Sustaining Virtual Communities of Practice,* Lisa Kimball and Amy Ladd observe that as organisations become more distributed, the relationships that exist between the people inside an organisation and those previously considered to be outside have become increasingly important. In addition, they argue that organisations have now begun to recognise the value of Knowledge Management and the ability to work in virtual groups to the organisation as a whole. In this chapter, they offer a lively selection of ideas, and examples of best practice, tips and illustrations from their work of training leaders to launch and sustain virtual CoPs. The "facilitator's toolkit" includes tips for chartering the community, defining roles and creating a culture that will help build a sustainable community.

Chapter 18, *The Use of Intranets: The Missing Link Between Communities of Practice and Networks of Practice?,* by Emmanuelle Vaast, is written from an academic perspective and presents the results of longitudinal case studies based in four different organisations. The chapter examines how the use of intranet systems by members of local CoPs begins to change the way the CoP functions and how it sees itself in relation to other CoPs. It also shows how the use of intranets in an organisation contributes to the emergence of broadly based Networks of Practice (NoPs). The chapter concludes with a discussion of the issues that managers should consider when implementing an intranet to support a CoP. To be successful Emmanuelle suggests that managers need to maintain a delicate balance in three key areas: 1) Initiative vs. Control, 2) Communitarian Principles vs. Competition, and 3) Official vs. Emergent Processes.

Section IV: Moving CoPs Forward

This is the final section in the book and it concentrates on looking at future developments and areas of interest.

Taking up the theme of NoPs, Robin Teigland and Molly McLure Wasko start this section with Chapter 19, *Extending Richness with Reach: Participation and Knowledge Exchange in Electronic Networks of Practice.* This chapter is also written from an academic perspective. Robin and Molly report on an empirical study at Cap Gemini. They explain that in an effort to replicate CoPs online, organisations are investing in information technologies that create intra-organizational networks, or Electronic Networks of Practice (ENoPs). These networks create electronic "bridging ties" between geographically dispersed organisational members and provide a space in which individuals can communicate with each other. In this chapter Robin and Molly compare the dynamics of knowledge exchange between ENoPs and traditional CoPs. They examine why people participate in the network, as well as examining whether participation in ENoPs has an impact on knowledge outcomes and individual performance.

In Chapter 20, *Trusting the Knowledge of Large Online Communities: Strategies for Leading from Behind,* John S. Storck and Lauren E. Storck take an academic perspective on a case study. The case study is of an online community of about 400 professionals, which is simply called "LG" (Large Group), and they use this to illustrate how a leader can develop the capacity to trust the group. Recognising that groups can be trusted is difficult for a leader. Modern managers, who are taught the value of using teams to achieve specific objectives, often find the idea of dispersed groups of people making decisions an anathema. Learning to trust in the knowledge of groups takes training, practice and courage. Using archives of discussions among community members, John and Lauren develop the leadership principles that support the approach of "leading from behind".

In Chapter 21, *Double Agents: Visible and Invisible Work in an Online Community of Practice,* Elisabeth Davenport moves us into looking at IT support for online CoPs. Elisabeth also writes from an academic perspective and reports on an ethnographic study of novice computer users (a loose association of small traders) in the tourism sector. In this chapter, Elisabeth draws on work by Paul Dourish in which he makes a case for an approach to design that takes account of both 'embodiment' and 'embeddedness'. An online knowledge network is embedded in a given domain, but it is also embodied in physical interactors working with machines. Novices who interact in this environment are thus double agents, working in a domain but also working with artefacts. The chapter concludes with some of the lessons that have been learned from this work.

Shawn Callahan, in Chapter 22, *Cultivating a Public Sector Knowledge Management Community of Practice*, gives us a practitioner's viewpoint of the history of an online CoP by charting the growth of Act-KM, an online CoP for practitioners in the public sector, from an initial meeting in 1998 to the present day online community of more than 550 people. Utilising the four domains of the Cynefin sense-making framework, Shawn analyses the ActKM community and provides a practical account of its history, purpose, guiding principles, goals, characteristics and dynamics. He concludes with a summary of the lessons learnt from the ActKM experience that others might find useful in cultivating a vibrant CoP of this type.

In Chapter 23, *Click Connect and Coalesce for NGOs: Exploring the Intersection Between Online Networks, CoPs, and Events*, Nancy White reflects in a lively and engaging manner on her experiences as a consultant and president of Full Circle Associates. She notes the shift of focus from "online communities" to more purposeful and focused online groups, including distributed CoPs, and provides a number of examples of how groups and individuals can "Click, Connect and Coalesce" in the online world. In particular, Nancy identifies the value of CoPs for Non Governmental Organizations (NGOs), and suggests that the catalysts of people and time-delimited events both stimulate the formation and growth of CoPs and help to capture and focus attention and resources around them. The chapter concludes with a list of factors to consider in the design of an online interaction space.

Perhaps appropriately, the final chapter in this book addresses an area that is frequently overlooked in the literature on CoPs: how to end them. In In Chapter 24, *Where Did That Community Go? Communities of Practice that "Disappear"*, Patricia Gongla and Christine R. Rizzuto deal with what happens to CoPs when they reach the end of their natural lives. Patricia and Christine write as practitioners and draw on their experience at IBM to address the question as to why a CoP might disappear. They discuss the factors related to the ending of individual communities and address three basic questions: 1) In what ways do CoPs disappear? 2) Why do they disappear? and 3) What are ways to help a community make that transition? In this chapter, Patricia and Christine walk the reader through the steps in a guide they have developed to aid easing a community's transition.

REFERENCES

Brown, J. S., & Duguid, P. (2000). *The social life of information.* Boston, MA: Harvard Business School Press.

Clark, H., & Brennan, S. E. (1991). Grounding in communication. In L. B. Resnick, J. M. Levine, & S. D. Teasley (Eds.), *Perspectives on socially shared cognition* (pp. 127-149). Washington, DC: American Psychological Association.

Hildreth, P., & Kimble, C. (2002). The duality of knowledge. *Information Research*, 8(1), paper no. 142. Available at http://InformationR.net/ir/8-1/paper142.html

Kimble, C., Hildreth, P., & Wright, P. (2000). Communities of Practice: Going virtual. In Y. Malhotra (Ed.), *Knowledge Management and business model innovation* (pp. 220-234). Hershey, PA: Idea Group Publishing.

Kimble, C., Li, F., & Barlow, A. (2000). *Effective virtual teams through communities of practice.* University of Strathclyde Management Science Research Paper No. 00/9.

Lave, J., & Wenger, E. (1991). *Situated learning. Legitimate peripheral participation.* Cambridge University Press.

Ponzi, L., & Koenig, M. (2002). Knowledge Management: Another management fad? *Information Research*, 8(1), paper no. 145. Available at http://InformationR.net/ir/8-1/paper145.html

Wenger, E. (1998). *Communities of practice: Learning, meaning and identity.* CUP.

Wilson, T.D. (2002). The nonsense of 'Knowledge Management'. *Information Research*, 8(1), 144. Available at http://InformationR.net/ir/8-1/paper144.html

Acknowledgments

First, the editors would like to thank the authors of the chapters in this book. The process of creating the book was very much a collaborative effort and would not have been possible without the patience, understanding and commitment of all involved. Particular thanks are due to the people at groupjazz for creating the on-line collaborative environment through which the authors could communicate and help each other.

Secondly, although most of the authors also served as referees for chapters submitted by other authors, we would also like to acknowledge the help of all those other people who were involved in the review process. We are sure that this has helped to ensure the high quality of chapters that form the finished version of the book.

Although not directly involved in the book, a note of thanks must also go to Andy Swarbrick from TecLAB at the University of Illinois, whose work as an undergraduate at the University of York provided the original inspiration for this book. Similarly, we must also thank the staff at Idea Group Inc. for their guidance and support through the eighteen months of work on the book.

Finally, in closing we would like to reiterate our thanks to all of the authors for their excellent contributions and thank our friends and families without whose ongoing support we would never have been able to complete this project.

SECTION I:

COMMUNITIES OF PRACTICE

Chapter I

Understanding the Benefits and Impact of Communities of Practice

Michael A. Fontaine
IBM Institute for Business Value, USA

David R. Millen
IBM Research Collaborative User Experience Group, USA

ABSTRACT

Organizations are increasingly providing Communities of Practice with resources to improve the exchange and flow of knowledge and information. However, as with any other significant investment, managers are naturally interested in, and are frequently called upon to justify, the impact that these communities have on individual performance, overall productivity and the bottom line. In this chapter, we present the results of work with thirteen Communities of Practice, focusing on how managers can collect community benefits via serious anecdotes and measure the impact that communities have on time use in knowledge work activities and on individual, community and organizational benefits.

INTRODUCTION

From the beginning of the industrial revolution through to the mid-1990s, the knowledge needed to compete and succeed in business was housed locally—within the co-located boundaries of the office, the city, the county and within formal worker groups who interacted daily. Today, however, in almost every aspect of business, organizations are pressed to fill the needs and wants of globally dispersed customers and suppliers, in real time and on-demand. At the same time, work teams have not only grown more complex and geographically distributed, but also their need to tap into the knowledge and expertise of their co-workers has never been more critical. To meet both of these challenges, organizations such as BP/Amoco, IBM, Montgomery-Watson Harza, Shell, Siemens, Johnson & Johnson, The World Bank, and Bristol-Myers Squibb have begun to support communities of workers, commonly referred to as Communities of Practice (CoPs), to increase the sharing of lessons learned, the exchange of insights and ideas and the transfer of expertise and hand-on experience.

Ethnographies of these communities reveal that sharing and exchange of knowledge occurs in a variety of ways. In a study of copy machine technicians, Orr (1996) reported that much of technicians' informal discussion took place in natural social interaction, for example, during meals, coffee breaks, and while driving to customer sites. The volume and detailed nature of the conversation supports the transfer of knowledge from the more experienced to the new technicians. Wenger (1998), in his research of a community within an insurance firm, describes how call centre employees exchange knowledge during group meetings and by handwritten notes passed among workers. Lesser and Storck (2001), in their study of seven CoPs in large, multi-national firms, describe how CoPs increase social capital and organizational performance in addition to reporting key value outcomes such as increasing customer response and creating new business opportunities. In their respective works, Teigland (2000) and Liedtka (2000) linked CoPs to an organization's competitive advantage and ability to deliver on-time customer performance. Finally, Fontaine and Millen (2002) reported that to support the sharing of knowledge in communities, organizations are increasingly providing the following resources:

- People: to fill certain community roles and manage the community's activities
- Activities: to bring the community together in meetings and events
- Technology: to facilitate the flow of knowledge and information between activities
- Content: to manage and share the explicit knowledge that the community creates

However, as with any other significant investment in resources, management is naturally interested in the impact that these community investments have on individual performance, organizational performance, overall productivity and, ultimately, the bottom line. As corporate investments in community increase, so does the scrutiny of the individual and organizational benefits of these investments. There is increasing pressure to augment the qualitative results with more formal measurement of the financial benefits and costs of the communities. In fact, measures of value are seen as being instrumental for communities to gain visibility and influence as well as to educate and guide their own development (Wenger, McDermott, & Snyder, 2002).

To meet this challenge, Knowledge Management (KM) researchers have considered various approaches to measuring the benefits of communities. For example, one approach has been to measure the time savings that accrue to various knowledge work activities because of IT investments (Butler, Hall, Hanna, Mendonca, Auguste, Manyika, & Sahay, 1997; Clare & Detore, 2000; Downes & Mui, 1998). A second approach has been to elicit detailed stories from knowledge workers that describe the benefits resulting from the use of various collaborative systems. These stories or serious anecdotes have been used to informally calculate the Return on Investment (ROI) for IT investment (Davenport & Prusak, 1998; US Navy, 2001). Finally, other researchers have employed various assessment models including Social Network Analysis (Schenkel, Teigland, & Borgatti, 2000), Balanced Scorecard (Roberts, 2000; Walsh & Bayma, 1996) and intangible asset valuation methods (Edvinson & Malone, 1997; Lev, 2001; Sveiby, 1997) to account for improvements in social connectivity, organization performance and intellectual capital value.

COMMUNITY VALUE RESEARCH

To understand the impact that these investments have on both community members and the organization, we studied thirteen communities in ten global organizations in two studies as part of our work with the IBM Institute for Knowledge-based Organizations and IBM Research. In the first study, undertaken in 2000, we interviewed 100 community members in seven global organizations. Working with KM and community leaders in these organizations, communities that were well established and had strong member participation were identified (Table 1 shows the mix of organizations and communities studied as well as the research methods used).

The findings from this study were published (Lesser & Storck, 2001) and a second follow-up study was undertaken in 2002 that used a mix of paper and electronic (web) based methods to administer a self-report survey to members of five communities. In total, 431 survey responses were received. The survey

Table 1: Community Value Research Studies (2000 and 2002)

Organization/Industry	Community	Research Method
2000 Study		
Aerospace & Defense Company	Manufacturing Engineers	Face-to-face interview
Global Development Organization	1. Land & Real Estate 2. Urban Development	Face-to-face interview
Global Software Firm	Software Designers	Face-to-face interview
Petro-chemical Company	Petro-chemists	Face-to-face interview
Pharmaceutical Company	Chemists	Face-to-face interview
Telecommunications Company	Project & Bid Managers	Face-to-face interview
US Defense Agency	Mathematics	Face-to-face interview
2002 Study		
Computer Software & Services Organization	1. Information Technology Architects 2. Software Asset Managers 3. Consultants	Web-based survey
Computer Hardware Firm	Engineers	Web-based survey
Petroleum Firm	Environmentalists	Web-based survey

was structured to gather information about the nature and frequency of participation within the community and to capture self-reported judgments about the benefits that result from community activities. More specifically, the 2002 study asked community members to report the following:

1) What benefits result from community activities, members' use of content and technology resources and overall participation?
2) In what ways has time spent in knowledge work activities changed as a result of the community? Is there evidence for an increase (or decrease) in worker productivity?

WHAT ARE THE BENEFITS OF COMMUNITIES OF PRACTICE?

Those who have worked with CoPs have long believed that they increase the level and flow of knowledge within an organization. That withstanding, how to measure and package this belief to convince senior management that actual value is being attained has been a struggle. The intangible nature of "sharing knowledge" is often difficult, if not impossible, to quantify. To help address this struggle, a list of measurable community benefits was compiled from the interview analysis with the seven communities who participated in the first study and a scan of community literature.

Table 2: Benefits Supplied by Communities of Practice

Communities of Practice have been reported as influencing one or more of following:

Ability to Execute Corporate Strategy	Job Satisfaction
Ability to Foresee Emerging Market, Product, Technology Capabilities and Opportunities	Learning and Development
Authority and Reputation with Customers and Partners	Learning Curve
Collaboration	New Biz Development
Coordination and Synergy	New Customers
Cost of Training	New Revenue from New Business, Product, Service or Market
Customer Loyalty Stickiness	Partnering Success
Customer Responsiveness	Problem Solving Ability
Customer Satisfaction	Productivity or Time Savings
Customer Service, Support and Acquisition Costs	Professional Reputation or Identity
Customer Turnover	Project Success
Employee Retention	Quality of Advice
Empowerment	Risk Management
Higher Sales per Customer	Supplier Relationship Costs
Idea Creation	Supplier Relationships
Identification and Access to Experts and Knowledge	Time-to-Market
Innovation	Trust Between Employees

As one can hopefully recognize from the benefits included in this list, what was once considered almost entirely intangible quickly becomes a list of benefits not far removed from those measures typically qualified and quantified in most, if not all, corporations. For example, all Human Resource (HR) departments administer employee satisfaction surveys designed to uncover the effects of job satisfaction on employee retention, learning and development, and the cost of training. Similarly, it is widely known that many organizations have quantified metrics that measure job satisfaction, its relationship to customer satisfaction and the direct link to increased revenue or sales (Heskett, Jones, Loveman, Sasser, & Schlesinger, 1994; Hoisington & Huang, 1999). Likewise, it would be hard to find a business executive who is not interested in project success, productivity, new business development and customer or employee turnover.

ASSESSING THE LEVEL OF COMMUNITY IMPACT

To better understand if communities really produced benefits, it was decided to start by directly asking the community members about the individual, community and organizational benefits that accrue as a result of their participation in community (Millen, Fontaine, & Muller, 2002). Our self-report survey, developed and administered in early 2002, asked community members about their participation, important success stories and the time use in various knowledge work activities (e.g., search tasks).

Table 3: Individual, Community and Organization Benefits

Type of Benefit	Impact of Community *It has improved or* *increased the following*	% Agree
Individual Benefits *What does participating in the community* *do for individuals?*	Skills and Know How	65%
	Personal Productivity	58%
	Job Satisfaction	52%
	Personal Reputation	50%
	Sense of Belonging	46%
Community Benefits *How does collective participation* *benefit others?*	Knowledge Sharing, Expertise and Resources	81%
	Collaboration	73%
	Consensus and Problem Solving	57%
	Community Reputation and Legitimacy	56%
	Trust Between Members	50%
Organization Benefits *How does participating in a community* *increase organizational efficiency, better* *serve customers/partners, and provide* *insights for the future of the firm?*	Operational Efficiency	57%
	Cost Savings	51%
	Level of Service or Sales	46%
	Speed of Service or Product	42%
	Employee Retention	24%

Focusing on what was perceived to be the most important sub-benefits within the laundry list of community benefits reported in Table 2, they were clustered and organized into three distinct groupings of benefits that accrue to members of CoPs. Survey respondents were asked whether participation, community activities and resources influenced fifteen specific impact statements (Table 3).

Individual Benefits

When people choose to participate in a community, they typically do so because they feel they may have something to gain, learn or benefit from. Obviously, some go to give or share their expertise, but at first, most people go to look for some piece of explicit or tacit knowledge: a document, a template, an idea or a solution. We refer to this personal gain as individual benefits.

When asked about individual benefits, 65% of participants agreed that their participation in the community and their use of community resources and activities increased their individual skills and know-how, and 58% felt they were more productive or had saved time in their job. Surprisingly, only 46% reported that they felt that participation in the community improved their sense of belonging in the organization.

Community Benefits

Community benefits consist of those that accrue to the "collective" community and are realized by connection, interaction and collaboration with others.

This interaction increases the awareness and access to the collective community members' expertise and experience. By knowing who in the community can help solve problems and share similar experiences, members can point to the community as a source of information that builds on their personal strengths and affects the organization's larger capabilities.

When asked about benefits to the community itself, almost everyone in the survey agreed that the community resulted in greater sharing of expertise, knowledge and resources between members. Additionally, more than 70% felt that collaboration had increased as a result of the community.

Organization Benefits

Even though personal and community benefits remain somewhat intangible, together they have the ability to influence tangible business outcomes, or what we term organization benefits. This is where the knowledge gained from participating in the community is applied to solve an actual business problem, and where the community's impact can be easily tracked and measured.

When asked about the impact on organization benefits, 57% of study participants indicated that they agreed that the community increased operational efficiency, leading to improved cost savings. Likewise, they indicated that they believed that the community's resources and activities increased sales and decreased costs. Finally, and surprisingly, only 24% reported that they believe that participation in the community has improved employee retention.

USING ANECDOTES TO UNCOVER BENEFITS

In addition to asking community members to assess the level of impact the community had on these three types of benefits, we asked respondents to share "serious anecdotes", i.e., stories that could be quantified and easily shared among members and executive sponsors (Davenport & Prusak, 1998). The hope was to learn how the knowledge shared, exchanged and transferred in various forms (expertise, documents, presentations, templates or client examples) was applied to solve an actual business problem. Specifically, each survey participant was asked to:

"Share a story when the use of one or more resources that you've received from participating in the community made your job easier, saved you time, helped you offer a new idea or solution, and/or assisted an important customer. If you saved time, costs, or increased revenue, please indicate the amount, if possible. Also, please indicate (1) What was the outcome of this event? (2) Who was impacted? (3) What may have been the potential cost if you didn't provide a solution?"

Table 4: Sample Anecdotes and Benefits Reported from the Total Community Value Study

Anecdote	Benefit
I was able to engage two mentors to assist in obtaining guidance and counsel. As a result I improved my relationship with the client and was able to leverage subject matter expertise from individuals to assess and provide recommendation on an IT architecture in only three to four weeks, saving weeks of time. And we signed a $4m contract that would have gone to a major competitor.	• **Improved Client Relationship** • **Time Savings** • **Increased Revenue** • **New Business**
I used the community's Q&A forum to ask a question related to a project I was working on. I received 10 or so responses. Some of my questions were answered outright whereas I received leads on where to find answers to other ones. It saved me time in that I didn't need to spend time searching the web or researching. I was able to get quick and precise leads on things I was interested in. Difficult to quantify saving but probably in the order of three to four days work.	• **Access to Knowledge** • **Time Savings** • **Ability to Execute**
Documents and templates from other community members saved at least 60% of my time for the project implementation process and around 40% during planning phase. It also helped with customer satisfaction, creating confidence that the project was conducted under effective methodology, process and procedures. Potential cost savings may be in excess of 30%.	• **Time Savings** • **Customer Satisfaction** • **Cost Savings**
The materials I received saved me and my teams between three and six months of research and distillation activities. That time allowed us to kick off the pilot program on time and more effectively than we likely would have done alone. I am convinced we benefited greatly from the improved skills. Certainly my performance review for last year would not have been as successful as it was if not for the level of expertise I gained from others.	• **Time Savings** • **Project Success** • **Employee Performance** • **Increased Skills & Know How**

Of the 431 people surveyed, over 120 provided impressive stories on how the knowledge they gained from interacting in the community helped them solve a business problem, improved customer satisfaction, closed a deal that might have gone to a major competitor, and most importantly, saved time. Table 4 highlights four representative anecdotes from our study and the benefits reported within each anecdote.

Suggestions for Collecting Anecdotes from Your Community

After working with these communities to report the value and benefits represented by serious anecdotes, three important lessons emerged that community and knowledge managers should warrant. First, the act of simply collecting anecdotes is not fully sufficient. Managers should conduct follow-up interviews with community members to assess the level of impact the community, minus other influences such as knowledge from other sources, serendipity, or interview bias, had on the anecdote reported. Second, managers should be conservative in their approach to report these benefits so as to not over-inflate the actual value or impact of the community. It has been our experience, however, that even if only a fraction of the benefits reported in the serious anecdotes is considered, there is still enormous payback for community investments. Finally, measurable benefits, i.e., time savings, increased revenue and cost savings, should be tracked, aggregated and reported to senior management on a periodic basis. Doing so sends a message that the community is continually delivering business value.

COMMUNITY'S IMPACT ON TIME USE

To address the community's impact on the time savings reported in almost all of the 120 anecdotes collected, the time spent in knowledge work activities was assessed to ascertain whether it changed as a result of the community and whether there was evidence for an increase (or decrease) in worker productivity.

Time Use in Knowledge Work Activities

To better understand the differences in time spent in knowledge work activities and the impact on community benefits, the active participants in the four communities (defined as daily or weekly participation) were compared with those who were less active (defined as less than once a month) and the analyses presented below. Specifically, members were asked to estimate the amount of time that they spent in each of the five clusters of knowledge work activities

Table 5: Mean Time Use for Knowledge Work Activities Time (HH:MM)

Knowledge Work Activities	I	II	III	IV	Mean
Looking for, accessing, or acquiring information from relevant sources (Searching)	1:50	1:18	0:58	0:52	**1:15**
Processing, evaluating or analysing information (Processing)	1:55	1:50	1:47	1:40	**1:48**
Solving problems and making decisions using job-relevant information (Decision-making)	2:06	2:15	1:50	2:10	**2:04**
Interacting or communicating with fellow community members (Interacting)	0:45	2:22	2:17	2:50	**2:03**
Coordinating, training, managing or advising others (Coordinating)	1:07	1:18	1:14	1:18	**1:21**
Total	7:43	9:03	8:13	9:33	**8:32**

shown in Table 5. These activities were adapted from a classification of work activities developed by the U.S. government (Jeanneret & Berman, 1995) and earlier work on interaction by Butler et al. (1997).

Analysing and Interpreting Time Use Results

The survey results showed that members in each of the four communities spent a majority of their time solving problems and making decisions, followed by looking for and processing information. Community members also reported significant amounts of time coordinating the work of others and interacting with fellow community members.

There are several possible ways in which time use could change across all work activities. It seems reasonable that the time spent in community events and interacting with other community members could result in increases in both interaction and coordinating activities. Additionally, some resources could reduce the amount of time spent on various work activities. For example, information portals, well-categorized and searchable document repositories and better social networks could result in reduced time spent in searching for, and possibly processing, information.

When specifically asked about changes in knowledge activities as a result of participation in the community, members generally confirmed expectations. Averaged across all four communities, there was a reported 2.1% decrease in searching time, a 0.8% decrease in information processing time, and a 0.9% decrease decision-making time. In contrast, the survey results also showed a 1.1% increase in interaction time and a 0.2 % increase in coordination activities.

Figure 1: Change in Time Use as a Result of Community Activities and Resources

While these amounts appear to be inconsequential, a simple extension of these daily percentages, a community member's loaded salary and yearly community participation, may equate to a significant increase in overall productivity.

Comparing Time Use for Active and Less Active Participants

To be sure that the changes in reported time use were related to community activities, the results of both the active and less active community members (see Figure 1) were compared. For both active and less active members, a decrease in time spent searching for information was reported. More important, however, was that across each of the five clusters, active members showed significantly more improvement then their less active counterparts.

One interpretation of these results is that increased interaction and coordination time is the voluntary price that active members pay for the benefits of decreased information searching and processing time. The improved social networking gained by participating in the community aids in decreasing time spent in unproductive knowledge activities, such as searching for information. The gain in search time for less active community members may be evidence of free-rider behaviour since less active members enjoy the benefits of better information sources (e.g., document databases). However, they may in fact spend little additional time supporting other community members. Overall, the results revealed that communities impact how members spend their time in various knowledge work activities, generally resulting in a more productive use of their time.

RECOMMENDATIONS FOR ASSESSING THE BENEFITS AND IMPACT OF YOUR COMMUNITY

In this chapter, three approaches to understanding the impact of Communities of Practice have been presented: anecdotes, time use, and individual, community and organization benefits. As one can well imagine, the combined results were of great interest to the community leaders, knowledge managers and business executives involved in the study. The use of a self-report survey increased understanding of the kinds of benefits reported by serious anecdotes and the impact on individual, community and organizational benefits. Importantly, the assessment of overall impact and reported time shifts in knowledge activities allowed community leaders to assess whether their investment strategies were sound and if the community program needed modification.

If knowledge managers and community leaders attempt to understand the benefits and impact of communities and employ some of the measures that have been highlighted in this chapter, it is suggested that what will be of most value is conducting an analysis that is not only relevant to the organization, but also to the stakeholders. Using self-report community surveys combined with collecting serious anecdotes may help to better justify a community's actual return on investment. Most importantly, however, tying the measures of the community (i.e., time savings, level of impact and anecdotes) to the larger objectives set by business executives will be paramount.

Finally, to ensure that measurement efforts are successful and meet these objectives, consider linking the reported community benefits and impact to the needs and wants of senior management by answering the following measurement questions efforts before beginning any community measurement initiative:

1) What types of measurement criteria are important to the stakeholders? Do they require quantitative data or would "one really great anecdote" suffice?
2) What is the community's larger purpose and objectives? What has it been asked to do or what has it suggested it would accomplish?
3) What is the KM strategy for the organization? How does the community address and impact what KM has been asked to deliver?
4) What is the organization's business strategy? What are the key initiatives underway that the community measures may be able to impact or influence?

REFERENCES

Butler, P., Hall, T., Hanna, A., Mendonca, L., Auguste, B., Manyika, J., & Sahay, A. (1997). A revolution in interaction. *The McKinsey Quarterly, 1*, 4-23.

Clare, M., & Detore, A. (2000). *Knowledge assets: A professionals guide to valuation and financial management.* Harcourt Professional Publishing.

Davenport, T. H., & Prusak, L. (1998). *Working knowledge.* Boston, MA: Harvard Business School Press.

Downes, L., & Mui, C. (1998). *Unleashing the killer app.* Boston, MA: Harvard Business School Press.

Edvinsson, L., & Malone, M. S. (1997). *Intellectual capital.* Harper Collins Publishers, Inc.

Fontaine, M. A., & Millen, D. R. (2002). Understanding the value of communities: A look at both sides of the cost/benefit equation. *Knowledge Management Review, 5* (3), 24-27.

Heskett, J. L., Jones, T. O., Loveman, G. W., Sasser, W. E., & Schlesinger, L. A. (1994). Putting the service-profit chain to work. *Harvard Business Review.* March-April, 164-174.

Hoisington, S., & Huang, T-H. (1999). *Customer satisfaction and market share at IBM Rochester, Baldrige.* Worksheet found at http://

www.baldrigeplus.com/Exhibits/Exhibit%20%20Customer%20satisfaction%20and%20market%20share.pdf [1999, July 27th]

Jeanneret, P., & Berman, W. (1995). Generalized work activities. In *Development of Occupational Information Network (O*NET) content model.* Utah Department of Employment Security.

Lesser, E., & Storck, J. (2001). Communities of Practice and organizational performance. *IBM Systems Journal, 40*(4), 831-841.

Lev, B. (2001). *Intangibles: Management, measurement, and reporting.* Washington, DC: Brookings Institution Press.

Liedtka, J. (2000). Linking competitive advantage with Communities of Practice. In E. L. Lesser, M. A. Fontaine, & J. A. Slusher (Eds.), *Knowledge and communities* (pp. 133-150). Butterworth-Heinemann.

Millen, D. R., Fontaine, M. A., & Muller, M. J. (2002, April). Understanding the costs and benefits of Communities of Practice. *Communications of the ACM, 45* (4), 69-73.

Orr, J. E. (1996). *Talking about machine: An ethnography of a modern job.* Ithaca, New York: Cornell University Press.

Roberts, B. (2000). A balanced approach. *Knowledge Management*, (September), 26-33.

Schenkel, A., Teigland, R., & Borgatti S. P. (2000). Theorizing Communities of Practice: A social network approach. Paper submitted to the *Academy of Management Conference*, Organization and Management Theory Division. ID No. 11307.

Sveiby, K. E. (1997). *The new organizational wealth: Managing and measuring knowledge-based assets.* San Francisco, CA: Berrett Koehler Press.

Teigland, R. (2000). Communities of Practice at an Internet Firm: Netovation vs. on-time performance. In E. L. Lesser, M. A. Fontaine, & J. A. Slusher (Eds.), *Knowledge and communities* (pp.151-178). Butterworth-Heinemann.

U.S. Navy. (2001). *Metrics guide for knowledge management initiatives.* United States Department of Navy, August.

Walsh, J. P., & Bayma, T. (1996). Computer networks and scientific work. *Social Studies of Science, 25*, 661-703.

Wenger, E. (1998). *Communities of Practice: Learning, meaning, and identity.* Cambridge University Press.

Wenger, E., McDermott, R. M., & Snyder, W. M. (2002). *Cultivating communities of practice.* Harvard Business School Press.

Chapter II

Overcoming Knowledge Barriers with Communities of Practice:
Lessons Learned Through Practical Experience

Eric L. Lesser
IBM Institute for Business Value, USA

Michael A. Fontaine
IBM Institute for Business Value, USA

ABSTRACT

Many organizations have invested a significant amount of time, energy and resources in overcoming intra-organizational barriers to sharing knowledge. Such barriers prevent individuals who are looking for knowledge from connecting with those who possess it. In this chapter, four common barriers (that the authors have seen in their work with knowledge-based organizations) have been identified that prevent two parties from coming together and sharing knowledge: awareness, access, application and perception. Based on their research and experience, they describe how Communities of Practice can be an important vehicle for breaking through each of these barriers and enabling knowledge to flow more effectively within organizations. In addition, practices are highlighted that organizations can put into place to provide effective support for these communities.

INTRODUCTION

Perhaps one of the most vexing problems facing organizations is the need to improve intra-organizational coordination. Firms, recognising the need to coordinate activities on a global basis, have spent significant time, resources and energy to bring together disparate functions and systems to eliminate these barriers. For example, pharmaceutical firms have long been organized by corporate functions, i.e., marketing, manufacturing, and research and development (R&D). Often these groups remained insular silos that lacked effective cross-functional knowledge sharing mechanisms. To address this challenge, many of these firms have created cross-functional drug discovery teams that support a drug candidate from the discovery phase through manufacturing and sales. Other organizations facing similar challenges have looked for similar ways of better coordinating their internal resources and activities.

Yet, despite their best efforts, organizations continue to be faced with additional barriers that inhibit the ability of their employees to share knowledge. Issues such as geographic boundaries, differences in regional cultures and a lack of awareness of others with similar interests make knowledge sharing a difficult activity. While these roadblocks are often not visible, and their boundaries not easily drawn, they represent a substantial challenge for many firms to overcome. In many of the globally-distributed companies and government organizations with which we have worked, we have seen a number of difficulties associated with finding critical expertise, transferring knowledge between locations and ensuring that individuals are appropriately recognized for sharing knowledge. Often, these impediments to knowledge sharing can significantly hamper firm performance, as organizations are unable to take advantage of one of their most valuable assets: their employees' know-how and expertise.

In this chapter, we outline how Communities of Practice (CoPs) can help organizations break through the barriers that impede effective knowledge sharing. A CoP is a group of individuals who regularly engage in sharing and learning based on their common interests or methods of working. Within communities, individuals interact with one another to solve problems, test new ideas, learn about new developments in their field and build a sense of affiliation with others in similar circumstances. Membership within CoPs often fluctuates, in terms of both the number of participants and the level of intensity with which people partake in the community activities. These communities can be either self-organized by members, or brought together by the organization to encourage this form of interchange between practitioners. Communities, through their ability to foster the development of connections, relationships and common context between knowledge seekers and sources, can help eliminate many of the common knowledge sharing barriers that plague even the most successful organizations.

BARRIERS TO SHARING KNOWLEDGE

At the heart of knowledge sharing lie two types of individuals: knowledge seekers—those who are looking for knowledge, and knowledge sources—those who either have the knowledge the seeker needs or who can point the seeker to another knowledge source. Effective knowledge sharing occurs when appropriate connections are built between one or more of these parties. Cross, Parker, Prusak and Borgatti (2001) suggest that there are four features of these relationships that determine their knowledge sharing effectiveness. These include: knowing what another person knows and thus when to turn to them; being able to gain timely access to that person; willingness of the person sought out to engage in problem solving rather than dump information; and a degree of safety in the relationship that promoted learning and creativity. Based on experience with many organizations to nurture and support communities, Cross et al.'s features have been modified to highlight four common barriers to knowledge sharing that CoPs help overcome:

- **Awareness:** Making seekers and sources aware of their respective knowledge
- **Access:** Providing the time and space for seekers and sources to connect with one another
- **Application:** Ensuring that the knowledge seeker and source have a common content and understanding necessary to share their insights
- **Perception:** Creating an atmosphere where knowledge sharing behaviours between seekers and sources are respected and valued

Awareness

In most globally dispersed organizations, finding "the expert" on a topic, particularly if the individual is not located in the same geographic area, is often a difficult, if not impossible task. Individuals, especially those who are new to an organization, have few tools to locate individuals outside of their own small personal networks. This problem is especially challenging in organizations that have been formed as the results of mergers and acquisitions. This is a problem faced not only by knowledge seekers, but by knowledge sources as well. Knowledgeable experts are often unaware of individuals who might benefit from their knowledge, making it difficult to proactively spread their insights. For example, in one of the organizations we worked with, a software programmer had a novel solution to a particular coding problem. However, this programmer was unaware of the fact that there were other programmers practising the same skills in different locations (other than his own group) who were wrestling with the same problem. The programmer had little awareness that others in their organization might benefit from his solution.

CoPs can be particularly useful in helping individuals become aware of the knowledge and skills of peers who perform the same or similar tasks within an organization. By creating a single place (either physical or virtual) where individuals can meet and interact with others, individuals can be exposed to the knowledge of a critical mass of like-minded practitioners (Lesser & Storck, 2001). As a member of a project management community in a large telecommunications firm stated:

"Undoubtedly, it [the community] has helped me to meet a lot more project managers than I would have done otherwise in joining [the organization]. And I know a lot through the Knowledge Management system. I have gotten to know a lot more people and am able to go and ask a lot more people the right questions. It definitely helps."

Communities can be particularly useful for individuals who are new to the organization, or who have been brought in as the result of a merger or acquisition. In one particular engineering and construction company, there is a CoP to help identify and share project management expertise that had been acquired by the firm as a result of two large mergers. Given that the firm has offices located all over the world, the community serves as a strategic mechanism for identifying expertise that has been critical in the bidding and execution of large projects.

Access

Even if the knowledge seeker and the knowledge source are aware of one another, it may be difficult for them to engage in a knowledge sharing dialogue. In some organizations, there may be limited incentives for the knowledge source to assist the knowledge seeker. For example, a partner in a consulting firm who is already spending a significant amount of effort on her own particular clients may have limited incentive to assist a new associate from a different practice, especially if helping this knowledge seeker will require a commitment of time, energy or other (already limited) resources.

We do not suggest that knowledge sharing is limited simply because of the self-interest of the knowledge source. Often, individuals are simply constrained by the amount of time they can allocate to helping others because they might be struggling to stay on top their own tasks at hand. For example, a 2000 study by Pitney Bowes and the Institute for the Future (Pitney Bowes, 2000) indicated that the average American worker receives over 200 e-mails per day and spends 47 minutes per day managing e-mail. Given the amount of attention spent on reading, reacting and responding to just this one form of communication, it is not surprising that time for knowledge sharing is often at a premium.

Another factor that should be considered is that knowledge sources may be confronted by multiple knowledge seekers, each asking similar questions. For example, a senior claims examiner in an insurance company may be asked to respond to dozens of inquiries about the same or similar topics from multiple call centres around the world. Each of these one-to-one encounters is not only time consuming, but also prevents individuals with more relevant questions from obtaining access to the knowledge sources.

CoPs can help balance a knowledge seeker's need for access with a knowledge source's need for time management. For the knowledge seeker, communities can be seen as a way of making personal connections with more experienced people in the organization (Lesser & Storck, 2001). Through these interactions, relationships are formed that can break down hierarchal boundaries and increase the probability that they will get a response to an inquiry. As another new employee who participated in a project management community in the telecommunications company stated:

"I feel more comfortable calling them (more senior practitioners). I know them more because they have seen my face; they know who I am. They know me as the (community) so they identify me...originally, they wouldn't necessarily pay me the same attention."

Further, communities foster the development of mentor/mentee relationships that can be valuable for both parties by connecting experienced subject matter experts with newer employees. Lave and Wenger (1991) call this process of newcomers learning the practices of the group Legitimate Peripheral Participation. Through community events and interactions, new employees are able to connect with more experienced practitioners who can provide them with insights and guide them in their career development. One of the senior community members within a multinational lending institution noted the importance of mentoring relationships within the community:

"It [the community] certainly has given me the opportunity to share some of what I have at this stage in my career. There are a lot of new entrants to the work force that are coming in and working on this and being able to have a way of registering institutional memory on this particular topic is critical ... The community has been doing a lot of mentoring. We're trying to do that more and more."

In addition to providing easier access to senior practitioners, communities can also help mitigate the number of requests for assistance that more experienced personnel encounter on a regular basis. Several communities with which we have worked have conducted both formal and informal training sessions to educate community members. This allows senior practitioners to share their knowledge with a larger audience and potentially reduce the number of basic inquiries made by less experienced individuals.

Application

Even if the knowledge seeker and knowledge source are able to find the time to connect and share knowledge, there is often difficulty ensuring that the knowledge is understood and applied properly by the knowledge seeker. From the knowledge seeker's perspective, they must be able to take the knowledge provided by the source and relate it to their specific situation. In many cases, this is easier said than done. In his study of 122 "best practices" transfers within an organization, Szulanski (1996) highlights the difficulty in this type of knowledge transfer. In many situations, the receiver of a practice often does not have the time, attention or experience to truly understand how the original practice actually worked. It is this "ambiguity" that makes the transfer and subsequent application of outside practices difficult to incorporate.

At the same time, it may not only be difficult for the knowledge seeker to apply knowledge from another situation, the knowledge source may be unwilling to share this knowledge for fear that the knowledge will be misused. For example, if a junior investment banker misunderstands the insights provided by a more senior member of the firm, it could potentially reflect badly upon the knowledge source that provided his or her insights in the first place.

Our experience suggests that communities can help facilitate the transfer of knowledge across firms by fostering regular dialogues between practitioners on day-to-day business challenges. For example, a community of environmental safety practitioners within a large, global petroleum firm met virtually on a regular basis to discuss remediation projects and other similar efforts. These discussions often required not only answers to specific questions, but also the background and context as to how that answer or solution was derived and applied to solve a previous problem. In interviews with these practitioners, community members felt they benefited significantly from these discussions with other community members as they specifically related to solving actual customer problems, or business challenges, using practices that had been "road tested" elsewhere in the firm (Fontaine & Millen, 2002).

Perception

In competitive work environments, knowledge seekers may find it difficult to ask questions at all. Often, the pressure to "know all the answers" makes it difficult for knowledge seekers to request assistance from others, especially from more experienced professionals. As a result, individuals do not seek out the best possible answer, but rather remain satisfied with an answer that seems "close enough".

At the same time, knowledge sources who are not explicitly recognized for their knowledge contributions may choose to focus their energies elsewhere. Given the reward and recognition systems in many firms, there often is little incentive to assist others, particularly those outside one's own department or business unit. In an atmosphere where rewards are allocated through the achievement of individual goals, it is easy for knowledge sharing to be low on an individual's list of priorities.

Communities can help address a number of issues regarding how individuals are perceived for their knowledge sharing efforts. The mutual engagement between community members often enables individuals to develop a reputation among the membership by giving them a forum to make their knowledge visible (Lesser & Storck, 2001). For example, within a community of software developers, a repository enabled individuals to be recognized for their contributions:

"If you've done some good work on a project, you can package it up and put it into the Tool Pool. That is well perceived by other developers around the world and it's a good way of getting your name known and raising your profile in the organization."

Communities can also hold events that can publicly recognize individual knowledge contributions. In one government organization that we have worked with, individuals could not easily receive spot awards or bonuses based on their willingness to share and reuse knowledge, due their agency's compensation system. However, each year they held a recognition dinner, funded by the community members themselves, to honour the members' contributions to the community.

OVERCOMING THE BARRIERS

In large, distributed organizations, enabling knowledge seekers and knowledge sources to effectively share knowledge is often a significant challenge. We have found that CoPs can help overcome four of the primary hurdles that prevent these exchanges from taking place. By helping individuals identify relevant experts, providing them with the time and space to build relationships and build common context and creating an environment where people are recognized for their contributions and are willing to explore new ideas, communities can go a long way in helping knowledge flow more smoothly across intra-organizational boundaries.

While these communities are often voluntary in nature, organizations can provide these groups with resources and tools that can make them more effective. Though each community is unique in the types of organizational support it requires, below are five general guidelines that can be applied to community efforts in the organization.

Provide a Central Place Where Individuals New to the Organization or Discipline Can Quickly Find Others

Communities, like most Knowledge Management (KM) initiatives, require some investment to facilitate knowledge sharing. Organizations can help communities by providing them with the resources that enable members to connect with each other. By providing time for members to interact in community meetings, training sessions and community forums, the seeds of trust needed to keep the conversations alive can be planted. Additionally, in this time of reduced corporate travel, the organization can also provide technologies that allow for the establishment of "virtual spaces" where members can access knowledge stored in documents, hold synchronous and asynchronous discussions with other members, have opportunities to get to know each other and engage in discussion.

Maintain Directory of Community Participants, Key Skills and Interests

To help with both physical meetings and virtual collaboration, many organizations provide their communities with directories that not only contain contact information (e-mail or office phone numbers), but also a listing of backgrounds, skills, interests and previous work experience. For example, a research community within a large technology company created a "face book" to help build trust and connections between individuals who were brought together because of a recent acquisition. We found that this helped to reduce some of the initial barriers when new members were asked to work on joint projects. By simply thumbing through the face book, members recognized common traits, backgrounds and areas where their expertise complemented that of others. Similarly, most online collaborative environments such as IBM's QuickPlace™ or eRoom's™ virtual workspace provide online directories. These spaces offer quick links to community members' contact information, and in some cases, instant messaging technology is incorporated into the space to provide real-time connectivity to experts.

Evaluate Submissions to a Repository to Ensure that the Explicit Knowledge Base is Current and Contains Relevant Material for Practitioners

In many communities, a significant amount of attention is placed on providing communities with repositories: technologies designed to capture and store structured or written knowledge. These repositories can range from shared file systems to expansive intranet sites. Firms that have effectively used these types of systems recognize the need for human intervention in identifying relevant information, soliciting content from practitioners, updating these spaces on a regular basis and eliminating materials that are no longer helpful or relevant (Fontaine, Burton, & Lesser, 2002). For example, a large US auto manufacturer requires that all submissions be routed to the appropriate community leaders in each of their assembly plants. Upon receiving these submissions via e-mail, the community leaders must indicate whether the material is relevant and applicable to their community's needs and to the job at hand (Stewart, 2001).

Foster an Environment where Practitioners Feel Comfortable to Test Ideas without Fear of Ridicule or Misappropriation

Providing an environment that allows community members to test ideas and try out new solutions is important to building a strong community perception built on trust. For example, at a pharmaceutical firm we worked with, a community came together to share knowledge about a particular new method for investigating chemical compounds. While traditional scientists were sceptical of this process, the community's open environment provided the right atmosphere for those more daring to showcase their groundbreaking ideas. Eventually, this technology achieved mainstream acceptance and the community was credited for enabling the company to remain on the cusp of scientific advancement.

Use Communication and Recognition Vehicles to Increase Visibility of Member Contributions and Reuse

Some organizations recognize and broadcast achievements of the whole community, while others single out key players for their accomplishments. We found that successful communities help overcome knowledge sharing barriers by recognizing and marketing achievements internally and externally, selling successes up to senior management via storytelling of community achievements and singling out key players for their accomplishments in front of their peers. Additionally, other organizations created incentive programs for sharing knowledge in the community through "peer nomination" or "knowledge in action awards".

CONCLUSION

In large, distributed organizations, enabling knowledge seekers and knowledge sources to effectively share knowledge is often a significant challenge. We have found that CoPs can help overcome four of the primary hurdles that prevent these exchanges from taking place: awareness, access, application and awareness. Communities can be a useful approach for helping individuals identify relevant experts, create physical and/or virtual spaces for individuals to meet and share content and foster an environment where people are recognized for their contributions and are willing to explore new ideas. Through the development of improved connections, relationships and shared context, communities can go a long way in helping knowledge flow more smoothly across organizational boundaries.

REFERENCES

Cross, R., Parker, A., Prusak, L., and Borgatti, S. (2001). Knowing what we know: Supporting knowledge creation and sharing in social networks. *Organizational Dynamics*, *30* (2), 100-120.

Fontaine, M. A., and Millen D. R. (2002). Understanding the value of communities: A look at both sides of the cost/benefit equation. *Knowledge Management Review*, *5* (3), 24-27.

Fontaine, M.A., Burton, Y.C., and Lesser, E.L. (2002, November/December). WorldJam: Shaping large-scale collaboration through human intermediation. *Knowledge Management Review, 5* (5).

Lave, J., and Wenger, E. (1991). *Situated learning: Legitimate peripheral participation.* Cambridge University Press.

Lesser, E., and Storck, J. (2001). Communities of Practice and organizational performance. *IBM Systems Journal*, *40* (4), 831-841.

Pitney Bowes. (2000). Pitney Bowes study reveals increased use of electronic communications tools among North American and European workers. *Pitney Bowes press releases* - July 24 and August 7, 2000.

Stewart, T. (2001). *The Wealth of Knowledge*. New York: Doubleday.

Szulanski, G. (1996). Exploring internal stickiness: Impediments to the transfer of best practice within the firm. *Strategic Management Journal, 17* (Winter Special Issue), 27-43.

Chapter III

Cultivating a Community of Practice Between Business and IT

Valerie A. Martin
Brunel University, United Kingdom

Tally Hatzakis
Brunel University, United Kingdom

Mark Lycett
Brunel University, United Kingdom

ABSTRACT

There is a perceived gap between the Information Technology (IT) and the Business function in many organizations, which can lead to poor working relationships and a loss of organizational effectiveness. In this chapter, we discuss an effort to bridge this gap through a program of Relationship Management (RM). The approach is based on the concept of cultivating a Community of Practice (CoP) and relies on facilitating relationships between people in order to share and leverage knowledge. This chapter describes a case study of a large financial services company and shows how the boundaries between Business and IT were spanned through a

Relationship Management Community of Practice (RM CoP). The outcomes of the work are embodied in a maturity model that provides a framework for practice and acts as a 'boundary object' enabling the gap to be bridged. The chapter illustrates how cultivating a CoP between Business and IT can be a holistic way to manage the dynamics of knowledge sharing in organizations.

INTRODUCTION

The perceived gap between the Information Technology (IT) and the Business function presents a major challenge for many business organizations. Poor knowledge of the issues that affect the other and ineffective communication can result in negative effects on knowledge sharing and leverage; this in turn can lead to poor organizational effectiveness.

In this chapter, we discuss a large-scale effort to bridge the gap, through the implementation of a program of Relationship Management (RM) in a large financial services institution. The sharing and leverage of organizational knowledge between Business and IT is a major focus of the RM initiative, the purpose being to bring about a 'one-team' vision and improve communication. Two major challenges are: (i) establishing a common vision and understanding between Business and IT and (ii) improving knowledge sharing.

This chapter aims to explore the nature of knowledge sharing and leverage between Business and the IT organization through an approach to Knowledge Management (KM) that is holistic in nature. The RM program reveals the process of improving knowledge sharing through the gradual spanning of the boundaries between separate functions, thereby cultivating a Relationship Management Community of Practice (RM CoP). We stress the importance of a holistic approach through the two main concepts of the Community of Practice (CoP): participation and reification. We also discuss the participative and facilitative role that the research team played in achieving these improvements.

In the next section, we argue that the Business/IT gap exists because of poor understanding of knowledge in organizations and propose Communities of Practice (CoPs) as an approach to overcoming this. This is followed by a section that introduces the case study and follows the progress of the RM program from inception, through the broadening of participation in the CoP, to sense making and evaluation. The following section discusses the improvements in knowledge sharing and leverage between Business and IT and highlights some concerns. In the final section, we discuss implications and some of the challenges brought up in the RM initiative and conclude that the findings offer an initial endorsement on the approach.

BUSINESS/IT RELATIONSHIPS AND KNOWLEDGE MANAGEMENT

Poor relationships, rather than a poorly integrated IT portfolio, may be at the root of poor knowledge sharing between Business and IT staff (Ward & Peppard, 1996; Peppard & Ward, 1999; Venkatraman & Loh, 1994; Schein, 1997). These poor relationships are a result of a lack of knowledge and differences in knowledge sharing styles. This poses two challenges for KM between Business and IT functions:

1. *Establishing a common vision/understanding between Business and IT*
    • IT is focused on Technology rather than being Business focused
    • Business expects efficient and fast solutions from IT, but gives them little guidance
    • Lack of a 'one-team' mentality and a lack of knowledge of each other's issues
2. *Knowledge sharing between Business and IT*
    • Poor communication and diverse knowledge sharing styles

The field of KM is diverse, spanning a multitude of areas and views. One of the most dominant, however, is the IT, tool driven view. KM sprang from the artificial intelligence movement where knowledge is viewed as a commodity that can be codified, stored and transmitted. Scarborough, Swan and Preston (1999) claim that nearly 70% of articles on KM are from the IT/IS areas and many of these are practice driven with the emphasis on explicit knowledge. Managers hope that these tools can be exploited to capture and retain knowledge within the company, and that this will encourage learning across functional boundaries.

This trend is also evident in academic literature. The most common use of technology in KM is to create a repository of so-called 'structured knowledge' (Davenport & Prusak, 1998). In analyzing the predominant views in KM, Schultze and Leidner (2002) claim that the vast majority of research in the area of KM in information systems falls under an approach which is concerned with codification of objective knowledge. This view is clearly the dominant view in KM. However, the weakness of this approach is the assumption that all knowledge can be made explicit and captured in a formal way.

It is questionable if this view can capture the nuances of more complex issues such as tacit mental models, relationships, degree of involvement and depth of knowledge in an information sharing community. People are active sense-makers who often share common views but also conflict and disagree. While they may like to make sense of things through codifying knowledge and formalizing processes, they often prefer informal dialogue and networks to share knowledge (Martin, Lycett, & Macredie, 2003). Knowledge in organizations is not simply about technology, no matter how sophisticated it is, but is a complex mix of people, technology, processes, relationships, dialogue, consensus and conflict.

Another related area of debate in KM is the division between tacit and explicit knowledge. Here the view is that knowledge is something more than an object that can be dealt with by formal, technology-based tools; the importance of tacit knowledge and the expertise that resides in people and communities must also be considered. In general, however, the tacit/explicit debate is mainly concerned with making tacit knowledge explicit rather than defining what tacit knowledge actually is, thereby assuming that tacit and explicit knowledge are mutually exclusive (Hildreth & Kimble, 2002).

Identifying this problem, Nonaka (1991) views tacit and explicit knowledge as being complementary rather than mutually exclusive. The values, know-how and tacit knowledge of people are interdependent with a more explicit type of knowledge; his well-known 'Knowledge Spiral' demonstrates the mutual dependency of both tacit and explicit knowledge. However, even this approach has its drawbacks; once again, there is the assumption that all tacit knowledge can be made explicit in some way (Hildreth & Kimble, 2002). Tacit knowledge cannot always be articulated, and if tacit knowledge cannot be articulated, then it cannot be made explicit.

Knowledge is complex and is neither purely tacit nor explicit, but dynamic and constantly changing. Hildreth and Kimble (2002) put forward the view that knowledge should not be seen as opposites but as complementary facets: a duality consisting simultaneously of 'structured' and 'less structured' knowledge. They argue that CoPs can be seen as a more holistic way of viewing and understanding organizational knowledge.

Communities of Practice

Wenger and Snyder (2000) describe a CoP as a group of people who are bound together informally through sharing expertise and enthusiasm for something. A CoP is built on collective learning over a period of time, which results in practices and social relations that reflect the expertise of the community.

Theories on CoPs propose an interdependent process of participation and reification of knowledge, which Wenger (1998) describes as the 'negotiation of meaning':

- Participation means living in the world in terms of being actively involved in social communities. However, participation can involve all kinds of relationships, conflictual as well as collaborative.
- Reification concerns giving concrete form to something that is abstract and this comes from manifesting the experience of the participants. Reification can take the form of tools, procedures, stories or language (1998).

Figure 1: The Duality of Participation and Reification (From Wenger, 1998, p. 63)

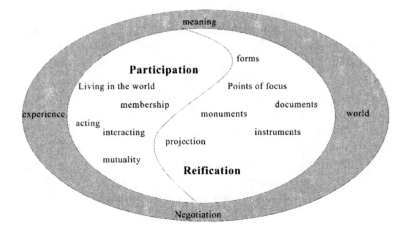

Participation and reification are inseparable: they are not a dichotomy. The concept of reification is closely related to the concept of a 'boundary object' (Star, 1989): an artefact around which CoPs can organize their interconnections. However, Wenger expands on this, believing that it is preferable to have people and artifacts travel together to take full advantage of the complementarity of reification and participation. Figure 1 illustrates the duality of the two concepts within a world of meaning, experience and negotiation.

The CoP provides an approach to implementing KM between Business and IT. A key theme is that a CoP cannot be managed or controlled, but cultivated. CoPs are fundamentally self-organizing and facilitators need to respond to them in a manner that respects their informal nature (Wenger & Snyder, 2000). In this chapter, we use CoP theory as a conceptual reference through which to view the RM process between Business and IT. We track the RM program in a case study company, showing how the concepts of participation and reification help to achieve better knowledge sharing and leverage between Business and IT, thereby building a Relationship Management Community of Practice (RM CoP).

THE CASE STUDY AND RESEARCH APPROACH

This approach was used to investigate RM and the Business/IT gap in Finco, a large financial services provider in the UK. This study is focused on their largest business unit, Retail Banking, and the perceived gap with their internal IT organization. Increasing competitive pressure within the financial services sector has led to the influence of each division on the processes of organizational innovation, strategy and change being fragmented. Because of this, the 'gap' has emerged as an area of organizational concern owing to problems in the areas of working relationships, knowledge sharing, communication and project planning and delivery.

The first phase of the research began when a Director of Finco decided to recruit a team of Relationship Managers (RMs) to be responsible for tackling the issues of the Business/IT gap. The director responsible for this initiative was the IT director for Retail Banking who had the remit of managing the IT function on behalf of the Bank. Although his title was IT Director, he was from a banking rather than an IT background. He put forward the following reasons:

1) IT people, being domain-focused, needed to broaden their thinking and learn to ask the right questions from business users.
2) Business users were challenging IT more because they know more about technology, but they still needed the cooperation and expertise of the IT people.
3) The Retail Banking units saw IT as expensive, slow and unresponsive.

These comments stressed the lack of vision and knowledge sharing between the two functions. In addition, some early interviews with Retail Banking and IT staff revealed concerns about the proposed RMs: RM should provide a conduit and not a blockage to communication between various parties and it should have a facilitation rather than a decision-making orientation. These concerns were especially prevalent amongst the IT staff and were an expression of a desire to build a genuine CoP between Retail Banking and IT where relationships would be equal and problems negotiable.

The second phase of the research began with the secondment of the research team to the new RMs. The research aims and objectives at this stage were to investigate and define RM best practices and to identify and describe the challenges the RMs faced when undertaking their new roles. This phase demonstrated increasing participation in the CoP, with the RMs reifying RM activities through identifying information and knowledge needs, diary keeping, note taking, following up phone calls and arranging meetings with people. In addition, they were also observed to act as intermediaries between Retail Banking and IT staff. Throughout this phase, the research team gradually established themselves as part of the widening RM CoP, engaging in dialogue with the RMs and other staff, taking notes and generally giving informal feedback to the RMs. The RM activities were documented on a daily basis, thus providing reification of knowledge for the community through discussion of the findings and relating this new knowledge to theory and practice.

The third phase was the development of the Relationship Management Maturity Model (RMMM), a reference framework for best practice in RM. The challenge we faced was to develop a model that could be used to help to define a framework for change and best practice for RM. There was a need for clear performance indicators and guidelines for RMs because RM has little theoretical grounding or documented practical applications. At the same time, the model also needed to incorporate guidelines for long-term sustainability of the RM CoP. The RMMM was the most important 'boundary object' in the research, as it helps to clarify RM best practices and to provide a roadmap for the future development of the RM CoP.

SOME IMPROVEMENTS AND SOME CONCERNS

The extent of participation in the RM CoP was hard to gauge throughout the process of observing the RMs, as interacting with people does not necessarily imply participation in a CoP. We defined participation in the RM CoP at this stage as being in favor of the RMs' work, as well as interacting with them. Eleven months after the introduction of RM, we undertook an evaluation exercise to collect feedback with regard to the degree that RM was perceived to have increased participation and improved knowledge sharing and leverage. The research team used Wenger and Snyder's (2000) suggestion that evaluation of a CoP may be done through story-telling and anecdotal evidence: therefore the interviewees were encouraged to talk as much as possible.

RM Successes in Knowledge Sharing

- **Better interdepartmental communication** - People were happier with communication and felt more involved. RMs have helped the organization share knowledge and expertise across departments and enabled both Retail Banking and IT people to learn about each other's concerns, considerations and limitations.

"The most prominent changes that RM has brought about are helping our understanding of IT issues, quality of communication and open and honest debates."

- **Ability for IT staff to get their voices heard in senior management agenda** - Lower ranking systems managers have admitted that it is easier to raise issues and lobby with RMs to press issues into the top management agenda, thereby speeding up communications.

"My view is that RM has effected immediate escalation routes and accessibility."

RM Successes in Knowledge Leverage

- **Improved quality of information for project planning** - The RM team have a first hand view of strategic direction in Finco as their manager sits on board meetings in which strategy and strategy amendments were decided. Frequent communication within the RM team have given them accurate strategic information and knowledge quickly. This has helped RMs to shape operational plans and advise on solving operational issues across and within Retail Banking and IT units in order to converge Business strategy.

"They are helping us to understand the issues and challenges facing the IT teams and how we can try to schedule projects taking into account dependencies and constraints."

- **Access to expertise** - The degree of direct access to colleagues' knowledge and expertise across divisions has increased considerably through the mediation of RM.

"My relationship manager is brilliant in this respect. Whenever I want something, I just have to call her. She will tell me what I need to know or find out for me or clue me in on what is happening and who I need to talk to."

Some Concerns

- **Dependence on RMs** - The increase in reliance on RM to ensure the delivery of IT promises, or at least to communicate enough information for Retail Banking to foresee issues and put contingencies in place, has created complacency and an unwillingness to instigate other links.

"I don't have time to go to speak to people within each of the departments of IT and there is no need as RMs get my job done ... if they weren't there the job would still be done as it used to, it won't be as efficient as now but it will get done eventually."

- **Perpetuation of the gap perception** - Although RM has formed a hub that brings together the organization it is doubtful whether integration capabilities have transferred to others within Retail Banking and IT units. The existence of the RM function as an effective alternative has introduced reluctance for direct interaction.

"Relationship Management has decreased instances of aggravation, but perpetuated the 'us-them' mentality."

These findings suggest that, apart from a few problems, participation has generally increased in the new RM CoP as it has developed over the first year of its implementation. Business managers in the wide network of branches appear to be taking part in the CoP, as are lower IT managers. Knowledge appears to be shared more effectively and sources of expertise sought out.

IMPLICATIONS AND CONCLUSIONS

The research so far has revealed many improvements in knowledge sharing and leverage in Finco, together with a widening participation in the RM CoP. There is already a clearer understanding of the others' issues, with RMs collecting information relevant to problem areas, thereby reducing uncertainty and speeding up information transfer between Retail Banking and IT. There is better access to sources of expertise and the RMs act as facilitators, co-coordinators and intermediaries to bring people with skills and knowledge together. In addition, the research team has been actively involved in facilitating the CoP and there is now a burgeoning RM CoP.

There are, however, a few issues of concern at this stage. In the Phase 1 interviews, the IT organization stressed the need for RMs to act as a conduit for knowledge sharing rather than a blockage. There are some issues here, as the evaluation exercise has shown. In terms of the RM CoP, there appear to be some adverse effects of RM. Instead of staff participating more in the RM CoP, it appears to be making them less participative than they were before. This

Figure 2: The Relationship Management Community of Practice

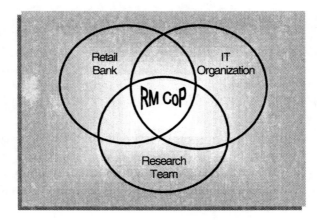

manifests itself as a dependency on the RMs to instigate relationships rather than people doing it themselves. This indicates that some staff have become lazier in their attitude to knowledge sharing and, in some ways, the RMs have caused a blockage to full participation in the CoP.

These issues may simply be 'growing pains' and not necessarily an indication of the future development of the RM CoP. This evaluation exercise was carried out after only a year of the RM program. The process of crafting a CoP does not happen overnight, but is a long-term process of change. It is probable that it will take some time for the RM concept to be accepted and integrated in the organization.

Implications

Our approach has provided insight into the following areas:

Knowledge Management and the Business/IT Gap

The perceived gap between Retail Banking and the IT organization in Finco has poor KM as one of the major causes. There is difficulty in establishing the leverage of knowledge and this is manifested through poor understanding of each other's issues. Retail Banking thinks IT is too insular and focused on technology and formalized processes, whereas IT staff think that they understand business needs better than Retail Banking understands IT needs. Poor knowledge sharing is manifested through an entangled organizational structure, where lines of reporting and responsibility are not understood and poor team working leads to communication blockages.

The prevailing models in KM theory are too limiting to explain a complex Business/IT gap based on poor vision and relationships between people. Simply implementing information systems as a way to improve knowledge sharing does not improve relationships. Knowledge is more complex than this, especially the tacit dimensions which are people-based, hard to define and often impossible to make explicit. Relationships are built not only on cooperation, but also on conflicts, discourse and discussion between parties; information systems may or may not be a part of this.

The concept of a CoP provides a reference framework through which to view the process of knowledge sharing and leverage in RM. This view shows how the two vital and complementary aspects of participation and reification can develop, combine and grow into a thriving RM CoP that can bridge the gap between Retail Banking and IT in Finco. There were many examples of both participation and reification in the case study; the most important were:

- The RMMM, which acts as a major boundary object between the research team, the RM team and the rest of the Retail Banking and IT staff in Finco. This model was developed through an iterative process of data collection, observation, dialogue, analysis and benchmarking data within the rapidly growing RM CoP. It is now complete and can act as a future reference for the RMs as they attempt to further develop the CoP.

- The three RMs, who were the people who travelled with the boundary object and the research team. In this case, they were all at the heart of the RM program, collaborating directly with Retail Banking and IT staff through direct communication and indirectly through the RMMM.

Cultivating a CoP for Practitioners

There is a need for Finco to have a good understanding of not only the successes achieved so far but also the glitches that are surfacing. In particular, Retail Banking may need to be careful not to impose their own agenda on the IT organization, especially as Retail Banking, in the form of the IT director, had originally conceived the idea of RM.

It appeared from the Phase 1 interviews that the IT organization actually does desire a genuine CoP to be cultivated through the RMs to enable them to respond better to business needs. The original meeting with the IT Director of Finco showed that the Business/IT gap issues were his own view on what he wanted the IT Organization to provide. Again, the concerns of IT in the Phase 1 interviews were that the RMs should provide a facilitation role, rather than a decision-making role.

The guidelines that the RMMM provides, however, are designed to enable the RMs to deal with these issues. The implication for practitioners is that care must be taken to realize RM as a long-term goal based on a CoP. This implies full participation and buy-in with no imposing of Business agendas, control or blame, to fulfil the self-organizing aspects of a CoP.

Conclusions

This chapter has described and discussed a large-scale effort to bridge the gap between Business and IT, through the implementation of a program of RM in a large financial services institution. The sharing and leverage of knowledge has been a major aspect of bridging the gap to overcome the lack of common understanding and poor communication.

After studying the problems of knowledge sharing and leverage between Business and IT, we have concluded that research in the understanding and management of organizational knowledge suffers from a dearth of holistic approaches. In view of the crucial issue of the Business/IT gap in organizations, we propose that CoPs may be the way forward for the study and understanding of knowledge in organizations. In this way, a broader understanding of KM may be achieved, as well as practical implications for the Business/IT gap. A strong CoP may be the basis upon which organizations integrate the IT organization with the Business for competitiveness in a knowledge-intensive global economy.

REFERENCES

Davenport, T., and Prusak, L. (1998). *Working knowledge. How organisations manage what they know*. Cambridge, MA: Harvard Business School Press.

Hildreth, P., and Kimble, C. (2002). The duality of knowledge. *Information Research, 8* (1). On the World Wide Web: http://informationr.net/ir/8-1/paper142.html

Martin, V.A., Lycett, M., and Macredie, R. (2003). Exploring the gap between Business and IT: an information culture approach. *Proceedings of ALOIS 2003, Action in Language, Organisations and Information Systems*, University of Linköping, Sweden, March 2003, 265-280.

Nonaka, I. (1991). The knowledge creating company. *Harvard Business Review, 69* (November/December), 96-104.

Peppard, J., and Ward, J. (1999). Mind the gap: Diagnosing the relationship between the IT organisation and the rest of the business. *Journal of Strategic Information Systems, 8* (1), 29-60.

Scarborough, H., Swan, J., and Preston, J. (1999). Knowledge management and the learning organisation—The IPD Report. *Report for the Institute of Personnel Development*, UK, October 1998.

Schein, E. (1997). *Organisational culture and leadership*. CA: Jossey-Bass.

Schultze, U., and Leidner, D. (2002). Studying knowledge management in Information Systems research: Discourses and theoretical assumptions. *Management Information Systems Quarterly, 26* (3), 213-242.

Star, S. L. (1989). The structure of ill-structured solutions: Boundary objects and heterogeneous distributed problem solving. *Distributed Artificial Intelligence, 2*, 37-54.

Venkatraman, N., and Loh, L. (1994). The shifting logic of the IS organisation: From technical portfolio to relationships. *Information Strategy: The Executive Journal*, Winter, 5-11.

Ward, J., and Peppard, J. (1996). Reconciling the IT/Business relationship: A troubled marriage in need of guidance. *Journal of Strategic Information Systems, 5* (1), 37-65.

Wenger, E. (1998). *Communities of Practice. Learning, meaning and identity*. Cambridge, MA: Cambridge University Press.

Wenger, E., and Snyder, W. (2000). Communities of Practice: The organisational frontier. *Harvard Business Review*, (January/February), 139-145.

Chapter IV

The Paradox of Communities of Practice:
Knowledge Sharing
Between Communities

Donald Hislop
University of Sheffield, United Kingdom

ABSTRACT

This chapter examines knowledge sharing between Communities of Practice, a relatively neglected topic of study. Theory and evidence is presented to suggest that knowledge sharing between communities is likely to be more complex than intra-community knowledge sharing, due to the lack of shared consensual knowledge or shared sense of identity which typically exists in inter-community contexts. In such situations, the development of trust is seen to be a key foundation which requires to be developed before effective knowledge sharing can occur. Three brief case studies are presented to illustrate the arguments made. Practitioner implications flowing from this chapter are twofold. Firstly, to facilitate effective inter-community knowledge sharing requires effort to be invested in developing the social relationship (and hence trust) between members from the communities. Secondly, organizations need to balance their efforts at building Communities of Practice with supporting inter-community interactions; otherwise they risk developing isolated and inward looking communities.

'The shared infrastructure of activity that makes cooperation the norm within particular communities of activity can act as a barrier to close collaboration with outsiders'

Blackler, Crump, & McDonald, 2000, p. 282

INTRODUCTION

One issue that has been relatively neglected by the Communities of Practice (CoP) literature is the dynamics of knowledge sharing between communities. Paradoxically, the characteristics of CoPs which facilitate knowledge sharing within a community may inhibit the sharing of knowledge between communities (Alvesson, 2000; Blackler et al., 2000). Consequently, the dynamics of knowledge sharing within and between CoPs are likely to be qualitatively different, with the sharing of knowledge between communities being typically more complex and more difficult (Brown & Duguid, 1998). This chapter sheds light on this neglected area by examining some examples of inter-community knowledge sharing and reflecting on the factors which affect the dynamics of such processes.

The paradox outlined above raises some interesting questions and dilemmas for organizational practitioners. To neglect supporting CoPs risks losing out on their undoubted advantages and benefits. Conversely, there is a potential risk that investing in CoPs may inhibit organization-wide knowledge sharing and fragment the organizational knowledge base through facilitating the creation of discrete, isolated and inward-looking communities.

The importance of examining inter-community dynamics is reinforced by the increasing use of team and project-based working by organizations. For example, team and project work are often multidisciplinary, requiring close collaboration between people from different disciplinary backgrounds and CoPs (Newell & Swan, 2000; Gherardi & Nicolini, 2002). Further, the use of such working practices also raises the issue of inter-project learning and knowledge sharing, as organizations attempt to avoid the twin problems of 'losing' project-based knowledge and reinventing the wheel (Prencipe & Tell, 2001).

The chapter is structured into three sections. The first briefly discusses the mainstream CoP literature, outlining its conclusions regarding the advantage of CoPs. The second section then examines the relatively unexplored issue of knowledge sharing between CoPs, using both positive and negative case study examples to illustrate the issues examined. Finally, the third section of the chapter reflects on the practitioner implications of the issues discussed.

COMMUNITIES OF PRACTICE AND INTRA-COMMUNITY KNOWLEDGE PROCESSES

Lave and Wenger define a CoP as a community of practitioners within which situational learning develops, which results in the community developing '... a set of relations among persons, activity and the world' (1991, p. 98). Extrapolating from this definition, CoPs can be seen to have three defining characteristics, all of which flow from the community members' involvement in some shared activity (see Table 1). Firstly, participants in a community possess and develop a stock of common, shared knowledge. Secondly, communities typically also develop shared values and a common 'world-view'. Boland and Tenkasi (1995) referred to the process of developing and communicating such views as 'perspective making'. Finally, and equally importantly, members of communities also possess a sense of communal identity (Brown & Duguid, 2001).

Increasingly, organizations are supporting and developing CoPs as part of their Knowledge Management (KM) initiatives, due to the benefits they provide in facilitating knowledge processes. Almost universally, the knowledge litera-ture considers CoPs advantageous for both individuals and organizations. Thus, they are argued to provide workers with a sense of collective identity and a social context in which they can develop and utilize their knowledge. For organizations, they can provide a vital source of innovation. The KM literature, which has utilized the CoP concept strongly, argues that they can facilitate organizational knowledge processes (Brown & Duguid, 1998; DeFillippi & Arthur, 1998; Hildreth, Kimble, & Wright, 2000; Iles, 1994; Lave & Wenger, 1991; McDermott, 1999; Raelin, 1997; Ward, 2000).

The utility of CoPs in enabling such knowledge processes is closely related to the elements that members of a community share, outlined above (see Table 1). The simultaneous existence of these elements enables knowledge processes for two primary reasons. Firstly, they make it easier to appreciate the taken for granted assumptions which underpin all knowledge. Secondly, the existence of these elements is likely to produce trust-based relations, creating social condi-tions that are conducive to knowledge sharing. KM literature suggests that supportive and positive social relations are an important pre-requisite for effective inter-personal knowledge sharing (Andrews & Delahaye, 2001; Rob-

Table 1: Characteristics of Communities of Practice

Defining Characteristics of CoPs
Body of common knowledge/practice
Sense of shared identity
Some common or overlapping values

erts, 2000). That such social relations are common within CoPs provides one explanation for why they are good knowledge sharing forums.

However, these advantages are focused primarily on intra-community dynamics. What is generally neglected in the majority of the CoP literature is the dynamics of inter-community knowledge sharing processes. These issues are considered in the following section.

THE DYNAMICS OF INTER-COMMUNITY KNOWLEDGE SHARING PROCESSES

As has been well illustrated by the majority of the CoP literature, the sense of collective identity and values and the existence of a significant consensual knowledge base within a CoP facilitate the processes of knowledge sharing. Arguably, however, the sharing of knowledge between communities is much more problematic due to the lack of both these elements. Thus, if CoPs create social conditions that are conducive to knowledge sharing, the character of social relations between people who are not members of the same CoP is less likely to. This section examines how a lack of shared identity, or a limited, consensual knowledge base can inhibit inter-community knowledge processes. The section concludes by presenting a positive example, which shows how it is possible to facilitate inter-community knowledge sharing, primarily through the development of trust.

Taking the issue of divergent identities first, the existence of diverging identities between different CoPs arguably complicates the knowledge sharing process through the perceived or actual different interests between communities and the potential for conflict this creates. A growing body of research shows that such factors can actively inhibit processes of knowledge sharing (Ciborra & Patriotta, 1998; Hayes & Walsham, 2000; Storey & Barnett, 2000). The following example reinforces these conclusions.

Neth-Bank is a Dutch bank which grew aggressively by acquisition during the course of 1990s. By the late 1990s, it had divisions in over 70 countries worldwide. At this point corporate management decided it was necessary to improve levels of co-ordination and knowledge sharing between divisions. A key element of their strategy to achieve this was the development of a global intranet, a project that was developed and managed by corporate IT staff. However, Neth-Bank had a strong historical culture of divisional autonomy, with divisions having operated completely independently from each other. Thus each division had controlled how it was organized, with the consequence that each division had its own working practices, IT systems, etc. For example, each division had its own intranet site (there were estimated to be at least 150 within the company), each with its own specific style, level of functionality, etc.

Thus, staff had a strong sense of identity with their division and possessed a body of specialist knowledge related to their division's particular customers, products, market conditions and internal ways of working. Therefore, the staff in each division had the three key attributes that characterize CoPs (see Table 1). The global intranet project experienced significant problems, however, as management staff from most divisions were hostile to the idea, primarily because they perceived the objectives of the project to be incompatible with their desire to retain divisional autonomy.

The global intranet project was significantly inhibited by the reluctance of staff from different divisions to collaborate and share knowledge, as the success of the project required them to do so. A significant part of the reason why corporate IT staff were unsuccessful in persuading divisional staff to do this was that they did little to improve the social relations between staff from different divisions. Instead, their strategy was technical in focus, being concerned primarily with putting an appropriate IT infrastructure in place, agreeing on protocols for site design, and defining style for pages and what content was suitable. This meant that the levels of trust between divisional staff were low, as nothing had been done to break down and challenge the historical antagonism that existed between divisions.

The other factor, which arguably complicates the sharing of knowledge between CoPs, is the distinctiveness of their knowledge bases and the lack of consensual knowledge that may exist. Further, not only can the knowledge of these communities differ, but their knowledge bases may also be based on qualitatively different assumptions and interpretative frameworks (Tsoukas, 1996; Becker, 2001). Brown and Duguid (2001) referred to these as 'epistemic differences', which significantly increase the difficulty not just of sharing knowledge between communities, but of fundamentally understanding the knowledge of another community and the assumptions it is based on. Thus, the limited degree of consensual knowledge that can exist between different communities can inhibit and complicate the sharing of knowledge. These issues are illustrated by considering the difficulties a French manufacturing company had in facilitating inter-functional knowledge sharing.

France-Co produces specialist components for military and civil aircraft. As part of the company's attempts to introduce new management practices following the end of the Cold War, it decided to implement an Enterprise Resource Planning (ERP) system, which was intended to improve levels of inter-functional knowledge sharing. This project represented an enormous challenge for France-Co, as two of the most important functions for this project, sales and production, had historically shared little information. These functional groups could be described as CoPs as they possessed their own specialist bodies of knowledge and staff had a strong sense of identity for the function they worked in. Further, the knowledge possessed by staff in these groups was highly tacit, being held largely in the heads of staff. This knowledge was typically developed through practice and very little of it was codified in any structured way. Finally, as with Neth-Bank's divisions, relations between these functional communities had historically been antagonistic.

As France-Co's ERP project developed it became apparent that the lack of knowledge sharing between these communities was proving detrimental to the project. Thus, initial attempts to implement the new system proved disastrous and had to be stopped. The main reason for this failure was that staff in both the sales and production function were not sharing the type of knowledge and information that was necessary for the success of the project. While this reluctance to share knowledge was partly related to the historical antagonism between these functions, it was also related to the specialized nature of the knowledge they both possessed. The specialist nature of their knowledge, combined with the extensive lack of interaction which had been typical, meant that they had a very poor understanding of how other functions worked or what their constraints and requirements were. Thus, even when staff from these communities were willing to share knowledge with each other, effectively doing so proved difficult as each had an extremely limited understanding of what knowledge was relevant, useful or important to other functions. As a consequence of these problems, not only was France-Co's implementation extensively delayed, but also the overall functionality of their ERP system was significantly compromised.

Arguably, a significant factor explaining these negative examples of inter-community knowledge sharing was the relatively low level of trust that existed between the communities examined. The importance of trust in facilitating knowledge sharing is increasingly being recognized, with a lack of trust likely to inhibit the extent to which people are willing to share knowledge with each other (Andrews & Delahaye, 2001; Davenport & Prusak, 1998; Roberts, 2000). To trust someone is to assume that they will honour their obligations, and trusting relations are based on, and develop from, an expectation of reciprocity. However, the nature of inter-community social relations, where the consensual knowledge base is limited, or where people have a limited sense of shared identity, makes the existence of trust less likely and the development of trust more difficult.

However, knowledge sharing between CoPs, while difficult and complex, is by no means impossible. This can be illustrated by examining an example where such knowledge sharing was successful. Swed-Co is a Swedish company which manufactures, services and rents specialist materials handling equipment such as forklift trucks. In the late 1990s, it had 11 nationally-based business units spread across Europe. These business units operated autonomously, with each being independently responsible for how they were structured and how their business practices were carried out. However, in contrast to Neth-Bank, relations between business units were not antagonistic. During the late 1990s, Swed-Co corporate management decided to implement an organization-wide ERP system to improve levels of co-ordination in its business units.

As a consequence of the high level of operating autonomy that had been traditional, staff in each business unit developed a strong sense of identity to their unit and each unit possessed its own body of specialist knowledge related to the character of its specific customers, market conditions and internal ways of working. Thus, Swed-Co's business units can be regarded as CoPs.

To develop and implement its corporate ERP system, the project manager (from the Corporate IS/IT function) created a multi-community project team involving staff from a range of business units. The project team was largely selected for the relevance of its knowledge of the IT systems and working practices in the different business units. The project team was given its own dedicated workspace at the corporate headquarters. The work practices utilized, which were developed with an awareness of and sensitivity to the 'people' issues underpinning knowledge sharing, involved divisional staff working closely together in a face-to-face context over an extended period of time. These work practices facilitated a process of what Boland and Tenkasi (1995) referred to as 'perspective making' and 'perspective taking', where business unit staff were able to develop an appreciation of the knowledge base of other project team members. This process simultaneously contributed to the development of trust between project team members.

The result of these working practices was that project team members were both committed to the aims of the project and were willing to share their knowledge as necessary, even though the project could be interpreted as threatening the historical autonomy of the local business units they worked in. Ultimately, Swed-Co's project was implemented largely on time, with planned levels of functionality, and could be regarded as relatively successful.

PRACTITIONER IMPLICATIONS

One of the main practitioner implications from the examples presented is that effective cross-community knowledge sharing requires a certain level of trust to exist and consequently requires a sensitivity to the character of inter-community social relations. Crudely, the reason for the success of Swed-Co and the failure of Neth-Bank and France-Co was that Swed-Co project management personnel showed a greater sensitivity to these social relations than project management staff in the other two organizations.

The reason for the need for trust and supportive social relations between communities attempting to share knowledge with each other is that, due to the lack of common knowledge and identity between community members, the initial level of trust and mutual understanding may not be high. Generally, a growing body of research shows that the character of social relations is likely to be a key factor shaping knowledge sharing dynamics (Andrews & Delahaye, 2001; Storey & Quintas, 2001; Robertson, O'Malley, & Hammersley, 2000; Scarbrough, Swan, & Preston, 1999). However, where knowledge sharing is between people from different CoPs, the character of the social relationship is especially important.

Further, the lack of consensual knowledge between communities means that for effective knowledge sharing to occur, a process of 'perspective making' and 'perspective taking' is necessary in order for people to begin developing a mutual understanding of the knowledge, values and assumptions possessed by people from other communities. It is only when such a foundation has been established that effective knowledge sharing is then likely to occur. The case of Swed-Co suggests that for these perspective making and taking processes to be effective it may be necessary for an extensive amount of face-to-face interaction to occur.

Finally, while there are undoubted organizational advantages to stimulating and developing CoPs, this chapter suggests that there are also some potential dangers if communities develop too strong a sense of community identity. Primarily, there is the potential that they may become insular, excessively exclusionary and unwilling to share knowledge outside of the community. Thus, it is important for organizations to facilitate inter-community relations as much as intra-community relations. For example, this could be done through creating social forums, which bring staff from different communities together in a social context, which allows them to improve their understanding of each other's perspective.

CONCLUSION

The subject of inter-community dynamics and knowledge sharing processes is much neglected by the majority of the CoP literature. Therefore, our current understanding of such processes is somewhat limited. This chapter has made a modest attempt to address this and contribute to an improved understanding of inter-community dynamics.

Empirically, the chapter has shown the difficulties involved in attempting to share knowledge across CoPs. The lack of consensual knowledge and diverging senses of identity that exist between communities represent two of the most important reasons why such processes are complex and difficult. Through all three examples, the chapter has shown how the character of inter-community social relations crucially shapes efforts to share knowledge between communities. The chapter therefore reinforces the emerging consensus in the contemporary KM literature, which emphasises the importance of human, cultural and social factors in shaping the character of knowledge processes.

The main practical conclusions from the chapter are twofold. Firstly, the achievement of effective inter-community knowledge sharing will require the communities involved to develop some level of trust and understanding of each other's knowledge base and assumptions, in a process of 'perspective making' and 'perspective taking'. There is therefore a role for organizational management to facilitate the creation of such conditions. Secondly, to avoid the potential danger of having exclusionary, inward-looking communities that are unwilling or unable to share their knowledge, organizational management can play a role in putting in place mechanisms to encourage communication and interaction across different organizational communities.

REFERENCES

Alvesson, M. (2000). Social identity in knowledge-intensive companies. *Journal of Management Studies, 37* (8), 1101-1123.

Andrews, K., and Delahaye, B. (2000). Influences on knowledge processes in organizational learning: The psychosocial filter. *Journal of Management Studies, 37* (6), 797-810.

Becker, M. (2001). Managing dispersed knowledge: Organizational problems, managerial strategies and their effectiveness. *Journal of Management Studies, 38* (7), 1037-1051.

Blackler, F., Crump, N., and McDonald, S. (2000). Organizing processes in complex activity networks. *Organization, 7* (2), 277-300.

Boland, R., and Tenkasi, R. (1995). Perspective making and perspective taking in communities of knowing. *Organization Science, 6* (4), 350-372.

Brown, J., and Duguid, P. (1998). Organizing knowledge. *California Management Review, 40* (3), 90-111.

Brown, J., and Duguid, P. (2001). Knowledge and organization: A social practice perspective. *Organization Science, 12* (2), 198-213.

Ciborra, C., and Patriotti, G. (1998). Groupware and teamwork in R&D: Limits to learning and innovation. *R&D Management, 28* (1), 1-10.

Davenport, T., and Prusak, L. (1998). *Working knowledge: How organizations manage what they know.* Boston, MA: Harvard Business School Press.

DeFillippi, R., and Arthur, M. (1998). Paradox in project based enterprise: The case of filmmaking. *California Management Review, 40* (2), 125-139.

Gherardi, S., and Nicolini, D. (2002). Learning in a constellation of interconnected practices: Canon or dissonance? *Journal of Management Studies, 39* (4), 419-436.

Hayes, N., and Walsham, G. (2000). Safe enclaves, political enclaves and knowledge working. In C. Prichard, R. Hull, M. Chumer and H. Willmott.

(Eds.), *Managing knowledge: Critical investigations of work and learning.* London: MacMillan.

Hildreth, P., Kimble, C., and Wright, P. (2000). Communities of Practice in the distributed international environment. *Journal of Knowledge Management, 4* (1), 27-38.

Iles, P. (1994). Developing learning environments: Challenges for theory, research and practice. *Journal of European Industrial Training, 18* (3), 3-9.

Lave, J., and Wenger, E. (1991). *Situated learning: Legitimate peripheral participation.* Cambridge: Cambridge University Press.

McDermott, R. (1999). Why Information Technology inspired but cannot deliver Knowledge Management. *California Management Review, 41* (1), 103-117.

Newell, S., and Swan, J. (2000). Trust and inter-organizational networking. *Human Relations, 53* (10), 1287-1328.

Prencipe, A., and Tell, F. (2001). Inter-project learning and outcomes of knowledge codification in project-based firms. *Research Policy, 30* (9), 1373-1394.

Raelin, J. (1997). A model of work based learning. *Organization Science, 8* (6), 563-578.

Roberts, J. (2000). From know-how to show-how? Questioning the role of Information and Communication Technologies in knowledge transfer. *Technology Analysis and Strategic Management, 12* (4), 429-443.

Robertson, M., O'Malley, G., and Hammersley, G. (2000). Knowledge Management practices within a knowledge-intensive firm: The significance of the People Management Dimension. *Journal of European Industrial Training, 24* (2-4), 241-253.

Scarbrough, H., Swan, J., and Preston, J. (1999). *Knowledge Management: A literature review.* London: Institute of Personnel and Development.

Storey, J., and Barnett, E. (2000). Knowledge Management initiatives: Learning from failure. *Journal of Knowledge Management, 4* (2), 145-156.

Storey, J., and Quintas, P. (2001). Knowledge Management and HRM. In J. Storey (Ed.), *Human resource management: A critical text.* London: Thomson Learning.

Tsoukas, H. (1996). The firm as a distributed knowledge system: A constructionist approach. *Strategic Management Journal, 17,* Winter Special Issue, 11-25.

Ward, A. (2000). Getting strategic value from constellations of communities. *Strategy and Leadership, 28* (2), 4-9.

SECTION II:

COMMUNITIES OF PRACTICE AND KNOWLEDGE MANAGEMENT

Chapter V

Investigating the Influence that Media Richness has on Learning in a Community of Practice:

A Case Study at Øresund Bridge

Andrew Schenkel
Stockholm School of Economics, Sweden

ABSTRACT

This chapter explores the influence that rich media has on learning in a Community of Practice (CoP) at a large multi-billion dollar infrastructure project, the bridge between Sweden and Denmark. The findings show that an increase in the number of deviations from customer requirement was associated with an organizational change that impeded the community from communicating through face-to-face interaction. In turn, it is suggested that the CoP studied could not reduce equivocality through collaborative narratives because of the absence of rich media. Thus it is argued that rich media are essential for effective learning in Communities of Practice (CoPs). The author hopes that the understanding of how communication influences learning will assist managers, through providing an understanding of the central role that communication has on learning, and researchers, through introducing the concept of equivocality and media richness into the domain of CoPs.

INTRODUCTION

How organizations prevent and manage problems is critical to organizational performance and long-term competitiveness. Changes in the detection and correction of problems are considered as learning (Argyris & Schön, 1995). However, not all problems that firms encounter are of the same quality. These differences can be understood in terms of equivocality (Daft & Lengel, 1986; Daft & Weick, 1984). The term equivocality refers to the existence of multiple and conflicting interpretations (Weick, 1979). In a highly equivocal situation, there are many possible meanings; people are not certain of what the relevant questions are to ask, or of the right answers to these questions (Weick, 1995). Solving problems requires a low level of equivocality, since long-term effective solutions to problems require that the situation is well understood (Buchel & Raub, 2001).

The concept of Communities of Practice (CoPs) offers a means to understanding how problems in organizations are solved (Brown & Duguid, 1991; Lave & Wenger, 1991) and how equivocality is reduced during the problem-solving process. CoPs are groups of people contextually bound in a work situation and applying a common competence in the pursuit of a common enterprise (Brown & Duguid, 1991; Lave & Wenger, 1991; Wenger, 1998; Teigland, 2000). It has been suggested that through patterns of exchange and communication, communities are able to reduce equivocality (Pava, 1983; Purser, Pasmore & Tenkasi, 1992; Teigland, 2000). Researchers in the field of CoPs (Lave & Wenger, 1991; Wenger, 1998; Brown & Duguid, 1991) have recognized the importance of communication in problem-solving. However, little distinction has been made between different types of communication media. The term communication in CoP literature has referred in a broad sense to all types of communication media. However, there are differences in media "richness", or the ability of a specific medium to convey and change understanding or to reduce the degree of equivocality (Daft & Lengel, 1986).

The goal of this exploratory research is to explore how media richness influences learning in a CoP at the Øresund Bridge, the bridge that connects Sweden and Denmark. The context of this study is thus a highly complex infrastructure project of immense size, with stringent quality requirements, a well-defined completion time and which is subject to harsh environmental conditions.

COMMUNICATING PRACTICE

The development and dissemination of the community's problem-solving ability is dependent upon a shared repertoire consisting of the community's routines, gestures, artefacts, vocabulary and understandings (Wenger, 1998;

1999). Brown and Duguid (1991) noted that through collaborative narratives a shared repertoire is formed, developed, maintained and reproduced.

Narration describes how people create and tell stories in order to improve their understanding of events. The telling of stories transforms incoherent accounts of events into coherent narratives. Stories have the advantage of flexibility and can therefore be adapted to each particular situation. The "richness" of stories can fill the gaps left by explicit manuals. According to Brown and Duguid (1991), story-telling helps people to develop an understanding of the situation that encompasses cause and effect.

Collaboration refers to how the shared narratives developed by communities involve both storytellers and listeners. Given the collaborative nature of stories, an individual member need not know everything about how to solve problems, but can draw on the cumulative knowledge of the community (Wenger, 1999). Collaboration serves not only as a means of developing and disseminating knowledge, but also as a way of reducing equivocality (Weick, 1979). Equivocality arises because meanings that people attach to situations are not objective and singular, but subjective, socially constructed and multiple (Weick, 1979; Berger & Luckman, 1966). The reduction of equivocality can be viewed as a series of iterative cycles in which "the community" discusses the problem at large, improving its understanding with each iteration (Weick, 1979), and as such communication is fundamental to the problem-solving capability of communities.

Communication Media and Problem Solving in Communities

It has been argued that reduction of equivocality is integrally linked with collaborative narratives (Teigland, 2000), a communication-based process. These narratives are developed through different communication media. However, few researchers in the field of CoPs have made a distinction between various communication media and their capacity for reducing equivocality.

According to a substantial body of literature in communication research, media vary in their ability to reduce equivocality (Daft & Lengel, 1986; Trevino et al., 1987; Markus, 1994). Communication may be conducted through a variety of media such as face-to-face meetings, telephone, e-mail, fax, paper-based messages and video conferencing. Media differ in their level of richness, or the extent to which they possess the following qualities: inherent capacity for immediate feedback, number of cues and channels, personalization and language variety (Yates & Orlikowski, 1992; Daft & Lengel, 1986). Daft and Lengel (1986) proposed that face-to-face communication is the richest communication, followed by telephone and written texts. Zmud, Lind and Young (1990) produced similar findings but included electronic mail and fax in their study; these were considered leaner than paper-based communication. Media richness theory prescribes that situations high in equivocality require the use of rich media to increase the overall clarity of the situation. It is argued that if lean media are used, they will not be rich enough to improve the understanding of the situation and a high level of equivocality will remain.

It is therefore suggested that in CoPs, where equivocality is reduced through collaborative narratives, the effectiveness of these narratives in solving problems is highly dependent upon the availability of rich media. If rich media are not present, the community's ability to learn is negatively affected. Thus, if rich media are exchanged for leaner media, there will be an increase in the number of deviations because it is no longer possible to reduce equivocality. Conversely, if lean media are exchanged, learning will be impaired.

STUDY DESIGN AND RESEARCH METHOD

This study uses data from Sundlink Contractors, the international contractor consortium that designed and constructed the Øresund Bridge, a five-mile, multi-level bridge. The focus of this study is a CoP that formed around a formal organizational unit, the Pylon Section. This unit was responsible for constructing the 200-meter-high pylons that support the bridge. While the Pylon Section is a formal group, it displays characteristics of a CoP since it has a shared repertoire in the form of common vocabulary, routines, understandings and artefacts. At the Pylon Section, the shared repertoire consisted of common means of detecting and managing deviations, a particular type of problem in the form of non-compliance with prescribed working processes. This study focuses on the management of one particular type of work-process deviation: repairs. These deviations took the form of honeycombs, blowholes and cracks. The terms "honeycombs" and "blowholes" represent a specific community vocabulary and describe different types of air pockets in concrete.

The common routines of this shared repertoire are based on a shared understanding of what is meant by a deviation and the procedures for detecting and managing deviations. There was a common procedure for controlling work processes against defined processes as well as procedures to manage deviations. The procedure for managing deviations included filling in a deviation report stating why the deviation occurred and proposing actions to repair the deviation and to prevent it from recurring. As an informal practice, departments would call the technically oriented support department before the deviation report was completed in order to inform them that it was on its way. This practice helped to ensure the approval of actions taken to remedy the situation. Further, the report constituted an artefact of the community and, in conjunction with this report, a vocabulary used to describe deviations emerged with words like "rat's hole" and "honeycombs" used to describe the deviation. Collaborative narratives were developed in informal meetings such as lunches or breaks, which were limited to section members and on-site locations.

The boundaries of this community were initially defined by management, but over time the boundary between formal and emergent became blurred because of homophily and geographical separation. Homophily refers to the phenomenon that people find similar people attractive and develop relations with others like themselves (Homans, 1950; Lazarfield & Merton, 1954). This principle could be compared to the expression "birds of a feather flock together". In this case, homophily was amplified by the physical layout of the work site since formal groups were geographically separated from other. As Allen (1977) has shown, physical proximity affects the frequency of communication and thus people in geographically separated groups tend to communicate and interact with each other.

Sources of Data

Three sources of data were used to explore how media richness influenced learning in this CoP. To explore learning at the Pylon Section, learning curves based upon the 31 repair deviations were constructed. Learning in this CoP was measured by examining and analysing the slope of the learning curve. The basic principle behind learning curves is that productivity is linked to the volume of production: a higher volume of production results from productivity increases due to learning. Thus, learning is indicated by changes in the cumulative output of "defective" units (Li & Rajagopalan, 1996). Since improvements are (all other things being equal) more difficult in absolute terms once a previous improvement is made, the learning curve normally follows a logarithmic decline in the form of a straight line with a negative slope (Yelle, 1979). The learning curves were produced by calculating and plotting on a monthly basis the cumulative total of repair deviations, divided by the cumulative total of concrete produced.

Qualitative data on media use were gathered. Interviews were conducted on a project-wide level with managers, supervisors, superintendents and engineers involved in the deviations. Finally, data on media richness were gathered through a survey in which members of the Pylon Section were asked to assess the richness of media.

MANAGING DEVIATIONS: SPECIFIC INSTANCES OF LEARNING AT THE PYLON SECTION

To understand the influence of media richness on learning in CoPs, an organizational change affecting communication patterns was chosen as the point of departure for this study. This section begins by describing the organizational change that occurred at the Pylon Section. Thereafter, the effect of this change on communication patterns was analysed. Media richness is then examined at a point after the change was established. The final part of this section seeks to understand whether changes in the richness of media had a corresponding effect on the learning curves of the Pylon Section.

The Organizational Change

In the spring of 1996, the massive concrete steel structures that formed the base of the pylons were shipped out to sea with the assistance of a giant floating crane. In conjunction with the move, there were two organizational changes. Firstly, the production group responsible for the pylons was divided into two operative groups and moved out to sea. Secondly, the production units became separated from the department's land-based support office. Before the move, both the production and support office were located on land in close proximity to each other. This separation is of interest since the Pylon Department went to the Support Department for advice in terms of how to prevent deviations from recurring. However, the two changes did not affect the main activities of the Pylon Section, which consisted of placing steel reinforcement and pouring concrete as well as how the groups were working.

How the Change Affected Communication Media

The interview data revealed that the organizational change affected two communication patterns. Firstly, the division of the Pylon Section into two production units meant that the formerly single unit was no longer co-located. For people in the East and West Pylon Sections to meet, they had to take a ferry. The ferries connecting the pylon units operated only a few times a day, and a round trip could take two or more hours. It is therefore suggested that the conditions for informal face-to-face interaction on a regular basis ceased to be present when members of the section were no longer co-located.

Secondly, the data revealed that communication between the Pylon Section and the department's support office changed in two ways. Firstly, attendance at the department's formal weekly meetings declined when people from the Pylon Section had to take a ferry to attend meetings. With slim resources and a tight production schedule, attending meetings was cumbersome and time-consuming. Further, the separation of the Pylon Section from the department's support staff meant that informal interaction between them was impeded since a meeting required that one of the parties take a ferry. Another member described the relatively low frequency of interaction between the Pylon Section and the department's support staff as follows:

"The superintendent is out a lot (away from the sub-section). The department manager is not out often, and the section head is out two times a week. The

superintendent is out everyday and the quality control engineer is out two to three days a week."

Informal interactions provide the context for the exchange and development of the collaborative narratives that constitute the shared repertoire.

The lack of face-to-face meetings could have been compensated for by using other media. However, the move out to sea restricted telephone usage since there were no fixed cables that connected the Pylon Section with the mainland. The lack of fixed telephone lines also curtailed the use of communication based on traditional telephone technology such as e-mail and fax. Cellular telephones, an alternative that is not dependent upon fixed telephone lines, were found to be an unreliable and limited form of communication.

To compensate for the restrictions on communication, people used walkie-talkies, a medium with limited access and poor voice quality. Firstly, access to walkie-talkies was confined to selected members of the East and West Pylon Section as well as some members of the department's administrative office. Secondly, the quality of transmissions was lower, as only one person could speak at a time.

How the Change Affected Media Richness

The previous section highlighted how the organizational change affected communication with all types of media at the Pylon Section. As the focus of this study is on media richness, we now examine the extent to which "rich" media were affected by the organizational change. To explore this question, quantitative data on the perceived richness of three types of communication media at Sundlink—face-to-face meetings, e-mail and telephone—were studied, with no difference being made between traditional telephones and cellular telephones. These media were rated according to five different qualities that influence richness. A scale ranging from one to seven was used, with seven indicating that

Table 1: Face-to-Face, E-Mail and Telephone Richness

Variable	Face-to-Face Richness		E-mail Richness		Telephone Richness	
	Mean	s.d.	Mean	s.d.	Mean	s.d.
Give and receive a quick answer	5.63	1.06	3.25	1.67	5.25	0.89
Express how you feel	5.50	1.31	2.50	1.51	5.50	0.93
Exchange and interpret different signals	5.75	1.04	2.75	1.58	4.63	1.30
Express nuances	5.88	1.36	2.63	1.77	4.50	0.93
Exchange sensitive information	6.00	1.19	3.13	1.81	5.00	1.20

the medium possesses a particular quality to a high degree and a one, to a low degree. In other words, a seven would indicate a medium that was very rich in that quality and a one, a lean medium. The results in Table 1 indicate that face-to-face meetings were the richest media overall and e-mail the leanest. In all qualities, the telephone was rated lower than a face-to-face meeting but somewhat higher than e-mail.

Media Richness and Learning

Thus far, it has been suggested that that the organizational change, the Pylon Section's move out to sea, influenced overall communication patterns. It is suggested further that the effect was to impede the use of rich media in the form of formal and informal face-to-face meetings as well as the use of fixed and cellular telephones. In a problem-laden environment, the absence of rich media should be accompanied by a change in the learning curve since the community is less able to use collaborative narratives to reduce equivocality, with consequent effects on the level of learning in the community. In terms of learning curves, an increase in equivocality would be associated with a learning curve that has a positive slope and a decrease in equivocality associated with a learning curve that has a negative slope, if all other conditions are held constant.

To explore this question the learning curve of the Pylon Section was examined. As can be seen in Figure 1, the learning curve of the Pylon Section has a negative slope followed by a positive slope. Specifically, the cumulative number of repair deviations was decreasing until period four, where the slope of the curve is broken and turns positive for one period. Thereafter, the curve has a slight negative slope for three periods followed by a positive slope for the following 13 periods. The negative slope for the Pylon Section corresponds to the period when there was a single, united Pylon Section located on the land, while the positive slope is for the period when the two separate section units were located at sea.

In sum, media-richness theory suggests that when equivocality is high, rich media are required to reduce equivocality. In the case of the Pylon Section, the organizational change curtailed access to the rich media of informal and formal face-to-face meetings and the telephone. The next best alternative to face-to-face communication in this case was the walkie-talkie, which was not rich enough to reduce equivocality. Consequently, successive improvements could not be made. Media-richness theory suggests further that the richest medium available to the people of the Pylon Section was not rich enough for them to develop and disseminate a shared repertoire that could reduce the level of equivocality—an explanation evidenced by the positive slope of the learning curve.

Figure 1: Repair Deviations: Honeycombs, Blowholes and Cracks

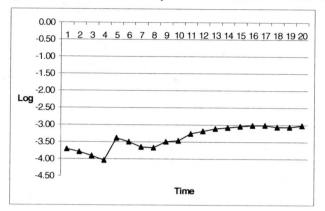

CONCLUSION

Solving problems is considered one of the fundamental activities of firms. The concept of CoPs offers a means for understanding how problems are solved and knowledge is developed in dynamic environments. This study found that two related organizational changes affected communication possibilities in terms of the richness of available media, and that in turn the number of deviations increased as shown by the positive slope of the learning curve. Specifically, the organizational changes impeded face-to-face communication and telephone communication, both rich media. In view of the change in learning curves and changes in communication media, it is suggested that when CoPs do not have access to rich media in equivocal situations, learning in the form of the correction and detection of deviations is impeded.

The change in communication can be viewed as influencing the communication patterns of the Pylon Section, a CoP and its ability to develop and exchange narratives. Thus, it is suggested that when communities do not have access to rich media in equivocal situations, equivocality cannot be reduced sufficiently to permit formulating effective actions to prevent deviations from reoccurring. This suggests that if there is a mismatch between the level of equivocality of the situation and the richness of the media used for communication, learning in CoPs will be impeded. When deprived of rich media, CoPs facing highly equivocal situations will fail to solve their problems.

MANAGERIAL IMPLICATIONS

This study has several implications for practice. Firstly, it highlights the impact of an organizational change on communication patterns and consequently on learning in CoPs. This suggests that managers need to consider carefully how changes can impact on communication media as well as the overall level of equivocality. Managers should consider what happens to available communication media as a result of changes. For example, is the availability of rich and lean media impacted upon? Further, changes can impact on the nature of work, which can lead to both an increase and decrease in equivocality. Thus, managers must pose the question of how change impacts on the equivocality of situations and whether "rich" enough communication media are available for communities to solve their problems. Similarly, this chapter has highlighted the pivotal role of communication in learning in CoPs, particularly the role of rich media. This suggests that the ability to communicate through rich media is fundamental to learning in CoPs and, to a large extent, a prerequisite for community-based learning. Moreover, if managers are to encourage effective and efficient community-based learning, they need to pay attention to the richness of available media that community members have at their disposal as well as the equivocality of problems these communities are dealing with. This process needs to be continually examined since the nature of problems that communities are dealing with change as well as the overall ability of the community to solve the problems. This suggests that rich media are important for communities in their early emergent stage when they are dealing with equivocal problems and that, over time, problems become less equivocal as knowledge of how to solve problems is integrated into the community's repertoire. Consequently, rich media become less important over time and lean media more important.

REFERENCES

Allen, T. J. (1977). *Managing the flow of technology: Technology transfer and the dissemination of technological information within the Rand Organization.* Cambridge, MA: MIT Press.

Argyris, C., and Schön, D. (1995). *Organizational learning* II. MA: Addison-Wesley.

Berger, P., and Luckmann, T. (1966). *The social construction of reality.* London: Penguin Books.

Brown, J. S., and Duguid, P. (1991). Organizational learning and Communities of Practice. *Organization Science, 2* (1), 40-57.

Buchel, B., and Raub, S. (2001). Media choice and organizational learning. In M. Dierkes (Ed.) *Handbook of organizational learning and knowledge.* Oxford: Oxford University Press.

Daft R. H., and Weick, K. E. (1984). Toward a model of organizations as interpretative systems. *Academy of Management Review, 9* (2), 284-295.

Daft, R. L., and Lengel, R. H. (1986). Organizational information requirements, media richness and structural design. *Management Science, 3* (5), 554-571.

Homans, G. C. (1950). *The human group.* New York: Harcourt Brace.

Lave, J., and Wenger, E. (1991). *Situated learning: Legitimate peripheral participation.* Cambridge: Cambridge University Press.

Lazarsfeld, P., and Merton, R. (1954). Friendship as social process. In M. Berger, T. Abel. and C. Page (Eds.), *Freedom and control in modern society.* New York: Octagon.

Li, G., and Rajagopalan, S. (1997). A learning curve model with knowledge depreciation. *European Journal of Operational Research, 105* (1), 143-154.

Pava, C. (1983). *Managing new office technology.* New York: Free Press.

Purser, R. E., Pasmore, W. A., and Tenkasi, R. V. (1992). The influence of deliberations on learning in new product development teams. *Journal of Engineering and Technology Management, 9* (1), 1-28.

Teigland, R. (2000). Communities of Practice in an Internet firm: Netovation vs. on-time performance. In E. Lesser (Ed.), *Knowledge and communities.* Newton, MA: Butterworth-Heinemann.

Trevino, L. K., Daft, R. H., and Lengel, W. (1987). Media symbolism, media richness and media choice in organizations. *Communication Research, 1* (5), 553-57.

Weick, K. E. (1979). *The social psychology of organizing.* New York: McGraw Hill.

Weick, K. E. (1995). *Sensemaking in organizations.* Thousand Oaks: Sage.

Wenger, E. (1998). *Communities of Practice: Learning, meaning and identity.* Cambridge: Cambridge University Press.

Wenger, E. (1999). Communities of Practice: The key to a knowledge strategy. *Knowledge Directions, 1,* Fall.

Wenger, E. (2000). Communities of Practice: The key to knowledge strategy. In E. Lesser (Ed.), *Knowledge and communities.* Newton, MA: Butterworth-Heinemann.

Yates, J., and Orlikowski,W. J. (1992). Genres of organizational communication: A structurational approach to studying communications and media. *Academy of Management Review, 17* (2), 299-326.

Yelle, L. E. (1979). The learning curve: Historical review and comprehensive survey. *Decision Science, 10* (2), 302-328.

Zmud, R., Lind, M., and Young, F. (1990). An attribute space for organizational communication channels. *Information Systems Research, 1* (4), 440-457.

Chapter VI

CoPs for Cops:
Managing and Creating
Knowledge through
Networked Expertise

Maarten de Laat
University of Nijmegen and Utrecht University, The Netherlands

Wim Broer
Police Education and Knowledge Center, The Netherlands

ABSTRACT

Managing knowledge in large organizations is a challenge in itself. Modern views on Knowledge Management (KM) focus not only on finding ways to capture and distribute corporate knowledge but also provide ways through which knowledge can be shared, discussed and created. Different types of organizations have different approaches to KM. From general descriptions of these approaches, parallels to the Dutch police will be presented. This chapter discusses how KM within the Dutch police is an integral part of the organization and how explicit and tacit knowledge is shared to create new corporate knowledge. The authors present examples of how Communities of Practice (CoPs) within the Dutch police play a role in both sustaining and developing their own practice, and how these communities are crucial to the learning organization.

KNOWLEDGE MANAGEMENT IN A LEARNING CONTEXT

Organizations are increasingly confronted with the problem of managing and creating knowledge in order to respond flexibly to changes in their working environment. They realise that sharing and creating knowledge brings a competitive advantage. Organizations are transforming into learning organizations and expect their workers to become lifelong learners. According to Marsick and Watkins (1999, p. 12), learning is "the process that makes the creation and use of knowledge meaningful". Huysman (in press) observed that learning and working become interrelated when the practice of knowledge sharing helps workers to do their work better and more efficiently. Providing space in the organization for workers to establish networks can therefore be a powerful way to facilitate workplace learning. Workers tend to form networks of expertise spontaneously: to facilitate individual learning, collaboration and to discuss work related problems together. Sometimes these networks transform into a Community of Practice (CoP). In a CoP, employees who share a common interest for the field they work in, come together on a regular basis to help each other, solve problems and to share and create knowledge collaboratively (Wenger, 1998). Knowledge sharing and meaning making are two of the core activities of CoPs. It is within this social community structure that workers learn from and develop their practice in a natural way and integrate it with their day-to-day work. Nursing and managing this process is one of the crucial conditions for fostering a learning organization.

The notion of CoPs was first proposed by Lave and Wenger (1991) who described them as groups where learning takes place through a process of Legitimate Peripheral Participation. The central issue in learning is about becoming a practitioner, not about learning about practice. According to Brown and Duguid (1991), workplace learning can best be understood in terms of communities being formed and personal identities being changed. This approach draws attention away from abstract knowledge and situates it into the practices of the communities in which knowledge takes on significance. A CoP defines itself along three characteristics (see Wenger, 1999):

- *What it is about* - A joint enterprise as understood and continually renegotiated by its members
- *How it functions* - Mutual engagement that binds members together into a social entity
- *What capability it produces* - The shared repertoire of communal resources (routines, sensibilities, artefacts, vocabulary and styles) that the members develop over time

These characteristics can be helpful to identify CoPs in organizations. However, what is more important is not the question as to whether a network is a CoP or not, but whether the framework is used to support learning and KM in the workplace (Glasweg, 2002). CoPs can be found in every organization, but the ways in which they operate and are rewarded differ.

KNOWLEDGE MANAGEMENT IN DIFFERENT ORGANIZATIONAL TYPES

Not every organization is the same, not only in how they are structured but also in how they manage their knowledge. We will use Mintzberg's (1989) classification as a lens to illustrate different approaches to KM and organizational learning.

Machine Organization

This type of organization has a central bureaucracy with formalized procedures. There is a strong hierarchy in the organization and the communication and change processes are top-down oriented. This type of organization operates in a stable environment where work is standardized and repetitive. In this environment, according to Ståhle (2000), emphasis is placed on explicit knowledge ready to put in manuals and procedures. KM is focused on providing corporate knowledge throughout the organization. Learning in this type is characterised by the acquisition of the organizational knowledge necessary to carry out the job (Huysman, in press).

Professional Organization

A professional organization is bureaucratic as in a machine organization, but power is decentralised. It operates in a complex changing environment. It tries to understand the environmental changes aiming to create standardised work procedures. The key to the functioning of a professional organization is to create domains or divisions within which professionals work autonomously. Changes are made through professional judgement and collective choice but with administrative approval. In this type, Ståhle (2000) points out that the organization fosters continuous, self-directive development, which is mainly based on standardised work procedures. A lot of dialogue is needed and the flow of information has to be interactive. Learning in this situation is characterised by exchanging individual knowledge with the aim of re-using it throughout the organization (Huysman, in press). KM is focused on establishing an interactive knowledgebase created through social networks.

Table 1: Organizational Structure and Knowledge Management

Organizational configuration (Mintzberg, 1989)	Knowledge Management Approach (Ståhle, 2000)	Organizational Learning (Huysman, in press)
Machine organization		
Predictability Manageability	Explicit knowledge Data-warehousing	*Retrieve*: individual acquisition of organizational knowledge
Professional organization		
Continuous controlled development Autonomous domains/divisions	Explicit and tacit knowledge Looking for shared meaning	*Exchange*: sharing individual knowledge in order to re-use it
Entrepreneurial organization		
Organic structure constantly changes. Roles constantly change creating innovation	Tacit knowledge Intense networking (in and outside the organization)	*Create*: community knowledge creation through sharing and co-construction of networked expertise

Entrepreneurial Organization

This structure is characterised by a simple, informal and flexible organiza-tion. It operates in a dynamic environment ready to respond to external demands. The director controls the activities through direct supervision. Creating innova-tion and investment in networks is a way to interact with its environment. Knowledge is intuitive and potential; intensive networking inside and outside the organization serves in the process of creating new knowledge (Ståhle, 2000). Learning in this type of organization is focused around the social construction of knowledge by establishing networks through which workers can share their expertise and create new knowledge (Huysman, in press).

These three classifications are summarised in Table 1. The classifications presented are ideal type descriptions, which help us understand the complexity in real organizational contexts. As organizations grow, they become more complex. They can be in crossover zones from one type to one other.

The Dutch Police Force

The Dutch police operate like many other organizations in a dynamic and rapidly changing environment. Police work has grown more complex, for instance due to more and frequently changing laws and regulations. It is important to carefully manage these changes so that all police officers have the same up-to-date knowledge about their work. The police strive for controlled development through understanding the changes in the working environment. This organization therefore has many features in common with a professional organization. The organization can be described as a mock bureaucracy because of the well-developed occupational culture of the police officers (Punch, 1984). Due to the nature of their work, police officers are used to reacting immediately, taking responsibility and directing their work alone or together with their colleagues. Consequently, there exists a well-developed solidarity with each other. The police administration has overall responsibility for police work but,

Table 2: Organizational Structure and Knowledge Management in the Dutch Police

Police organization		
Organizational configuration	Knowledge Management Approach	Organizational Learning
Rather decentralised, continuous and controlled development	PKN: Presenting explicit knowledge and looking for shared meaning	PDN: sharing knowledge with the aim to validate and standardise

due to its nature, the work itself cannot be directly supervised. This creates space for some horizontal decentralisation. Within the police organization there is a strong division between various domains. Within these domains, knowledge is shared with the aim to develop and create new standards to be implemented throughout the organization. Because of this, the organization relies on the skills and knowledge of its workers to produce standardized products and services (see Table 2).

In a professional organization, it is important to make the flow of knowledge interactive. KM in these organizations needs to create opportunities for sharing knowledge by creating relationships between the workers. Networking serves the process of keeping up to date: to solve work related problems and (in doing so) creating new knowledge that could be re-used throughout the organization. Within these expertise networks, members share and appropriate tacit knowledge with the aim of sustaining and developing their own practice. To foster these relationships and to stimulate networked expertise the Police Education and Knowledge Centre created a nationwide intranet (see Figure 1). Its structure is based on three pillars, the Police Knowledge Net (PKN), the Police Discussion

Figure 1: Relationship Between PKN, PDN and the E-Campus

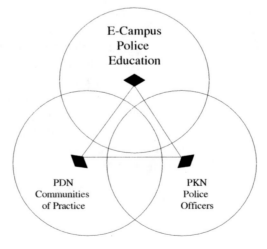

Net (PDN) and the E-Campus. This makes it possible for learning and working to meet and become integrated in the workplace.

The interaction between PKN (presenting explicit or hard knowledge), PDN (sharing tacit or soft knowledge) and the E-Campus (online courses and personal development plans) offers a powerful basis for organizational learning.

Innovation through CoPs

Large organizations, like the Dutch police force (50,000 employees), deal with a wide range of specialized knowledge, which needs to be updated and adapted frequently. However, police officers do not often work together in a physically shared space. They discuss work related problems during ad hoc meetings, coffee breaks and by telephone. Police officers throughout the country tend to keep close contact with one another and this is how CoPs spontaneously emerge within certain areas of expertise. They acknowledge the need to share knowledge to solve shared problems and to generate new standards. Providing CoPs with ICT-tools like PDN and PKN can be an advantage in bringing officers together. PDN for instance facilitates communication between participants of (existing) CoPs and helps them to stay in touch. It offers the possibility of collaborating online over time and space. Due to these developments, there is a growing number of CoPs trying to manage their networked expertise. Recent developments are the existence of hybrid networks where both operational as well as professional knowledge is shared and discussed in CoPs. This interaction is of great value because integrating working and learning highlights the importance of tacit knowledge and recognizes that work experience leads to organizational and educational innovation.

In the next section, three examples of CoPs within the Dutch police will be presented. The examples will address how police officers have established CoPs in which knowledge is shared, created and appropriated around problems and issues that matter in their work. The first example will be about a CoP the members of which investigate the field of human trading and prostitution. It presents a good example of how CoPs can be organized in face-to-face meetings using the PKN to present their knowledge domain. The second example will be of a CoP that works in drugs prevention by using the PDN to exchange and generate knowledge. The third example will be a CoP that concentrates on developing work processes. In this example, the focus will be on discussing experiences of the members being engaged in online discourse.

Example 1: CoP Investigating Human Trading and Prostitution

In 2000, the prostitution business was legalised in The Netherlands. This meant a significant change for the police. Work procedures and practice would differ radically from the previous situation. To prepare and manage this changeover, police officers working in this division gathered together to share knowledge about this new phenomenon. They established a CoP by inviting criminal investigators throughout the country that would have to deal with the change. What started of as a group of five grew to a community of 45 members.

They arranged monthly meetings to exchange experiences, identify problems and try to solve them. Generally, these meetings had the following structure. First, the chairman presented new developments and provided feedback on previously developed practices. After that, all participants gave an update on their regional work experiences. This identified good practices, recognised problems and allowed everyone to help each other on concrete questions. Sometimes these problems needed more attention to find an appropriate solution. Small focus groups within the CoP were formed to study these problems and present their findings during a following meeting. These focus groups were carefully formed so that their outcomes would reflect the reality of the police practice throughout the country. The focus groups were a successful format for this community to learn from each other, to create knowledge and solutions for their reformed practice and to develop new educational offerings and online courses.

The second half of the meetings was either reserved for these focus groups to make arrangements and/or work together or were based on a presentation by a guest speaker. Due to high levels of commitment and engagement and their shared interest in developing their practice, this community was very successful in both learning from each other and in developing their practice. Because of the monthly face-to-face meetings, the need for PDN was small and it was mainly used for distributing agendas and documents. The PKN was used to present explicit and validated knowledge. These web pages were updated frequently when new standards and general knowledge developed within the CoP became validated and therefore ready to be presented throughout the whole police force and the E-Campus.

Example 2: CoP on Drug Prevention

The drug prevention CoP has a similar structure to the CoP in the previous example. This CoP consists of 46 members who are conducting drugs-related investigations throughout the country. Due to the need for fast communication around emerging questions within the field, they decided to use PDN to share knowledge and propose immediate questions.

The way members participate in CoPs provides insight into the process of knowledge sharing. A discussion space provides ideal possibilities to study interaction patterns between the members of a network. However, insight in communication patterns within a certain network alone is not enough. The content of the discourse must be taken into account. This way information can

Figure 2: Interaction Pattern within the Network

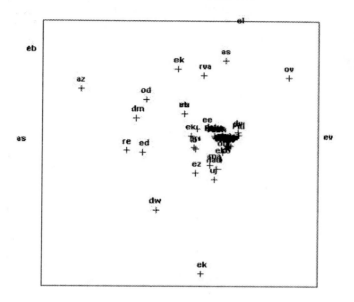

be gathered about the nature of the discourse. To visualize the interaction patterns a multi-dimensional scaling plot was created.

Figure 2 shows that the interaction between the members is rather centralized. The members cluster around those members considered to be at the core of the CoP. There are no subgroups and most of the members are somehow involved within the discourse. To study the nature of the discourse we coded 177 messages that were shared in the period of January until June 2001 (see Table 3).

Most of the communication (72%) between the members of the CoP corresponds to Phase 1 (sharing or comparing information). This was expected because the purpose of this CoP is information sharing and discussion of work-related problems. New trends related to drugs cases are being shared between members. Different work experiences sometimes lead to discussion in which participants seek to further explore, support or identify statements of other members. This is indicated by the 20% that corresponds to Phase 2. Only 8% of the messages were coded as Phase 3. This shows that the members are occasionally negotiating the terms they use and collaboratively try to solve a work-related problem.

The challenge this CoP faces is how to transform their mainly tacit knowledge into organizational standards so that it can become accepted as formal explicit knowledge. The PKN institution provides knowledge brokers and content managers to assist the CoPs to formalise their knowledge in order to submit it to an assigned group of specialists who research and teach this

Table 3: Construction of Knowledge (Gunawardena, Lowe, & Anderson, 1997)

Phase I: Information Sharing/comparing	Messages	Percentage (in total)
Opinion	40	
Corroboration	19	
Clarification	14	
Definition	55	72%
Phase II Discover/ explore concepts		
Identifying	14	
Disagreements	1	
Restating	20	20%
Phase III negotiation/ co-construction		
Negotiation of terms	9	
Identification of agreement	2	
Compromise	1	
Integrating	2	8%

particular domain. Once the expert group has given its approval, it will go to a so-called policy board, which formally validates the knowledge before it is disseminated through the PKN and E-Campus.

Example 3: CoP within a National Support Staff on Crime Detection

This community consisted of eight participants. They responded to a letter sent by the national support staff presenting a work-related problem. The problem was about how to identify and describe general work-processes used in the field of criminal investigation. They discussed the problem online over a two-month period. The participants agreed to start with an open discussion on the subject 'work-processes'. The discussion was then divided into various perspectives where the participants contributed according to their knowledge of this subject. At the end, this project was evaluated with a questionnaire and a group interview to gain information about their experiences with working together online.

Most of the participants (60%) agreed that they were collaboratively creating new knowledge about 'work-processes', but they pointed out that they need to grow more into building upon the ideas of others. They also mentioned that there was a lot of confusion about the concepts being used and that they needed to clarify the goal of their study and to give more direction to the discussion. Nearly all the participants (80%) indicated that they know enough about the topic to be able to take part in the discussion. If they lacked certain information, they would search for relevant information, consult colleagues, and try to stimulate the other participants to explain certain issues. They thought that the quality of the written notes varied from good to reasonable. Their overall impression of discussion was good but the discussion faded later on. A possible reason for this is summed by one participant as:

"There is too little structure to guide our discussion, the notes contain valuable information but what does it bring to us?"

The questionnaire pointed out that there was less coordination during the discussion and that a more structured or goal directed approach is necessary. The participants point out that more coordination and structure would help them to achieve agreement and extend their knowledge about the problem. It seems that the activities the participants carried out are more discussion oriented than extending existing knowledge or new information. However, they appreciate the possibility of knowledge sharing. This is promising for the support of working with CoPs in organizations.

These examples exemplify the process of managing and sharing knowledge in order to learn from each other. Creating new knowledge, standards and procedures in CoPs is a means of stimulating and integrating learning and working throughout the organization. By creating relations between PKN, PDN and the E-Campus the police emphasise the iterative process KM. Within this process, it is clear that CoPs are a relevant player in managing knowledge by critically questioning, innovating and assimilating corporate knowledge in a fast changing working context. In this case, we see that the CoPs are formed by the workers themselves—they are not forced to create and participate in CoPs by the organization and membership is purely voluntary. This shows that CoPs emerge spontaneously around issues that matter in the organization. Community members are willing to share information together as long as it helps them to do their work better. However, knowledge sharing in ICT-based environments is still somewhat new. The first example, where the community had regular face-to-face meetings, seemed to be most successful in organizing its learning activities. However, the other two examples indicate that the willingness to share knowledge and learn together is not so much the hurdle; it is how to organize networked expertise in way that it will result in satisfying collective outcomes. The second example shows that in an online environment the commitment and interest can be satisfying, but that they have difficulties in creating knowledge together. In example three, this is further indicated by the fact that it seems to be difficult to structure and regulate an online discussion.

DISCUSSION

The CoP literature discussed earlier in the chapter and the CoP examples that have been presented suggest that the focus of organizations in fostering KM should not only be understood from its context and structure. More attention needs to be given to the community and its social processes, instead of a limited focus on its practice. More investments on supporting group dynamics, social conferencing skills and problem solving techniques in online discussion environments are necessary to facilitate CoPs in their pursuit of appropriating and creating new knowledge about their work. Learning behaviour has to be stimulated by stressing the importance of finding promising answers for new and existing problems. This endeavour can only be successful if combined programs can be offered that are supported by sophisticated software and inspired by convincing leadership. Organizations should not only facilitate internal group processes but also support and reward the dissemination of community outputs. How this can be done is dependent on organizational structure and the approach to KM. In the case of the Dutch police validation, processes have to be followed carefully.

Supporting networked expertise stimulates the mixture of operational and professional knowledge. The more police officers experience the possibilities of online knowledge sharing, the more they feel the attractiveness of direct communication about operational cases. This allows them to benefit from the experience of their colleagues nationwide in their fight against criminals.

A last question to address is how to assess the Dutch developments in relation to the theoretical schemes presented by Mintzberg, Ståhle and Huysman. The police organization has a strong tendency to work pragmatically. So, the formal upper structure with its validation protocols and policy boards on the one hand is accompanied with more or less informal network arrangements on the other hand. Within the police, three occupational sub-cultures can be discerned: street cops, management cops and policy cops. While each sub-culture has its own set of conduct, it can be questioned how these cultural arrangements are influenced by the emergence of network tools, which offer the possibility to make crossovers between these subcultures. So far, it seems that groups of specialists within the police are interested in using online possibilities for sharing their expertise with colleagues.

Supporting networked expertise throughout the organization can bridge the gap between different sub-cultures and serve as a carrier to exchange and disseminate knowledge. CoPs provide the social structure in the organization for an interactive approach to Knowledge Management. This way CoPs make a valuable contribution to the professional organization.

REFERENCES

Brown, J. S., and Duguid, P. (1991). Organizational learning and Communities of Practice. *Organization Science, 2* (1), 40-57.
Glasweg. (Personal Communication). June 2002.

Gunawardena, C. N., Lowe, C. A., and Anderson, T. (1997). Analysis of global online debate and the development of an interaction analysis model for examining social construction of knowledge in computer conferencing. *Journal of Educational Computing Research, 17* (4), 397-431.

Huysman, M. (in press). *Knowledge hharing in practices: Towards a second generation of Knowledge Management.*

Lave, J., and Wenger, E. (1991). *Situated learning. Legitimate peripheral participation.* Cambridge University Press.

Marsick, V. J., and Watkins, K. E. (1999). *Facilitating learning organizations.* Vermont: Gower.

Mintzberg, H. (1989). *Mintzberg on management: Inside our strange world of organizations.* London: Collier Macmillan.

Punch, M. (1984). *Policing the inner city: A case study of Amsterdam's Warmoesstraat.* London: McMillan.

Ståhle, P. (2000). Knowledge Management as a learning challenge. *Lifelong Learning in Europe, 7* (1), 10-17.

Wenger, E. (1998). *Communities of Practice: Learning, meaning, and identity.* Cambridge: University Press.

Wenger, E. (1999). Learning as a social system. *Systems Thinker, 9* (5), 2-3.

Chapter VII

Communities of Practice in the Royal National Lifeboat Institution

Roger Kolbotn
Directorate for Civil Protection and Emergency Planning, Norway

ABSTRACT

This chapter concentrates on Communities of Practice (CoPs) in the volunteer organization Royal National Lifeboat Institution. It argues that overlapping CoPs throughout the organization are needed to deal with a variety of unstructured practices at sea. In addition, altruism and trust are vital elements for sharing and creating knowledge among volunteers in the organization. The author hopes this chapter will provide a practical understanding of CoPs. The author hopes the discussion of a volunteer organization will bring some new insights into the concept of CoPs.

INTRODUCTION

Communities of Practice (CoPs) have gained increased attention over the last few years. Both academics and practitioners have become more appreciative of the "...groups of people who share a concern, a set of problems, or a passion about a topic, and who deepen their knowledge and expertise in this area by interacting on an ongoing basis" (Wenger, McDermott & Snyder, 2002, p. 4). However, most research has concentrated on commercial organizations. This chapter looks at CoPs within a volunteer organization, the Royal National Lifeboat Institution (RNLI).

The RNLI was established in 1824 and provides a lifeboat service for the United Kingdom and the Republic of Ireland. Around the coasts are more than 230 lifeboat stations, whose lifeboats launch more than 6,000 times a year and rescue over 6,300 people. They are manned by largely volunteer crews (approximately 4,500) and every penny required to maintain the lifeboat service is raised from voluntary contributions.

Apart from the lifeboat stations, the RNLI has a large headquarters in Poole, England and six divisions around the United Kingdom and the Republic of Ireland where managers work.

This chapter focuses, first and foremost, on the work of operational volunteers in the RNLI, i.e., actually saving people at sea. The RNLI also has many thousands of other volunteers in areas like fundraising, public relations and water safety. The operational volunteers must be able to make decisions on their feet, often under extreme conditions. Especially during unforeseen and abnormal rescue operations, they must trust each other and rely on their intuition to get the job done. These rescue operations are extremely difficult to formalise since they often involve a variety of unstructured practices.

UNSTRUCTURED PRACTICES

In organizations, there is quite a difference between job descriptions and actual work (Brown & Duguid, 1998). Instead of going to inadequate manuals and documents, people communicate, share their knowledge and experiences and get the task at hand done. Most organizations today are complex, where formal mechanisms cannot keep up with the variety of unstructured practices.

In the RNLI, it is impossible for managers to create formal processes for volunteers that incorporate all the variety that happens during rescue operations. The following example underlines this. A rescue operation was video-recorded where a boat with three people was trapped next to a ferry. Two lifeboats worked together to solve the situation. However, the trapped boat suddenly sank and a woman was dragged under the ferry. One man was held by the collar just above the water by a volunteer. If the volunteer had let go, the person would have followed the woman under the ferry. The third man was next to one of the lifeboats, barely conscious and unable to get out of the water. In this situation, the lives of these people were in the hands of the volunteers. Due to teamwork and being capable of dealing with an abnormal and unforeseen situation, the volunteers were eventually able to save all three.

LEARNING BY PRACTICE
AND COMMUNICATION

The example highlights collective knowledge among volunteers - it shows that volunteers need to draw from each other's knowledge to save people at sea. It is not enough that one volunteer is performing at sea; they need to perform together.   In the abnormal situation where three people almost drowned, volunteers needed to apply their collective knowledge. This situation leads to new knowledge being generated among volunteers. Spender (1994, p. 397) argues:

"Collective knowledge is a dynamic concept in that it is not only held collectively but also both generated and applied collectively within the pattern of social relationships."

Collective knowledge leads to new learning taking place. Lave and Wenger (1991) have developed the element of learning in CoPs with their framework Legitimate Peripheral Participation. They argue that learning must be seen in relation to practice. Another example may help clarify this issue. Volunteers in the RNLI have phone pagers. If a situation requires a lifeboat, they respond immediately. It usually takes less than seven minutes from the pager going off until the volunteers have left the quay at Poole lifeboat station in Dorset, England. Moreover, seven minutes is the RNLI's national average launch time.   One reason for this fast response time is the collective and embedded knowledge in the work practices. Obviously, it is important for volunteers to have the theoretical understanding for launching a lifeboat. Nevertheless, a volunteer cannot learn to launch a lifeboat in seven minutes in a classroom. He or she needs to practice with other people.

Learning within CoPs involves communication and storytelling. Brown and Duguid (2000, p. 77) argue:

"Storytelling helps discover something new about the world. It allows us to pass that discovery on to others."

At Poole lifeboat station, communication plays a prominent part. Volunteers meet regularly on Thursday evenings to discuss both major and minor incidents during the previous week's training and rescue operations. After the meeting, most volunteers go to the local pub where they chat about "everything and nothing". Apart from the obvious trivial talks, this is also a place where stories are told about difficult and complex rescue operations. For instance, volunteers might talk about the limitations of a specific towing rope. This knowledge could be of great importance for the rest of the organization.

UNDERSTANDING AND FOSTERING COMMUNITIES OF PRACTICE

Managers in the RNLI must understand and foster the various CoPs among the volunteers. Wenger and Snyder (2000, p. 143) compare CoPs to gardening and claim:

"Although Communities of Practice are fundamentally informal and self-organizing, they benefit from cultivation."

However, there is a difference between understanding and fostering, and creating formal management structures. Managers in the RNLI are unable to institutionalise all the variety that happens at sea. The example above where three people were saved illustrates this point. In abnormal situations, volunteers must rely on each other and be able to work together. CoPs among volunteers have often been formed over a long period and hold valuable experience and knowledge. Thus, managers "...must see beyond its canonical abstractions of practice to the rich full-blooded activities themselves. And it must legitimise and support the myriad enacting activities perpetrated by its different members" (Brown & Duguid, 1991).

Most managers in the RNLI are aware of the collective and social elements at the stations. However, they do not try to control the stations in great detail. The RNLI is a practical organization. The primary concern for managers is to make sure that the stations and volunteers are performing satisfactorily. They appreciate what is working and deal with factors that do not work adequately. If a lifeboat station falls short, more formal processes are put in place by managers to improve the situation. A new competence-based training system for volunteers is mentioned below to highlight this matter.

PRACTICE AND PROCESS

Good practices at one station can obviously be beneficial for the rest of the organization. Still, it is also important to identify and deal with bad practices. In addition, managers must establish the right processes in order to implement and execute the significant ideas and insights that develop from practice. Brown and Duguid (2000, p. 74) argue:

"Finding the right balance is the central task for managers everywhere. It's embodied in a million business fads, and it transcends them all."

Getting the right balance between practice and process is without doubt a daunting task for managers!

The RNLI has introduced a more formal competence-based training system to lower the gap between practice and process. With the system, managers try to tap practices and spread them throughout the organization. However, given the many unstructured practices that happen at sea, the system is primarily designed to help volunteers acquire basic skills and knowledge. This includes obtaining local geographical knowledge, general seamanship and specific knowledge about boats and equipment. The intention is that the basic skills and knowledge help volunteers during unforeseen and abnormal situations. The system is also a guarantee that all stations hold to a minimum standard.

Volunteers in the RNLI form a diverse group as they come from all parts of society, including lawyers, doctors, factory workers, self-employed, fishermen and mechanics. These people bring new ideas, thoughts and knowledge into the existing CoPs. This knowledge is vital for the RNLI. In this sense, volunteers and managers must work together to find best practices and processes. Communication and overlapping CoPs between volunteers and managers are imperative for tapping into knowledge at the various stations and making it available for the rest of the organization. However, this is not easy! Unstructured practices and great variety are usually the norms at lifeboat stations and at sea.

One current example of overlapping CoPs between managers and volunteers is the development of a new lifeboat. During previous development projects, volunteers have not been actively consulted and lifeboats have had to be adapted to life at the stations after the launch. Many volunteers have questioned this approach. Now, when the RNLI is developing its new lifeboat, managers have brought volunteers more into the process. This has already led to changes in the design of the lifeboat. This is a situation where managers take advantage of knowledge among volunteers. Many volunteers have experience with other boats; they have seen both what does and what does not work.

MANAGING VOLUNTEERS

Mutual understanding and communication between volunteers and managers are crucial aspects, in part because of the difficulty of managing volunteers. Several managers contend that they need to be aware of pressures on volunteers. One manager underlined the difference between managing paid employees and volunteers. Managing paid employees, obviously within reason, is a less daunting task. While a paid employee in a commercial organization could be afraid of being fired, a volunteer might say: "What are you going to do, fire me?" This is clearly pushing things to extremes, but it illustrates one difficulty of managing volunteers.

Volunteers are the most important people in the RNLI. These are the people saving lives at sea and making sure the boats and equipment are in working order. In this sense, the RNLI is at the various lifeboat stations around the coasts and not at the headquarters or the various divisions. Managers are there for volunteers, not the other way around. Several managers underlined the fact that the headquarters and divisions around the country are only toolboxes for the stations. Without volunteers, the RNLI would not exist.

ALTRUISM

The thousands of volunteers around the coast work for free. Why are they doing this? What do volunteers get out of being part of the RNLI? These questions hold one key to why the RNLI survives.

Most volunteers feel a sense of being in an extended family where they work for each other. This is appreciated by the Operations Director in the RNLI. He argues that volunteers in the RNLI tend to go the extra mile for the organization. The RNLI has existed for more than 175 years and has acquired a very good reputation. The RNLI shirt attracts respect and admiration from people in the local community. This in turn influences volunteers. The RNLI is in a fortunate situation where volunteers feel so strongly about their work. Volunteers show passion and commitment and are genuinely interested in their work. Even though being a volunteer is hard work and sometimes dangerous, volunteers feel it is meaningful and rewarding.

Since volunteers are interested in doing the best job possible, each must be able to draw from others' knowledge and experience. Although they give a lot of themselves, they do not expect anything in return except for a simple "thank you" once in a while. This altruistic behaviour is a vital element among volunteers in the RNLI. It is necessary for the organization that people with extensive knowledge and experiences share this freely and openly with newcomers and other volunteers in the organization (Davenport & Prusak, 1998).

This altruistic element among volunteers must be supported. Winston (2002, p. 299) argues,

"Even if we have altruistic intensions, we may lack the courage to see them through. So where altruism exists, it should be treasured."

He argues further that the combination of instinct, emotion and reason are vital elements in relation to altruistic behaviours. Again, communication and overlapping CoPs between managers and volunteers are essential.

TRUST

Altruistic behaviour can also be linked to trust (see Fukuyama, 1995). A volunteer must trust the knowledge, experience and competence other volunteers have obtained, especially in abnormal situations at sea. A volunteer said that trusting the people next to you is the main thing during rescue operations. They are the ones who will pull you out of the water if you go under. In this sense, it is a very good reason for altruistic behaviour. Without trust, a volunteer would not be able to tap into and understand the knowledge and experience the others hold. This can lead to dangerous situations. If the people next to you are unable to carry out vital processes during abnormal situations, one might literally end up dead. This concept of trust also intensifies the importance of the collective and social elements where people work together.

Volunteers must also trust managers. Managers have the final say about what boats and equipment volunteers use. In dangerous situations, the boats and equipment must work satisfactorily. On the other hand, managers must trust volunteers. Considering that there are over 230 lifeboat stations around the coasts, managers in the RNLI are unable to supervise everything. The stations must be reliable. Volunteers must show up during rescue operations and perform. The concept of trust between volunteers and managers influences communication and overlapping CoPs.

IMPLICATIONS FOR THE RNLI

Volunteers make up hundreds of CoPs around the coasts in the United Kingdom and the Republic of Ireland. Without the knowledge and experience that exist in these CoPs, volunteers will not be able to do their jobs satisfactorily. Moreover, in abnormal and unforeseen situations the knowledge and experience that exists among volunteers are crucial. Knowledge and experience is often embedded in practice and virtually impossible for managers to institutionalise.

The RNLI has existed for over 175 years. In all those years, various CoPs have come and gone. However, the existing CoPs must be cultivated and new ones developed. Specifically, managers in the RNLI must be persistent in the future to enhance communication and overlapping CoPs between managers and volunteers. Managers have theoretical knowledge backed up by practical experience, whilst initially, volunteers often only have practical knowledge. Using the argument from Brown and Duguid (2000), the organization must be able to understand and foster the practices and have the right processes to spread the knowledge around the organization. Nevertheless, this is not easy, as unstructured practices are often difficult to get to grips with.

It is important to realise that the RNLI is a volunteer organization. It influences the CoPs that exist and are created. Altruism and trust, especially, are vital elements among volunteers. It is essential that volunteers share their knowledge freely and openly. Moreover, if volunteers cannot trust each other, the whole organization would fall apart. Volunteers put their lives on the line. In these situations, you will and must trust the person next to you.

IMPLICATIONS IN A WIDER CONTEXT

Volunteers in the RNLI must be able to deal with unstructured practices and great variety at sea. Further communication and overlapping CoPs throughout the RNLI are developing to get the right balance between practices and processes.

A link from the RNLI to commercial organizations may seem farfetched and of little practical interest to a wider audience. Nevertheless, this way of presenting the problems is also valid for commercial organizations.

Unstructured practices are part of most commercial organizations these days. Together, managers and employees must find ways of dealing with situations. That means communication and forming overlapping CoPs through-out the organization. In these situations, managers and employees must see beyond formal hierarchies and establish relationships vertically and horizontally in the organization.

In the RNLI, altruism and trust are vital elements for sharing and creating knowledge among volunteers. However, altruism and trust are not well established in the existing body of literature concerning CoPs. How do these concepts fit in with commercial organizations?

Altruism must be seen in relation to reciprocity and reputation. Many commercial organizations are built around reciprocity and reputation, where most people only share their knowledge if they think they will benefit from it (Davenport & Prusak, 1998). These benefits do not necessarily have to be money, but obtaining a better position or getting access to new knowledge.

In addition, altruism, reciprocity and reputation must be seen in relation to trust. Davenport and Prusak (1998, p. 34) argue:

"Without trust, knowledge initiatives will fail, regardless of how thoroughly they are supported by technology and rhetoric and even if the survival of the organization depends on effective knowledge transfer."

Every organization is different. Some can, for instance, have a high level of reciprocity among their members, while other organizations can have a strong sense of altruism in their work force. Nevertheless, trust is the underlying foundation for knowledge transfer and creation in both commercial and volunteer organizations.

REFERENCES

Brown, J. S., and Duguid, P. (1991). Organizational learning and Communities of Practice: Towards a unified view of working, learning and innovating. *Organization Science, 2* (1), 40-57.

Brown, J. S., and Duguid, P. (1998). Organizing knowledge. *California Management Review*, *40* (3), 90-111.

Brown, J. S., and Duguid, P. (2000). Balancing act: How to capture knowledge without killing it. *Harvard Business Review*, (May/June), 73-80.

Davenport, T. H., and Prusak, L. (1998). *Working knowledge: How organizations manage what they know*. Boston, MA: Harvard Business School Press.

Fukuyama, F. (1995). *Trust: The social virtues and the creation of prosperity*. London: Penguin.

Lave, J., and Wenger, E. (1991). *Situated learning. Legitimate peripheral participation*. Cambridge: Cambridge University Press.

Spender, J. C. (1994). Knowing, managing and learning. A dynamic managerial epistemology. *Management Learning*, *25* (3), 387-412.

Wenger, E., and Snyder, W. M. (2000). Communities of Practice: The organizational frontier. *Harvard Business Review*, (January/February), 139-145.

Wenger, E., McDermott, R., and Snyder, W. M. (2002). *Cultivating Communities of Practice*. Boston, MA: Harvard Business School Press.

Winston, R. (2002). *Human instinct. How our primeval impulses shape our modern lives*. London: Bantam Press.

Chapter VIII

Innoversity in Communities of Practice

Susanne Justesen
Innoversity Network, Denmark

ABSTRACT

This chapter is about innovation in Communities of Practice and introduces the term innoversity, which describes the role of diversity in fostering innovation. The chapter sets out to discuss when and under what circumstances of innovative practice diversity should be encouraged, as opposed to similarity. The chapter furthermore explores the following questions: 1) What actually is innovation? 2) How does innovation take place in Communities of Practice—and when does it not? 3) Why is diversity in CoPs important in fostering innovative practice? and finally 4) What can be done to foster innovation within and among Communities of Practice? This chapter therefore sets out to describe innovation in Communities of Practice, and what can be done to foster such innovation.

COMMUNITIES OF PRACTICE

Communities of Practice (CoPs) emerge among people who experience a mutual engagement in a shared practice around which they share a common repertoire of knowledge (Wenger, 1998; Brown & Duguid, 1991). "What makes engagement in practice possible and productive is as much a matter of diversity as it is a matter of homogeneity" (Wenger, 1998, p. 75). But according to different fields of research such as social psychology, network theory and

Figure 1: The Similarity — Diversity Continuum

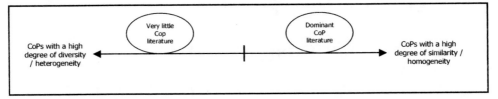

diversity theory, we have solid evidence that birds of a feather tend to flock together, which is usually described by the term *homophily* (McPherson, Smith-Lovin & Cook, 2001). The tendency towards homophily in organizations has been thoroughly documented by Byrne (1971), Kanter (1977) and Ibarra (1992). These findings illustrate why most self-emerging Communities of Practice tend to be based more on similarity than diversity. However, even though the majority of CoPs tend to be homogeneous, CoPs that emerge among highly diverse individuals deserve our attention as well. This chapter sets out to explain and illustrate why such diverse CoPs provide for an interesting new approach to working with innovation and innovative practice in organizations.

Self-emerging CoPs can be described according to their degree of diversity. Most CoP literature focuses primarily on more homogeneous CoPs (Lave & Wenger, 1991; McDermott, 1999; Wenger, McDermott & Snyder, 2002), whereas only very few theoreticians have dealt with the more diverse CoPs (Hildreth, Kimble & Wright, 2000, Justesen, 2001), as illustrated in Figure 1 below.

This distinction between similarity and diversity in CoPs becomes particularly interesting when dealing with innovation. This chapter sets out to explain why diverse CoPs are likely to be innovative, and how this perspective on innovation in CoPs, known as innoversity[1], may bring about a different approach to working with learning and innovation. The word 'innoversity' combines the words innovation and diversity, as diversity becomes crucial especially when considered in the context of CoPs (Justesen, 2001). This chapter therefore explores the dynamic relationship between diversity and innovation in CoPs and what can be done to facilitate and sustain CoPs that strengthen innovation and new thinking.

DEFINING DIVERSITY

In this section, diversity is described as an important vehicle for providing for innovation in Communities of Practice, and an explanation is given as to why this is so. Before venturing into this, however, a clarification of the term diversity is necessary. Diversity, as the term is used and applied in this chapter, refers to diversity in techne (skills and abilities) and cognition.

Using this definition the author would argue that being a woman, Asian and homosexual in an otherwise male, Caucasian and heterosexual organization does not necessarily provide for diversity. Diversity only exists if being a woman, Asian and homosexual influences the way she is categorised by others (i.e., as similar or dissimilar to themselves), if her skills and abilities are different (i.e., techne), and/or if her values and perceptions (i.e., cognition) of the world around provide for diversity (Raghuram & Garud, 1996; Justesen, 2001).

Similarity-attraction theory explains how individuals are more comfortable with others perceived to be similar to the self (Lazarsfeld & Merton, 1964; Berscheid, 1985; Northcraft, Polzer, Neale & Kramer, 1995; Byrne, 1971). Human beings prefer being with others with whom they perceive a similarity of values, beliefs and interests. The rationale offered for this observation is that similarity is: a) reassuring because it reaffirms our beliefs, b) serves as a signal that future interaction will be free of conflict, and c) engenders a sense of unity, all of which are interpersonally rewarding (Byrne, 1971).

Similarity in this definition, therefore, is when people perceive each other as similar (pertaining to the very same identity groups) and share a set of values, beliefs and interests. Diversity exists in a setting where people perceive each other as being dissimilar (more different than similar) in terms of values, beliefs and interests.

INNOVATION AND INNOVATIVE PRACTICE

Innovation is when knowledge from previously separated domains is exchanged and combined in new ways (Nahapiet & Ghoshal, 1998; Hargadon & Sutton, 2000; Justesen, 2001). The result of this innovative practice is innovation when and only when this combination of domains leads to the successful diffusion of a new product, process or service (Schumpeter, 1934). Innovative practice is therefore not merely about getting new ideas and the generation of an invention, but equally about the successful exploitation and diffusion of that invention.

Amidon (2002) further strengthens this perspective when she defines innovation as the practice of creation, conversion and commercialisation. Innovation and innovative practice therefore rely very much on the existing knowledge networks in an organization, and how such networks of conversation allow for or prevent different domains of knowledge from being connected in new and meaningful ways.

Drucker (1985) argues that it is exactly the organization, understood as the patterns of relationship between people in that organization (Stacey, 2001), which provides the most important premises for innovation. Drucker (1985) describes seven contextual sources of innovative opportunity or discontinuities

Table 1: Drucker's 7 Sources of Innovation

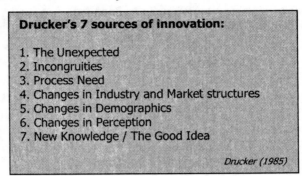

Drucker's 7 sources of innovation:

1. The Unexpected
2. Incongruities
3. Process Need
4. Changes in Industry and Market structures
5. Changes in Demographics
6. Changes in Perception
7. New Knowledge / The Good Idea

Drucker (1985)

and determines innovative practice by the organizational ability to exploit these contextual opportunities when they arise.

Viewing the organization as a constellation of CoPs within which the naturally emerging patterns of relationships provide for combination and exchange of knowledge, meaning and experience (Wenger, 1998) makes CoPs a natural unit of analysis for a better understanding of innovation and innovative practice within organizations.

INNOVATION AND LEARNING IN COMMUNITIES OF PRACTICE

CoPs can be described as the context for situated learning, but in most cases, learning and innovation are co-situated practices. This relationship between learning and innovation is important in that innovation builds on prior learning and most often is path-dependent (Arthur, 1989; Cohen & Levinthal, 1990), i.e., dependent on prior learning within that particular domain. Learning in CoPs is where "learners are acquiring not explicit, formal 'expert knowledge', but the embodied ability to behave as community members" (Brown & Duguid, 1991, p. 48).

Learning in CoPs is described as a process in which the 'competence regime' of the knowledge domain 'pulls' the experience of the individual (usually the newcomer) until there is enough overlap between the experience of the individual and the core competences of the domain for the person to be a fully competent member of the community (Wenger, 1998; Justesen, 2001). This is illustrated in Figure 2a.

It needs to be stressed that the competence regime does not necessarily equal the most experienced core members of the community; just as the 'new (in)experience' does not necessarily refer to peripheral members, but instead symbolises the competencies important to this particular domain of knowledge and this particular community at this particular moment.

An example of such learning can be found in a Danish software company that produces Enterprise Resource Planning (ERP) systems. Until about four years ago, the whole organization was dominated by a rather inaccessible computer-language, understandable only to software engineers and highly skilled IT people. This high-tech culture was perceived positively by most of the employees. It defined who they were and was important in the way they carried out their everyday work and exchanged insights with each other. But then management realised that the company was well underway towards designing software for users like themselves, i.e., other experts and colleagues in the field, thereby effectively losing touch with the normal end user who did not have the same skills, needs and understanding. The most evident result of this was the end user manuals accompanying the software: they were only understandable to other software engineers, and end users were starting to complain that they wanted less functionality and more usability.

Management then began hiring "end user specialists", who were to play an equal part in the development process and who were to turn the documentation into user-friendly documentation. End user specialists had very diverse backgrounds, but they all shared a keen interest in customer needs, and it was their responsibility to provide for those needs during the whole development process.

The engineers regarded the end user specialists as newcomers to their territory, and no matter the intention of management, the end user specialists never managed to change anything. Instead, they learned the expert language, and were eventually pulled by the existing domain, without the existing domain

Figure 2a: Learning in a CoP Competence Regime Pulling the Experience of the Individual   *Figure 2b: Innovation in a CoP Experience of the Individual Pulling the Competence Regime*

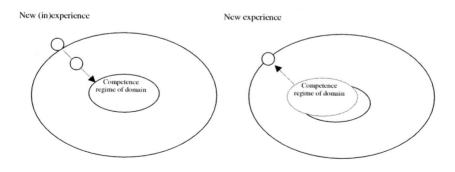

being pulled by them. The result of this was learning, but not innovation. The 'competence regime' developed and negotiated by the engineers over several years was simply too strong, and the engineers were too tightly knit together for anyone from the periphery to participate enough to be able to change anything about software development.

The group had simply become too homogeneous and specialised over time so that nothing from the outside could persuade them to make any changes—they were to a certain extent executing 'group think' and would primarily focus on providing for others to learn, not themselves. So what happened instead was that the end user specialists over time learned 'how things are done around here'— they learned to speak the highly specialised IT-language—and only very few things did actually change.

Innovation—as illustrated in Figure 2b, is what happens when the new experience is able to pull the competence regime and move into a different direction by challenging the existing regime with new knowledge, thereby igniting innovation and the redefinition of the regime, maybe even the creation of a whole new competence regime.

An example of such innovation can be found in another Danish company which produced a so-called actuator device able to expand from just 3 cm to the incredible height of 80 meters. The device was discovered several years later by an enthusiastic entrepreneur, who was not part of the original development project. He was convinced that the actuator had potential and went ahead and turned it into a skunkwork project. From the periphery he could see what no one else could see, and eventually managed to persuade both the community who originally discarded it, the organization and, not least, the market. The product is expected to be highly successful and has already received attention from a long list of different industries such as spacecraft, the car industry, elevators, product designers, architects, etc.

Whereas Figure 2a illustrates the diffusion of existing learning and knowledge in a CoP, Figure 2b illustrates the creation of new knowledge domains (such as the different usages for the above device) on the boundaries between previously separated communities. This happens when the competence regime of the domain is either redefined and renegotiated (incremental innovation) or when a completely new knowledge domain is created (radical innovation), followed by the social construction of a new competence regime.

But innovation breeds a need for learning as well, so the construction of new knowledge domains (innovation) should therefore be illustrated as an iterative process between the practice of innovation and the practice of learning, as illustrated in Figure 3.

So, whereas learning provides for more knowledge about an existing domain, innovation is about the exploration and creation of new domains, both of which are caused by the interaction between new experience and the compe-

Figure 3: Learning and Innovation in CoPs

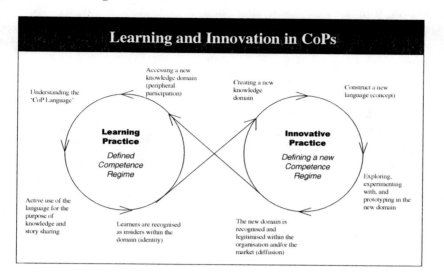

tence regime. However, when will this interaction result in innovation and when will it 'merely' result in learning?

This somewhat 'generic' difference between innovation and learning requires a discussion of what it is within a knowledge domain that will allow for invention and new thinking to take place, and in the following section it is argued why diversity should be seen as at least one important means for developing new knowledge domains.

THE ROLE OF DIVERSITY IN INNOVATION

From among a range of different theoretical fields and scientific traditions, five drivers of innovation have been identified and labelled 'Innoversity Drivers' (Justesen, 2001) because each of these drivers establishes diversity as an important source of innovation in and among Communities of Practice.

Innoversity Driver #1: Absorptive Capacity

The term absorptive capacity was introduced by Cohen and Levinthal in 1990 and describes the ability to learn and develop new knowledge, and how this capability is enhanced in a context characterised by diversity. Cohen and Levinthal (1990, p. 128) define absorptive capacity as "the ability to recognize the value of new, external information, assimilate it, and apply it to commercial ends". Furthermore, they argue that "the organization needs prior related knowledge to assimilate and use new knowledge" (1990, p. 129), which is based on the assumption that prior knowledge increases both the ability to absorb new knowledge into memory, and the ability to recall and use it. Diversity is seen to drive organizational absorptive capacity by increasing "the prospect that incoming information will relate to what is already known", and Cohen and Levinthal (1990, p. 131) continue: "In addition to strengthening assimilative powers, knowledge diversity also facilitates the innovative powers by enabling the individual to make novel associations and linkages."

Diversity in CoPs therefore allows for a multiplicity of knowledge paths which makes the organizational path dependency more flexible. Absorptive capacity, however, not only benefits from this complementarity of skills, but also builds up and enables the necessary organizational ability of reacting to changes in the environment, i.e., requisite variety, which is Innoversity Driver #2.

Innoversity Driver #2: Requisite Variety

The second driver, requisite variety, originated within the natural sciences but was applied to knowledge creation by Nonaka and Takeuchi (1995) due to its focus on variety in techne and cognition, and how such variety may influence problem solving and decision making.

Ashby's (1956) law of requisite variety from the natural sciences is described as "the larger the variety of actions available to a control system, the larger the variety of perturbations it is able to compensate" (Heylighen & Joslyn, 1993). The essence of this law is that a system (such as an organization) can control something, such as the discontinuities in the environment or Drucker's sources of innovation, to the extent that it has sufficient internal variety represented within the organization. Having a diversity of resources available allows for effective combination and exchange internally and therefore for innovation and the creation of new knowledge domains.

Diversity in techne and cognition naturally enhances requisite variety, which also allows for sustaining a wide variety of different skills and methods to be used for dealing with unforeseen contingencies and opportunities in the external context. Diversity also drives the existence of multiple interpretations of particular events by events being interpreted from a range of different perspectives, while simultaneously allowing for immediate action (due to the immediate availability of resources and the enhanced absorptive capacity). Requisite variety and diversity thereby allow for multiple and diverse interpretations of new opportunities and sources of innovation, which are necessary for in-depth inquiry into these opportunities to be pursued. Furthermore, this may lessen oversimplification or premature decision making, which is one of the primary enemies of innovation (Yogesh, 1997).

Innoversity Driver #3: Network Variety

Network variety is highly important in detecting new opportunities in the external world and environment, but even more so in the creation of new knowledge. Several studies of networks (Ibarra, 1992; Lazer & André-Clark, 2000) document the existence of network homophily, which means that individuals tend to 'construct' their networks with similar others and primarily connect in what Ibarra (1992) calls 'homophilous ties' spanning multiple networks.

These findings suggest that diversity in organizations results in equally diverse networks 'spun' around the organization. This means that if people are connected internally across and spanning traditional social categories—for instance in CoPs—the diversity in networks means enhanced access to a wider variety of external connections, and thereby also to a wide variety of knowledge domains. Having ties to diverse parts of the broader social system will yield non-redundant information to a given node (Granovetter, 1973).

CoPs composed of diverse members can therefore tap into broad networks of contacts, making it likely that useful new information will be incorporated into decisions, which can enhance responsiveness to rapidly changing organizational environments (Donnellon, 1993). Diversity may, in this way, contribute to an organization's monitoring of environmental turbulence, just as interaction with the environment is enhanced, which makes it more likely that any useful new information will be discovered and brought to the organization (Lipnack & Stamps, 1993).

These findings are also supported by different studies of team formation, where diverse teams are found to be more likely to communicate with others outside of the team, which was seen to lead to greater innovation (Ancona & Caldwell, 1992; Schneider & Northcraft, 1999).

Innoversity Driver #4: Creative Destruction

Creative destruction is old, and in many ways misunderstood, thinking. When originally introduced by Levitt (1962, p. 128), he described it as follows: "being willing to destroy the old is the heart of innovation and the means to enormous profits", and he continues, "creative destruction is a useful motto not simply because of its purposeful and ringing sound but because it creates an organizational disposition towards entrepreneurial audacity. Its constant quest is to create progress through obsolescence" (Levitt, 1962, p. 129).

According to Thomas and Ely (1996, p. 80), diversity can "help companies grow and improve by challenging basic assumptions about an organization's functions, strategies, operations, practices and procedures." However, challenging organizational assumptions is not enough to achieve innovation; it only works if the challenges are being listened to. Only too often, experts tend to ignore whatever does not support their particular expertise, as illustrated by the history of science. In order to be able to benefit from the mechanisms of creative destruction, challenging members need to be granted the necessary legitimacy by the CoP at large to be able to challenge the existing competence regime.

Diversity may therefore be seen as an important driver of creative destruction, due to diversity's potential of offering dissimilar "what if" assertions, allowing conversation to become more dynamic, and enabling a creative destruction and questioning of status quo, and the testing of previously held assumptions (Sutton, 2001; Mathews & Wacker, 2002).

Innoversity Driver #5: Problem Solving

Finally, the last driver, problem solving, is inspired by Leonard (1998), and her emphasis on the importance of shared problem solving—where diversity of perspectives is argued to enhance problem solving routines and processes. Problem solving skills can be perceived as a set of routines employed to respond to changes or threats, or as knowledge about how new knowledge is created, i.e., as a practice shaping the knowledge in the organization (Andersen, 2000).

Diversity can be seen to drive problem solving and the development of organizational problem solving skills, due to diversity offering different options and points of view - which is highly important for problem solving (Leonard, 1998). According to Thomas and Ely (1996, p. 85), "employees frequently make decisions and choices at work that draw upon their cultural background - choices made because of their identity-group affiliations." However, it needs mentioning that it is not the variety among individuals' social category memberships that produces synergy; it is the variety in techne and cognition that we associate with diversity which allows for innovative idea cross-fertilisation (Northcraft et al., 1995).

Cox (1993) advocates that diversity may be seen to drive creativity and problem solving by generating a multiplicity of points of view to confront problems. Supporting this idea is the notion that a variety of perspectives can stimulate non-obvious alternatives (Nemeth, 1986).

This position is supported by findings maintaining that top management heterogeneity predicts innovativeness in banks (Jackson & Associates, 1992; Schneider & Northcraft, 1999). As an example of how diversity drives problem solving, Ivan Seidenberg, chairman and CEO of Bell Atlantic Corporation, states, "Diverse groups make better decisions." With telecom going through mammoth changes in technology and competition, Seidenberg figures that what Bell Atlantic needs most is "more diversity of thinking. If everybody in the room is the same, you'll have a lot fewer arguments and a lot worse answers" (Colvin, 1999).

Figure 4: How Similarity/Diversity May Foster Either Complex or Abundant Learning and Innovation

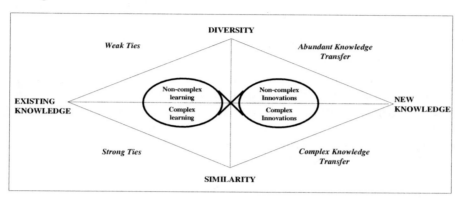

INNOVERSITY IN COMMUNITIES OF PRACTICE

Thus far, learning and innovation have been described as interdependent processes in CoPs, and as such lead to an expansion of existing knowledge (learning) or new and applicable knowledge (innovation), which can be depicted as a double-loop-process as depicted in Figure 3, and may take place in CoPs characterised by either similarity or by diversity. This is illustrated in Figure 4.

Figure 4 also illustrates the type of innovation and learning that can be expected in each setting, where specialised and complex knowledge require a higher degree of similarity to be shared and exchanged, as opposed to less complex kinds of knowledge (Katz & Lazer, 2001). In a study by Hansen (1999), it was found that there is a relationship between tie strength (among similar others) and the complexity of information being transmitted; highly specialised and complex knowledge requires the bandwidth of strong ties. Weak ties, on the other hand, work best for conveying less complex knowledge.

Even though similarity in a CoP is important when the knowledge being transferred is highly complex or specialised, diversity will be highly beneficial to innovation in a range of different settings. According to a study on intra-organizational networks by Katz and Lazer (2001), diversity within a group provides for a more diverse set of external ties, at the cost of internal connectedness; whereas similarity provides for a higher degree of internal cohesiveness but is often externally poorly connected. With innovation being often dependent upon external connectivity (Drucker, 1986), diversity becomes highly important.

The traditional description of CoPs focuses on the very essence of the community to exist and evolve from the sharing of language, social constructions and narratives, thereby constituting a certain degree of similarity through the sharing of a particular domain of knowledge. Diverse CoPs exhibit similar patterns of behaviour, although the diverse CoP will have access to abundant knowledge transfer from multiple external ties, which is unlikely to be the case in a more similarity-based CoP.

Such a process can be illustrated by the following example from a project among free agents in Copenhagen who wanted to better understand creativity. They felt like were on deep water when setting out to do so - and decided to name themselves 'Skibet', which in Danish means 'the ship'. 'Skibet' can be described as a small CoP where the participants have been brought together by mutual engagement in a common practice field: creativity. The members all have a keen interest in learning and developing their creativity. The three participants may be described as highly dissimilar and representing very different social identity groupings.

What is primarily interesting about Skibet is how their participation in 'Skibet' (where they aim to develop a creativity product) seems to allow them to play with identity roles; they put their normal identity on hold for a moment, and investigate the creativity possibilities offered when doing so. The way the participants in Skibet play with identity roles makes them experience creativity (their practice field) in practice: what it means to be creative, and how the 'stepping out of existing identity groups' allows for creativity to flourish. This way their engagement in creativity not only becomes a matter of creating a creativity product, but also a matter of learning from their own engagement in creativity activities.

For instance, when Peter (film-maker) 'allows' the other two participants to do the filming in a movie they are making about creativity, they have found creativity to be enhanced in two ways: first of all because Birgitte and John are not restricted by the do's and don'ts of the film-world, because they are not part of it themselves; and secondly, because Peter learns from their creative destruction of his 'way of doing things'.

This example can be seen to illustrate one way in which diversity can be important in learning and innovation, first of all from the identification with a certain practice field and how that can be an important source of cohesiveness in an otherwise diverse group of people. Secondly, because of how they seem to develop their competences within the field of creativity, this innovative practice in itself makes them embrace diversity as an important means for them to be able to engage in creativity the way they do.

Another important aspect of diversity illustrated by this example is the importance of trust, which is described by Fonseca (2002, p. 9) in the following way:

"The emergence of trust is required to sustain the anxiety-provoking conversations, characterized by redundant diversity experienced as misunderstanding, which are required for innovation to emerge."

HOW TO FOSTER INNOVERSITY IN COMMUNITIES OF PRACTICE

The innoversity drivers and Drucker's seven sources of innovation illustrate how important it is to systematically encourage a certain degree of diversity in CoPs, and both IBM and LEGO are very much aware of this. "Bringing in new or divergent points of view was also a technique used to spark innovation within a community at IBM. Outside influences were valuable to provide for new thinking" (Lesser & Storck, 2001). At LEGO, this need for diversity in working with innovation is reflected in their new team-model within product development, which requires every new team to be diverse in terms of both culture and profession, thereby providing for as many different viewpoints as possible.

The very first step in working with innoversity begins with a thorough understanding of existing networks of learning and knowledge sharing within the organization, to understand who speaks to whom about what, and especially who does NOT speak to whom about things they SHOULD be talking about. This is most effectively done by making use of the methodology of Social Network Analysis to locate existing and emerging Cops and competence regimes.

When the most strategically important CoPs have been identified, they should then subsequently be analysed from the perspective of each of the five innoversity drivers to understand whether they would each benefit from a higher degree of similarity or diversity, according to the level of complexity of their particular knowledge domain. If the level of similarity is perceived to be too high, the CoP needs facilitation in understanding the importance of diversity and will need assistance in identifying and 'inviting in' potential new members who will minimise the likelihood of group-think and increase innovative practice within that particular CoP.

CONCLUSION

In a decade where innovation becomes increasingly important, organizations need to be able to also capitalise on CoPs characterised by diversity, and not merely those characterised by similarity, even though these are more frequently described in existing CoP literature. To enable a conceptualisation of the existence of different levels of diversity and similarity in CoPs, this chapter initially enabled the categorisation of CoPs along different dimensions such as learning and innovation, similarity and diversity, complexity and abundance, and new experience and existing experience.

From these different categorisations it was found that CoPs characterised by a high degree of similarity in techne and cognition will have a tendency to be internally well-connected and cohesive, which allows for the easy transfer of highly complex and specialised forms of knowledge, but with the risk of fostering group-think and with relatively few external links. CoPs characterised by a high degree of diversity in techne and cognition are likely to be less cohesive and poorly internally connected, whilst being externally well connected, and with a more diverse set of external ties. Such a CoP will therefore be more likely to be able to be innovative in their ability to learn about and exploit the seven primary sources of innovation described by Drucker (1985).

Both types of CoP are therefore important to innovation and innovative practice, but this chapter illustrates why diverse CoPs deserve more credit due to the advantages such CoPs exhibit in terms of absorptive capacity, requisite variety, network access, creative destruction and problem solving.

CoPs, as they have been described here, are self-emerging, and even though CoPs may be aided and facilitated by management, they are created from within and not from the outside. To develop a recipe for 'building' a CoP among dissimilar individuals is, however, beyond the scope of this chapter. Within the scope, however, is providing for an increased awareness of the importance of diversity in and among CoPs, along with a vocabulary and a theoretical framework from which future research may attempt to develop such methodology.

The general applicability of innoversity (the dynamic relationship between innovation and diversity) should therefore be relevant to organizations interested in improving their innovative practice by an increased understanding of when to sustain CoPs dominated by similarity and when instead to sustain CoPs characterised by diversity.

REFERENCES

Amidon, D. M. (2002). *The innovation superhighway.* New York: Butterworth-Heinemann.

Ancona, D. G., and Caldwell, D. F. (1992). Demography and design: Predictors of new product team performance. *Organization Science, 3* (3), 321-341.

Andersen, L. B. (2000). *Innovation in firms—A study of problem solving processes.* Thesis, Dept. of Industrial Economics and Strategy, Copenhagen Business School.

Arthur, W. B. (1989). Competing technologies, increasing returns, and lock-in by historical events. *Economic Journal, 99* (394), 116-131.

Ashby, R. (1956). *Introduction to cybernetics.* New York: John Wiley.

Berscheid, E. (1985). Interpersonal attraction. In G. Lindzey and E. Aronson(Eds.), *Handbook of Social Psychology*, 2, (pp. 413-484). New York: Random House.

Brown, J. S., and Duguid, P. (1991). Organizational learning and Communities-of-Practice. *Organization Science, 2* (1), 40-57.

Byrne, D. (1971). *The attraction paradigm*. New York: Academic Press.
Cohen, W. M., and Levinthal, D. A. (1990). Absorptive capacity: A new perspective on learning and innovation. *Administrative Science Quarterly, 35*, 128-152.

Colvin, G. (1999). The 50 best companies for Asians, Blacks, and Hispanics. Companies that Pursue Diversity Outperform the S&P 500 Co. *Fortune*, Monday, July 19.

Cox, T. (1993). *Cultural diversity in organizations*. San Francisco, CA: Berett-Koehler.

Donnellon, A. (1993). Crossfunctional teams in product development: Accommodating the structure to the process. *Journal of Product Innovation Management, 10*, 377-392.

Drucker, P. F. (1985). *Innovation and entrepreneurship*. Oxford: Butterworth-Heinemann. Fonseca, J. (2002). *Complexity and innovation in organizations*. London: Taylor and Francis Books Ltd.

Granovetter, M. (1973). The strength of weak ties. *American Journal of Sociology, 78* (6), 1360-1380.

Hansen, M. T. (1999). The search-transfer problem: The role of weak ties in sharing knowledge across organization subunits. *Administrative Science Quarterly, 44* (1), 82-111.

Hargadon, A., and Sutton, R. I. (2000). Building an innovation factory. *Harvard Business Review, 78* (3), 157-166.

Heylighen, F., and Joslyn, C. (1993). The law of requisite variety (modified August 2001). In F. Heylighen, C. Joslyn, and V. Turchin (Eds.), *Principia Cybernetica Web* (Principia Cybernetica, Brussels). On the World Wide Web: http://pespmc1.vub.ac.be/REQVAR.html [September 1st 2002]

Hildreth, P. M., Kimble, C., and Wright, P. (2000). Communities of Practice in the distributed international environment. *Journal of Knowledge Management, 4* (1), 27-37.

Ibarra, H. (1992). Homophily and differential returns: Sex differences in network structure and access in an advertising firm. *Administrative Science Quarterly, 37*, 422-447.

Jackson, S. E. and Associates. (1992). *Diversity in the workplace: Human resources initiatives*. New York: Guilford Press.

Justesen, S. (2001). *Innoversity—The dynamic relationship between innovation and diversity*. (Working Paper 6/2001). Copenhagen Business School, Department of Management, Politics and Philosophy.

Kanter, R. M. (1977). *Men and woman of the corporation*. New York: Basic Books.

Katz, N., and Lazer, D. (2001). *Building effective intra-organizational networks: The role of teams*. (Working Paper). Kennedy School of Business, Harvard University.

Lave, J., and Wenger, E. (1991). *Situated learning—Legitimate peripheral participation*. Cambridge University Press.

Lazarsfeld, P. F., and Merton, R. K. (1964). Friendship as social process: A substantive and methodological analysis. In M. Berger, T. Abel, and C. H. Page (Eds.), *Freedom and Control in Modern Society*, (pp. 18-66). New York: Octagon.

Lazer, D., and Andre-Clark, A. (2000). *Knowledge in the network*. Paper from Kennedy School of Government, Harvard University. Available http://www.ksg.harvard.edu/teamwork/Knowledge%20in%20the%20network21.doc [September 25, 2002]

Leonard, D. (1998) *Wellsprings of knowledge*. MA: Harvard Business School Press.

Lesser, E. L., and Storck, J. (2001). Communities of Practice and organizational performance. *IBM Systems Journal*, *40* (4), 831-841.

Levitt, T. (1962). *Innovation in marketing: New perspectives for profit and growth*. New York: McGraw-Hill.

Lipnack, J., and Stamps, J. (1993). *The Teamnet factor: Bringing the power of boundary crossing in the heart of your business*. Essex Junction: VT Oliver Wright Publishers.

Mathews, R., and Wacker, W. (2002). *The deviant's advantage*. New York: Crown Business.

McDermott, R. (1999). Learning across teams: The role of Communities of Practice in team organizations. *Knowledge Management Review*, *4* (8), 22-30.

McPherson, M., Smith-Lovin, L., and Cook, J. M. (2001). Birds of a feather: Homophily in social networks. *Annual Review of Psychology*, *27*, 415-444.

Nahapiet, J., and Ghoshal, S. (1998). Social capital, intellectual capital, and the organizational advantage. *Academy of Management Review*, *23* (2), 242-266.

Nemeth, C. J. (1986). Differential contributions of majority and minority influence. *Psychological Review*, *93* (1), 23-32.

Nonaka, I., and Takeuchi, H. (1995). *The knowledge creating company*. New York: Oxford University Press.

Northcraft, G. B., Polzer, J. T., Neale, M. A., and Kramer, R. M. (1995). Diversity, social identity, and performance: Emergent social dynamics in cross-functional teams. In S. E. Jackson and M. N. Ruderman (Eds.), *Diversity in Work Teams*, (pp. 69-96). Washington: American Psychological Association.

Raghuram, S., and Garud, R. (1996). The vicious and virtuous facets of workforce diversity. In M. N. Ruderman., M. W. Hughes-James, and S. E. Jackson (Eds.), *Selected Research on Work Team Diversity*. Washington: American Psychological Association.

Schneider, S. K., and Northcraft, G. B. (1999). Three social dilemmas of workforce diversity in organizations: A social identity perspective. *Human Relations, 52,* 1445-1467.

Schumpeter, J. A. (1934). *The theory of economic development: An inquiry into profits, capital, credit, interest and the business cycle.* Cambridge, MA: Harvard University Press.

Sessa, V. I., and Jackson, S. E. (1995). Diversity in decision-making teams: All differences are not created equal. In M. E. Chemers, S. Oskamp, and M. A. Costanzo (Eds.), *Diversity in Organizations—New Perspectives for a Changing Workplace,* (pp. 133-156). Thousand Oaks, CA: Sage Publications.

Stacey, R. D. (2001). *Complex responsive processes in organizations.* London: Routledge.

Sutton, R. (2001). *Weird ideas that work.* Free Press.

Thomas, D. A., and Ely, R. J. (1996). Making differences matter: A new paradigm for managing diversity. *Harvard Business Review,* (September/October), 79-90.

Wenger, E. (1998). *Communities of Practice—Learning, meaning and identity.* Cambridge University Press.

Wenger, E., McDermott, R., and Snyder, W. M. (2002). *Cultivating Communities of Practice.* Boston, MA: Harvard Business School Press.

Yogesh, M. (1997). *Knowledge management in inquiring organizations.* New York: Brint Institute.

ENDNOTES

[1] This perspective on innovation was developed by the author and presented in the paper "Innoversity - The Dynamic Relationship between Innovation and Diversity" (Justesen, 2001). The word innoversity has (in Denmark) been recognised as a general term for this relationship, by being quoted in the Danish Encyclopedia of Management (2001).

Chapter IX

User Networks as Sources of Innovation

Anders Lundkvist
Stockholm University School of Business, Sweden

ABSTRACT

In the computer and software business, it is common practice to involve users in problem solving and sharing of experiences, not only between a company and individual users but also between groups of users. Although customer support has gained some attention in recent years, a more intriguing thought would address users as a source of innovation. What if users themselves, or in interaction with other users, would, in addition to solving specific problems, also develop and share new knowledge that influences products within companies? In connection with this notion is the question as to how companies can come to relate to these networks of users. The empirical case study in this chapter was generated from a long-term study during 1998-1999 with Cisco Systems and the company's groups of users. Of particular interest to this study was the use of the Cisco newsgroup, which is available on the Internet. The conceptual framework was generated from the emerging theory of Communities of Practice (CoPs). By using this framework, user networks were recognised as peripheral and yet vital sites of innovation. This implies new strategies for management of innovation as the creation of spaces for interaction with and between users and addressing networks rather than individual users.

INTRODUCTION

One problem relating to new product development is that customers or users may be unacquainted with the technique and its use and are thus unable to evaluate the benefits. Furthermore, users may have difficulty articulating their needs, in that these needs are embedded in daily practices. Traditional market research would therefore be inadequate to provide companies with sufficient information about their customers. Von Hippel (1988) suggested that if users address key issues in their own specific context, new ideas could be more easily generated. To focus on the practice of customers or users has also been proposed as a successful, but less applied, way of understanding customers (Dougherty, 1992).

Later research (e.g., Von Hippel, 2002a) has adopted the concept of a community-based perspective on users and customers as innovators. Here the interactions among people are essential. Franke and Shah (2001) noted that it is by linking people to each other that innovators are provided with powerful resources. Such a perspective differs from traditions of new product development (Jelinek & Schoonhoven, 1990; Leonard-Barton, 1995) in which attention is turned to internal roles, resources and competencies (e.g., managers, engineers, researchers and experts).

In the field of innovation theory, there thus seems to be a growing interest in customers as innovators. Some novel thoughts include users and customers being recognized as connected, which turns attention away from the individual user to the network or context. Von Hippel (2002b) further defined user networks as user nodes interconnected by information transfer links which may involve face-to-face, electronic or any other form of communication.

Whereas the notion of user networks has grown out of advances in innovation theory, there are evident links to Communities of Practice. Common links are the view on: (1) innovation as generated from practice in everyday life, (2) the situated nature of learning and (3) joint rather than individual problem solving. This chapter explores user networks as sources of innovation and how they relate to the emerging theory of CoPs. Using the unified view of working, learning and innovation (Brown & Duguid, 1991), this chapter proposes that user networks are a peripheral, yet vital, site for innovation.

Communities of Practice

Earlier studies of CoPs observed that workers found their own ways of creating new work patterns, which are often different from those formally prescribed. From these observations, three central processes of CoPs emerged: social construction, collaboration and shared language. By adapting to these three processes, participants were engaging in joint problem solving. Thus, the focus in CoPs is not the individual or his or her cognition, but rather the interaction among participants.

Becoming a member in a CoP is a process over time. By exchanging "war stories" from the frontier of practice and engaging in common activities, participants move from peripheral to fuller participation (Lave & Wenger 1991) and thus not only change personal identities, but also contribute to development and change in the community. Wenger (1998) further noted that participants develop "multimemberships" as they move between different communities and combine the simultaneous influences from multiple communities.

There appears to be some features in CoPs that would be of benefit when studying how customers and users engage in joint problem solving, namely: participation, collaboration and shared language.

Innovation in Communities of Practice

Many researchers (e.g., Brown & Duguid, 1991; Wenger, 1998) have noted that CoPs provide a novel view of how knowledge is created and of the process of innovation. One's action only becomes meaningful in relation to the actions of others. What is subsequently produced is not a socially rational consensus but a sense of collective identity (Gergen, 2000). This view is fundamentally different from other perspectives (Grant, 1996; Nonaka & Takeuchi, 1995), where knowledge is individual and subject to being transferred, integrated or combined.

As Brown and Duguid (1991) propose, innovation cannot be separated from the work and learning that takes place as people engage in everyday social life. Further, the source of innovation lies on the interface between an organization and its environment. This position is far from the traditional view of innovation in which innovation is looked upon as a disruptive process carried out by experts in certain organizational functions.

INTRODUCTION TO THE STUDY

The main attribute that the members of the CoP described in this chapter have in common is that they are customers and use equipment from a larger supplier of network systems, namely Cisco Systems. Rather than focusing on Cisco Systems, this study is concerned with the interactions among users. A few notes about Cisco Systems, however, may provide a better understanding of the business context.

Cisco Systems is in the networking business, where it develops and provides technologies and equipment for Internet and computer communication. With the commercialisation of the Internet in 1992, the market grew rapidly and Cisco Systems expanded with other networking equipment companies, becoming the leading and dominant provider in the network market during the 1990s.

Growth and new technology brought new challenges to Cisco. The first challenge concerned recruitment of a large enough support staff that would meet the divergent demands from the growing market. The second challenge concerned issues related to developing leading edge equipment when customers and users are unacquainted with the use of new equipment. To overcome these challenges, Cisco built information strategies that would enable automation of support, customer self-service and customer-to-customer support. However, enabling customer self-service in this way was not only a way of reducing the organization's administrative load. It could also be viewed as a complementary strategy for product innovation in that the use of equipment sparks information sharing among customers, which, in turn, generates new suggestions for the further development of products.

Data Generation

The customer and user networks case study provided in this chapter was generated over a long period. During 18 consecutive months, from February 1998 to July 1999, 27,185 postings to the Cisco Usenet group comp.dcom.sys.cisco were downloaded and analysed. Communication patterns between participants were studied using Social Network Analysis (see Wasserman and Faust, 1994, to provide an overview of techniques and methods). One common criticism of Social Network Analysis is that it gives an understanding of who speaks to whom (i.e., the notion "the self-in-relation to specific others"), but provides less understanding of the context as to why people communicate with each other. In this case, communication patterns and findings from the study were used to ignite discussions in three workshops involving 60 users from 11 companies. From the intense discussions that followed, questions and problems relative to CoPs emerged. Please note that in the following text, identities, where given, have been changed to provide anonymity.

The presentation of the study is structured as follows:

- First, an illustration is provided of one innovation process in CoPs: the movement from peripheral to fuller participation.
- Second, a discussion is presented on problems and opportunities related to CoPs.
- Third, a brief discussion on how Cisco chose to approach the CoPs is introduced.
- Finally, CoPs as sharing innovation processes between companies are examined.

Peripheral Participation

In 1997, David Johansen became employed as a network technician at a larger university. His job was to provide a well functioning email and server network for more than 45,000 people, including students, researchers and staff. David shared this task with three other experienced colleagues. This was an exciting and challenging task in that the network required perpetual attention and development. It was also evident that the four technicians needed constant support from network suppliers. However, often neither they nor the suppliers found immediate solutions to their problems.

David started to address the newsgroup comp.dcom.sys.cisco with postings for help. During the first six months in 1998, David was the most frequent participant in the newsgroup and recognized as a beginner or a "newbie", exclusively asking for help rather than providing assistance. Subsequently, these interactions started to change as David began to reply to the needs of others. David's responses not only included information gained from earlier conversation threads but sometimes went on to extend the original problem with new innovative solutions. It became apparent that David often participated in conversations with longer threads, such as when five or more people interacted on the same topic or generated more than 20 postings. This form of conversation indicated a complexity in the topic and a situation where none of the participants could easily provide an answer. It was not a matter of simply transferring information about technical issues among participants. There were often new and unfamiliar problems in which participants had to co-operate by exchanging ideas, trying them out and then sharing new experiences again.

During the next six months, David posed less than 15 questions; however, he was involved in 185 conversations regarding complex problems with many other contributors. David had started to become recognized as an important contributor to the newsgroup. Because David's email address was shown in the postings, David started to receive questions posed not only to the newsgroup but also to his own private email address. David, who then addressed the issue in the newsgroup, considered this an annoyance. David simply did not have the time to reply to all the incoming questions. He asked people not to mail him directly and observed that the newsgroup provided a much greater opportunity in that it gave access to a much wider range of support. It was also a way of lessening the burden of having to participate in newsgroups with a large variety of topics.

From Peripheral to Fuller Participation

There were different indications of David's process of becoming a core member in the newsgroup. First, David may not be the best expert; yet, he was contributing to conversations and problem solving with others. Second, on another level he was also participating in the process of creating norms and ways of behaving in the newsgroup. Third, others recognized David as an important contributor. This third indication was noted in one posting to David, addressing the "routing elite":

"Hi there, I have a related question I put on another mailing list. Without reply : -(Now I bring this before the routing elite, hoping to get an answer."

From the study, it became evident that members of the newsgroup could be grouped according to levels of participation. First, only a few people participated in this process through time, moving from a peripheral to fuller participation. Second, most people only occasionally participated in the newsgroup by asking questions or giving answers. These people maintained a legitimate, but nevertheless peripheral position in the newsgroup. We found that this did not imply that they were newbies or less experienced technicians, however. On the contrary, some were recognized as legendary routing experts, but because of lack of time or for other reasons, they did not participate to the same extent as others.

Problems and Opportunities with User Networks

The discussions in the workshops generated some intriguing questions concerning how participants in CoPs solve their everyday problems. It was apparent that participation in Internet newsgroups or mailing lists was considered as important to maintain or develop personal skills. This was explained, as in the case of David, because peers were to be found outside their own organization. David noted:

"There is no way the few of us could possibly understand or solve problems with new equipment. The people that we would like to discuss these issues with are simply not here. But they are always available out there."

Thus, for David and many other participants, the shared practice is not within the organization, but with fellow technicians in other organizations. Practice in this way transcends boundaries of organizations and provides an opportunity for interaction among people and the sharing of experiences.

During another workshop, a support manager elaborated on the need to employ staff with extended social networks, as this would speed up problem solving and provide new resources for innovation. The support manager explained this in the following terms:

"It is commonly known that if you recruit one talented technician, you will get twenty for free."

This and other remarks turned the discussion to whether it is acceptable for the organization to take advantage of its employees' personal and social networks. All participants agreed on the necessity to employ social networks in their daily work. However, it was another question as to whether it was acceptable to make use of these networks, especially because participants were required to make use of the formal tools available inside the organizations (e.g., intranets and knowledge bases). One participant was very explicit about the problem: if social networks were identified and made known, corporate managers, by nature, would try to formalise and control them, a fact that would make everyday work harder. Consequently, the issue of CoPs was considered a highly delicate matter, one requiring a new managerial understanding.

How May a Company Benefit from a User Network as a Source of Innovation?

How a company may exploit networks of users is illustrated here by how Cisco approached the newsgroup. Although Cisco had no authority or control over the newsgroup, support staff and product engineers monitored the newsgroup conversations.

The company's Technical Assistance Centre (TAC) noted that many conversations in which David participated provided valuable recommendations on the use of equipment and novel ideas for new configurations. To Cisco, it became important to develop a standpoint regarding the valuable conversations in the newsgroup. There were fears that David and other participants might have extensive communication in private email sessions in addition to the publicly available newsgroup. In this situation the TAC within Ciscos Support Department asked David if he was interested in becoming an 'official helper'. David's new email address was in itself a symbol of how people may transcend boundaries of formal organizations:

"David.Johansen@cisco.com, University of xxx".

This showed that David was officially legitimated by Cisco as a participant in the newsgroup. At the same time, the email address showed that David was still upholding a position as a technician at the University. By approaching David, Cisco was really approaching the network of users.

The Periphery as a Site for Innovation

A point which is emphasised by the theory of CoPs is that participants transcend different communities. As an example, David's work involves not only the use of Cisco equipment but also hardware and software from several other suppliers.

When a user moves among different newsgroups or contexts, the user is actually bringing experiences from one situation to another. The newsgroup could be described as belonging to the periphery. Participants create, share and recreate experiences from other situations, which might be their office, company or other communities. In bringing these other experiences, the members make the newsgroup a site for innovation (Brown & Duguid, 1991).

This argument would imply that innovation could be a process involving companies not only through agreements, partnerships or joint ventures but also

Figure 1: User Networks as a Site for Sharing Innovations Among Companies (Inspired by Brown and Duguid, 1991)

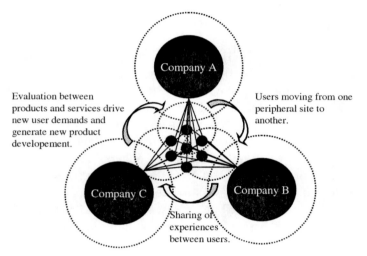

through various interactions among users. Thus, users have become creators and sources of innovation to companies.

CONCLUSION

As we learned from the workshops described, CoPs are a powerful tool for creating an understanding of how innovation, work and learning are interrelated. The beauty with CoPs is that they are not limited to specific contexts and organizations but transcend boundaries, as in the case study in this chapter where customers and users share interest and practice.

This study involved participants normally engaged in developing and providing the latest communication technology. One might assume that sharing experiences in this CoP would not be likely to arouse controversy. However, findings from this study indicate that CoPs were a delicate issue for participants and managers to handle. Organizations still seem to consider information sharing through informal and social networks as something that ought to be controlled through "proper" channels. Nevertheless, participants recognised the newsgroup and other boundary crossing activities as important for innovation in daily work life.

Another issue concerned the boundaries of practice. As in the case of David, it is not necessary that members of the same organization share the same culture or practice. To David and his close colleagues the CoPs provided an opportunity for personal development. In this specific case David's supervisor encouraged interactions with participants outside the organization as a way of enriching the daily work of the individual. In other organizations, managers might try to direct attention to internal interactions as a means of encouraging problem solving and sharing within the organization, which would neglect the peripheral site for innovation.

It is evident that CoPs challenge dominant perspectives on innovation processes. Consider that few participants describe themselves as innovators; rather, they are just trying to make sense of the events of everyday life. In a recent article, Dougherty (2001) called for "reimagining" the differentiation and integration of work for sustained product innovation. How companies may perceive innovation in CoPs becomes a strategic issue. Recognising interactions with customers and users as sources of innovation would demand strategies for companies to maintain relationships with CoPs emerging from customers. One strategy presented in this chapter was to identify those participants who had become known as important contributors. It was further noted that this approach addressed the interactions between users rather than individual experts.

REFERENCES

Brown, J. S., and Duguid, P. (1991). Organizational learning and Communities of Practice. *Organization Science*, *2*, 40-57.

Dougherty, D. (1992). A practice-centred model of organizational renewal through product innovation. *Strategic Management Journal*, *13*, Special Issue Strategy Process: Managing Corporate Self-Renewal, (Summer, 1992), 77-92.

Dougherty, D. (2001). Reimagining the differentiation and integration of work for sustained product innovation. *Organization Science*, *12* (5), 612-631.

Franke, N., and Shah, S. (2001). *How communities support innovative activities: An exploration of assistance and sharing among innovative ssers of sporting equipment*. Sloan Working Paper #4164, August. Massachusetts Institute of Technology/Sloan School of Management.

Gergen, K. J. (2000). *The saturated self: Dilemmas of identity in contemporary life*. New York: Basic Books.

Grant, R. M. (1996). Toward a knowledge-based theory of the firm. *Strategic Management Journal*, *17*, Special Issue: Knowledge and the Firm (Winter, 1996), 109-122.

Jelinek, M., and Schonhoven, C. B. (1990). *The innovation marathon: Lessons from high technology firms*. Oxford: Blackwell.

Lave, J., and Wenger, E. (1991). *Situated learning: Legitimate peripheral participation*. Cambridge: Cambridge University Press.

Leonard-Barton, D. (1995). *Wellsprings of knowledge. Building and sustaining the sources of innovation.* Boston, MA: Harvard Business School Press.

Nonaka, I., and Takeuchi, H. (1995). *The knowledge-creating company.* New York: Oxford University Press.

von Hippel, E. (1988). *The sources of innovation.* New York: Oxford University Press.

von Hippel, E. (2002a). *Horizontal innovation networks—By and for users.* Working Paper #4366-02, June. MIT Sloan School of Management.

von Hippel, E.(2002b). *Open source projects as user innovation networks.* Working Paper 4366-02, June. MIT Sloan School of Management.

Wasserman, S., and Faust, K. (1994). *Social network analysis: Methods and applications.* Cambridge University Press.

Wenger, E. (1998). *Communities of Practice: Learning, meaning, and identity.* Cambridge: Cambridge University Press.

Chapter X

Building Customer Communities of Practice for Business Value:
Success Factors Profiled from Saba Software and Other Case Studies

Brook Manville
Saba Software, USA

ABSTRACT

Most discussions of Communities of Practice (CoP) place them in the context of a primarily internal-to-the-organization approach to managing knowledge. The construct, however, has application across the entire value chain of an organization, including the domain of a company's customers. This article explores the strategic value of building Customer Communities of Practice (CCoPs), learning networks among customers of a company whose win-win value proposition helps customers gain valuable insights from other peers while also providing the sponsoring company with a means to further innovation, loyalty and deeper insights into the markets they serve. The analysis suggests three types of CCoPs, including business to consumer, business to business, and communities of channel distributors. Case studies of each are presented and an especially extensive treatment is offered of the second type based on the author's experience of building a CCoP for his own software company. The discussion concludes with several lessons learned and practical guidelines for building successful CCoPs in any industry.

INTRODUCTION

When Communities of Practice (CoPs) captured the attention of business leaders during the 1990s, the predominant application was to foster and support learning networks of practitioners within the traditional boundaries of an organization. Though most founding fathers of the CoP concept envisioned communities as cross-boundary constructs (e.g., Wenger, 1998; Brown & Solomon-Gray, 1995; Brown, 2000; AQPC, 2000; Wenger, McDermott & Snyder, 2002), enthusiasm for largely internal Knowledge Management (KM) programs during those years branded CoPs as part of the great unseen and informal network of learning to be tapped within every enterprise. Today that assumption still largely prevails and indeed many organizations are moving to develop internal knowledge communities as part of their overall learning and KM approach.

This chapter argues that, in addition to more common internal versions of CoPs, there are opportunities for creating a comparable system of relationships, motivations and learning processes of these networks among customers of an enterprise (e.g., Lesser, Fontaine & Mundel, 2002). Indeed, approaches, techniques and design principles of these Customer Communities of Practice (CCoPs) are emerging among pioneering experiments that can guide their development in other companies. The chapter further argues that development of CCoPs is both timely and strategic for the benefits they can confer for increasing customer loyalty, innovation and the deepening of market understanding for a sponsoring company. At the same time, customers who participate in CCoPs can benefit from professional growth and knowledge about organizational improvement within their own companies. At their best, CCoPs are win-win networks that help both the sponsoring company and the members who join in such a community.

However, CCoPs do not spontaneously emerge, nor can they be developed without due attention to the fundamentals of CoP architecture (developed from Wenger, McDermott & Snyder, 2002, p. 23): *context, knowledge domain, people, practices* and *governance.* Analysis of some recent case studies and especially the experience of my company, Saba Software, will highlight relevant themes for success applicable to other situations.

Our discussion is organized around these questions:

- What are CCoPs? How do they differ from other CoPs?
- What business or organizational value do they potentially promise? What is the business context that makes them strategically valuable now?
- What can be learned from practice? Case studies of CCoPs and a detailed examination of CCoPs at Saba Software.
- What are the success factors for building successful CCoPs and what pitfalls to be avoided?

What are CCoPs?

As always, definitions can be all-important and at the same time controversial. The recent definition of Wenger, McDermott and Snyder (2002, p. 4) of a CoP is a good starting point:

"A group that shares common concerns, problems, or passion and who deepen their knowledge and expertise by interacting on some ongoing basis."

Adapting it to the customer context, we can say that CCoPs are groups of customers of a particular company who interact on some ongoing basis for those same reasons. The customer identity of this kind of CoP implies a shared relationship with a provider of goods or services whose offerings are part of the group's common concerns; but as subsequent examples will show, common experience with a company's products or services may be only the pretext, or only part of the reason, that the CCoP forms. At the same time, as long as we identify the CCoP as a customer group, some fundamental tie to the core provider of goods or services that define the customer relationship remains a core element of this form of CoP. As such, there is always some element of a commercial relationship between providers and users, if not to the fore, at least in the background of the network.

Purists may object that as soon as any kind of commercial relationship becomes part of a community, it cannot truly be a community. However, there are already plenty of CoPs which function at least partly as marketplaces rather than purely altruistic learning exchanges. Perhaps more importantly, as experience shows, companies can take advantage of the social and organizational dynamics of CoP type relationships in ways that benefit all participating members. CCoPs need not be the exploited tool of the provider organization; indeed, if one sets out to build a CCoP for only that purpose, it will almost certainly fail—or devolve into something less.

Many companies, particularly those in the technology industry, have established user groups or customer advisory boards, which are arguably a precursor to CCoPs. However, most of these are not true communities, focusing little, or not at all, on cross-member learning or collective development of a domain of knowledge. Instead they are (in the worst case) merely marketing PR—customer representatives brought together periodically to provide references for sales support or the illusion of collaborative product development, nourished by golf outings and fancy dinners. Less cynically, they are advisory groups which provide periodic input to a company's product/service development, but whose activities yield no collective betterment of the membership.

A fundamental distinction between these false communities and true CCoPs is the structure and operating relationship between sponsor and participants. Do they operate primarily as spokes to the hub of the sponsoring company or more as a multi-lateral network of equals committed to advancing the state of the knowledge domain—working with, as opposed to for, the sponsoring company? In some cases, CCoPs may even work independently of the company that is the core provider of goods and services that defines the domain of the group. That said, there are expanding examples of user groups that are being run, or run themselves, as true CoPs, cases of which we will look at in greater detail later.

Some analysts and commentators of CCoPs have endeavoured to segment different kinds of CCoPs. In an interview with Diane Hessan (CEO of Communispace, Inc), November 15, 2002, Hessan identifies three basic forms of CCoPs:

1)   *Type 1:* Business to Consumer, in which a company creates a CCoP to test and develop new products for retail markets
2)   *Type 2:* Business to Business, in which a company creates a CCoP among wholesale users of its products/services, to foster new product development and increase loyalty
3)   *Type 3:* Channel Communities, in which a company fosters CCoPs among resellers or distributors of its products and services, for similar reasons

This segmentation may have some value for understanding audience, knowledge domain and approaches to group development. At the end of the day, however, they share some common features - specifically a blend of commerce and learning, around a defined domain, in which both sponsoring company and participant members all benefit from the development of professional relationships, knowledge exchange and professional growth.

What is the Business Value of CCoPs?

CCoPs represent potentially valuable forums in which a company's goods and services, or the supporting processes thereof, are discussed, analysed, criticized and (potentially) improved. They represent a unique listening post and live laboratory generally freed from the constraints and biases of traditional sales situations or the one-on-one transactional relationship between vendor and buyer. The social dynamic and processes of multiple users of the same product or service coming together, discussing those products/services (or ideas for new ones) outside of a commercial negotiation offers a unique and potentially insightful exchange of business intelligence. Because CCoPs also foster inter- (and also intra-) company relationships, they can also create different and deeper bonds between company and customers. They also provide a larger umbrella of learning that surrounds membership in the customer community. This umbrella can both encourage new customers to join and helps the sponsoring company add more value to all customers in the future. CCoPs can also seed demand for a company's product and services in new companies as members of the customer community take on new jobs or roles in other organizations, while still leveraging the knowledge and relationships of the core community.

Several customers of Saba Software (my own company) for example, are today building communities among their own customers with role-based learning programs, with the expectation that the professional growth and expertise of practitioners will drive more demand in the future as they move to other jobs. As one executive explained:

"We know the buyers and users of our storage products are very professionally mobile; if we can build a generation of users certified in our technology, they will drive more demand for our products when they move onto their next and bigger job."

The evolution of customer communities is tracking trends in today's global economy and leading-edge organizations. At the most basic level, customer communities represent yet another instalment of the ongoing development of the knowledge revolution, which Drucker and many others framed a generation ago (e.g., Drucker, 1993; Davenport & Prusak, 1998). For a long time, this revolution was seen as fundamentally an internal matter of leveraging the skills and experience of knowledge workers, but organization after organization has come to realize that a vast complement of knowledge and understanding can also be tapped from one's own customers. User groups, focus groups and advisory bodies, of course, reflected the earliest manifestations of that understanding, but CCoPs, because of the greater intimacy and win-win potential that they represent, are an obvious next step of evolution.

CCoPs and Market Trends for Solutions and Co-Creation

Two other related trends in today's economy are similarly paving the way for development of CCoPs - the increasing demands of customers less for simple transactional purchase of products and more instead for integrated solutions and/ or applications, e.g., "don't just sell me the engine, help me save costs in designing our car around it", or "don't just sell me the software, make it work with all the other systems and tools I need to drive more revenue in my sales force" (Sharma, Lucier & Molloy, 2002).

Complementary to this pull for solution and application is the understanding of companies that they can create more value, faster—and higher barriers to entry—if they move beyond the traditional over the wall design of products to actually co-creating them with those who will invest in them—the customers (Prahalad & Ramaswamy, 2002). Once one acknowledges the need for co-creation and/or solution-delivery, it becomes clear why creating and nurturing a community of user customers can provide such benefits. A company that can create and sustain customer communities related to its products, services and overall strategy can expect to drive higher revenue, deeper customer loyalty (and thus future revenue), more innovation and deeper sustainable advantage in terms of higher switching costs. That said, the essential thing to understand—and the real value of CCoPs for those belonging to one—is that the bonds of community membership are as much about the participants learning and benefiting from the experience and problem-solving with one another as they are about the business value derived by the sponsoring company.

CASE STUDIES OF CCoPs
Accelerating Innovation with a Type 1 CCoP

Given the marketplace and economic trends, there is, not surprisingly, an expanding universe of examples of CCoPs. One of the better-documented cases of a Type 1 (Business to Consumer) CCoP is provided by Hallmark greeting cards. Originally, these were formed to gather and test new ideas for greeting cards and were sponsored by gifts, coupons and other material incentives for members to participate, similar to a focus group. Over time, however, the Hallmark consumer groups evolved into true communities in which members began to participate based on learning and helping one another.

That transition was facilitated by creating community segments that Hallmark initially used to pinpoint tastes and preferences (e.g., grandparents, mothers with children, Hispanics). The commonality of each constituency soon evolved into a basis for collateral learning (e.g., mothers trading tips about childcare, managing kids, homework, etc.). Hallmark, aided by the Communispace tools and facilitators that supported the groups, soon realized that the more continuous conversations and relationships within the group—acting as a CCoP and not just a focus group—had much greater value. With a minimum of support and ongoing facilitation, the groups became self-sustaining and ultimately generated several new product ideas, which have led to measurable commercial value (revenue-generating products). Another Communispace client, a major consumer goods manufacturer, embarked on a similar program and found that the initial rewards for participation were soon leapfrogged by community members' interest in getting to know one another and exchanging household tips. The company reported several new product ideas generated by their CCoPs, at much lower cost than traditional market research.

Aligning Distributors and Increasing End-Customer Value with a Type 3 CCoP

An example of the Type 3 CCoP (Channel Customers) was documented by Hubert Saint-Onge and Debra Wallace, who led the development of a virtual strategic capability network among insurance agents who are resellers of insurance products of the Canadian financial services company Clarica (Saint-Onge & Wallace, 2003, p. 116). In this type of CCoP, the customer community stands as a best-practice sharing and learning network whose capabilities grow for the purpose of (a) helping members of the channel be more successful in serving their customer needs and thus also tying the channel more tightly to the sponsoring company, and (b) driving more value indirectly to the ultimate consumers of the company's products and services by increasing the capability of those who sell to them.

Accelerating Market Development, Innovation and Customer Loyalty with Type 2 CCoP

Because of my personal experience building CCoPs at Saba Software, this case study offers an opportunity for some more detailed commentary, both about what and how to. Saba Software is a mid-size provider of technology platforms for managing human capital, training and performance in large organizations. Saba was founded in 1997, went public in 2000 and is today a $50 million company acknowledged to be the leader in its market space. Type 2 CCoPs (Business to Business) have been a key element of Saba's strategy from its earliest days. The business value derived from their development has been confirmed both by the company's leadership and by the over 60 customer organizations that have participated in the networks.

Business Value

For Saba, the CCoPs have contributed directly to new product development with measurable financial return; they have also been an invaluable vehicle for helping the company develop its strategy, offerings and positioning against competitors. And finally, the communities have been a key differentiator helping to drive company loyalty and customer satisfaction; the meetings of the CCoPs are both a forum in which many customer problems are resolved in real time and one in which Saba's commitment to customer success is demonstrated and reinforced. In a recent management planning session, the leadership of the company ranked our CCoPs as among the top 10 strategic assets of the organization.

Customers have also acknowledged the business value of these communities for them. They are often cited as a key purchase differentiator in independent customer satisfaction surveys and members of the community in other diagnostic surveys have echoed repeatedly the value derived from collaborative problem solving, best practice sharing and benchmarking and professional development derived from participating in the networks. As one executive joked:

" ... these meetings are some of the best professional therapy I've ever had!"

Developing CCoPs at Saba: A Historical Perspective

These communities did not invent themselves, nor were they created quickly. However, they were seen as an early critical dimension of our company's strategy. From the first, the founders of the company pursued a strategy of not just building software but also creating an ecosystem of partners and customers whose collective knowledge and learning would both accelerate the development of the overall market, deepen our own product innovation and also increase differentiation from competitors. Stated in other words, CCoPs were founded to both build a new set of opportunities and, at the same time, distinguish the Saba brand as not just about a certain set of products, but also about relationships, knowledge and momentum-building professional development among an extended community of stakeholders. The stated goal was to increase the pace of market development and build a leadership position for Saba and its customers within it.

The first steps were to create an advisory board of key customers, companies that had early on bet on Saba's technology and worked with the company to refine its features and functionality. Because the software was targeted to automate and transform a broad range of previously manual processes and also to provide new capabilities, the working relationship between Saba and these customers (initially training directors or HR executives) was intense and necessarily co-dependent. As Saba was endeavouring to create a new market, these customers were also endeavouring to create new ways of working in their organizations. Like it or not, company and customers were all joined at the hip: their success depended on Saba and vice versa. Each side was yoked together in the business of organizational transformation.

That understanding set the context for Saba working with its customers not as a bilateral advisory group, but much more valuably as a multi-lateral learning community. From the earliest days, it was recognized that all participating customers had something to learn from Saba and from each other; Saba in turn had lots to learn from each of them and from the exchanges among them. Those conversations inevitably had the effect of surfacing invaluable tacit knowledge about human capital processes; that is, insights, understandings and perspectives known but not necessarily documented. As the first user group formed, it soon became clear that the social and professional dynamics were in place to make it a true learning community—a forum for exchange, learning and growth for all participants.

Protocols and Working Practices of the CCoP

As Saba leaders in this program, my colleagues and I also understood that for that kind of community to evolve, a context would have to be established that would encourage such a development. Working with the core members of the group—and doing so in a participative and democratic way—we identified protocols and working practices that helped foster the kind of community culture that would be truly win-win for all concerned.

Firstly, it was acknowledged that all participants (including Saba) shared a common domain—how to best use Saba software in the context of certain common business roles and objectives (e.g., managing training and learning in a corporate context). With that stated, members were recruited who were both actively engaged with those practices and who also had the interest and need to reflect upon practice for greater learning and improved performance in their organization. Secondly, ground rules were established that the work of this community was to be non-commercial and multi-lateral; that it could not become just a sales or marketing forum for Saba, though Saba could obviously benefit from participation in other ways. Thirdly, participants worked together to set a climate of openness and sharing, coupled with largely self-governing decision-making (see Manville & Ober, 2003): customer members elected their own officers, developed working and learning agendas, schedules and operating arrangements with Saba as a non-voting participant. Fourthly, the community kept a focus on real work and real benefit for participation—an objective to ensure that there was value for participation and that discussions and working sessions were practical and workplace-oriented, not theory.

Adding Structure and Formality

Over time this group evolved to a larger and more structured community—naming itself the global customer advisory board (GCAB)—which elected its own members and officers, developed and pursued a formal learning agenda and also pursued a series of ad hoc working projects (e.g., how to integrate third party content into the system; how to pursue a change program and govern the learning function in a decentralized organization). Some of these were aimed to educate Saba about future needs and requirements; others instead intended company-to-company sharing of best practices or techniques related to managed learning. Saba colleagues and I worked increasingly closely with this board and the project teams, building learning relationships and also doing all we could to continue to support the cross-member exchange as well as the transfer of best practice and insights into our own Research and Development (R&D) group. Through specific communications vehicles (newsletters, website, conference calls) and occasional face-to-face meetings that explicitly combined real work with a little light-hearted fun (evening out at a baseball game, trip to sponsoring company's manufacturing plant for a visitor tour, etc.) we helped the group develop a sense of community that was social as well as professional—but always prioritising the latter as the real focus of our meetings.

These face-to-face meetings of the GCAB were in fact, by design, hosted not at Saba but at one of the members' business locations, with participants taking turns to provide the sponsorship in terms of meeting rooms, facilities, etc. In addition to providing a more neutral and customer-centric setting for the meeting, the hosting of the event also gave the sponsoring company the chance to invite various managers and other contributors to the meeting, which offered them the opportunity for their own networking and professional growth. Saba normally provided some subsidy for a group dinner or similar, but each company paid its own expenses to travel to the location, reflecting the expectations of both making a contribution to the community's work and symbolizing value given for value received instead of being on a Saba junket. Meetings at the different company locations were administratively managed by the sponsoring company, with the senior member executive of that company also playing some kind of leadership role in the proceedings. Saba's role in these meetings was limited to light facilitation, helping to structure the discussion, document decisions and plan for future projects and meetings. In all cases, however, the meeting was convened for and by the customers and not Saba; in many cases, the group took the discussion in very different directions than had first been planned.

All of the Saba CCoPs came to combine at least some face-to-face meetings with virtual teleconferences or exchanges using such tools as virtual classrooms. The general philosophy that evolved generally held that periodic in-person meetings were necessary to build trust and relationships, as well as foster more detailed problem solving together. Interim virtual meetings, inevitably shorter and less costly, were efficient ways to work on a well-defined project (such as meeting planning, or collecting requirements for a new product), but could not themselves sustain the culture of a community dedicated to professional growth and development. Those sub-communities (regional communities, see below) that minimized their face-to-face meetings tended to be overall less productive and less valuable for all members (by their own admission) than those that met for regular in-person events. (For some general discussion about the role of face-to-face interaction versus virtual exchanges in building communities, see Nohria, N. and Eccles, R.C. (1992) or Rheingold (1993)).

Second Generation Sub-Communities

After about a year, awareness and interest in user communities began to rise in other Saba customer organizations. Since it was not possible to add easily any further members to GCAB and since the interests among at least some of the members were beginning to diverge, Saba took the step of decentralizing and segmenting. We began to institute a next generation of smaller, more local and/ or specialized networks to complement the central GCAB. In design, the local communities were intended to draw from some of the same people on the GCAB, but they also potentially included members of other organizations and/or other members of the same organization who by function or seniority might not be appropriate for GCAB.

The meetings of these sub-communities were designed to be more informal and in cases of face-to-face gatherings, would require less travel. Thus, members of the Eastern regional user group were mostly located near New York or New Jersey; the Midwestern group tended to cluster near Chicago and Minneapolis; the Western group got its start with a critical mass of companies in or near Silicon Valley. The work of these smaller communities tended to be similar to that of GCAB, but involved either more technical and hands-on knowledge sharing, or clustered around a more focused industry experience, e.g., among technology companies in the western region or pharmaceutical companies in the East. At the time of this writing, there are now five vital regional user communities; three in the United States, one in Asia Pacific and one in Europe.

At about the same time, another opportunity for community learning cropped up in the form of special interest groups or networks. Some of these emerged from the discussions of GCAB or regional groups (e.g., FDA-regulated interest group, an outgrowth of the pharmaceutical companies in the East), others arose naturally as Saba customers interested in certain requirements reached out to one another in their eagerness to develop their businesses on the basis of benchmarking and best practice sharing (e.g., companies in the for-profit learning business).

In developing both the regional and special interest groups, all of the same principles of GCAB applied (self-governance, focus on the practical, etc.). In every case, Saba played a facilitative and infrastructural role and let the participating companies set the agenda and processes for their work. At the same time, Saba took care to keep these communities linked to its business and products, to ensure that the feedback and learning implied in their discussions would benefit its future strategy and that Saba could in turn be responsive to questions and requirements of customer members.

To increase the coverage and stewardship of the communities, Saba regional account managers (part of the Customer Support organization) took on the role of community facilitators. Through mutual consent, the program of all the groups' meetings also included periodic visits by key Saba executives and facilitators did all they could to develop a climate of ongoing and open exchange between customers and Saba leaders - but again, as a complement to customer-to-customer learning and dialogue.

Looking Ahead

At the time of writing, there are now eight separate (albeit somewhat overlapping, including both regional and special interest-focused) customer-learning communities. As Saba's customer base grows and the knowledge required to pursue technology-based human capital management becomes more sophisticated, we envision the number and specialization of communities to also increase. With the business value already established from these communities—increasing innovation, market understanding, customer loyalty, etc.—the future challenge for Saba is how to derive even more benefit and make the learning from the communities more integral to the company's strategy-making process.

There are also a range of organizational and design challenges that must be considered as the CCoP program expands. Saba is now wrestling with questions such as:

- Should we continue to encourage organic growth and steady expansion of more and more communities? Are there limits to the complexity implied? Will there be diminishing returns that lessen the value of more growth in the future?
- How much should Saba endeavour to manage the communities going forward? To date the company's role has been developmental and facilitative, but will the program cross a boundary requiring a decision to play either a more active or a less active role?
- Is there a larger scale model for governance linking local and special interest communities more tightly together and/or with the GCAB that should be developed? What would that look like?

Many of these questions reflect the same future questions that will be faced by any company developing CCoPs. If CCoPs are as valuable and timely for other companies as they have been for Saba - and if the trends towards customer co-creation, collaborative development of solutions and cross-boundary knowledge networks remain firm—we should imagine CCoPs becoming a more common imperative for every organization. From a strategic perspective, the challenge will be no longer be "why build these?" or "how to build these?" but rather "how to scale them?" and "how to govern them?" as they become part of the increasingly complex ecosystems of the modern and knowledge-based organization.

LAUNCHING AND SUSTAINING CCOPS: SUMMARY FACTORS FOR SUCCESS AND PITFALLS TO AVOID

In the meantime, our research and practice has revealed some common factors for success in launching and sustaining CCoPs. Similarly, the investigation has shown some all-too-familiar pitfalls to avoid. Because every situation has its own set of business and organizational challenges, we articulate these factors as a series of suggested guidelines supported with a list of relevant diagnostic questions. These can be used to identify the relevant factors for any particular case. We close this essay by documenting these, following the basic framework of CoP architecture developed from the work of Wenger, McDermott and Snyder (2002).

CONTEXT

Success Factors

- Understand and clarify the business value of creating a CCoP: What would be the benefit to the sponsoring company? What would be the benefit for participants? Are the value propositions to all members clear?
- Understand the metrics of success: What would success look like? How would you measure value? How would the participants measure their value?
- Understand organizational readiness: Is there willingness on behalf of the sponsoring company to make a contribution—in time, resources and attention—to building and participating in CCoPs? Is there interest and willingness to make a commitment on the part of customers themselves?
- Establish an expectation and climate upfront of mutual learning: Though this is a given for any CoP, it is particularly important that the CCoP create an environment of mutuality and constructive exchange between the customers and the sponsoring company. Customers must not be made to feel like they are merely being farmed for their knowledge, gathered to be sold to, or that they should be operating as a collective bargaining group intent on zero-sum negotiation about product features or functionality with the sponsoring company.

Pitfalls

- Trying to launch a CCoP without the clarity of value, purpose or benefit to both the sponsoring organization and the potential members.
- Trying to launch a CCoP without the support or commitment of colleagues in the company, or the resources to support it.

- Launching a CCoP whose intent, spoken or unspoken, is overtly commercial for the sponsoring company only, or lacks the constructive mutuality of a multi-lateral learning community.

KNOWLEDGE DOMAIN

Success Factors

- Having a well-defined focus of issues, themes and topics that will guide the community's work. Though this will likely emerge and evolve over time, there must be at least some kind of starting hypotheses about what these are, ideally developed collaboratively by the members themselves. The work of the community must be to continually define and articulate the boundaries of their shared interests.
- Keep the focus practical and on real work. As a Community of Practice, the CCoP no less than any other learning network should maintain a focus on real work—learning and reflection based on active engagement in workplace settings. Though there is always some value in integrating theory into learning practice, nothing will kill off a CCoP faster than to turn it into an academic meeting.
- Being sensitive to competitive conflicts. Though, in this era of co-opetition, more and more companies are learning how to balance collaboration and competition, there are inevitably areas of conflict that will crop up, particularly in special interest groups, along industry lines or, in other cases, along functional lines. In building a CCoP one must be sensitive to such things, face and discuss openly potential conflicts; if there are areas that must be either kept confidential or treated as off limits, better to be explicit about that and avoid the tension and guardedness of what's left unsaid.

Pitfalls

- Failing to articulate the boundaries of the domain, or make any effort to define areas of joint inquiry.
- Failure to avoid the easy temptation of purely academic or theoretical discussions.
- Relying on relationships and socializing as a substitute for work of the community.
- Ignoring the potential dangers of competitive conflict or trying to obscure them when they arise.

PEOPLE

Success Factors

- Having the right people in the room: Whether face-to-face or virtual, the meetings of the community will be successful only if those participating feel they are spending time with fellow practitioners from whom they can learn and who they feel are in some sense of the word professional peers. A customer joining a CCoP will want to feel that he or she is engaging with others of comparable knowledge, both in terms of organizational level and practical experience, and also engaging with others facing comparable challenges in their professional work.
- Having the right behaviours in the room: Along with the right people must come the right behaviours; the basic things—listening, respecting others, being constructive, being attentive, etc.—cannot be taken for granted, and indeed a good facilitator will take careful steps to ensure that the right environment is struck in the meetings of the community. Participants who are regularly disruptive or are otherwise misaligned with the CCoP interests have to be removed from the group.
- Overlapping memberships: It may be that as the CCoP grows, it will spawn the development of complementary or separate communities focused on a particular subset of the original domain of knowledge, for example. This is not necessarily to be discouraged and indeed reflects what is a natural evolution of learning knowledge development. There is no reason to try to restrict membership to only one community when participation in two or even more can benefit the individual and indeed the communities themselves.

Pitfalls

- Not being clear—as a group—about the kind of people who would ideally become members (based on knowledge, role, etc.).
- Being afraid to deny someone from participating because "the customer is always right" or "the group has to be flexible and open towards all".
- Trying to control membership in any or several communities that are naturally evolving around relevant domains of knowledge.

PRACTICES

Success Factors

- *Creating and sustaining a learning agenda:* developing a specific list of topics (updated periodically) that the group collectively wants to pursue and help one another grow from.

- *Creating and sustaining learning infrastructure:* putting in place the administration and support mechanisms to make participation smooth and productive—meeting schedules, teleconference and/or web access for meetings and communications, minutes and archives of previous meetings, etc.
- *Creating and sustaining learning processes:* pursuing a combination of both formal and informal discussions, presentations (e.g., case studies) combined with informal networking, socializing, etc.
- *Combining virtual meetings with at least some face-to-face:* Although debates rage among practitioners and commentators about whether purely virtual communities are better/stronger, worse/weaker or about the same as more traditional communities which meet face to face, our experience suggests that at least some personal interaction goes a very long way to making the customer community productive. Because the multilateral, as opposed to hub and spoke, relationships between customers and company are so important, it is all the more important that customers get to know one another and develop the kind of cross-company networks that add to the value proposition of the CCoP.

Pitfalls

- *Under-appreciating the importance of infrastructure and management:* Just because it is administrative does not mean it is not important. Such things are a critical part of the glue of a CCoP, just as for any CoP.
- *Not balancing the formal and informal:* Any learning community, CCoP or otherwise, will be choked if it turns into a stiff classroom experience; similarly it will make little progress if it is merely a floating 'bull session'. Combining both structured presentations and informal exchange is critical.
- *Letting the sponsoring company be dominant or customers dominant in meetings:* Though it is important for the sponsoring company not to overwhelm the proceedings, it must also not shrink and be a silent and passive observer. Customers expect some engagement with the sponsoring company and similarly the sponsoring company must be eager to encourage customers to participate actively and freely. All around the table (virtual or otherwise), participants must feel like they are contributing on some regular basis and are being heard as they do so.
- *Resisting the opportunity to engage in at least some face-to-face meetings:* In today's budget-strapped world and dwindling amounts of disposable time, there will be inevitable calls to just "go virtual". That's fine to get started, but the community will likely only develop so far if there are no in-person meetings eventually. Face-to-face events can be occasional, and once held, the relationships formed can be extended for a long time in the future through interim virtual exchanges.

GOVERNANCE

Success Factors

*   Engaging the community to govern itself. In order to avoid turning the customer community into a simple or one-way advisory board, it must have a large degree of autonomy in setting its domain, people, processes and decisions. That means giving the CCoP the opportunity to choose such things on their own, elect their own officers, set their own agendas, etc. The sponsoring company can and should play a role here—but as a non-voting member at the table. This is not so much an issue of control, but of alignment—ensuring that the CCoP contributes benefit to the company in the same way that the CCoP must expect the company to contribute to it.

*   Build networks of networks. As a CCoP grows and expands and new or sub-communities form, natural questions of governance will arise about the prerogatives of one community versus another. Though there is no single structural design for governing multiple communities that have interconnected or linked memberships, as a general principle, helping them develop as a "network of networks" seems to yield good results—let each new community define its own domain and practices and find ways to let decisions or perspectives developed in one be carried over and built into the agendas of other (e.g., by overlapping memberships of particular participants). One might alternately pursue a more hierarchical structure—in which sub-communities' work rolls up to a more senior group (for example, made up of "best and biggest customers" or representatives from lots of regional or specialist groups)—or, taking a more horizontal approach, create mechanisms and processes in which relevant perspectives and decisions in each community are carried over to others, without creating an overall steering or governing authority at a higher level. In all cases, there is value to finding mechanisms to interconnect the learnings of multiple communities, working across a broad customer base of the sponsoring company.

Pitfalls

*   Trying to control CCoPs so they become nothing more than marketing channels for your company.
*   Abandoning any participation in the governance of the CCoP and thus missing opportunities for aligning CCoPs for business value.
*   Ignoring opportunities for achieving overall scale among multiple CCoPs by under-investing in creating connections among them.

ACKNOWLEDGMENTS

Thanks to Diane Hessen, Amy Keill, Bill Snyder and the editors and contributors of this volume for comments and suggested improvements on previous drafts of this article.

REFERENCES

American Productivity & Quality Center. (2000). *Sustaining and building Communities of Practice: Continuing success in Knowledge Management.* Houston, TX: American Quality & Productivity Center.

Brown, J. S. (2000). *The social life of information.* Boston, MA: Harvard Business School Press.

Brown, J. S., and Solomon-Gray, E. (1995). The people are the company. *Fast company,* November, 78-82.

Davenport, T. H., and Prusak, L. (1998). *Working knowledge. How organizations manage what they know.* Boston, MA: Harvard Business School Press.

Drucker, P. (1993). *Post-capitalist society.* New York: Harper Business.

Lesser, E., Fontaine, M., and Mundel, D. (2002). *Learning from the connected customer: Enhancing customer websites with community.* White Paper. IBM Institute for Knowledge-based Organizations.

Manville, B., and Ober, J. (2003). *A company of citizens. What the world's first democracy teaches leaders about creating great organizations.* Boston, MA: Harvard Business School Press.

Nohria, N., and Eccles, R. C. (1992). Face to face: Making network organizations work. In N. Nohria and R. C. Eccles (Eds.), *Networks and organization: Structure, form and action,* (pp. 288-308). Boston, MA: Harvard Business School Press.

Prahalad, C. K., and Ramaswamy, V. (2002). The co-creation connection. *Strategy and Business, 27,* (2nd Quarter), 50-61.

Rheingold, H. (1993). *The virtual community: Homesteading on the electronic frontier.* Reading, MA: Addison-Wesley.

Saint-Onge, H., and Wallace, D. (2003). *Leveraging Communities of Practice for strategic advantage.* Woburn, MA: Elsevier Science.

Sharma, D., Lucier, C., and Molloy, R. (2002). From solutions to symbiosis: Blending with your customers. *Strategy and Business, 27,* (2nd Quarter), 38-48.

Wenger, E. (1998). *Communities of Practice: Learning, meaning and identity.* Cambridge, UK: Cambridge University Press.

Wenger, E., McDermott, R., and Snyder, W. (2002). *Cultivating Communities of Practice.* Boston, MA: Harvard Business School Press.

SECTION III:

COMMUNITY OF PRACTICE DEVELOPMENT

Chapter XI

Creating a Multi-Company Community of Practice for Chief Information Officers

John Moran
Global Gateways, Inc., USA

Lee Weimer
Weimer Collaborative, USA

ABSTRACT

This chapter presents a case study of the creation and evolution of a fee-based, multi-company Community of Practice (CoP) for Chief Information Officers (CIOs) in the San Francisco Bay Area over a six-year period. It describes the principles, processes and practices required to form and maintain a trust-based, face-to-face learning organization where members share accumulated knowledge. Additionally, it states some of the individual, collective and Information Technology industry benefits and results that have accrued from member participation in the CIO Community of Practice. The authors hope that the description of this CoP will foster the same sense of excitement for would-be practitioners that they feel.

TODAY AT A CoP MEETING

It is early 2003 and you have just finished dinner as a guest of the Silicon Valley Chief Information Officers' (CIO) Community of Practice (CoP). On the way home, you reflect on the meeting and the day's activities. Several points strike you as interesting. There seemed to be a genuine level of trust and respect among the more than 20 members, each from a different company, participating in the lunch discussions about their soon to be published book, *CIO Wisdom* (Lane et al., 2003). They had different ideas on how the book royalties should be distributed from the scholarship fund they had established, but that high level of respect never waned.

As they moved into the presentation part of the meeting, you soon realized how much experience, depth and interest the members had in their profession. The members' questions probed the presenters for information and several members willingly shared their own experiences with the subject matter. The interchanges were rich and fascinating and it was evident that both presenters and members were learning from each other. This learning/sharing environment continued throughout the afternoon as progress on a joint project was updated. Additionally, a departing member, whose division had fallen victim to reorganization, shared the resumes of his best and brightest with the hope his colleagues and friends could both benefit and help. Later in the day, the members chose the topics and suggested potential presenters for future meetings.

As they broke to head for the dinner part of the meeting, you began to notice a mood shift to a much lighter tone. At dinner, there was a combination of personal, professional and jovial conversations. You noticed that some of the more experienced members were having mentoring sessions with one or two of the newer members, while others at the table were discussing their latest high tech product purchase. A thought occurred: here over good food and wine, there continued to be learning, trust and community building—what a great resource this CIO Community of Practice (CoP) would be.

IN THE BEGINNING

The authors had been working with CIOs from a few different companies through having monthly lunch discussions. These CIOs are responsible for an organization's entire Information Technology and infrastructure, including computer hardware, software, and networks. They are responsible for recommending strategic technology initiatives, and once the decision is made, the CIO is charged with making the implementation successful. In order to recommend technology strategies, they have to keep current with the changes and products in the global IT industry. They are employed in multiple companies involved in the design, marketing and manufacturing of high technology products and services in an area south of San Francisco, California, known as Silicon Valley.

During these lunches, the topic of making the meetings more formal and creating a best practices forum was discussed. The concept was intriguing and it was decided to investigate the idea. Questions provided a starting point— Would CIOs from different companies be willing to share information and learn from each other? Since CIOs are extremely busy and are on-call 24x7, would they have the time and interest in a learning community? If there were interest, how would they want it structured? Face-to-face? E-meetings? Would the participants be open to sharing with direct competitors in the group? How would the approach differ from other already existing learning forums? Would they be willing to pay for the facilitation of the meetings?

To answer some of these questions, five people (3 CIOs and 2 facilitators) were called together in the autumn of 1997. The meeting started with a definition of the term CoP:

A Community of Practice is a group of people who are brought together by a desire to learn more about a common class of problems/opportunities. Community members accelerate business results and add value by collaborating directly, using one another and outside resources, to learn and teach each other. Members find themselves drawn to one another by a force that is both professional and social.

Several ideas were discussed. However, the principal question of the dialogue was: Could an alternative way be created for these people to meet and share ideas that would address needs and desires not currently being filled? As a result of this meeting, several of our questions were answered. The most important answer was yes, there was an interest and a willingness to move ahead with the idea of a CoP. This group of three CIOs would form the "core members" of the CoP. It was agreed that the first "real" meeting of the CIO Community of Practice would be in early 1998. It was also agreed that the facilitators, with input from the CIOs, would be responsible for identifying and inviting additional CIOs to participate in the CIO CoP.

These early discussions in 1997 helped set the baseline principles for the CIO CoP. The core members already knew each other and had a level of trust between them. They established the community's field of interest or "domain". Thus, the core team's "Field/Domain of Interest" became: *Leadership and Management of Information Technology.*

Another important point to come out of these early meetings was the group's interest in being "practical". They made it quite clear that they wanted to hear from others who were investigating or implementing IT products, rather than from academics or from vendors making sales presentations. Thus, they established the "Practice" part of Community of Practice as being: *Real World IT Practices—Methods, Successes and Failures.*

The final principle for our CIO CoP was the "community building" aspect, i.e., building the trust and relationships that would allow the community to grow larger than the core members. We decided the format should be face-to-face meetings that included presentations, discussions and dinner. The purpose of the dinner was to create a very relaxed atmosphere for building relationships and trust among the members. Thus, the "Community" part of Community of Practice was created through:

- Face-to-face meetings, including dinner
- Meeting summaries distributed to all members
- Public and private e-mails and phone calls among members and facilitators

Since this was to be a CoP involving several different companies, the baseline roles for the facilitators were also established. The facilitators were responsible for:

- Finding qualified speakers for meetings
- Facilitating the actual meetings of the CoP
- Writing meeting summaries and distributing speaker presentations
- Growing the CoP by identifying and enrolling new members

THE EARLY YEARS: GROWING THE CIO CoP

Of all the facilitators' responsibilities, enrollment was everything in the early years. The goal was member growth to a "critical mass", which was defined as 12 members, so that with 50% attendance, there would be at least six people in the room. Identifying, contacting and inviting potential members and speakers required hours of research, phone calls, e-mails and face-to-face meetings. We became "knowledge managers", building databases for potential members and speakers, searching the Web for company profiles and interesting topics. The greatest challenge was to convince all parties, from the CIOs to the potential speakers, that their time would be well spent with the CoP. Over time, these responsibilities became easier as knowledge and experience increased and the membership grew. As facilitators, we were learning right along with the members.

From the beginning, subject matter for the meetings was driven by whatever problems or opportunities were foremost on the individual minds of the members. We, as facilitators, had considerable room to influence both topics and presenters, but both choices came first from the members. The members are very busy executives who attend many meetings and are "on call" for IT emergencies. These facts made any progress in actually scheduling and facilitating the meetings to maximize the number of members in attendance also a challenge. The CoP started with day-long meetings every other month. When that did not work too well, day-long meetings every month were tried and finally migrated to monthly half-day meetings.

There were high points and low points in growing this CoP. There would sometimes be ten members in a meeting, but on one particular occasion only one member showed up to hear two speakers. Through it all, the core members stayed and persevered. No one was beating down the door to mingle with the little band in the beginning but as it grew, the idea of being able to be heard by a relevant number of executives, all in one room in an informal, intimate atmosphere, began to take on a life of its own.

THE CoP AND ITS CULTURE EVOLVES

Those first three core members drove the CoP in style, subject matter and expectations. These were Silicon Valley veterans, who knew each other and were well familiar with the benefits of sharing problems and solutions with colleagues from many years of interaction at various conferences and roundtables. Having been part of the history and story of Silicon Valley, they respected each other's role in the creation of the unique positions they each held and appreciated both what had been and how it was changing. There has always been a realization with the CIOs that they are making this up as they go along - their companies, their products, their roles - because nothing like it has ever existed before. That is why they wanted to hear what was going on in their colleagues' heads and businesses. Much more depended on it than just their own personal success. They saw the CIO CoP as a means of sharing that "tacit knowledge" i.e., that knowledge carried in their heads that had been built through trial and error experiences.

As the CoP has grown, some of the characteristics of people who have (or will) become members have been identified. First, they like both individual and group learning opportunities: clarifying and polishing their own ideas and views with the quick wits, deep experience and honesty that can take place only in the company of those they know and trust. In the meetings, they test one another's knowledge of their industry and grow mutual respect. Over dinner and wine, they delve further: who is this person, how do they live, what do they believe? Those who have seen the benefit are the "joiners" one sees in every membership organization: those with an ever-present sense of curiosity and an attitude that there is always something to learn. Naturally, if you are benefiting from an experience, you share it with others you like and respect, and over time, members willingly provided the names of colleagues to be invited to join the CoP.

The CIO CoP has continued to grow in members and each meeting usually has one or more guests who are evaluating the value of the CoP for themselves.

At times companies have contacted us requesting to present to this community. As a result, members have grown freer in their willingness to express themselves: voicing their frustrations with products that fail to live up to their promises, or companies that treat them as hostages instead of valued customers and partners. They are emboldened by their group strength and by what their collective companies represent in both influence and buying power. Individually, as professionals, they are more willing to demand the truth, to challenge the hype and tell it like it is. That is the real gift of the CoP opportunity and what makes members feel so good. They are heard, whether it is expressing an opinion about a vendor's service or a daughter's educational experiences.

As a result of the whims of "success and failure," there is a great deal of empathy in the group, a sensitivity expressed in wry humour and nodding heads as members feel ever more confident in expressing their fears and foibles. There is lots of horse-trading in how to deal with challenging situations and people, as well as the testing of new ideas and other colleagues' thoughts picked up along the way.

The varieties of companies, along with the distinct personalities of the members, bring new perspectives and knowledge to the participants. An opportunity for each member's company to present itself is built right into every meeting since each company "hosts" a CoP meeting in successive order. Over time the habit of using the CoP as a focus group for new products and services has evolved. This adds a valuable dimension to the CIO's investment for the rest of his company and gives members additional ability to shape their surroundings and industries. The "speed" culture of the Silicon Valley lays the expectation that things will be handled now. It also creates the conditions for constant turnover and mobility—a great challenge to continuity of the CIOs themselves and to the CoP.

CONTINUING THE EVOLUTION: THE DESIRE TO CONTRIBUTE

The CoP was created as a learning and sharing organization. The core members had experienced the "bang and bust" cycles of the high tech industries of Silicon Valley and they wanted to share their experiences with others. This sharing started early through mentoring new, younger members as they entered the community. With the maturing of the community came additional opportunities for sharing, collaborating and using the CoP for leverage and influence.

As numbers grew, the group quickly began to measure the possibility that they might act collectively as a buying consortium. This idea has evolved into using their numbers for leverage in their interactions with other businesses to effect contract terms and negotiating positions. Another opportunity to share and mentor arose when we were asked by the CIOs to form a similar CoP for their IT Directors. The CIOs saw this new CoP as an opportunity for them to act as coaches and discussion leaders for their closest protégés. This was envisioned to not only inform and expand knowledge, but to close a gap between internal industry disciplines and to grow these direct reports to their highest potential.

Most recently, through the contacts of one key member, the CIOs have realized the amazing feat of writing a book collaboratively, combining their experiences and knowledge to produce a "how to" text for current and future Information Technology leaders. Finally, the book has led to a new project: the establishment of a scholarship fund for the next generation of IT professionals. The fund was initially conceived to hold the proceeds of the book but is now being considered for an ongoing endowment to match the life of the CoP.

These projects have created a dimension of the "Practice" that has taken it far beyond its original goal of seeding and growing a learning community. It is spilling over to nurture a new cohort of IT professionals: some fresh from school, some already well into their careers and others looking to go further. These projects have grown within the group a sense of purpose and capability most natural to seasoned veterans, but also a sense of being part of something good and larger than themselves. In addition, this sense of purpose has only served to emphasize further the CIOs' dedication to one another and their craft.

Just as the original CoP has been used as a model for the new Directors' group, we are also attempting to reproduce our success in other geographic locations. The Silicon Valley CoP continues to evolve and is close to expanding beyond an optimal number of members. There are also the challenges of "splitting" the group into two and resolving the various cultural, geographic and facilitation issues that will accompany the division. Some of those who have worked with the CoP have seen the promise of the concept as well as the real results and are interested in expanding the CoP concepts further. We have always believed there is the possibility of reaching beyond the parameters of practising CIOs to encompass other professionals in other locations dealing with rapid change in their industries.

SUMMARY AND LESSONS LEARNED

The experience of facilitating the CIO CoP over the last several years has taught us a number of very valuable lessons. CoPs are reproducible by putting together a "core group" that will fund and promote its growth once they are convinced of the CoP value. The three principles that a CoP are founded on are:

- A shared Field (or Domain) of Interest
- A desire for the practical (Practice) within the Field of Interest

- A willingness to spend time building trust, respect and relationships with the community members

If these principles are in place, there are various roles the CoP facilitator can play; however, the key role is assisting the CoP to grow and evolve in membership and culture. The experience of facilitating the CIO CoP indicates that:

- A monthly meeting is frequent enough to build relationships while less frequent meetings are not.
- Speakers as a source of information and discussion stimulation are important.
- Members need to make their own decisions on topics and operating ground rules.
- Size counts—in the CIO CoP, there was an initial goal of having at least six members present for meetings. The optimal number is 25-30.
- The social aspect of the meeting (dinner) is invaluable both to demonstrate value added and to ensure camaraderie.
- Key to success is a facilitator who understands the industry of the members and can "speak the language".
- Continuous effort and dedication to keeping the organization fresh, along with the belief that the CoP is owned by its members, can ensure its stability.

REFERENCES

Lane, D., and Members of the Silicon Valley CoP. (2003). *CIO wisdom.* Upper Saddle River, NJ: Prentiss Hall PTR.

Chapter XII

Viable Communities within Organizational Contexts:
Creating and Sustaining Viability in Communities of Practice at Siemens AG

Benjamin Frost
Siemens AG, Germany

Stefan Schoen
Siemens AG, Germany

ABSTRACT

This chapter is about the question of what creates and sustains viability in Communities of Practice (CoPs) embedded in an organizational context. Experience with successful CoPs at Siemens AG has shown that even though most of them differ greatly from each other in many aspects, they all share five common factors that are necessary for the viability of a CoP. These five factors are introduced in the following pages. They represent an approach that can be used to analyse and improve CoPs that do not seem to be viable and as a guide for CoP members and moderators to maintain viability in their own CoPs.

INTRODUCTION

Communities of Practice (CoPs) are one approach to Knowledge Management (KM) that has proved to be very successful at Siemens AG. Like many other international companies, Siemens AG has a globally distributed organizational structure and is embedded in a very dynamic environment. In this context, CoPs create a significant benefit for the company, as they connect the different organizational units and enable the flow of knowledge between them.

Siemens understands a CoP to be a group of experts of different organizational units who are held together by a special interest in a business relevant topic. There are numerous such CoPs at Siemens. They exchange and create knowledge on various topics like specific products, markets, software solutions, functions or working methods. Some of these CoPs integrate employees from all over the world, while others focus on employees of a specific business unit or a region. The various CoPs differ greatly in their sizes. Some of the CoPs at Siemens are very small and have only 10 or 15 active members, while others are large, up to a couple hundred of members.

CoP members meet in large conferences, in smaller personal or virtual meetings, and they share a common IT platform. While conferences serve the exchange of knowledge that is relevant to most of the CoP members, smaller personal or virtual meetings can be held with only some of the CoP members. This is a practical solution, especially when members have a need to share knowledge on more specific topics that apply to only some of them, e.g., the practical implementation of a software solution in the context of one business unit. The IT platform with multiple functionalities (e.g., file storage, time schedules, news channels and discussion forums) enables the exchange of knowledge on a virtual basis. Most CoPs at Siemens have a moderator who coordinates the activities within the CoP. This includes the coordination of CoP meetings (e.g., facilities, agendas with presentations or workshops and the focus of the meetings), the coordination of platform activities (e.g., structuring content and making sure that requests on the IT platform are answered) and the management of the members (e.g., inviting and adding new members). In many cases, the moderator also moderates the meetings. Often the moderator is supported in the tasks by a core team of active CoP members (Schoen, 2001; Davenport & Probst, 2002).

Since CoPs can offer a great benefit for the organizations, companies want to utilize this potential for their own competitive advantage. However, the active involvement of employees in CoPs requires time and resources, and companies want to make sure it is well invested. CoP members can only get long-term value out of the CoP if it is active and alive. In addition to that, the CoP becomes more attractive for new members the more active and alive it is. It is therefore also of importance to the company, as well as to the members, that the CoP is viable.

The term viable refers to a CoP that is active and alive, creating a benefit for the organization in which it is embedded. It means that it maintains its own identity in the long-term. This chapter is about the question of what creates and sustains viability in CoPs. It identifies five common factors that are necessary for the viability of CoPs. These factors, as described in the following paragraphs, have been modelled according to the viable system model by Stafford Beer (1985).

The viable system model sets conditions for any viable system that are both sufficient and necessary. According to the model, each viable system must contain five subsystems that ensure that certain factors are provided. Simplified, the first system deals with the management of the production of goods and services, and the second with the coordination of the subsystems. The third system deals with the overall optimisation of current activities, the fourth with the future and the environment and the fifth is about the normative aspects (values). Each of the five factors described below refer to these subsystems of the viable system model.

The development of factors for viable CoPs integrates the long-term experience of the authors with building and supporting CoPs, multiple interviews with other CoP moderators and the results of a survey of over 50 CoPs at Siemens. Some of the most significant results are mentioned specifically in the next paragraphs.

FACTORS OF VIABLE COPS

Just as for any viable organization, it is a basic precondition that a viable CoP creates a significant benefit. Thus, a CoP gains its legitimacy as it creates value for the individual members and for the organization as a whole. The surveys of CoPs at Siemens have shown that there is a relation between the viability of a CoP and several items that describe the benefit for the individual CoP members: CoP members gain fast access to information, they are able to establish a network of contact persons and their participation in the CoP increases the quality of their work. In addition, there is a distinct connection between the viability of a CoP and the items that describe the benefit for the organization in which the CoP is embedded: the CoP adds value to the company and the benefits of the CoP are greater than the time and resources invested.

Factor 1: Organizing and Facilitating Community Activities

The service (or "product") a CoP delivers is that it provides knowledge to its members. The "management activities" needed for this to take place are to organize and facilitate CoP activities. This is the first factor of a viable CoP.

There are various activities such as conferences, workshops and the use of a common IT-platform. The CoP carefully selects a portfolio of activities that fits the needs of the individual CoP. These activities need to be facilitated and well organized. Most CoPs at Siemens use personal meetings and the use of the IT platform to supplement each other. However, some CoPs focus only on face-to-face collaboration and others only communicate virtually via the IT platform. As part of Factor 1, both face-to-face meetings and the IT platform need to be addressed.

Each viable CoP at Siemens has its own individual rhythm which is flexibly adapted whenever needed. The frequency of the meetings and the duration of each meeting depend on the needs of the CoP members and can vary widely between CoPs. The rhythm of the CoP is influenced strongly by its main purpose. For example, a CoP that focuses on helping other members in small day-to-day problems will meet in a different rhythm from a CoP that focuses on the stewardship of a knowledge area. In addition, the local distribution has a significant influence on the rhythm of the CoP. In most cases, the rhythm of the CoP is completely self-organized. However, sometimes it is helpful if the moderator initiates a discussion about the rhythm of the CoP.

The meetings held by the CoP can be formally organized or be spontaneous in nature (e.g., ad hoc meetings). The formal CoP meetings have a set agenda that has been worked out before the meeting. Viable CoPs at Siemens create meeting agendas, which can include presentations, workshops or panel discussions. Setting up the agenda is an important organizational task and in most cases coordinated by the moderator. The agenda should be attractive and challenging. Many CoPs make sure that there is enough time for personal communication in between the presentations and structured discussions. The items for the agenda are suggested by the CoP members who are often actively involved in the planning of the agenda and provide input. Often the CoP members come up to the moderator with ideas by themselves, while in other cases the moderator has to initiate the process. The IT platform is used in addition to personal communication to gather topics, ideas and questions for the agenda that are meaningful for the CoP. Whenever there are too many items, only the most important topics will be discussed during the meetings. Sometimes items are discussed on the platform in preparation for the meeting. Interesting presentations and contributions are key to the viability of the CoP. One needs to identify the speakers and contributions that provide value to the CoP.

The moderation of the meetings is another significant key success factor for viable CoPs. It almost goes without saying that the environmental conditions, like the facilitation of rooms or catering, and the organizational aspects, like sending out the invitations with the agenda or providing support with hotels, need to be considered as well, even though their influence on the viability is rather small.

The organization and facilitation of activities on the IT platform are also an important part of this first factor. The features of the platform provide the technical infrastructure for virtual collaboration. Common features on the platform include discussion forums, urgent request functionality, news, document management and forms for structured knowledge objects. Viable CoPs carefully select which features of the platform to use in order to support the communication processes of the CoP.

CoP members share their knowledge on the platform as they upload documents, ask questions and provide answers. Viable CoPs pay special attention to the usefulness of the contributions on the platform. This means that the CoP is viable when the members can use the knowledge received via the platform in their tasks. In addition to that, the content of the IT platform of a viable CoP must be of an appropriate quality that meets the expectations of its members.

As knowledge is stored in the platform, a content structure serves as a navigation aid for members searching for documents but also for those who want to upload files. The content structure grows organically and is adapted according to the needs of the CoP. The uploading and organization of content is done as part of the activities on the platform. The moderator discusses the content structure with the CoP members whenever there is a need to do so. Ideally, the members of the CoP participate in organizational activities on the platform and support the moderator in his tasks.

Factor 2: Connecting People and their Knowledge

The second factor describes the coordination between smaller parts of the CoP (subgroups or individuals). The coordination of the knowledge needs and haves of subgroups or individuals in the CoP takes place as people and their knowledge are connected. People and their knowledge connect in order to identify who can provide knowledge they could use. Even though all of the CoP members contribute to this task, the moderator plays a special role in facilitating this process.

CoP members connect in many different ways. In most cases, CoP members connect to each other as they meet new CoP members during the meetings and simply talk to each other. However, when there are many members who do not know each other or the CoP is very large, it is helpful to implement certain elements in the agenda, like introductions or little games, which help the CoP members to connect to know each other personally. Some CoPs use creative elements in the meeting rooms like boards with member profiles or with questions that are to be answered. Coffee tables with topics, where CoP members who are interested in that specific topic can meet during breaks in the meeting, also support the connecting of CoP members.

The viability of CoPs at Siemens links closely with the extent to which members connect to each other by themselves. The members who have questions get the answers from other CoP members and members with similar questions connect together to develop a solution. If the questions are larger in nature, those members can continue to discuss problems and solutions independently of the specific meetings. Often the moderator acts as a contactor, trying to connect CoP members with similar work assignments. A group of active core members in the CoP supports the moderator and helps to connect CoP members. In many instances, CoP members come up with questions and ask the moderator for suggestions of people who would be able to answer them. When a moderator has a good idea of who is working on which topic, he or she can refer them to other CoP members. Experience has shown that most moderators who have this kind of overview keep in close contact with the CoP members.

In addition to the face-to-face meetings, CoP members can also connect on the platform. Here people and their knowledge often connect when users ask questions in the discussion forum or chat rooms. Similar to the situation during the face-to-face meetings, other CoP members with the same problem can identify each other as they answer the same question or provide additional knowledge. This requires that, on the one side, members communicate whatever they want to know, and on the other side, that members are willing to make that knowledge available.

Experts in certain knowledge areas can also be found when members search for documents that provide information on the authors or contributors. The platform should support easy retrieval of documents and include information about contributors. Many CoPs support this with a "yellow pages" functionality on the IT platform where CoP members can find basic information about the knowledge areas of other members. Furthermore, the moderator identifies open questions that have not been answered on the platform and tries to address those who might help.

Factor 3: Finding a Common Focus

The third factor for a viable system is the overall optimisation of activities. The content and extent of current activities are directed by the common focus of the CoP. Finding a common focus is the third factor of a viable CoP and it gives overall direction for the community - it is when the community decides on what they actually want to do and it determines meeting agendas or frequency of activity.

A common interest in a relevant topic binds the CoP members together. Viable CoPs have a clearly defined topical focus. The current and future relevance of the focus of the CoP is key to its viability. It should be relevant for both individual members and the company. The focus of the CoP determines who will participate in future activities and how much time CoP members are willing to invest. It also determines the extent to which knowledge is shared either during the meetings or on the platform.

Many CoPs have a certain topic or problem area on which they will immediately want to focus; other CoPs may have to find their focus over time. Viable CoPs regularly rethink the CoP focus and actively involve the CoP members in finding a new focus whenever needed.

The common focus can be found and maintained in several ways. Just as with the other factors mentioned earlier, it can be either completely self-organized or processes can be initiated by the moderator. If during the discussions in face-to-face meetings or on the IT platform the CoP finds out that there is a common need to talk about or work on specific knowledge areas, it will automatically sets its focus to this area. If this is not the case, the moderator starts the discussion. If he or she is to plan the next meeting, he or she has to know the needs of the CoP members in order to meet them. For that reason, the moderator initiates a discussion on the focus of the CoP.

Factor 4: Interacting with the Community Environment

The fourth factor of a viable CoP deals with the environment and the corresponding changes for the future. CoPs that are embedded in an organizational context have an internal and an external organizational environment to monitor and interact with.

In the internal environment, the individual CoP members and the CoP as a whole interact with the management. Even though the management does not control the CoP activities, the CoP benefits greatly from the support of the management. Viable CoPs receive the support of the management. The management also influences the CoP as they define the business strategy and make decisions that mark the future range of activities of the organization. If the management, for example, decides that the company will take a different focus on a topic, the CoP might also have to readjust its focus in order to generate a benefit for the company. The individual CoP members also need the support of their superiors, since work time is invested in the CoP that could otherwise be used directly for the work in the projects. It is important to convince superiors of the benefit to the company as a whole. It is also important to convince them of the benefit to the projects and individual organizational units for which the CoP members work. The viability of the CoP is closely connected to the support of the individual members by their direct superior.

Part of the internal environment is new potential CoP members. Viable CoPs promote themselves in various ways to attract new members. Members recruit members, and CoPs have web pages that provide basic information about the CoP and can be found via search engines. Siemens also has a central CoP directory integrated in the employee portal, where employees find an overview of existing CoPs with additional information about the purpose, topic, members or moderator.

Regarding the external environment, viable CoPs monitor and consider the development of the knowledge area outside of the organization as far as relevance to them. This takes place in various ways. During the CoP conferences, external speakers and contributors are invited to share their insights and to make sure the CoP is informed about external developments. CoPs can also be in contact with other companies, universities and research institutes. Some CoPs consciously monitor the external environment as they report any information that might be interesting to the CoP either in meetings or on the platform. Some CoPs regularly scan resources, like articles in magazines, newspapers and web pages and provide interesting contributions to the CoP.

Changes in the environment of the CoP can have a massive impact on its future development. Viable CoPs discuss these changes to find out how they will affect the future development of the CoP.

Factor 5: Living the Community Values

Values and rules set the normative framework for a viable CoP. To make sure that that these values are put into practice is the fifth factor of a viable CoP.

Trust and openness are two essential values of a viable CoP. Only when CoP members trust each other are they willing to share the knowledge they have. Trust is also necessary for CoP members to ask questions, as they reveal what they do not know. In a CoP where trust has not been built, some CoP members might hesitate to share knowledge. At Siemens we found that face-to-face meetings, where CoP members get to know each other personally, help greatly in building an atmosphere of trust in the CoP. Openness goes tightly along with trust, since CoP members communicate more openly when trust is established. This goes along with a type of culture where not only best practices are openly shared, but also mistakes and lessons learned. This is what viable CoPs do. In many cases, the knowledge about others' mistakes can be very valuable, because their repetition will be prevented.

In viable CoPs, there is a balance between giving contributions and taking solutions from others. This is the normative basis for the long-term viability of a CoP. Only if there are enough members who are willing to give, can others take. However, if it is always the same ones who provide knowledge, they might not be motivated to contribute in future. Even if members who receive help from others are unable to give knowledge to others (e.g., because they are newcomers), they can provide feedback on how the knowledge has helped them and sometimes have constructive suggestions for additional improvement.

Some viable CoPs set explicit rules they want to live by. These can refer to the communication within the community (e.g., feedback rules) or can affect the behaviour of the community members. Whether the values and rules are explicitly written or implicitly lived, it is important for the CoP members to make sure that everybody accepts them and sticks to them. Mostly, the members themselves live by example and give feedback to others when they do not comply with the CoP values. In addition to that, the CoP moderator approaches this matter whenever necessary and helps to provide positive conditions. Viable CoPs seen in Siemens have also demonstrated that they address their values on a regular basis.

SUMMARY

CoPs as implemented at Siemens are very different in their nature. Viable CoPs share five factors which have been described in this chapter and which have a special relevance for the viability of the CoP:

1) Viable CoPs effectively organize and facilitate CoP activities on a regular basis and thus provide the infrastructure for the exchange of knowledge across organizational boundaries.
2) Viable CoPs actively connect those CoP members who have questions with those who can provide answers.
3) As they work together, viable CoPs find a common focus that directs the activities of the CoP. This focus is reconsidered whenever needed.
4) Viable CoPs monitor and interact with their environment and are able to adjust changes in future developments accordingly.
5) The normative setting for a viable CoP is provided by values like trust and openness, and a balance between giving and taking.

While a viable CoP meets each of these factors, CoPs achieve this in multiple ways. How a CoP actually does it depends strongly on the individual needs of the CoP. In most CoPs at Siemens these factors are self-organized by the CoP members, where the moderator (or members of a core group) initiates the corresponding process.

REFERENCES

Beer, S. (1985). *Diagnosing the system for organizations*. Chichester, UK.
Davenport, T., and Probst, G. (Eds.) (2002). Knowledge Management case book. *Siemens Best Practices,* 2nd Edition. Munich.
Schoen, S. (2001). *Gestaltung und Unterstützung von Communities of Practice*. Munich.

Chapter XIII

Best Practices:
Developing Communities that Provide Business Value

Wesley C. Vestal
American Productivity & Quality Center, USA

Kimberly Lopez
American Productivity & Quality Center, USA

ABSTRACT

Organizations continually look for ways to do more with less. One of the most important methods today for helping improve the company bottom line involves linking experts in Communities of Practice to find, share and validate best practices, ideas and solutions. This chapter examines how several best-practice organizations select Communities of Practice, provide support for their ongoing work, develop specialized roles to sustain their efforts, and use technology to bolster the rich tacit knowledge exchange offered by these entities. APQC has also developed a list of critical success factors for Communities of Practice and questions to help organizations develop those factors from its research on Knowledge Management over the last eight years.

INTRODUCTION

Organizations of all forms have always contained smaller, informal communities. However, what is emerging in the new workplace is the recognition of Communities of Practice (CoPs) as boundary-spanning units responsible for finding and sharing best practices, stewarding knowledge and helping community members work better. This new role for communities is emerging because organizations now consciously nurture and harness relevant knowledge.

The American Productivity & Quality Center (APQC), a non-profit research and advisory services firm that helps organizations adapt to rapidly changing environments and build new and better ways to work, has researched many of the leading examples of successful CoPs. For APQC, CoPs are networks of people—small and large—who come together to share ideas with and learn from one another in physical and virtual settings. A common purpose or mission holds these communities of practice, of interest, and of learning, together. They are sustained by a desire to share experiences, insights and best practices.

For the past 25 years, APQC has been identifying best practices, discovering effective methods of improvement, broadly disseminating findings and connecting individuals both with one another and with the knowledge, training and tools they need to succeed. During these efforts, it has found a number of useful practices that organizations, in both the public and private sectors, use to cultivate CoPs. In taking a step away from an academic perspective and focusing on APQC's original research, this chapter will examine practical factors in cultivating CoPs, specifically: the selection of a community, gaining support and establishing resources, roles and development, ongoing facilitation, and technology support.

SELECTING A COMMUNITY

To begin, the organization must determine what communities it should develop and sustain. This decision should be driven by the knowledge sharing and overall business strategy of the organization. Formal CoPs should help their members improve their performance, and by extension that of the organization's bottom-line. APQC's 2001 benchmarking report, Building and Sustaining Communities of Practice (APQC 2001a), found that the following criteria were used by best-practice organizations when looking to select a Community of Practice (CoP) to support.

- The CoP must relate to a business need. It should not focus on additional work, but instead on existing tasks and responsibilities.
- The CoP, with guidance, must be able to demonstrate results such as enhanced revenue or profitability, enhanced management and business

process capability or reduced cycle time. For many organizations, results are demonstrated in terms of reduced mistakes.

- It is important to select a community that energetically desires to address an issue. The CoP must satisfy a legitimate need in the organization.
- Again, with guidance, lessons from the CoP should be transferable throughout the organization.

In APQC's research, best-practice organizations typically depended on their Knowledge Management (KM) Advisory Group (a cross-functional group of senior leaders who drive strategy and results) to identify and select formal communities. However, these same organizations also recognize the efficacy of the many informal communities that naturally spring up and collaborate. The Advisory Groups should understand how these support the organization and provide any tools that will make their collaboration more effective. Selecting a community that meets the above criteria will assist in gaining the necessary support and resources.

GAINING SUPPORT AND ESTABLISHING RESOURCES

Once an appropriate CoP has been identified, the prospective leaders of the community should put together a business case and plan that outlines the mission, vision and benefits of the CoP. APQC's 2001 benchmarking report, Managing Content and Knowledge (APQC 2001b), details that a business case should include:

- Background and strategic context
- Evidence of need
- Potential benefits, outcomes and indicators of success
- Organizational accountability for planning and design
- The initial investment requested
- Resources and their source
- Development plans

In addition to a business case, support for CoPs should be gained by promoting the potential benefits of the CoP to the appropriate process area management teams through short presentations, workshops and examples from benchmark organizations.

In addition to management support, organizations with a large number of CoPs may find it necessary to create and maintain a central support group. This group can standardize development, facilitation, change management, project management, communication and IT support. In many of the organizations

APQC has researched, the central support group is tied to a corporate-level KM initiative and is tasked with linking CoP activity to the organization's strategy.

The central support group also ensures that community findings are disseminated across the organization. For many organizations that choose to create CoPs—such as APQC members Schlumberger, Best Buy Company, the U.S. Army Medical Division, and Siemens AG—there is a general consensus that business groups and regions often fail to share valuable knowledge across functional lines and that knowledge-sharing efforts should work from a common set of standards and processes. The central support group should work with both communities and functional group management to address these issues by:

- Establishing common standards for portals, collaboration, architecture and tools
- Engaging a cross-functional and multi-level "design team" to create a CoP that meets the community's needs for knowledge sharing, capture and reuse
- Helping prospective CoP members understand how, why and when to participate in a CoP
- Providing project management expertise and tools to ensure a timely design and launch of the CoP
- Training individuals on CoP processes and tools
- Developing IT tools to connect widely dispersed members and to house legacy information
- Measuring and marketing CoP successes

The report Building and Sustaining Communities of Practice (APQC 2001a) found four models for central support among best-practice organizations.

- The Board Support Model - Each CoP provides a facilitator that serves on a board that is responsible for guiding the direction and the outcomes of the community.
- The Community of Leaders Support Model - Each community leader works within a community of CoP leaders to set goals, prioritise projects and champion community activities.
- The Central Staff Support Model - If the organization does not have a corporate KM initiative, central staff, in the role of community administrator and community leader, provides both technology and training, and monitors the activity of the community.
- The Functional Level Support Model - This model combines the central KM group with functional-level CoP support groups. CoP support groups reside in functional areas and facilitate the development and growth of communities in those areas.

ROLES AND DEVELOPMENT

After the Advisory Board has selected a CoP opportunity for the organization, the next step in creating successful communities is to select a sponsor to champion the community and a design team to create the initial community framework. Begin by having a conversation with the CoP sponsor to answer the following questions:

- What role do you see yourself playing in the community's development?
- How will we know we have been successful?
- What results would you like to see?

Based on the interviews and recommendations of the community sponsors and business stakeholders, a design team of 10 to 12 people should be formed to create the strategic and tactical plans for a successful CoP. This team will create a charter, select a project, create infrastructure, design rollout plans, foster support for KM and monitor the results of the CoP. The design team will become the initial "charter members" of the community and will be responsible for creating the CoP operational framework.

The business leader working with the KM core team should recommend design team members. The business leader should empower the group and provide overall vision. In addition to the front-line users from the business, the following groups should be represented on the design team to provide support: human resources, internal change agents, Information Technology (IT) and marketing or communications.

ONGOING FACILITATION

As CoPs mature and evolve, their membership, sharing styles, meeting frequency and business goals will inevitably change. Such shifts should not simply be allowed, but encouraged. APQC found that some organizations have initially created communities in all functional areas, which can lead to CoPs that do not have a compelling business need, dynamic membership or leadership, or a viable value proposition. Other organizations created CoPs that worked well and solved a specific set of problems, but slowly deteriorated as the need for their expertise diminished. In both cases, a central support group can monitor when it is appropriate to refocus or remove CoPs that no longer serve a viable business function.

For example, APQC studied an oil and gas company that created more than 90 CoPs during the late 1990s and 2000. After reflecting on the support and resources required by these CoPs, the company set out to identify the characteristics of their successful CoPs and determine a course of action for unsuccessful communities. An examination of a representative sample of CoPs from the major lines of business (exploration, production, and refining) showed that not all CoPs provided either business or personal value to members. Some communities had no discernable activity for longer than a month (due to lack of leadership, lack of compelling business need or too general a focus). In the most successful communities, however, several members indicated they could not accomplish their daily tasks without accessing community members. In both cases, the central KM group provided insight, refresher training and publicity (where appropriate) to enhance results and boost participation. When appropriate, the support group also set a new objective for a community or redeployed the resources elsewhere.

Despite the assistance from support groups, CoP members need to own the knowledge and content they use to solve problems, create new solutions and mentor each other. In essence, the support group should provide the field on which the communities play—the boundaries, tools, and support infrastructure. However, the communities themselves determine the rules, length and method of play.

TECHNOLOGY SUPPORT

IT tools such as knowledge repositories, people finders, bulletin boards and collaborative software (databases of best practices, expert locators, chat rooms and tools like NetMeeting) help to facilitate sharing beyond face-to-face interaction. APQC has found that best-practice organizations typically create an IT tool to support CoPs. These can be as simple as a threaded discussion bulletin boards or as complex as a full portal with discussion space, knowledge repositories, collaborative tools, web crawlers, people finders and supplier information.

Such support is a critical success factor; even if a CoP is small enough to fit in one room or building, members will probably benefit from having a means to store frequently used knowledge, tips or ideas. Creating an electronic "bread crumb trail" will allow new members to hasten their speed to competency, reduce the time spent searching for expertise or information and create a sense of ownership within the community itself.

CRITICAL SUCCESS FACTORS

CoPs need strong leadership, a compelling business case, sufficient technology to enable communication and an intense people focus to be successful. Even with this infrastructure, connecting widely dispersed people from various backgrounds is very difficult. Nearly every organization has as many failures as successes in this field. APQC has found some critical lessons from CoP success stories.

The following traits for the successful cultivation of CoPs originated from APQC's work with communities. These traits summarize the key lessons from this chapter. The associated questions can help community leaders, central support groups, KM practitioners and management to focus on that crucial middle ground that enables functioning, strategic CoPs.

1) A compelling, clear business case for all involved:
   • What value does belonging and participating in the CoP have for an individual?
   • What value does it bring a department if one staff member takes time to participate?

2) A dedicated, skilled facilitator or leader:
   • Does the CoP leader have the skills to facilitate an organic, outside-of-line responsibility group?
   • Does the CoP leader have a vision for moving the CoP forward?

3) A coherent, comprehensive knowledge map for the core content of the CoP:
   • Does the group call on frequently used common content, topics or knowledge that should be pulled into one shared space?
   • Can all members of the CoP understand and identify the sources and recipients of knowledge within the community?

4) An outlined, easy-to-follow knowledge-sharing process:
   • Do people know how, what, and when to share and reuse knowledge?
   • Are community members able to access and reuse knowledge from others or a shared space easily?

5) An appropriate technology medium that facilitates knowledge exchange, retrieval and collaboration:
   • Does it include a repository of community content and/or knowledge?
   • Is the technology supported by the organization's IT group?
   • Does the technology meet the needs of community members? Did they have input into the look, feel, and content?

6) Communication and training plans for members and others outside of the CoP:
   • Do existing community members (and prospective members) understand why they should participate? Have they heard success stories and do they know the mechanics of the CoP?
   • Is there a self-training or short program that shows individuals how to share and find knowledge from each other?

7) An updated, dynamic roster of CoP members:
    • Are CoP members able to access others with their interests quickly and easily?
    • Do members have tools that assist with rapid, one-to-many communication?
8) Key metrics of success to show business results:
    • Does the CoP have a documented measurement system to show how it is meeting its business value proposition?
    • Is there a plan for collecting, reviewing, sharing and validating metrics?
9) A recognition plan for participants:
    • Can participants recognize "what's in it for me?"
    • Is the recognition scheme built into the HR process and is it part of the development or evaluation process?

CoPs are many things to many people. For management, they may serve as a locus of knowledge and mentoring. For members, they may serve as a networking forum and answer depot. To the organization, they may provide innovative solutions to problems or reduce turnover by providing "homes" for employees and strengthening the social fabric of the organization. On the other hand, CoPs may be seen as irrelevant corporate initiatives, overhead, time wasters or silly exercises in teaming or handholding. The difference depends on how well an organization has united its people around solving business problems.

People have been organizing themselves into communities since the dawn of time; it is a natural state that most individuals will thrive in. Organizations have only begun tapping back into this basic structure because the break up into departments, locations and business units has isolated employees. When cultivating a community, APQC advises a business to search for those naturally occurring networks. Help to support them and broaden their scope by providing IT support, management backing and business goals. Look to see where natural networks do not exist, but should. The result will be the transfer of local know-how to collective information that promotes the standardization of practices across operations and regions.

REFERENCES

APQC. (2001a). APQC Benchmarking Report. *Building and sustaining Communities of Practice*. APQC. (2001b). APQC Benchmarking Report. *Managing content and knowledge*.

Chapter XIV

Building Sustainable Communities of Practice

Bronwyn Stuckey
The University of Wollongong, Australia

John D. Smith
Learning Alliances, USA

ABSTRACT

The authors have both been involved as designers, producers and facilitators of CPsquare's Foundations of Communities of Practice Workshop (www.cpsquare.com). Through that ongoing exposure to learning and leading in Communities of Practice (CoPs), they became convinced that stories about CoPs play a crucial role in motivation and learning for community leaders. Within communities, the swapping of stories is a means by which local theories of cause and effect are developed and contextualized. These stories provide powerful ways of invoking context, of framing choices and actions and of constructing identity (Bruner, 2002). From the context of a Community of Practice (CoP) concerned with the cultivation of CoPs, (i.e., the Foundations workshop) there is strong anecdotal evidence that stories are of equal value to practitioners and researchers alike. As part of an extended research activity, and parallel to this growing conviction about stories, Stuckey analysed the Frequently Asked Questions (FAQs) raised over six iterations of the workshop. The ten most frequently asked questions became the basis of semi-structured interviews held with the developers and managers of the communities described in this chapter. The chapter presents the essence of seven community cases and is intended as an enticement to explore the full case descriptions and community stories (which are beyond the limitations of this printed publication) at http:// www.cpsquare.org/cases/.

INTRODUCTION

Is it a community or not? This is a very common question and often quite a valid one. The reporting of this series of case studies was guided by a question posed by Etienne Wenger (2002) in response to the Community versus Network debate, "Will the group benefit by being viewed as a community?" Each of our cases reinforces the notion that one's view on this matter depends significantly on one's role or place in a community. People near the core of a community experience the community features more readily, while people on the periphery may see only a looser network. Our respondents, who all were close to the core of the communities, would answer Wenger's question with a resounding "Yes", for they all have envisioned their groups as communities and that vision in turn drives the opportunities for the group.

This chapter gives a taste of some of the energy, vision and effort it takes to build effective CoPs. The cases selected vary across geographical, techno-logical and sectoral dimensions in the hope that you will find useful insights for your own community development efforts, whether inside organizations or across organizations, in educational, government or business settings. Each case is exemplary in its field and renders insights into the intricacy and complexity of issues that arise in building communities. Each of the interviewees was not only a leader in their community but also a highly respected practitioner in their domain. The goal in this chapter is to present the community, the leader, and the community's situation in an authentic and accessible way.

The focus of this chapter is on the topic most frequently of interest to novice community leaders and designers: building a community. This building phase can be mapped directly against the stages of CoPs proposed by Wenger, McDermott and Snyder (2002, pp. 68-69). The building phase of community covers the Wenger et al.'s stages of potential, and coalesces through to mature where the sense of group, individual agency and the dynamic of the community are being built.

The importance of CoPs and their generative capacity has been argued extensively (Wenger, 1998; Wenger et al., 2002; Williams & Cothrel, 2000; Davenport & Hall, 2002) and elsewhere in chapters of this book. How to cultivate communities has also received extensive study, and whether you subscribe to the explicit design principles in The 5Ps of Joseph Cothrel (2001), The 9 Design Strategies of Amy Jo Kim (2000, pp. xiii-xiv), or the 7 Design

Principles of Wenger et al. (2002, p. 51), you will find rich value in the cases offered in this chapter. The story elements are presented not as a restatement of theory, but as a distillation and aggregation of effective strategies in the words of the community leaders themselves. This brings new meaning and clarity to the theory, rules and principles.

THE COMMUNITIES

The following communities are presented in alphabetical order: Australian Flexible Learning Community; ChevronTexaco's Operational Excellence Communities; CompanyCommand.com; Government Online International Network; Knowledge Management for Development; MirandaNet Fellowship and Switched On Leaders.

Australian Flexible Learning Community
Australian National Vocational Education Initiative Providing Professional Development

The Australian Flexible Learning Community is an instrument of the Australian Flexible Learning Framework. The community began in 2000 under a five-year plan to support the take-up of flexible learning in the Australian Vocational Educational and Training sector when the vocational and further education sectors faced a climate of great change. It has evolved to its present title and presence as part of the Framework's mission to encourage, but not mandate, flexible learning and online technology. The Australian Flexible Learning Community provides professional development to the vocational education and training sector across Australia. The community has more than 3,500 members who share resources and interact with each other in a web-based environment.

While the domain is clear, this community embraces a field that is shifting rapidly; it includes some one hundred different training areas and 75% of the workforce is part-time. All of the community activities take place online, although members have opportunities for face-to-face contact and activities through other Framework programs. In addition to the formal online activities and resources available to the community, the social contact it provides has proved important to members facing sometimes very trying work environments. As the community manager explained:

"Most members work in organisations with vertical structures, the community interactions are horizontal, allowing a different type of interaction and sharing between various individuals and groups. Senior executives are very supportive. The site has senior support to be irreverent at times and

have fun.   We try to achieve a balance between 'strategic and serious' (credibility) and warm and engaging."

ChevronTexaco's Operational Excellence Communities

Management Orchestrated Groups in the Service of Strategic Corporate Goals

ChevronTexaco is made up of many independent companies operating in over 180 countries, each focusing on a specific area or function such as oil exploration, refining, Information Technology or sales. The corporation has a successful history with formal and informal CoPs, most notably the successful communities built around best practices in refinery operation. ChevronTexaco has begun to employ the community approach in new domains. The corporation is leveraging its expertise in areas of management focused on Operational Excellence. The approach initially involves project teams designing practices (processes and tools) in various strategic areas, beginning with motor vehicle safety, contractor safety, reliability improvement and repetitive stress injury prevention. These teams expand and evolve into CoPs charged with supporting and sustaining the implementation of those practices.

The initiative is clearly setting an aggressive development agenda while being careful to create a workable ownership of the goals with links between each community and the existing cultural and operational environment surrounding it. The knowledge analyst charged with developing these communities explained that:

"What would tell me it's a community is that the sharing and use of successful practices and lessons learned become the largest deliverable."

CompanyCommand.com

Community in the US Army Ramping Up the Learning Curve for Command Excellence from Within

The seeds of this group were sown in 1992 with conversations among young practitioners sharing stories, books and tools they found valuable when preparing to take command posts. CompanyCommand.com is now a community with a mission to develop excellence in the practice of military command. This community allows those with ambitions for command to connect to a larger world, introducing them to many styles of leadership and issues of battle-ready command. It creates an opportunity for the learning curve to begin well before officers actually take command of a company and the learning and contribution continues through their years in command and beyond. Through personal contacts, face-to-face seminars, discussions on the website and repositories of trusted and tested tools, past, present and future commanders become laterally connected.

The CompanyCommand management team is focused on serving the needs of a specific customer: practising company commanders. While staying true to the ethos and tradition of the US Army, the community has developed and become valued because of its independence. CompanyCommand's management and facilitation team is in itself a highly effective CoP. A community leader described:

"The key to success is to be a laser beam focused on improving leadership at the company level. We are acutely aware that the people we are seeking to connect have tremendous demands on their time, are continually deployed around the globe and spend little time sitting in front of a computer. The day we lose focus on adding phenomenal value to our specific audience-leaders in the field-is the day that we become irrelevant."

Government Online International Network
Learning About e-Government Across International Boundaries

The Government Online International Network community began in 1995-1996, when a group of civil servants decided that they wanted to continue meeting after the completion of a G7-sponsored Information Technology project. They discovered that informal contact with colleagues was an opportunity to learn about current and future technology issues facing their governments. As their relationships and sense of community developed, the simple practices and infrastructure that they evolved turned out to be a good framework of essentials for a moderately sized informal community. The community meets once a year for a three day face-to-face meeting and communicates regularly through an email list of some 80 members. The community organizes two or three projects each year, studying topics ranging from e-government in general to specific opportunities in the use of technologies such as XML.

Members of the community are all civil servants in government agencies concerned with Information Technology. The community itself does not receive any ongoing government funding or have any resources of its own. Although agencies sponsor the participation of individual members and benefit indirectly, the emphasis is on relationships between and learning of individual members, not governments per se. A community leader explained:

"Government people can be happy to see issues raised even if not tied back to them or credited. Ideas are more 'royalty free' and the idea itself might be more important than who brought it into the group. Sometimes they might even use the group to push a agenda at home."

Knowledge Management for Development (KM4Dev)

Supporting International Development Organizations in Knowledge Management

KM4Dev, which was formed after a face-to-face meeting in June 2000, is a community focusing on Knowledge Management (KM) issues in international development organizations such as donor agencies, civil society organizations, multilateral organizations and governments. Several organizations have supported the face-to-face events that launched and then developed the community, although Bellanet (a non-profit international secretariat based in Ottawa, Canada) has been its biggest supporter. Bellanet has developed infrastructure to enhance the basic email list services that make it possible to reach low-bandwidth areas in developing countries. It currently has about 240 members on the list. Community facilitators at KM4Dev described the community's stage of development as being:

"... mid-adolescence to early adulthood. This has happened in the last six months. We have come to this point after growth spurts. This growth is heading us into changing what are we about."

This community is described more fully in the chapter "Click Connect and Coalesce for NGOs: Exploring the Intersection between Online Networks, Cops and Events" by Nancy White.

MirandaNet Fellowship

Research and Educational Consultancy Through a Practitioner Community

The MirandaNet Fellowship began its evolution in 1992 as a research project under the sponsorship Toshiba called The Miranda Project; at the time, this involved 15 classroom educators and researchers. At the close of the project, people wanted to maintain the community and it was decided to establish MirandaNet. An ongoing stream of research, assessment and demonstration projects, some funded, others supported by volunteers, have provided a rich environment for learning and sharing. The community has a clear trajectory for its 150 members who apply, or are recommended for membership, as MirandaNet Scholars. After publishing within the community or making a clear contribution, MirandaNet Scholars become Fellows, who are the inner circle of and mentors to the larger community.

International MirandaNet has Fellows in more than 15 countries. There are seven local chapters run by Fellows in Australia, Bulgaria, China, the Czech Republic, England, Ireland and Northern Ireland. Members are part of a consultative organization where professionals talk, listen and collaborate with government, industry, teacher educators and researchers. MirandaNet Fellows in essence provide services for each other. The Director of MirandaNet described her role as operating:

"... a dating agency, hooking up people with others. Bringing in groups of teachers from abroad, sponsors from industry and teaming best practice with a action research."

Switched On Leaders

Asia-Pacific Business-to-Business E-Commerce Competitors and Collaborators

Switched On Leaders was born out of the need to develop new knowledge and practical insights around contemporary issues facing businesses. E-Hubs Asia, an earlier incarnation of the community, proved unsustainable because the experience and interests of members did not align with the changing business context. Switched On Leaders is now a niche community and membership is by invitation only. The common areas of interest include: customer leadership, enterprise agility and networked value chain. The members are e-business practitioners, executives, consultants, government policy makers, marketing leaders, supply chain managers, academics, entrepreneurs and small business owners.

The Switched On Leaders community has a high level of discussion and inquiry across very different national cultures and organizational settings: even when members are natural competitors. When describing his community the manager of Switched On Leaders said:

"The community has been growing organically. It's global. It has members mostly from Asia-Pacific, then from the States and the rest in Europe or South America. Our main purpose has continued to be learning, sharing and diffusing knowledge about best practice-and looking for innovative ways of improving the practice."

BUILDING A SUCCESSFUL COMMUNITY OF PRACTICE

What was learned about the effective strategies for community building? Strikingly, while technology plays an important role in each community's life, much of the focus and energy is not on technology but on personal contact and the development of social capital. The groups represented here use everything from simple email lists to highly designed websites and combinations of technologies, teleconferences, face-to-face conferences, workshops and social gatherings to motivate and facilitate communication, cooperation and collaboration.

In each case, the insights available from the community manager's story offer authentic and relevant experience far beyond that which may be gleaned from examining a website or email archive. What follows are the most relevant and powerful lessons to be learned for community building that surfaced from the seven communities. These lessons are presented as actions to scaffold shared value, engagement, knowledge creation, trust, ownership, collaboration, validation and reification within the community.

Tune In and Respond Strategically to Current Ethos of the Practice and Needs of Prospective Members

All of the case communities began with a clear focus on the issues that surround the practice and its practitioners. For MirandaNet the combination of the depressed professional status of teachers and the newness of Information and Communication Technology (ICT) in the curriculum created a climate ripe for a community where teachers could gain professional standing and opportunities to work in professional teams. For ChevronTexaco, operational excellence required a participatory model where teams develop the processes and tools that business units may implement for organizational improvement. It is worth noting that ChevronTexaco's history with CoPs allows them to strategically plan for community development through project teams, which expand and morph into CoPs.

For Switched On Leaders, CompanyCommand.com and MirandaNet the ethos of the relative practices required a very professional community space. Quality, integrity, standards and a strict domain focus have been vital to build reputation and attract members and leaders in the field. As one member of CompanyCommand.com stated:

"I often find that the information offered on these pages bridges the gap between the 'school-house' answer to leadership challenges and the 'boots-on-the-ground' answer."

Switched On Leaders embraced the cultural ethos of the Asia Pacific region to provide a focus and meet a need of various business practitioners not met in any other environment.

The Australian Flexible Learning Community and its vocational education teachers and trainers, united in one practice of vocational education but spread across a staggering diversity of fields, roles and levels of experience, required a friendly non-threatening environment where first steps to becoming involved could be as simple as a poll or a competition or a game. The Australian Flexible Learning Community has to balance the tensions of being attractive and engaging to a workforce reluctant to use online technology while leading and influencing change in culture; the focus is on driving need as well as responding to it. For the Government Online International Network the practice of e-government in very diverse governmental settings requires frank but diplomatic sharing, collaboration and project development all anchored to members' local political concerns and strategies. Direct ties to strategic initiatives and branding may well have expedited the membership growth for ChevronTexaco and the Australian Flexible Learning Community. Over time, being part of a national framework has given the Australian Flexible Learning Community goodwill, brand recognition and credibility. What appears on the website is of obvious importance to the clientele faced with embracing flexible learning. While being largely independent communities, both MirandaNet and CompanyCommand.com strongly support initiatives of their respective sponsors, and have gained respect and growing acknowledgements from their sponsoring agencies.

Sharing and publishing resources meets a current and pressing need for time-starved practitioners and serves to attract a great percentage of members to community websites where they may eventually discover more than repositories or resource portals. As the developer for ChevronTexaco's communities says:

"All it takes is for them to find one valuable piece of information on the site and they're hooked."

All seven communities offer access for members to retrieve and publish resources, instruments and tools of their respective practices. This is clearly a success but also a concern for community managers in so far as community members who participate only by accessing resources may not be moved to become active contributors. Indeed, some communities resist making resources available for that very reason. The following invitation from the "Ideas and Stories" section of CompanyCommand.com suggests one way that stories can generate deeper contribution:

"Stories: Tell us a short story that describes a company command experience, good or bad. Hearing about something that really happened, in a story format, is usually much more meaningful than simply being told what you should do. When you reflect on someone else's experience this way, you come much closer to learning the lessons, good and bad, that the story teller learned, without actually going through it."

Use Conviction and Experience to Make Vision Possible

Within ChevronTexaco, there is a ten-year history of the development and application of formal and informal CoPs. Those ten years have led to the conviction in some senior managers that CoPs can effectively be harnessed to serve the strategic goals of the organisation. The same can be seen in the Australian Flexible Learning Community, based on a conviction that a community approach is especially important in a field dealing with emerging technologies and new practices.

The importance of conviction and passion is borne out on a very personal level by the founders of CompanyCommand. Their personal experiences of the positive value of sharing stories of command have shaped the vision of their community. At the outset, they had never heard the term "Community of Practice" but they knew that there was a wealth of untapped experience to be shared - and that it could better prepare new commanders to meet the challenges of their chosen role. That conviction still carries through today when each copy of the community-related book 'Taking the Guidon' (Allen & Burgess, 2001) is personally annotated by the authors, Nate Allen and Tony Burgess, to acknowledge the purchaser and offer an invitation to join them in the web space.

Personal commitment, vision and high standards are all evident in the Switched On Leaders, MirandaNet and CompanyCommand.com stories. In each case the community's leader committed personal time, money and other resources and, to some extent, continues doing so to realize their community vision. This personal commitment and belief makes founders into 'community evangelists' and evangelism plays a large part in the first steps taken by each of these communities. It has been a key element in attracting new members as well as corporate or organizational acceptance for the community. The respect and financial support for the community that evangelists garnered was vital to carry on a professional level of work. For MirandaNet the community's association with industry was vital to support the professional nature of the projects and consultancies delivered by the community. The high quality action-research programs and projects would not be possible if supported purely by volunteer activity in an already overworked and depressed profession. For Switched On Leaders, personal contacts among members facilitated the community growth. The US Military Academy at West Point, New York has offered four tenured positions to sponsor the CompanyCommand.com management team who, until that point, had largely devoted their own free time to position the community in its current high regard.

It is true to say that the managers and facilitators at the heart of each of the seven communities carried deep convictions about the value of their communities. They each carried a vision for how that community would affect the practice even though management of such a group was a totally new experience for them.

Structure Clear Roles and Put Your Members to Work

For at least three of the communities reviewed, a clear structure for membership roles and progression had been sculpted from the outset of the community. Progression and levels of involvement may well serve to be an attractant to community members looking for professionalism and quality and it certainly makes clear the pathways for moving into the centre of the community.

ChevronTexaco's operational excellence initiatives are based on the formation of cross-functional project teams, which include some senior managers. The mandate for those teams is to develop strategies for operational improvement in the focus areas. After the design phase the team will hand responsibility over to the communities charged with assisting business units in implementation of the strategies. Some members of the project teams will progress to be leaders in the communities and new people will join them. The ChevronTexaco plan acknowledges the different roles of project teams and communities and clearly acknowledges the effectiveness of CoPs as a tool to support innovation and evolution of practice.

For MirandaNet the progression is more individually focused as members move from scholar to fellow. Members apply or are nominated to join the community and are accepted as scholars. When they have collaborated and have had research or written works approved for publication to the community, they can progress to become fellows of MirandaNet. In that progression, resources and funding become available for collaboration in research projects. Fellows may then be called upon to mentor new scholars in the community. New members are supported in professional activities by the community and have a clear pathway for deeper involvement, as they become ready to do so.

For Government Online International Network the structure allows an international community to flourish in a controlled fashion, where the administration and decisions are made at the national representative level. The community has a national representative for each of the 25 countries. The representatives nominate new members, projects and activities for their country and are part of the core of the community. Given the political nature of the domain, a structure and protocol of this nature is reassuring to the busy executive and senior level civil servants who are members of this community.

Beyond the ChevronTexaco workplace implementation communities, two other communities have both structured membership roles and put their members to work in community-focused projects. The Government Online International Network and MirandaNet both support member involvement in strategic projects. For MirandaNet, that involves being part of a consultancy team working on industry or government-funded research projects. In the Government Online International Network, members offer up project proposals to the community at the annual meeting and invite others to join. Projects are endorsed and move forward if there is an adequate level of member interest and support to realize the project goal.

Several other community managers said that they were developing smaller, more bounded (time and activity) and more focused nodes to stimulate deeper levels of member contribution and to continue developing community ties. Two communities had already incorporated such small group project work as mainstream to the community. Additionally, some earlier members of Switched On Leaders have self-formed consortia and consultancy teams to tender for projects, and while these collaborations are encouraged as a goal of the community, they are not part of its formal structure.

Grow From the Recognized Value of Being Together

MirandaNet and Government Online International Network both developed out of small groups formed for a discrete task or initiative, where members recognized the value of being together and were reluctant to disband after the task was completed. For these groups the first experience of being together was face-to-face, although other modes of community activity may also work. Indeed the weight of evidence supports the notion that face-to-face contact is valuable in early community building, particularly for motivating members and creating bonds between them.

All seven featured communities have a key role for face-to-face activities, whether strategically designed or enabled through related workplace activities or initiatives. These activities play a role not only in building ties but also in raising the professional status of the individual and the group.

- Australian Flexible Learning Community - teams never meet in this community but many members will meet through other initiatives
- ChevronTexaco - work team teleconference and existing communities
- CompanyCommand.com - seminars, management team meetings
- Government Online International Network - annual three day meetings in a host country
- KM4Dev - sponsored meetings, workshops
- MirandaNet - five workshops and recommended education conferences
- Switched On Leaders face-to-face meeting and personal contacts

Going online and exploiting the Internet extended the membership and enriched the connectivity of all of these communities, but it was essential that the building of the communities could draw upon other non-technological resources. That is part of why the face-to-face beginnings can support a faster ramp up of community, for only the tools are new if you already have relationships. Still, the Internet plays a crucial role in these communities. For example, without shared space on the Internet, Army company commanders would not be able to connect laterally as they currently are doing. In addition to bringing company commanders together with their peers, as a CompanyCommand.com manager says, the Internet brings:

"... the generals and the company commanders into the same coffee shop."

For the new online technologies, it was important to make the first experiences successful and non-threatening and to draw a clear boundary around a potentially vast domain for discussion. The communities reviewed were somewhat polarized in their approach to this issue. For the Australian Flexible Learning Community and MirandaNet, the friendly, social and fun task offerings (offline or online) were vital for their member professions. A tension can be seen between being credible, professional and relevant for busy practitioners, yet remaining informal and friendly. Communities such as CompanyCommand.com, Switched On Leaders and KM4Dev need to be focused on the slice of the domain important to the members. For these communities the value creation is high if there is scrupulous adherence to standards and to topics currently relevant to the practice.

All community leaders spoke of their ongoing load and a continual drive to raise the level of contribution and active involvement above the current norm (consistently described as a 5-10% figure for those now at the centre). Constantly working to engage members is a high priority and it is not by accident that this final feature connects back to the first, because staying in touch with the ethos, norms and needs of the members is ongoing and at the heart of all effective communities.

CONCLUSIONS

The work of cultivating a CoP cannot depend on formulaic recipes or quick-fix solutions. Community leaders were engaged in an ongoing process of development and self-design that responded to opportunities and challenges as they arose. The leaders of the CoPs in this study were engaged variously in the full range of political, organisational, technical, social and financial activities during the life of their communities. Building community depends on the passion and personal involvement that community leaders bring to their work and the vibrancy of the core group attracted to the centre of the community. To support sustainable growth, the commitment of the core members to invest time, effort and take significant risks must parallel their familiarity with the landscape and understanding of the needs of practitioners. That same commitment informs an understanding of the high standards that make a community viable and suggests how those standards play out in practice. While these community leaders are taking advantage of the Internet and the tools it currently provides, they are uniform in their understanding of the importance of sociability and community beyond the constraints of any technological platforms. Opportunities for face-to-face interaction were capitalized on, sought out and/or designed to integrate effectively with other media.

The complexity of each community described in this chapter was remarkable. Each contained a series of ongoing conversations and activities braided into a larger whole where all members see different strands of the community as well the practice around which the whole is formed. The leaders of these communities initially make some of the largest contributions and benefit most by being able to see the broadest picture of what's taking place in their communities. Where a team led the community, it was remarkable to find how close that group was and how vividly it displayed the characteristics of a CoP. Looking out from the middle there is also a rich and well-tended periphery in each of these communities attracting people from diverse backgrounds and perspectives.

The growth and development of these communities was due to a deep commitment to integrity and did not depend on marketing gimmicks of any sort. Growth came slowly by word of mouth. Pivotal in that growth was the calibre of leaders at the helm. Each community leader was unerringly attentive to new resources, new topics, new members and new ways of hosting the community's conversations. The openness of these leaders to new thinking brought a gradual but steady evolution to the conversations, the means of being together, and to the practice itself.

ACKNOWLEDGMENTS

Many thanks to the following community leaders and managers:

- Rose Grozdanic, Project Manager, Australian Flexible Learning Community, http://flexiblelearning.net.au/community
- Darron Padilla, Webmaster/Knowledge Analyst, Operational Excellence Communities, ChevronTexaco
- Major Peter Kilner, Editor and Community leader, US Army CompanyCommand.com, http://www.CompanyCommand.com
- John Gøtze, Webmaster, Government Online International Network, http://www.governments-online.org
- Lucie Lamoureux and Allison Hewlitt, Community Managers, Knowledge Management for Development (KM4Dev), http://open.bellanet.org/km
- Christina Preston, Director, MirandaNet Fellowship, http://www.MirandaNet.ac.uk
- Aseem Prakash, Community Director, Switched On Leaders, http://www.businessconfigurator.com

REFERENCES

Allen, N., and Burgess, T. (2001). *Taking the Guidon: Exceptional leadership at the company level.* The Centre for Company-Level Leadership.

Bruner, J. (2002). *Making stories: Law, literature, life.* New York: Farrar, Straus and Giroux.

Cothrel, J. (2001). Building an online community—The five P's. *IEC Symposium, Seamless integration of the Internet into your marketing program.* June 1, 2001, http://technologyexecutivesclub.com/prebuildingan.htm [last accessed January 2003]

Davenport, E., and Hall, H. (2002). Organizational knowledge and Communities of Practice. In B. Cronin (Ed.), *Annual review of Information Science and technology 2002,* (pp. 171-227). Medford, NJ: Information Today.

Kim, A. J. (2000). *Community building on the Web: Secret strategies for successful online communities.* Berkeley, CA: Peachpit Press.

Wenger, E. (1998). *Communities of Practice: Learning meaning and identity.* Cambridge, UK: Cambridge University Press.

Wenger, E. (2002). *Lisbon dialog on Communities of Practice.* Open Discussion Session, Setubal, Potugal, June 24.

Wenger, E., McDermott, R., and Snyder, W. (2002). *Cultivating Communities of Practice: a guide to managing knowledge.* Boston, MA: Harvard Business School Press.

White, N. (2003). Click connect and coalesce for NGOs: Exploring the intersection between online networks, CoPs and events. In this volume.

Williams, R. L., and Cothrel, J. (2000). Four smart ways to run online communities. *Sloan Management Review,* Summer, 81-91.

Chapter XV

How Information Technologies Can Help Build and Sustain an Organization's CoP:
Spanning the Socio-Technical Divide?

Laurence Lock Lee
Computer Sciences Corporation, Australia

Mark Neff
Computer Sciences Corporation, USA

ABSTRACT

Communities of Practice (CoPs) are seen as a primary vehicle for knowledge sharing across large and disparate organizations. It is therefore expected that technology will play a critical role in enabling global CoPs. The usefulness of Information Technologies (IT) to support CoP activity in two large, but quite different, global organizations is analysed and common themes developed. BHP Billiton is one of the world's largest diversified resource companies, with a strong industrial heritage and a mix of blue and white collar workers and levels of IT literacy. CSC is one the world's leading IT service providers, with a highly IT literate staff and a relatively sophisticated IT support environment. Both organizations could be considered early adopters of the CoP concept. This chapter tracks their evolution and the lessons learned along the way. The common themes arising from comparing and contrasting these two experiences mostly reflect the socio-technical challenges faced when enabling CoPs by the use of IT. In both organizations, the adoption of the newer collaborative tools is slower than anticipated, with the tried and tested face-to-face, teleconferencing and e-mail alive and well. The rule of people first, technology second is reinforced in both organizations. Technology adoption was far more successful as a response to CoP demand than a technology push. Where technologies are deployed, the level and degree of support was critical. The commitment of CoPs to a particular tool is fragile and easily lost through inconsistent performance of the technology. As well as facilitating CoPs, IT also plays an important role in developing measures and metrics for supporting CoPs as a value adding business resource. The ability to digitally track CoP activity provides an additional value-adding role for IT. While the usefulness of IT to support CoPs has largely been oversold in the past, BHP Billiton and CSC are two organizations that have persevered and learned from their respective experiences, to the extent that IT is now playing a key role in sustaining healthy and valuable CoP programmes.

INTRODUCTION

Communities of Practice (CoPs), as effective vehicles for knowledge sharing, are fast becoming the cornerstone of Knowledge Management (KM) programmes around the world (Wenger & Snyder, 2000). The majority of CoP "early adopters" are global organizations looking to leverage their knowledge across widely distributed organizations. With geographical separation comes the need to use technology to sustain contacts within the communities, in many cases, a "necessary evil". The human sensitivities associated with CoPs are often not well respected by the current class of collaborative IT systems. What works and what does not will often be a case of trial and error. While the heavy use of IT is not a necessary pre-condition for successful CoPs, there is sufficient evidence now that those organizations with successful CoP programmes will make better use of technology than those that do not. Leading organizations like Buckman Laboratories, BP, the World Bank, IBM, Schlumberger and Xerox all make effective use of IT systems to support their CoPs (Collison & Parcell, 2001; Edmundson, 2001; Lesser & Storck, 2001; Fulmer, 2000; Pan, 1998).

This chapter describes the experiences of two "CoP early adopter" companies in BHP Billiton (BHPB) and Computer Sciences Corporation (CSC).

In this chapter, CoPs are defined as informally established groups, driven to collaborate by a common purpose or discipline. Global CoPs (also referred to as Networks in this chapter) are often formally sponsored by senior management; however, most CoPs are informally formed as "bottom up" initiatives.

BHPB is the world's largest natural resources company with operations in over 100 sites world-wide, including many remote area sites. CSC is one of the world's largest IT companies with over 90,000 staff operating at 400+ sites. BHPB is very much an industrial company with a large mix of blue-collar and white-collar workers with varying levels of computer access and literacy. CSC on the other hand has a staff profile with extremely high levels of computer access and literacy.

Both companies have global reach and a strong need to leverage their knowledge across their respective organizations. Networks and CoPs are seen as ideal vehicles for achieving this goal, without the need to overcomplicate the formal organizational structures. The global nature of some of the CoPs is problematic in itself. The inability to have regular face-to-face contact presents some serious challenges to sustaining effective global CoPs.

Both BHPB and CSC have addressed these challenges over the past decade or so. The following case studies will trace the evolution of CoPs and the use of technology to support them over this time. The experiences of both companies will be compared and contrasted before some common themes and lessons are drawn from experiences to date. The lessons learned should be broadly applicable to organizations across all industry sectors.

THE BHP BILLITON STORY

BHPB was formed as a result of a merger of BHP and Billiton in 2001. BHP was formerly Australia's largest corporation with global interests in mining, petroleum and steel. Billiton was a large South African based mining house, with operations spanning all continents. This story reflects the BHP experiences leading up to and including the merger with Billiton and subsequent de-merger of BHP Steel. While it could be argued that BHP had been practising KM for decades, it was the BHP services division (IT, Engineering and Transport) that initially introduced KM into BHP in the mid 1990s. The programme became organization wide in 1999, with the establishment of a corporate Knowledge Management programme and the appointment of a Chief Knowledge Officer. In recent years, BHPB has followed the path of similar early adopters like BP and Xerox in embedding KM into day-to-day business operations (Collison & Parcell, 2001). The Corporate Knowledge Management programme has now been integrated into its overall business improvement / operating excellence function.

Figure 1: CoP Evolution and Technology Adoption at BHP

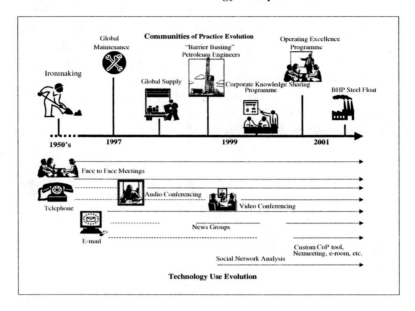

BHP Community Evolution

The earliest identifiable Community of Practice within BHP was the Steel Ironmaking Practices Network. This network can trace its origins to before the Second World War. The ultimate success of the Ironmaking community led to its replication within other disciplines, initially within the Steel divisions and then throughout the other divisions of Minerals, Petroleum and Corporate functions. Figure 1 identifies some of the key CoPs that have evolved from the CoP model established by the Ironmakers.

While the Ironmakers were all Australian based, the first truly global communities were established for Maintenance Engineering and Supply. These global networks were formed through the amalgamation of previous divisional communities and spanned the continents of the Americas, Europe, Africa, Asia and Australia. Within the Petroleum division, the global Petroleum Engineering Network undertook an innovative "Barrier Busters" programme whereby any "barriers to knowledge sharing" were identified and systematically addressed (Balnaves & Busch, 2002). The Petroleum Engineering Network has now delivered many millions of dollars of value to BHPB's bottom line. In early 2000, a corporate Knowledge Sharing programme was established with a major focus on facilitating effective CoPs. With the BHPB merger in 2001, the key responsibility for knowledge sharing moved to the global Operating Excellence (OE) programme. The OE programme has specific responsibility in facilitating identified global networks in areas like Maintenance, Mine Planning, Mining Operations, Processing and Supply.

In 2002 BHPB divested its Steel businesses, and along with it a majority of CoPs. Prior to the Steel divestment, there were over 200 identifiable CoPs within BHPB. Since the divestment, BHP Steel has managed to sustain and grow its CoPs within its now independent business. At the same time, BHPB has continued to successfully grow and sustain its CoPs under the guidance of its Operating Excellence programme. CoPs are now well established vehicles for knowledge sharing across both organizations, with many examples of tangible benefits arising from their respective activities.

Technology Use Evolution

Figure 1 also loosely tracks the technology adoption cycle in support of the building and sustaining of CoPs. What is quickly apparent is the adoption process for new technologies is slower than one would anticipate, with the older technologies (e.g., telephone, audio conferencing) not being superseded by newer collaborative tools. The other key feature is there is no single best tool. Across the whole portfolio of CoPs, there are good examples of use for all the identified support technologies.

A survey conducted in 2001 asked community members what technologies they thought best supported them in sustaining community activity (using a preference rating of 5 = best and 1 = worst). From nearly 500 respondents, the strong preference for face-to-face contact is not surprising. The use of e-mail and the telephone still dominated over the newer technologies, though the use of the newer collaborative tools is now slowly improving.

The BHP Billiton CoP Support Tool

In 2000, the Corporate Knowledge Programme sponsored the development of a custom CoP support tool. The intent was to provide a facility that could be freely available to the 20,000+ intranet users to form and run their own CoPs. A key principle adopted was that there should be no barriers to knowledge sharing for staff at any level. Allowing staff to establish and run their own CoPs was a clear reflection of this principle in action. The tool provides the basic functions of electronic discussions, document sharing, news broadcasting, requests for help and a directory of members. Additionally, statistics are collected to assist the Knowledge Sharing programme to monitor and improve on the CoP programme as a whole.

The CoP tool has now been in operation for over two years, during which time close to 200 communities have been formed with over 2,500 members. Figure 3 illustrates a typical CoP shared space. The tool menu on the left shows the functions for the sharing of documents, news items, member profiles, web links, project information, discussions on topics of interest and responses to

Figure 2: Preferred Technologies for Supporting CoPs

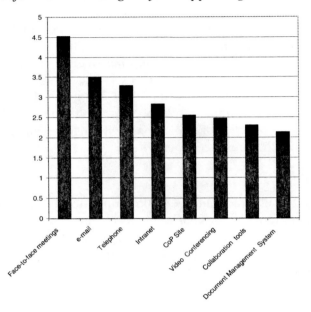

specific requests for assistance. The most recent contributions are highlighted on the respective CoP home page. While the adoption rate is healthy, it is still represents only around 10% of the potential audience of intranet users. It would also be naïve to assume that all of the established "electronic communities" were active CoPs. The CoP statistics on "hits" show that 20% of the CoPs represent

Figure 3: The BHP Billiton CoP Tool

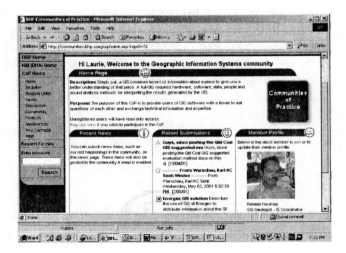

close to 70% of the activity, so it is still early days for the effective adoption of the tool.

Measuring and Monitoring CoP Activity

While concepts of CoPs and measurement may seem incongruous to some, in the corporate context any investment needs to demonstrate a return, which invariably means measurement and/or benchmarking. That said, measurement systems need to be sensitively designed to complement, rather than undermine, the essentially voluntary nature of CoPs.

In this context, statistics collected from the CoP tool usage are used by the co-ordinating team to assist with "nurturing" more so than "controlling" CoP activity. BHPB have also made use of Social Network Analysis (SNA) to help assess the "health" of its CoPs. Prior to the launch of the Global Maintenance Network (GMN) in late 1997, SNA was used to provide an "as-is" picture of knowledge sharing relationships amongst maintenance engineers world-wide. The GMN was the result of the amalgamation of several divisional maintenance engineering networks, numbering some 2,000+ engineers. SNA is a technique for mapping relationships within an organization or group. Some 1,000 engineers were asked to nominate their "trusted advisors" to assist in developing the relationship map (Figure 4). The analyses identified potential weak points in the Network, providing opportunities to "engineer" some collaborative activities to help strengthen the Network (Lock Lee, 2001).

This figure illustrates the knowledge sharing connections between and within business units. The satellites represent different business units and connections within those units. The links between the arcs in front of the satellites indicate inter-business unit connections. Each line indicates a link between two individuals.

A key finding from the study was that formal business unit boundaries are far greater barriers to knowledge sharing than geographic separation. For example, a particular business unit had more numerous connections between operations spanning the Pacific Ocean than to peers in other business units who were geographically co-located.

The GMN also operated the Company's most successful on-line discussion group. Some experiments were conducted with using discussion data to non-intrusively map connections over time. Figure 5 illustrates the evolution of CoP electronic interactions over time from the GMN launch. While the results were preliminary, it was felt that the data did reflect to a reasonable extent the nature of the activity in the Network.

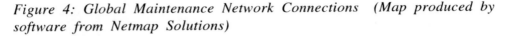

Figure 4: Global Maintenance Network Connections   (Map produced by software from Netmap Solutions)

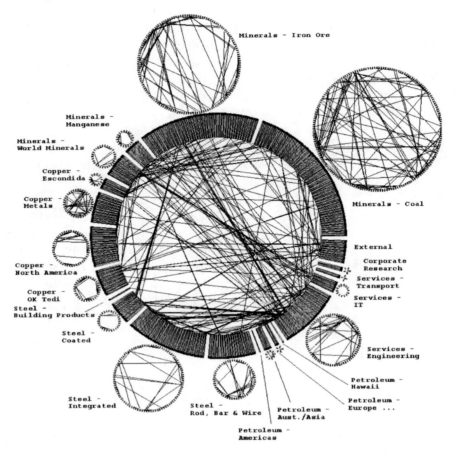

BHP Steel Divestment

The formation of the Global CoPs in areas like maintenance, safety and project management were aimed at facilitating collaboration across business divisions. They have been quite effective in quickly assimilating new acquisitions. Divestments, however, have the potential for undermining Global CoPs by removing potentially key members. In April of 2002, the re-structuring of the BHPB business was completed with the divestment of the BHP Steel division. The business separation was conducted over a 12 month period. The impact on the BHPB CoP programme was one of the considerations in the process. Those CoPs initiated by the Steel Division within BHPB were the most mature CoPs.

Figure 5:   Discussion Group Activities—Over Time

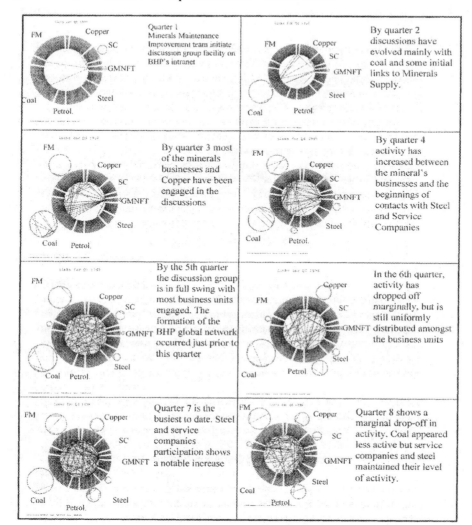

To understand the potential impact on the CoP programme (specifically where CoPs with cross divisional membership might be undermined by the loss of Steel members), the CoP tool membership data were used to identify CoPs at risk (Figure 6).

This "map" provides an overview of CoP membership as extracted from the CoP tool. The black circles are BHP Steel members with connections to CoPs (triangles). One can clearly see the polarisation of "Steel" CoPs, which was good news for the separation as the impacts would be minimal.

Figure 6: CoP Membership by Business Division (Map produced by the Pajek software)

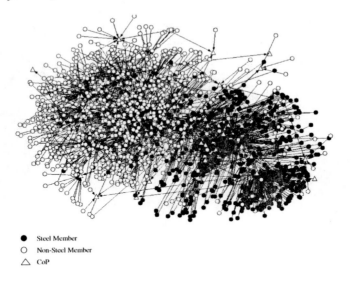

●   Steel Member

○   Non-Steel Member

△   CoP

For the identified "CoPs at risk", the CoP leader was interviewed to assess the potential impact of losing steel members from the CoP. With the separation, BHP Steel now has its own copy of the CoP tool, with the majority of CoPs operating and unaffected by the change.

BHP Billiton Lessons Learned

Technology enablement of BHPB CoPs began in earnest from the 1980s to the point now where Communities have literally a smorgasbord of support technologies to choose from. The major lessons from this experience could be summarised as:

- For CoPs, technology use is discretionary. There is no single "best support tool". The differing styles and cultures across communities will often dictate the style of support they will seek.
- Face-to-face meetings are absolutely essential to successfully launch and sustain a community. The value in the use of technology may simply be in sustaining activity between meetings.
- CoPs will use a mix of technologies, driven by what is pragmatic for the group overall. To ensure no member is disadvantaged they will often choose the lowest common denominator (perhaps explaining the continued popularity of e-mail and the telephone).
- For effective CoPs, technology is not a barrier. For ineffective CoPs it is always a barrier.

Figure 7: CSC's Knowledge Environment

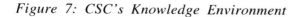

- Trying to launch a CoP by first establishing a "shared electronic space" will often fail. It needs to be people engagement first, then technology support following as a response to a demand.
- New technology introduction needs champion/s to sustain its use beyond the inevitable teething stages.
- Investment in technical support is critical. New technology will often fail. If support teams can have it up and running again quickly, then frustrations will be minimised. Coaching in the "social protocols" of virtual work can also help CoP members to quickly become more comfortable with a new media.
- Technology-enabled CoPs can be an effective vehicle for corporate departments in developing and then implementing global initiatives where cross business activities are the norm (e.g., safety practices, environmental practices and project management).

THE CSC STORY

Computer Sciences Corporation was founded in 1959 and is one of the World's leading consulting and Information Technology service providers. CSC has grown rapidly through IT outsourcing acquisitions in the past decade. Now with over 90,000 employees operating in some 700 sites and 70 countries, the need for an effective KM environment had been apparent from an early stage.

Figure 8: History of CoPs within CSC

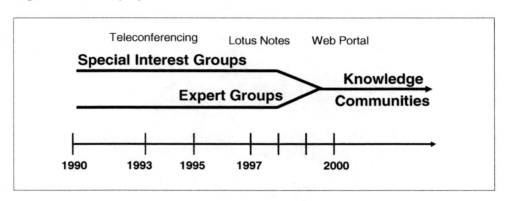

CSC's Knowledge Environment

CoP (called Knowledge Communities within CSC) are One of the Four Quadrants Making Up CSC's Knowledge Environment

CSC's knowledge communities are horizontal communities of experts and practitioners that cooperate to build and share knowledge around business topics that impact the organization's performance or ability to adapt to business changes. These communities play an important role in building and accelerating the flow of tacit knowledge within the company. They support business developers and delivery managers seeking expertise to address challenging business problems. They support practitioners in developing their own knowledge and expertise. They provide a forum for collaboration that accelerates the rate at which the organization innovates and enables CSC to maintain its thought leadership in disciplines important to its success.

- *Knowledge Base.* CSC's knowledge base captures explicit knowledge providing CSC employees with the information, methods, learning programs and tools that enable them to work effectively in cross-organizational teams. Communities play a key role in organizing the knowledge base to meet the needs of their members and in maintaining the business value of the knowledge base over time.
- *Knowledge Infrastructure.* CSC's knowledge infrastructure provides employees with the tools needed to participate in knowledge communities and to take advantage of their services.
- *Knowledge Processes.* Processes for aligning investments in the knowledge environment with the strategy and goals of our business, launching and operating knowledge communities, managing the quality and structure of the knowledge base.

Figure 9: Types and Roles of Communities in CSC

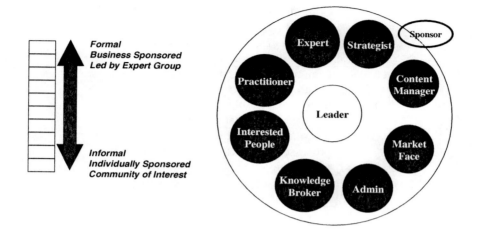

CSC Community Evolution

CSC's experience with communities stretches back over a decade. Early on, CSC focused on stimulating communities of interest—informal groups focused on networking practitioners. They then chartered expert groups and gave them specific responsibilities for reviewing and recommending best practices, engineering new knowledge assets and supporting requests for assistance from business developers, practitioners and delivery teams. They expanded expert groups into expert and practitioner networks to diffuse expert group results more effectively. Then CSC began to look for means to strengthen the communities' business focus and to align community investments with CSC business goals on both the global and local levels. They worked with community leaders to mature their processes for supporting and operating the communities. They explored different community funding models: funding for leaders, funding for members and funding of community projects. Some of its business units began to converge their organizational and community models.

Today within CSC, knowledge communities number in excess of 500. These communities focus on business topics related to business development, business drivers, core competencies, solutions, market drivers and/or industries. Other examples include project management, system architecture, supply chain solutions, client relationship management, JAVA programming and outsourcing transition management. They include formal and informal communities. Formal communities are sponsored globally or at a business-unit level and are charged with specific goals such as the engineering of new knowledge assets, identification of best practices and recommendations for their use, demonstration of CSC's thought leadership and point of view in external forums, mentoring

Table 1: CSC Communities—Levels of Maturity

Level 5	Communities are responsible for delivering business results
Level 4	Business value is clearly a focus of community action
Level 3	Community leadership well established. Communities recognised as a source of thought leadership. Community processes and roles well established.
Level 2	Informal communities in place. Community processes and roles not well established. Leadership issue is in early phases.
Level 1	Some social forms may exist within the organization.

practitioners and identifying experts to assist business developers and delivery managers in addressing client needs. Informal communities are sponsored by individuals and often focus on topics such as emerging technologies that may be critical to the business in the future.

The larger, more formal communities will have members acting in most of the roles identified. For communities of interest there may simply be a leader and interested people. CSC has developed a methodology for launching, operating and supporting communities based on experience that stretches back over a decade. This methodology reflects its knowledge about the roles that a community must establish to increase its maturity and its business value to an organization—roles such as expert, practitioner, interested person, knowledge broker, content manager and strategist or thought leader.

CSC experience showed that communities grow through a natural evolution as they mature (Table 1). Communities initially focussed on connecting people and sharing knowledge, progressing to a focus on developing knowledge in support of key business initiatives and demonstrating thought leadership. Communities in their most mature form have directly impacted the strategy of the business; some have even become formal constructs within an organization, chartered with the delivery of business results. For example, the global systems architecture and global project management CoPs now have formal roles in establishing company standards and designing company-wide training programmes.

CSC's focus has evolved into establishing joint communities with its clients and partners focused on topics of interest to them and making these communities accessible through shared knowledge environments.

Figure 10: CSC Portal

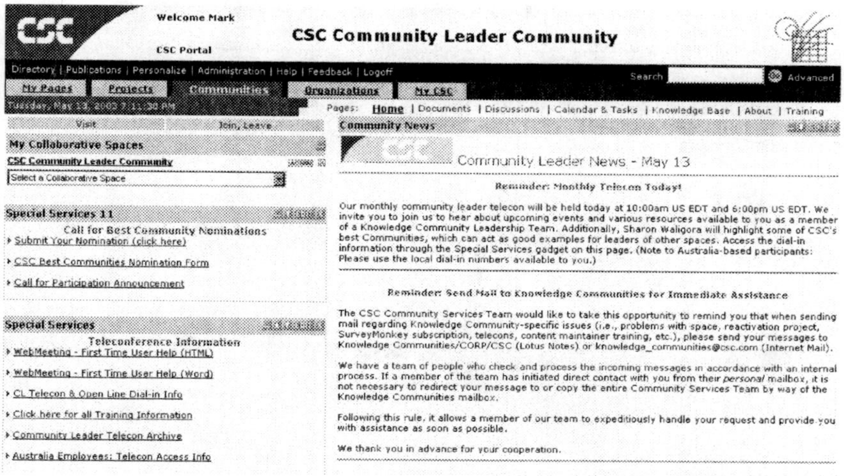

Technology Use Evolution

From the early 1990s, communities relied on teleconferences and e-mail to sustain their activities. The introduction of Lotus notes in the mid-1990s provided a richer environment for supporting communities, enabling customised repositories and discussion areas to be self-maintained by the communities. In 2000, CSC introduced an enterprise-wide portal solution based on technology from Plumtree. The CSC portal is now a one-stop shop for enterprise information across CSC and provides a home for the knowledge communities as well as project teams and organizational units.

The portal provides communities with their own electronic space. Community members are able to post information "assets" informally into the "knowledge base". These assets may be working documents or documents of general interest to the community members. A more formal process is used to post documents to the CSC enterprise-wide repository. Assigned community members are used to get information assets for inclusion in the enterprise wide repository. The portal also supports community discussions, broadcasts and member lists.

Another powerful and often used feature of the knowledge environment is the "Request for Assistance" (RFA) function. This function enables staff members to post a request for assistance on any topic by addressing the request to those communities who are most likely to be able to help. The RFA repository can also be searched to see if your request has already been answered previously. Each community has a member assigned to facilitate the rapid response to requests for assistance addressed to their community.

Figure 11: Western Integrity Center Shared Community Space

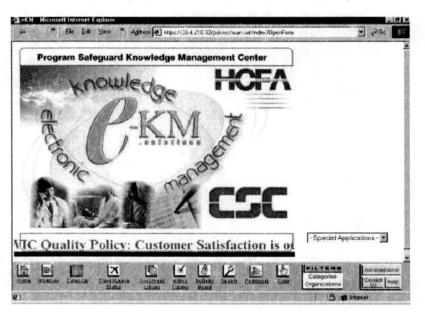

The CSC Corporate Knowledge Programme (CKP) team has played a critical role in the establishment, awareness building, training and support of the technical infrastructure supporting communities. The CKP is a distributed team with key nodes in the US, Europe and Australia. The CKP effectively facilitates a formal knowledge community around the use and continued improvement of the knowledge environment.

In support of CSC's growing focus on enabling community formation with its external customers, partners and suppliers, CSC has developed a web-based tool called "e-KM", which provides a shared electronic space for communities which form across multiple organizations. e-KM can support multiple communities with basic functions for document and link sharing, discussions, news, personal calendar sharing and action tracking. An example of e-KM use is a cross-organization community formed to identify and prevent Medicare fraud in 12 western US States. Called the Western Integrity Center, the community is made up of a geographically dispersed collection of experts in statistics, data base administration, programmers, special investigators, specialized nurses, a physician and an attorney.

What has CSC Learned about Communities?
• Successful communities require strong sponsorship, effective leaders and clear business alignment (both at a global and local level). For a global organization like CSC, technology use is unavoidable. A standard environ-

ment like the CSC portal can greatly assist their operations, ensuring that no members are disadvantaged through lack of the appropriate tools.

- Providing access to the community support environment via the Internet can ensure staff members working from client sites will not be disadvantaged by less than ideal connectivity with their community colleagues.
- Communities need social as well as professional interaction if they are to thrive. Social interaction is often only achievable for some, at the annual business and technology conference. Technologies can, however, help sustain energy between these annual events.
- Regular virtual "recharge" events are needed to keep the communities alive. Synchronous technologies are preferred, usually teleconferencing, sometimes supported by conferencing software. Video conferencing has proved problematic, too costly and not robust enough.
- Some communities like the CSC Research Services Alliance network have been using instant messaging (IM) to assist with sustaining contact. Experience to date is that IM is not for everyone, with usually only a core regularly making themselves available. Social protocols need to be developed (e.g., how you leave a chat session without appearing rude). Again, this tends to be less of an issue if the members are well known to each other (i.e., social interactions have previously been experienced).
- In developing shared knowledge environments for inter-company communities, CSC found it was far simpler to make use of a completely separate tool hosted on the Internet than to try and extend its internal portal for external use, where security issues became quite problematic. Additionally, community participants are likely to feel more comfortable in using an "independent" tool.
- Measurement systems around community participation and activity are a useful proxy measure for the degree of business value achieved. Anecdotally, the most active communities are generating the most business value.

COMMON THEMES AND LESSONS LEARNED

BHP Billiton and CSC are quite different companies with quite different staff profiles with respect to blue collar/white collar mix and levels of IT literacy. What they do have in common is the global nature of their respective businesses and their commitment to using CoPs as a primary vehicle for knowledge sharing across their global operations. As one might expect, CSC's use of technology is much more pervasive than with BHP Billiton. Being a technology company whose assets are mainly human, CSC has invested heavily in ensuring that its people can connect with each other effectively. Penetration of usage is still relatively low with respect to potential users, with BHP Billiton CoP tool users being around 10% of the potential users and CSC's at around 50% at the time of writing, but usage rates are still growing rapidly for both organizations.

Both organizations have developed customised environments to support their CoPs. The BHP Billiton system is built mainly with Microsoft Web Development tools and CSC's systems using a mix of Lotus Notes and Plumtree. Both organizations use these tools to help monitor CoP activity as a proxy measure for business value, with BHP Billiton taking additional steps over the traditional "Number of members" and "Hits" measures to look at the social network implied by the data.

It is commonly accepted that CoPs are predominantly social artefacts, and on the surface, both organizations are performing equally well and facing similar challenges, independent of the level of technical sophistication. The common themes emerging are:

- Without face-to-face contact, CoPs will struggle to survive. Technology can at best sustain communities between face-to-face events and perhaps reduce the number of face-to-face events required.
- The technology choice needs to respect the "lowest common denominator" members such that no member is excluded from participation for technical reasons. One advantage CSC has is its fairly rich "base level".
- Technology alone will not launch and/or sustain an effective community. Both organizations have a substantial number of ineffective CoPs (i.e., have established an electronic space but have very little activity).
- Technologies must be robust and well supported. The slower adoption of newer technologies is more related to supportability than acceptance. The drop off in video conferencing use and the continued reliance on teleconferencing by both organizations is reflective of this.
- Measuring the business value of CoPs is problematic given their less formal mode of operation. Membership, activity levels and relationship maps have all anecdotally provided useful proxy measures for business value. Specific "stories and anecdotes" appear to be the most useful mechanism for communicating business value from CoPs.

SUMMARY AND CONCLUSIONS

For global organizations like BHP Billiton and CSC the use of technology to help develop and sustain CoP activity is essential. Both organizations have undertaken some innovative technology developments to help facilitate their respective CoP programmes, with varying degrees of success. Technology has clearly played an important role in enabling local communities to go global.

The common challenge for both organizations has been largely socio-technical. Both organizations have adopted new technologies, but at a slower rate than expected and without leaving behind the older tried and tested technologies. Despite CSC having a more sophisticated and pervasive technical environment than BHPB, both organizations' CoP members would still nominate, in order of preference: face-to-face, teleconferencing and e-mail as the prime connectivity channels.

Perhaps the key lesson learned by both organizations is that while experimentation with new technologies is encouraged, the rolling out of the next technical increment needs to be all-inclusive (not just in some areas, to some people). Supportability is key. If time challenged community members are inconvenienced in any way, they will fall back to the tried and tested. Technology use by CoPs cannot be mandated, so the technology has to "earn its keep" by providing the appeal and reliability that CoPs could not do without.

ACKNOWLEDGMENTS

We would like to acknowledge John Vucko, Barbara Busch and Charles Balnaves from BHP Billiton for their contributions and comments on the BHP Billiton story.

REFERENCES

Balnaves, C., and Busch, B. (2002).Creating and nurturing a knowledge sharing culture in a high performance technical group. In *Proceedings of the Society of Petroleum Engineers Inc. International Conference on Asia Pacific Oil & Gas on creative solutions for maturing basins and new frontiers*, October 6-8, 2002.

Collison, C., and Parcell, G. (2001). *Learning to fly*. UK: Capstone Publishing.

Edmundson, H. (2001). Technical Communities of Practice at Schlumberger. *Knowledge Management*, (May/June).

Fulmer, W. (2000). *The World Bank and Knowledge Management: The case of the Urban Services Thematic Group*. February, Harvard Business School.

Lesser, E., and Storck, J. (2001). Communities of Practice and organizational performance. *IBM Systems Journal*, January.

Lock Lee, L. (2001). Knowledge sharing metrics for large organizations. In D. Morey, M. Maybury, and B. Thuraisingham (Eds.), *Advances in Knowledge Management: Classic and contemporary works*, (pp. 403-419). MIT Press.

Pan, S. L. (1998). A socio-technical view of knowledge -sharing at Buckman Laboratories. *Journal of Knowledge Management*, 2 (1), 55-66.

Wenger, E., and Snyder, W. (2000). Communities of Practice: The organizational frontier. *Harvard Business Review*, (January/February), 139-145.

Chapter XVI

Building a Community of Practice:
Technological and Social Implications for a Distributed Team

Pete Bradshaw
Anglia Polytechnic University, United Kingdom

Stephen Powell
Anglia Polytechnic University, United Kingdom

Ian Terrell
Anglia Polytechnic University, United Kingdom

ABSTRACT

This chapter looks at the work of a team of remote workers and how they have developed into a Community of Practice (CoP). It explores the roles that technology and communication methods have in the formation and development of the community. In telling the story of the progression from a team of individuals to a CoP, the chapter provides a practical guide to others wishing to do the same.

Two aspects of the work of the team are considered in depth:

- *Building communication systems across a Distributed CoP*
- *Building commitment, ownership, engagement and focus in a Distributed CoP*

The team and community on which the chapter is based is one of some 20 people working remotely for Ultralab, a learning, technology and research centre in Chelmsford, UK. The work of the team is online facilitation for the National College of School Leadership (NCSL). The team meet together approximately four times a year, using an online community space, the Facilitators' Forum, as their day-to-day working space.

INTRODUCTION

Wenger argues that 'Communities of Practice are everywhere' (Wenger, 1998, p. 6) and goes on to cite the example of the family, neighbourhood and informal workplace grouping, leisure clubs and societies. He further explains that Communities of Practice (CoPs) are central to learning, saying:

"... engagement with social practice is the fundamental process by which we learn and so become who we are" (Wenger, 1998: Abstract).

With the use of new information and communication technologies, remote working is becoming more common. Where workers are engaged in a CoP, it is now possible for this to be distributed, whereas previously a degree of co-location was the norm (Brown & Duguid, 1999.) This chapter is a practical guide focusing upon the key features of the development, work and collaborative support of a geographically distributed team that shows characteristics of a CoP, and that uses new technologies. The focus is on one of the teams at Ultralab, a research and development unit based at Anglia Polytechnic University (APU) in Chelmsford, England. Ultralab's work or 'domain', using Wenger's term, is research into, and creation of, 'delightful' learning experiences using new technologies. This forms the central mission for all Ultralab work and is the focus for collaborative engagement.

Some 60 people work for Ultralab, either full or part-time. Approximately 40 of these are based at Chelmsford, working on a large number of projects, either individually or, more often, in teams. The remainder, some 20 people, are remote workers who, with four Chelmsford based staff, work on a project that is developing online learning communities for the National College for School Leadership (NCSL). These communities include Talking Heads, an online community for head teachers (school principals) and communities that provide online support for programmes of professional development.

Ultralab's organizational structure can be described as "The Operating Adhocracy" (Mintzberg &Westley, 1992) where the organization relies on informal "mutual adjustment" as the method of coordinating efforts. Handy (1991) describes both 'task' and 'person' cultures; the former being dynamic, flexible and suitable in creative organizations and the latter being focused upon individual self-direction, motivation and autonomy. At Ultralab, a particular culture, 'the way we do things around here' (Deal & Kennedy, 1983, p. 14) has been developed to suit a flexible, dynamic and creative research and development unit. Staff work collaboratively and are encouraged to work across different projects. Leadership is 'distributed' across 'the lab' with younger and less experienced staff often taking leading roles in managing and directing projects. Hence, both collaborative task culture and individual person culture are features of the distributed teamwork. The challenges of knitting together a distributed team trying to work in a truly collaborative way more readily associated with co-located workers are formidable. The team has developed a number of work practices and strategies to help it to address the significant challenges it has faced.

In the outline of practical strategies that follows, two issues are dealt with, each in the context of the use of technologies in a distributed CoP:

1)   Building communication systems
2)   Building commitment, ownership, engagement and focus

Building Communication Systems Across a Distributed CoP

Establishing the core mission around which team members can engage in a collaborative venture can be seen as the first practical task of building a distributed CoP. Further, as we have shown, there is building a task and person culture that allows teamwork and individualism to flourish. The culture needs to develop autonomy, self-direction and independence yet also build collaboration and teamwork focused upon particular tasks, and distributed among sub-groups. Dynamism and the ability to change and reorganize teams rapidly is essential to match the changing demands of projects and tasks.

With the mission established, the first area that we will discuss here is the building of systems of communication that connect both individuals (one to one) and groups. While being at a distance, these groups and individuals are working on this common mission and set of tasks.

Development of Community Software at Ultralab

The Ultralab team facilitating NCSL communities, from its establishment in the first quarter of 2000, has used collaborative software tools in its daily work. The team's development towards a CoP was largely, but not exclusively, made possible by the use of such software and the collaboration and communication tools it provides.

This team is known as 'the facilitation team'. Through its daily working practices over the past three years, it has established a clear domain for its work (school leadership), is engaged in common practices (facilitation) and has reified and negotiated meaning in these practices (Wenger, 1998). Thus, it shows signs of being a CoP, one that is able to accommodate new members through their Legitimate Peripheral Participation and apprenticeship and interaction with core members.

Having community software available and ready at hand is central to the success of building a distributed CoP. More than this, however, is the willingness to commit to the use of community software for conversations and sharing of information.

Guided by Ultralab, software was developed by Oracle (think.com) and built on the principles of:

- Community creation and ownership by members
- Tools that allow the user to create discussions and other items
- Universal access through any web browser on any machine anywhere in the world
- Scalable size of user base
- The primacy of asynchronous communication

The use of asynchronous rather than synchronous communication allows for reflection and consideration before posting comments. Being web-based and avoiding the need for client software enables access at a time and place of convenience to the individuals in the distributed team. The choice of a 'flat' structure of user privileges empowers and enfranchises community members.

This use of think.com has been complemented by the lab's use of Centrinity's First Class (http://www.centrinity.com/) for internal conferencing, e-mail services and synchronous 'chat' facilities.

Other forum, message board and community-ware products are available and many provide adequate to good community environments. It is, however, important that before deciding upon a particular platform the likely community is scoped to ensure that the platform will be able to deliver.

Through the design of our own solutions and the use of proprietary and bespoke software, we have honed our use of online community tools. There is no one choice that would fit all CoPs and compromises may need to be made. Table 1 lists issues for practitioners when choosing community software.

Online Asynchronous Discussion: The Community 'Bulletin Board'

The work of this team and its development into a distributed CoP has been primarily carried out using think.com. The Facilitators' Forum (FF), a community space built with the tools of think.com, was the first, and remains the most significant, tool in the work of the CoP. Its purpose is for communication, sharing ideas, and developing understanding: in short, a place of learning.

Table 1: Issues to be Considered When Designing or Selecting Community Software

Projected size of the community
Learning architecture: how conversations and resources will be
structured
Range of tools available, e.g., styles of conversations, calendars, upload
facilities
Projected costs
Software sophistication and resultant training implications for
community members and facilitators
Hosting options and resultant hardware and technical support required
Scalability options
Administration of community membership
Is there a sustained history of product development?

We have found that it is important to keep a high degree of consistency with the layout of the FF. Changes in the information architecture should be slow and evolutionary, not radical, as this leads to a feeling of dislocation amongst users and, for some, it takes a long time to re-orientate and find those regular accessed resources and conversations.

At the heart of this consistency is the daily bulletin board (BB). For many months, this was a simple single-thread asynchronous discussion. After a review, this developed into first three, and then five, threads with which the flow of the conversation is maintained. The BB convention has colour-coded entries depending upon the thread: blue for dialogue about work, green for social interactions, red for "must read", black for information giving, and purple for items carried forward from "yesterday", i.e., the previous day's BB. These categories match the variety of community members' needs; for example, those who wish to engage in social banter as a part of their daily work can do so.

A key feature of the BB is the breakout discussions and activities that flow from, and return to, it (see Figure 1). Throughout the day, the BB is used to springboard other conversations on a specific topic. These are then included in the top of the BB to run for a period of time appropriate to their context. Thus, asynchronous discussions are used to lead to the formation of either rapid action teams (RATs) or longer-term action groups to undertake the work of the CoP (Figure 1).

The BB requires three kinds of management and facilitation:

1)   Housekeeping, archiving and tidying. A rota is used for this with individual community members producing daily summaries, with the important "must read" items being carried over into the next day's BB. An archive is also maintained of important documents and specific conversations for future

Figure 1: Use of the BB for Break-Out Discussions and Teams

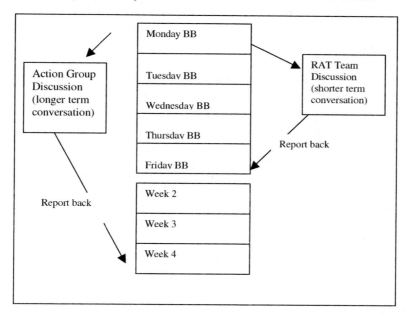

reference. Members of the facilitation community find this invaluable for referring back for the detail of past discussions, while those who have not been able to access the FF for a period of time use it to 'catch up' with the 'community history'.

2)   Facilitation of the conversation, which involves everyone making summaries of ongoing conversational threads, as appropriate, to move the dialogue along, picking up points and so on.

3)   Leading and structuring the dialogue so that it focuses on key issues and the development of the agenda of the teams, with this leadership role distributed through and across the teams. Strategies for using a tool such as the BB to develop community are listed in Table 2.

Table 2: Strategies for Using an Asynchronous Conversation Tool for Developing Community

Encourage frequent and regular use as a way of working
Use for news, updating, sharing as well as discussions and conversations
Encourage social communication and humour
Colour code
House keep for access and navigation
Involve everyone
Make sure conversations are completed and lead to action

The use of the FF is at the heart of the social cohesion and process of negotiated meaning that goes into making the CoP. The FF consists of ongoing and time-limited debates, an archive of summarised knowledge, and is the virtual embodiment of the community. When new staff are employed and join the team, they are inducted into the community through activity in the FF. At first, this will be limited to the use of the BB, but, as the newcomer becomes closer to the core work of the community, they will begin to access all of the tools and resources across the FF space, i.e., as a form of Legitimate Peripheral Participation (Lave & Wenger, 1991).

Synchronous Group Discussion: The Telephone Conference

Telephone conferencing is at the heart of building good communication in the team, with a weekly phone conference attended by representatives of its main working groups. The purpose of the conference is to exchange and update on progress and to discuss team issues. The agenda for the meeting is created by conversation in the asynchronous BB and any papers are made available in the community or by e-mail. In addition, other resources that would be used in a face-to-face meeting or diagrams that may be created on the 'fly' are also circulated; these visual aids to conversations require thought and preparation in advance of the meeting. Phone conferences are used by smaller teams and action groups to convey information to the wider community—often via the central team acting as the 'hub'.

Different phone systems have been experimented with. They fall broadly into two categories, those where the host phones out to the participants and those where the participants phone into a password protected 'meeting room' hosted by a third-party organization. Experience has shown the latter to be a far more efficient, albeit more expensive, option as the onus is on the participants to join the meeting and rejoin themselves, minimising the disruption to the overall meeting should they experience difficulties.

Systems have also been established where phone conferencing is integrated with web-based sharing of documents and interactive whiteboard tools. Frequent phone conferencing helps to connect the team and promotes engagement in team activities rather than the sometimes more isolated world of the text-based bulletin board.

A chair leads the phone conference meeting, balancing the contributions of all the speakers. Identifying each speaker as positions on a clock face allows participants to have a visual image and the chair not to miss asking for contributions from each person in turn. A minute taker is essential. Minutes are posted, as the meeting progresses, in the same asynchronous conversation that was used for the agenda. The minute taker works at a hands-free telephone, so

Table 3: Lessons from the Community's Use of Telephone Conferencing

- Use frequently
- Chair to ensure contributions from everyone
- Use a clock face to position participants
- Verbally check individual action points and agreements with all present
- Have a minute taker with a hands free telephone
- Set strict time limits
- Circulate agenda with attached discussion documents and other supporting resources and aids to the conversation

that they can type and listen. Table 3 lists lessons from the community's use of telephone conferencing.

The phone conference, a relatively recent addition to this team's armoury of tools, is an essential resource for providing the social bond between team members and for establishing the nuances of meaning and purpose that define the community's practice. Supporting the asynchronous work, the phone conference's regularity provides a weekly marker for the team's work.

Synchronous Group Discussion: Text-Based Online Discussions

Synchronous online conversations in text have been used by the community, taking advantage of First Class conferencing software, MSN Messenger and other software platforms. At first, these discussions took place on a weekly basis at a fixed time. This reduced in line with need. No agenda was set; the meetings were seen simply as a means of sharing the week's experiences, both successes and setbacks. These events served to promote the social maintenance of the group, by 'mending fences' where the pressure of the previous week had caused friction. They also played a part in building cohesiveness in the team and reducing the feeling of isolation. Latterly, they have become an informal way of communicating used by small groups of individuals, particularly to solve problems, clarify a point raised in another form of communication or relieve any sticking points in actions that had been planned.

This small group use of synchronous messenger services, which is a form of 'instant messaging', has contributed hugely to reducing feelings of isolation as it increases social awareness. Remote members report benefits as being able to ask questions of colleagues that require rapid answers and to have social conversations. This use can be compared to that of talking to colleagues on an adjacent desk, when making a cup of coffee at the machine or in the kitchen or around a water cooler. Many of the remote members log onto the system at the start of the day and leave it running throughout, setting the controls to show whether they are at their computer or 'away'. The presence of others on the system is reported as giving a feeling of 'virtual co-location', supporting the social cohesion of the community. Table 4 lists the lessons learnt from the use of synchronous online discussion.

Table 4: Lessons Learned from the Use of Synchronous Online Discussion

Encourage synchronous discussion between groups and individuals
Chair and structure the discussion firmly
Save discussion text in an archive

Synchronous Group Discussion: Full Use of Technology

Monthly meetings are held for all staff at Ultralab. Those at Chelmsford can attend face-to-face, whereas for remote community members the meetings are broadcast live over the Internet. This uses a combination of technology - video/phone conferencing, synchronous chat and, most recently, desktop-sharing applications. Video and audio are streamed using 'iVisit' to provide a 'video wall' of images of several remote workers and a view of the room used for the meeting face-to-face. Applications such as Webex and NetMessenger have enabled sharing of computer desktops between remote workers. These allow numerous participants to give over control of their desktop over to a presenter for demonstrating a piece of software. Further, documents can be worked on collaboratively with these applications. The use of technology in this way is in its infancy and is still not technically robust.

Phone conference kit allows remote workers to participate through audio and an ongoing synchronous chat is maintained in First Class where all can contribute, ask questions and seek clarification. Effective use of this requires 'spotters' in the face-to-face meeting who relay questions and contributions to the whole meeting where appropriate. In addition, a couple of 'writers' keep an ongoing description of points made, agreements, etc. This stream of text forms the basis for a subsequent digest of the meeting.

Other synchronous activities have been used for collaborative working over a short timescale. For example, one exercise was to analyse data collected in a collaborative team research journal. The discussion centred upon creating categories of data. Ideas were shared online, small groups discussed them using instant messenger and telephone, and responses were posted into an asynchronous text-based conversation. A summary of the discussion and action points was drawn out by individual members appointed to the task.

Video conferencing is being piloted amongst remote members of the facilitation community, being dependent on connections and hardware. It is heavily dependent upon the user's 'bandwidth' (connection speed) for the quality of the user's experience, and broadband access will, in the future, become essential.

Table 5 lists the recommendations from our practice for the use of these diverse technologies.

Table 5: Recommendations for the Use of Diverse Technology for Synchronous Discussions

- Invest in technical support
- Invest in good quality equipment
- Use spotters to support the remote participants
- Use writers to capture and summarise the conversations

Synchronous Discussion: The Mobile Phone

Each member of the facilitation community is issued a mobile phone. This enables conversations to take place with clients and contacts in the online project areas, using both text and voice messaging. Members of the community have also found them useful for the retrieval and sending of email, and accessing of the Internet.

Naturally, considerable use of the phones is made for one-to-one discussions between community members. This is felt to be an essential channel of communication, giving access to each other on a 24-hour basis, no matter where in the country they are located.

Table 6 lists the recommendations from our use of mobile phones in developing the social cohesion of the community.

Table 6: Recommendations for the Use of the Mobile Phone

- Use mobile phone technology to connect team members
- Be conscious of the appropriate time to use phone conversations - sometimes it is much better than email or community conversations

Face-to-Face Meetings

Face-to-face meetings, in the form of conferences, are held bimonthly by the community. They are seen as an integrated whole of the community practice, a natural extension of the overwhelming majority of the community work, which is carried out in a distributed way.

Asynchronous conversations are used to lead into the face-to-face as preparation and to take further issues and plans following the face-to-face. The agenda is drawn up in negotiation between the remote members of the community and the centrally based project leaders. Striking the balance between the two parts of the community is important so that the whole community has a feeling of ownership of the agenda, while also addressing issues that are more pressing from a project leadership and management perspective. This requires a great deal of discipline by the community, with all members fully engaging in the process. Table 7 lists the purposes of face-to-face conferences.

Table 7: Purpose of Face-to-Face Conferences

- Integrate face to faces with online activity
- Optimise the use of time at face-to-face meetings by having online discussions before, during and after the event

The face-to-face conference works in the same way as the phone conference in developing the team's negotiation of purpose and meaning. That it does so over a much longer period, and with wider participation, allows the CoP to develop in a much more secure way, with its procedures and purposes reified by all.

Building Commitment, Ownership, Engagement and Focus in a Distributed CoP

The use of technology to build effective communication among distributed workers is not the only area of practical concern. There is also a major area of practical activity focused upon building commitment, ownership and engagement with the core focus of the team's work. These factors affect any team collaboration. Wenger (1998) emphasises the need for engagement in CoPs, but the engagement required here is more complex when a team is distributed and individuals could, potentially, work in isolation.

However, maintaining communities at a distance with a large and diverse project is difficult. We have already outlined how having a mission or focus for our work and building a culture helps to establish commitment, engagement and ownership. In addition, in building this culture, we are concerned with sharing vision and values, planning through involving people, working collaboratively and developing an identity.

Vision and Values

According to Senge (1990, p. 206), 'Shared vision...is a force in people's hearts.' Binding the community together is a sense of purpose and direction, underpinned by a set of values. In the wider Ultralab team, the commitment is to building and researching delightful learning using new technologies. The facilitation community is committed to working in collaborative partnerships within Ultralab and with other organizations and individuals. The notion of empowering users is central to our work and this extends naturally to the members of the facilitation community itself.

Team meetings, both online and face-to-face, are frequently characterised by discussions about what the facilitation community is trying to achieve and the scope and definition of its work. This vision is established through the description of the community's work to others, and the interpretation and negotiation of these principles in its daily work. This is particularly evident in the processes used for planning.

Planning Through Involvement

One of the major and regular themes in the cycle of discussions is the process of planning. The facilitation community's work is both trying to achieve development of school leadership communities and to research that development at the same time. Central to the approach and a key to gaining involvement and commitment is the process of collaborative planning.

Fullan (1991) refers to the 'meaning' of educational change and sees a process of change focused on developing understanding. In this he argues that plans are important but do not necessarily on their own lead to change. Participants need to understand what their changed practice looks like. Wenger (1998) also regards negotiation of meaning as an important part of the development of understanding practice.

Thus planning in our CoP might be described as a process of negotiation and peer review, where intentions are focused and refocused on the key objectives of what is to be achieved, how it is intended to be achieved, and who is going to do what. The process involves using the technology discussed earlier to debate, dialogue, discuss and indeed argue. In this process, clarification and ownership develops. Guidelines developed from our practice are shown in Table 8.

Table 8: Guidelines for Collaborative Planning

- Negotiate clear outcomes
- Negotiate priorities
- Negotiate resources required
- Negotiate review process
- Negotiate tasks that will achieve outcomes
- Negotiate what will count as evidence of achievement
- Negotiate who will be involved in each area
- Negotiate who will do what by when

The Planning Hierarchy

Large complex projects, such as that engaged in by the facilitation community, have different levels of planning. We distinguish two or three distinct levels. These levels have developed over time and inform the working practice of the community. Through understanding and sharing in the development of these levels and interactions, remote community members become closer to its core.

Firstly, there is the level of the whole community and this forms the overall project plan. The detail, however, is found in the plans of various sub-groups, for example groups responsible for maintenance and development of school leadership communities, teams focused on specific medium and long-term tasks and rapid action teams (RATs), who are formed to achieve specific goals in short-time periods.

Peters and Waterman (1986, p. 126) regarded the small group as 'the basic organizational building blocks of excellent organizations' and valued their flexibility, adaptability and ability to focus on a task. In the Ultralab projects, we observe many small groups and teams, and co-ordinating them all is an issue that is at the basis of the approach to planning.

Clearly, co-ordination between plans of the various groups and the overall plan is a central feature of much of the negotiation. This is facilitated by the 'central team' of four Chelmsford-based staff focusing on specific areas, groups and teams, and taking responsibility to co-ordinate these plans with the emerging whole project plan (see Figure 2).

To assist in this process, the community makes use of a range of bespoke and project-specific databases, implemented either in-house using Filemaker Pro

Figure 2: The Planning Hierarchy

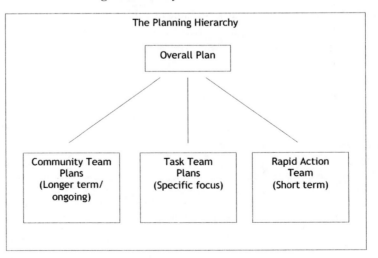

or hosted externally by project partners. These provide all members of the community with collaborative tools, which allow for the sharing and refinement of plans and for the sharing of data.

Collaboration: Research and Writing

Planning actions together, focused upon an agreed mission, leads to collaborative action by the team as a whole, and within sub-groups. The facilitation community has a clearly defined purpose—the development and research of the domain of online learning communities. Focusing this even more, it is engaged in collaborative research and writing, using the asynchronous online environment as a shared journal, archive of data and forum for analysis. A key feature has been the presentation of papers for peer-critical review. This has occurred at face-to-face discussions and in online discussions.

Distributed Leadership

Inclusive and effective leadership is distributed (Miles & Murray, 2001). This is manifested in the community of facilitators by the establishment of numerous working teams and sub-groups. It could be argued that many of these also show signs of being separate CoPs, but that is beyond the scope of this chapter.

These teams and sub-groups have different functions, and they have different leaders. These leaders are coordinated by the central team and are engaged in two-way dialogue to enable this co-ordination. They also feed reports into the weekly meeting process and post them online, inviting the team, the wider facilitation community and Ultralab staff members to comment.

Building a Community and Reducing the Feeling of Isolation: Presence and Identity

Team building and how it fosters a sense of community can be problematic at the best of times and it is, perhaps, more difficult and requires greater attention when distributed. For our community, the particular issues that have arisen are how to minimise the feeling of isolation, how to foster collaborative working and a sense of the integration of the remote and co-located teams. By presence, we mean a sense of audience, feeling of a shared place and development of identity that we take for granted at face-to-face meetings or when we work together in a shared space. As well as work-related tasks, there is also the social maintenance role of this space.

Tuckman's (1965) widely used model for team building, "forming, storming, norming, performing", predicts the stages that a team must pass through as it moves from a loose collection of individuals to a cohesive group. Parker (1990) identifies many features that mesh well with a CoP approach such as the opportunity for "participation", "civilised disagreement" and "open communication". There are however difficulties with seeing a structured 'formal' team as a CoP in that their informal nature creates a tension in defining "clear roles and work assignments" (Parker, 1990), or "challenging objectives which everyone understands and wants to achieve" (Honey, 1994).

By definition, participation in a CoP is voluntary; this may be ideal, but it is not an option for an organization basing its organizational and management process around CoP philosophy. The concept of contracting (Cockman, Evans & Reynolds, 1992) when working as a member of a team sits ill at ease with the notion of voluntary participation in a CoP. The concept of Legitimate Peripheral Participation (Lave & Wenger, 1991); that is, an individual's relationship to the core of a community, whose practice is made accessible by its members, is problematic in a team working towards goals and objectives. The ability to simply withdraw from a conversation or a community and, hence, move away from the core is unhelpful in a workplace situation.

Identity

The use of technologies, working in a remote team and the sharing of domain, practice and community require members of staff to establish an identity as a member of the Community of Practice (Wenger, 1998).

Co-located staff expose their identity in a range of environments including the ad hoc comments about the work in progress, in team discussions and in social interactions. Text-based communication does not always convey a person's full identity and therefore identity can become an 'accident of the environment'. Furthermore, identity is located in tasks and therefore can arise from those tasks that we are closely associated with. For example, a 'training team' can quickly be associated with a particular identity. There is also the identity the CoP member would like to portray.

Care is needed to ensure that the sparseness of the medium (Bradshaw, Chapman & Gee, 2001) does not give a false impression of the meaning and identity of contributors. The remoteness of the team and the tension between these identities require constant checking and reaffirming of purpose and, hence, identity.

Goal Slippage

Constant peer monitoring and review is a central feature of the distributed community. Distribution can mean, however, that goals can be displaced and focus lost quite easily. This is particularly true in the work of establishing online communities. The software used is based upon the principle of empowering users to create spaces and conversations. We have noted that this ease, although a fundamental principle of the work of the facilitators, can lead to the goal of creating beautiful spaces and activities rather than focusing on the more difficult task of working with potential participants to ensure that they contribute to the community. We have termed this online goal slippage.

This slippage is accelerated where teams are working remotely, unless the community continually shares and reviews its goals. This is a key function of the central team and a responsibility of all members of the community. This constant review and negotiation can be a source of friction for those members who favour a more autonomous and pragmatic approach to their day-to-day work.

Clarity of Communications and Developing Group Understanding

The harsh nature of typewritten text in an online environment is well understood, and the oft-quoted maxim of always assuming good intent when reading an email or contribution to an online conversation is good enough advice to be repeated as a mantra at every opportunity. Despite this understanding, the community still suffers periodically from misinterpretation and the subsequent discordance that it brings. On the other hand, tension can be good to help unleash creativity (Wenger, 2002) and if a culture of critical feedback is the norm, then messages can be seen as healthy 'plain talking'.

Moving Forward Together

We have also found that careful thought needs to be given when assessing the time taken for particular conversations and therefore progress towards objectives (Bradshaw, Powell & Terrell, 2002).

Our experiences confirm the observations made by Rheingold (2000) that online communities are particularly suited to generating ideas and exploring positions, but less good at achieving consensus or making joint decisions. The ability of individuals to choose to withdraw from conversations and activities and to hide in the anonymity of online space requires explicit checking of agreements. Silence cannot be taken as assent. This tendency, and its subsequence time consumption is countered by the practice of posting direct messages, making it explicit that feedback is required, rather than more general requests, which assume collaborative teamwork will take place.

CONCLUSION

Developing a remote and distributed team into a CoP is a process that takes time and that is aided by the use of technologies. Even when the members of the team are engaged in a common task, the dislocation caused by not working in a common space must be overcome by continually checking on goals and working practices. Of prime importance are the methods of communication employed to build cohesion and to develop the community's shared understanding of goals, development of knowledge and sense of belonging. Through a combination of synchronous and asynchronous tools, reification of working practice, participation in daily discussions, task teams and distributed leadership, the facilitation team at Ultralab has overcome these challenges. By negotiating meaning in this way, the team shows signs of being a CoP according to Wenger's terms (1998).

REFERENCES

Bradshaw, P., Chapman, C., and Gee, A. (2001). *NPQH interim developments.* http://www.ultralab.net/papers [November 29, 2002]

Bradshaw, P., Powell, S., and Terrell, I. (2002). *Online communities—Vehicles for professional learning?* http://www.ultralab.net/papers [November 29, 2002]

Brown, J. S., and Duguid, P. (1999). *The social life of information.* Boston, MA: Harvard Business School Press.

Cockman, P., Evans, B., and Reynolds, P. (1992). *Client centred consulting.* London: McGraw Hill.

Deal, T., and Kennedy, A. (1983). Culture and school performance. *Educational Leadership, 40* (5), 14-15.

Fullan, M. (1991). *The new meaning of educational change.* London: Cassell.

Handy, C. (1991). *Gods of management,* 3rd Ed. London: Century Business.

Honey, P. (1994). *101 ways to develop your people without really trying! A managers guide to work based learning.* Maidenhead: Peter Honey Publications.

Lave, J., and Wenger, E. (1991). *Situated learning.* Cambridge: Cambridge University Press.

Miles, S., and Murray, E. (2001). *Leadership challenges.* http://www.heidrick.com/publications/pdfs/Leadership_Challenges.pdf [November 29, 2002]

Mintzberg, H., and Westley, F. (1992). Cycles of organization change. *Strategic Management Journal, 13,* 39-59.

Parker, G. (1990). *Team players and teamwork.* San Francisco, CA: Jossey-Bass.

Peters, T., and Waterman, R. (1986). *In search of excellence.* New York: Harper Row.

Rheingold, H. (2000). *The virtual community: Homesteading on the electronic frontier,* revised edition. Boston, MA: MIT Press.

Senge, P. (1990). *The fifth discipline: The art and practice of the learning organization.* London: Century Business.

Tuckman, B. (1965). Developmental sequences in small groups. *Psychological Bulletin, 63*, 384-399.

Wenger, E. (1998). *Communities of Practice. Learning, meaning and identity*. Cambridge: Cambridge University Press.

Chapter XVII

Facilitator Toolkit for Building and Sustaining Virtual Communities of Practice

Lisa Kimball
Group Jazz, USA

Amy Ladd
Group Jazz, USA

ABSTRACT

The boundaries of a Community of Practice (CoP) have changed significantly because of changes in organizations and the nature of the work they do. Organizations have become more distributed across geography and across industries. Relationships between people inside an organization and those previously considered outside (customers, suppliers, managers of collaborating organizations, other stakeholders) are becoming more important. In addition, organizations have discovered the value of collaborative work due to the new emphasis on Knowledge Management— harvesting the learning and the experience of members of the organization so that it is available to the whole organization. This chapter offers a practical toolkit of best practices, tips and examples from the authors' work training leaders to launch and sustain a virtual CoP, including tips for chartering the community, defining roles, and creating the culture that will sustain the community over time.

INTRODUCTION

Virtual Communities of Practice (CoPs) enjoy interactive environments that give their members the chance to engage with other members through a series of tools such as chats, document postings and community discussions at any time from any place. In traditional CoPs, individuals often interact between meetings in one-on-one conversations. In a Virtual CoP, the group can continue to meet as a group in ways unbounded by time or location.

THE CHANGING NATURE OF COMMUNITIES OF PRACTICE

The boundaries of CoPs have changed significantly because of changes in organizations and the nature of the work they do. Organizations have become more distributed across geography and across industries. Relationships between people inside an organization and those previously considered outside (customers, suppliers, managers of collaborating organizations and other stakeholders) are becoming more important. In addition, organizations have discovered the value of collaborative work due to the new emphasis on Knowledge Management (KM)—harvesting the learning and the experience of members of the organization so that it is available to the whole organization. All these changes in organizations have changed how CoPs evolve and how they operate. Communities have changed with regard both to membership and to projects.

As work in organizations becomes more complex and everyone strives to do more with fewer people, it is increasingly difficult to get the time and other

Table 1: Key Changes in Communities of Practice (Adapted from Eunice et al., 1998)

FROM	TO
Fixed membership	Shifting membership
All members drawn from within an organization	Members can include people from outside the organization (clients, collaborators)
The community comes alive during periodic face-to-face meetings	The life of the community is ongoing (as much happens between meetings as during meetings)
Members are co-located organizationally and geographically	Members are distributed organizationally and geographically
Interests of the group are fairly static	Interests of the group change frequently
Leadership is provided by an individual or small group	Leadership is widely distributed and changes over time

resources required to bring CoPs together face-to-face to maintain momentum. Most "virtual CoPs" operate in multiple modes including having face-to-face meetings when possible. The challenge to innovators in the field will be the need to integrate these virtual practices into their current community building strategies as well as to learn how to continually improve virtual group process.

Example

A large teachers' organization was a leader in developing and promoting new standards for teaching maths at all levels. However, due to summer institutes and other training programs reaching only a small number of the tens of thousands of math teachers in the U.S., they knew that getting teachers to adopt the significantly new ways of teaching required would not happen just because the standards were published.

The organization joined with public television in an initiative to produce and distribute a set of videos that showed real teachers in real classrooms using the new ideas. According to Donald Schon (1983), an author in the field, professionals learn best when they have the opportunity to apply knowledge, reflect on their experience and get feedback from peers and mentors. Unfortunately, a teacher's schedule does not provide any time for conversations with peers during the day and they do not have a lot of energy for meetings at the end of the day.

The videos were distributed and the teachers could watch them in their own time. They then had access to an online discussion forum to connect with other teachers and share reactions to the videos, brainstorm classroom applications and share stories of their own instructional design with others.

Having the online space made it possible for teachers to share experiences with each other, about which new approaches were working, which were not working, and how they felt personally and professionally about the changes. For example, a teacher in Illinois could use great ideas that were working in a fifth grade classroom in Texas. As one math supervisor said:

"Simply accessing information about different lesson plans and new techniques would not have been nearly as useful as hearing from a fellow teacher about something that really worked with real kids. That is where the rubber meets the road. That is what makes a teacher willing to try something new."

LAUNCHING AND LEADING A VIRTUAL COMMUNITY OF PRACTICE

There has been a lot of excitement about the potential of online community networks to provide new environments for projects, professional development conferences and other innovative learning activities among groups of people. However, online experiences can be frustrating and disappointing when interaction with others in the group results in information overload, topic drift or conversations that are just not all that valuable. The good news is there are ways of making such long-distance learning work. Facilitation is the key. The fact is that leading a group of individuals in an online community requires all the finesse and skill of facilitating a workshop or classroom experience in person. When online, everything you have ever known about designing and facilitating group process must be carried over to this medium.

Example

For most global corporations, establishing effective avenues for improving collaboration across the enterprise is strategic. Fred S., Director of Learning and Knowledge Management at a major computer company, felt that finding effective ways to share knowledge throughout the organization was key to the company's ability to develop and unify common business unit strategies. The company already had plenty of databases and other tools to access information. What they needed was a better way for people to share experience interactively while being fully aware that they could not afford to bring people together from around the globe. When they convened their community virtually, they didn't just create a space to exchange documents and static reports, they designed and facilitated activities—like storytelling—that allowed new knowledge to emerge from the group process.

TEMPLATE FOR SUCCESS:
15 TIPS FOR A VIRTUAL COMMUNITY
OF PRACTICE LEADER

This section focuses on how the Community Leader can facilitate a successful virtual CoP. We will guide you through tips and templates to launch, lead, and sustain your virtual CoP.

1)   *Create your Community of Practice Charter*

Begin by framing your community. Create your Community Charter (see Figure 1). Why does your community exist? What will members get out of it? What is it about (also, what is it NOT about)? Is the purpose to exchange information? To generate new ideas? To learn and explore? A CoP can have many purposes—and these purposes may evolve and

Who?
What?
When?
Why?

Figure 1: Community of Practice Charter

Community of Practice Charter
Community Name
Short Description (50 words or less)
Themes, sound bites related to our community we could use to convey the meaning to others. 1. 2. 3. 4. 5.

What are some topics that would fit well into our Community of Practice?	What are some things this particular community will NOT be about?

change over time—but it is important to be explicit about what the purpose of the community is at the beginning.

Think ahead by thinking through what some of the indicators of success will be and what the potential obstacles could be for your community members. What factors will make the most difference in the quality of the participants' experience? As a community leader, you need to think about the key messages you want to get to participants about your community and include them in the charter.

2)   *Define Membership and Assign Roles*

Update Membership Directory Monthly

Make it clear who is an eligible member of your community and highlight your participants. Think about how your membership is as it stands today and how it might grow over time. Create a definition that will be adaptable to growth and change in your group. Document membership by creating a directory and select a tool that allows you to build in a Profile Feature or add a linked membership directory. Add individual and group pictures. Ask questions to find out more about the people in your community. Knowing the people in your group well will make a tremendous difference as you try to work together, make decisions and resolve conflicts. Try to find out as much as you can about the people in the group. Send out a Community Member Survey to get started. Consider publishing the results of the survey in the Community Documents area so that each member can learn about his/her colleagues.

Once membership is identified, you can assign roles. Identify roles in the community and assign different members a variety of activities to launch on the site. One of the things you might consider is "rotating the facilitator" so everyone in your community has a chance to show some leadership. Other ideas to draw attention to membership include creating a welcoming ritual or icebreaker that you can offer for newcomers such as a check in section in the cafe where community members can announce that they are here.

3)   *Establish Norms*

> *Check in*
> *Every Day*

How will your members communicate? When is the right time to report on something in the community and when is the right time to use the phone or email? Tell your participants how often you anticipate they should be checking in. Establish norms for response time when new material is posted. Create guidelines for participation and publish them in your community document folders.

Heavy-handed guidelines and rules about behaviour are usually boring. However, it never hurts to be explicit about the kind of atmosphere you are helping to create. What adjectives would you like to see describe your community? Do you hope it will be supportive, deep, amusing, fast moving, reflective, cutting edge, information-intensive, risky, silly, focused, unfocused? What styles and behaviours would help or hinder the atmosphere you want? Thinking about these questions will help you figure out what you could be doing to guide your virtual CoP.

4)   *Frame the Invitation*

Build anticipation for the launch of your community ahead of time with "coming soon" notices. Send a "Welcome Kit" (see Figure 2). Receiving an official welcome kit from the community leader can encourage community members to participate in the group and provide tangible reminders to stay involved.

Figure 2: Welcome Kit Template

Welcome Kit Template
Sample items in a Welcome Kit could include:

- A Note Card Invitation to join the Community
- Printouts of articles on Communities of Practice
- A 3 x 5 Card with the URL to your Community
- Little box of chocolates or candy
- Frame with picture collage of all the group members in it
- Community leader & support contact information
- List of FAQs
- Community rules of engagement

Schedule an activity for the first week so that participants have a purpose for making this a new part of their routine. Hold a "Virtual Party" where everyone meets on the phone to launch the kick-off. Send an email or paper invitation with all the community charter and the access information so community members will have something to keep by their computer to remind them to check the community daily. Document the activities that you launched so newcomers can see that the experience occurred. The goal is to welcome your community members and encourage them to participate and get excited about the opportunity to engage.

5)   *Create the Ambience*

> *Create a "Water Cooler" component to replicate hallway networking*

Your community has its own culture; there are many things that you can do which will give your virtual community its own flavour. Think about ways to use the first posting or documents to set the tone. Think about how you model formatting, the "voice" of postings and messages and how you respond to things written by others. One of the first projects your community can work on could be to come up with an appropriate nametag. You can set a formal, official name that clearly communicates what the community is about, and then create a fun nickname for use within the group. You can take the exercise further by creating a community logo for to use in your group communications. A community mascot or metaphor can help participants identify with their community and help to distinguish this community from others in your organization.

6)   Celebrate the Launch

> *Just because we are a Virtual CoP, doesn't mean we can't still see each other face-to-face!*

Host a kick-off face-to-face event. As excited as we are about the way technology can enable virtual communities, there is no substitute for a face-to-face meetings to kick-off. If time and budget allow for a face-to-face event, one of the best times to take advantage of its benefits is at the beginning when a community is forming. If budget does not allow for face-to-face meeting at this point, try a teleconference, videoconference or some other synchronous event to kick things off. Bring the community together to share the vision and principles and to begin forming effective group work.

Follow up your real time event with an online opening reception forum where participants can spend time getting to know each other before jumping into the work. Try some icebreakers and games. Start the group out with some light-hearted, fun activities to break the ice and allow community members a chance to get to know each other, familiarize themselves with the technology and feel comfortable working as a group.

One example is "Word Association". Type in the word Community and then ask everyone to type the first word that comes to their mind when they see the previous word. Keep it going for a few days and see how many words are evoked! Another fun game is to allow the group to build a story together. This works very well in virtual CoPs. Start the game off with an instruction post explaining that each participant should respond to the last message below and add the next sentence of the story. Participants should feel free to add in a graphic to illustrate their contributions. As a leader, you can help the story along if it gets stuck, or wrap it up when it runs out of energy.

7)   Model Conversation

> *Practice principles of good facilitation*

Think about what types of conversations would be good for members of the community to be having and set the tone in your headings and descriptions. Are there some conversations that would be right for only a sub-set of the community? Participating in a virtual CoP will be new to most of your members and they will feel more comfortable adding to the discussion after someone else has already started. We recommend utilizing "Ringers". Ringers are the people that the Community Leader lines up ahead of time to seed the discussion space with cheerful, inviting, warm responses to model participation for newcomers.

Create separate areas for breakout teams to meet in the community. All questions need to be responded to, but distinguish questions that need to be answered by you from ones that others can answer.

8)   *Create Community Connections*

> **NOTICE**
> *"Friday is the last day to register for the Annual Housing Conference"*

Assign "buddies" and break into subgroups. When the community starts, and when any new members are added, assign each participant one or two colleagues to be their "buddies". Encourage buddies to contact each other via email or by telephone and to introduce themselves. Each participant can make sure that his or her buddy is informed about upcoming events and is able to use all of the necessary tools. During the course of the community lifecycle you can try to break the group up into pairs or small groups to work on pieces of the project together. Relationships between members of your community will be the glue that holds it together and it will be what allows your goals to be met. Spotlight some of the interesting parts of your community. What is going on in the news that would be good to highlight in your community? Scan for conferences, white papers, speaking engagements, social occasions and newsworthy issues to introduce to your community. Make your community a place where your participants know to go to find out what is happening!

9)   *Check in Regularly*

> *Assign a role to someone who has been absent*

How is your community doing? Engage disengaged parts. If some members have been "absent" for a while, send them an email or give them a call to check in. Ask them if the community design is meeting their needs or if they have suggestions for new activities or discussions.

Develop a calendar of milestones, deliverables and activities. Decide upon a schedule for completion of milestones and deliverables. Send that schedule in a calendar format to everyone in the community. You can create an HTML Calendar and link it in your community so that everyone can access it online. Include scheduled events and periodic check-ins, as well as holidays and other significant events that may affect timing. If you have a widely dispersed community, participants may not be aware of scheduling conflicts that are unique to each other.

10)   *Reinforce participation*

> *Send private feedback via email*

There is nothing worse than making your first contribution in a new medium and having it ignored. One of the most effective things you can do as a community leader is to acknowledge people's postings by responding to them or acknowledging the point they made. Some readers feel that they should not write anything unless it has "substance" and you can let them know that adding a post that says, "I'm enjoying what others are saying" or "Thanks for taking the time to share that," is a worthy contribution to the group.

Encourage participants who add good material by sending them private "thank you notes" via e-mail as well as by public acknowledgment in the community space. Alternatively, if you have someone who is writing "too much" or using a format that is difficult to read (all upper case or no spaces between paragraphs), you may want to give them private and constructive feedback (e.g., "I think people would be able to respond to your ideas more if you put spaces between your paragraphs" rather than "Your posts are much too dense!")

11) *Pace your Community*

> *Take a weekly temperature of the pace*

The "rolling present" refers to the phenomenon that what is considered "the present" for a community member will differ depending on whether they sign on four times a day, or once a week, or have not been on for a month. If you have a couple of members who sign on four times a day, they may make it difficulty for the majority of the group to get engaged - it will all be going by too fast. You may need to do some things to slow it down.

Provide cues to participants so they know which items are "hot" and active. You can put this information in an e-mail message or in a posting to the first topic in a discussion board. Sometimes it is useful to have one topic with the current "agenda" so if people read the posts to only that thread, they would get a picture of what is going on in the community this week. Assess the community on a weekly basis because you will see a lot of variation from day to day, week to week. At the end of each week, ask yourself about the pace of the community and the range of material added.

Add Fresh Material. Even if there are many active participants in your community, it is important to keep adding new material to keep the community fresh and keep it "growing" in the qualitative sense (as well as quantitative). Add "Coffee Talks" with weekly topics. Invite Experts to your community for a chat or featured discussion. If something new is about to happen, send an email "hot news" bulletin to the group to give them a heads up!

12) *Keep discussion on track*

> *A solution to topic drift could be to create a new discussion thread*

You may experience topic drift, as a natural outgrowth to conversation (just like happens face-to-face). It is important that you do not make people feel bad for having strayed off topic, but it is also important that you bring the discussion back to your session's objectives. You can do this with a simple note like, "Over the last few responses, we've sort of drifted away from our topic, and I'm wondering if anyone could respond to X" which draws people back to the question.

13) *Summarize the Discussion*

"Now that we have all had a chance to give input, let's move to the decision making phase."

"Weaving" is a term used in online community networking to refer to the process of summarizing and synthesizing multiple response and/or messages in a community space online. This gives participants a chance to "start fresh" or take off in a new direction. The weaving message tells people, "Here is where we've been, here is where we are right now and here is where we might want to go next". It can identify issues/questions where there is agreement or where there are still a lot of questions pending or more information needed. Weaving can help keep the community members from "spinning their wheels in the same groove".

14) *Housekeeping*

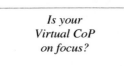

Archive finished Discussions

Delete or archive discussions that are out of date or seem "old" (with the exception of some special items you may want to keep for reference or because they are "jewels"). You can put copies of postings in the documents folder if you think people may want to read them again later. If a discussion thread generates a lot of discussion, summarize and possibly start spin-off threads to manage the flow. If there is a lull in a discussion, it could be time to post a wrap up message and close it. The right amount of time to keep material will differ depending on the nature of the group - the important thing is to think about it.

15) *Evaluate and Make Changes*

*Is your
Virtual CoP
on focus?*

Is your virtual CoP growing as anticipated? Celebrate success by reporting it in your community. Make note of changes that you are making to improve your site. Are you on focus? Are there critical goals that need to be met and are things in place to ensure these goals are met? Include your community membership in assessment and evaluation of the site to ensure their buy-in for success.

SUCCESSFUL VIRTUAL COMMUNITIES OF PRACTICE DO NOT HAPPEN BY CHANCE!

Facilitating a group of individuals who meet virtually in a CoP is not unlike facilitating face-to-face meetings or seminars: fruitful learning experiences do not happen by chance. While virtual communities can take on a life of their own, they benefit from attention to the design of the launch and ongoing facilitation of the community.

Example

A global pharmaceutical company identified high potential managers in different regions as an advisory group for top management. Their periodic face-to-face meetings were interesting and enjoyable but they felt that somehow the group should be able to have a bigger impact. When the group was convened as part of a Virtual CoP, they were struck by the potential value of being connected continuously rather than just for a few hours every few months.

However, perhaps more importantly, they "discovered" one of their members in a new way. Because English was not his first language, he spoke with an accent and a very soft voice. As a result, he had not been a very active participant in face-to-face meetings and people did not have much of a sense of his experience and ideas. Conversely, his online contributions were brilliant and his peers were very excited about the new ideas and insights he brought to the table. One of his colleagues said:

"Now that I have gotten to know him online, I am very motivated to take the time and make the effort to HEAR him in our face-to-face meetings."

Idea Factory

Here are 10 ideas for activities that you can implement in your own Virtual CoP!

1) **Storytelling:** Storytelling is increasingly recognized in business as a way to engage an audience to be able to personally connect to an issue. Using storytelling around a topic of interest easily establishes a personal relationship between the issue and the audience. Enhanced through digital media and shared via the web, these stories become a powerful tool for improving understanding about the issue.

2) **Guest Speakers:** Identify a presenter or expert in the field. Convert their PowerPoint presentation into HTML so participants can click through it at their convenience. Following the presentation, participants can pose questions and responses. The Guest Speaker logs on once or twice a day to engage in the conversation. Online presentations such as this have a start and a finish, typically one week. Alternatives to PowerPoint include digital video, audio recordings for the web and simple text posting by a presenter.

3) **Resource Pool:** Post links to popular websites, conferences, community calendars, white papers, photo galleries of participants—anything relevant to your area that you think participants would benefit from by having easy access.

4) **Bibliography:** Browse Amazon.com by topic keyword search. Many websites that host information in your area already provide bibliographies, so that might be a great place to start! Once you've identified a good book on topic you can send the author an email and see if he/she is interested in leading a "Meet the Author Session". Create a virtual book tour where participants can find out more about the book and meet the person behind the pages.

5) **Question and Answer Interview Sessions:** Think of a topic for a particular week and identify someone with expert knowledge on that issue. Interview them and post the transcript. Similarly, you can identify two or three experts and create a panel discussion where they are in a sense having a discussion with each other. This can be recorded or available as a digital audio link.

6) **Hot Topics Featured:** Link current events and world happenings to your site. Have a Topic of the Week category and invite participants to respond to how these current events are affecting them personally.

7) **Virtual Exhibition Hall:** Do you know of companies, organizations, and vendors that would like to reach your audience? Create a "Virtual Exhibition Hall" of websites to introduce them to participants. Create a web page that overviews them and provides the summary information to participants to give them the "hook" to contact that party for more information.

8) **Schedule a Chat:** Schedule a chat to add an activity to your community! Participants love a chat: it's quick, has a beginning and an end, has a specific topic of interest and provides a way for them to connect with each other in "real time".

9) **Weekly Reminders:** Send weekly updates and summaries to your community members via email. It serves as a summary of what has happened all week to give them a "birds eye view" of all the exciting activities as well as providing them with a trigger to check back into the discussion area or to participate in synchronous events (chats, phone calls, etc.).

10) **Create a Newsletter:** Write a brief newsletter or email announcement that features news and noteworthy aspects from your community. Feature participant profiles, popular discussions or news from a chat that was scheduled. Send it out via regular mail or email to remind people of all the great things happening in your community.

REFERENCES

Eunice, A., Kimball, L., Silber, T., and Weinstein, N. (1998). Maximizing team learning through boundaryless facilitation. In P. Dodd and J. Morris (Eds.), *Pushing the boundaries: Learning organization lessons from the field.* ASTD. Kennedy Press.

Kimball, L. (2001). Managing distance learning: New challenges for faculty. In R. Hazemi and S. Hailes (Eds.), *The digital university: Building a learning community.* UK: Springer.

Kimball, L., and Digenti, D. (2001). *Leading virtual teams that learn: Methods, tips, and techniques for increasing virtual team effectiveness.* Boston: Learning Mastery Press.

Schon, D. (1983). *The reflective practitioner: How professionals think in action.* Basic Books.

Chapter XVIII

The Use of Intranets:

The Missing Link Between Communities of Practice and Networks of Practice?

Emmanuelle Vaast
Long Island University, USA

ABSTRACT

This chapter examines how members of local Communities of Practice (CoPs) have appropriated intranet systems and how their use of these systems has contributed to the emergence of more broadly based Networks of Practice (NoPs). CoPs are groups of interacting agents who share common activities and knowledge. NoPs are composed of people who are geographically separate but who still share work-related practices. This chapter argues that intranet systems provide the means by which members of local CoPs can overcome geographical distance and connect with other CoPs to create NoPs. This argument is based on four case studies that relate how individual CoPs have implemented, managed and used specific intranet sites and how this use has strengthened their local Community of Practice (CoP) as well as fostered links with a wider Network of Practice (NoP).

INTRODUCTION

To deal with worldwide competition, shorter product life cycles and challenging marketing demands, organizations have to learn. When organizations learn, they are able to create new innovative products and processes and to explore new strategic options (Cohen & Levinthal, 1990; Dodgson, 1993; Fiol & Lyles, 1985; Virkkunen & Kuutti, 2000). Communities of Practice (CoPs) emerge as people work closely together, do their job better and improvise in the face of unexpected issues. CoPs are central to organizational learning; as their members share activities, they develop a sense of a common identity and culture (Gherardi & Nicolini, 2000; Liedtka, 1999; Wenger, 1998). Furthermore, geographically separate, local communities whose members have strong links and interact on a daily basis can be linked to each other through the (at least partial) sharing of knowledge and activities. Thus, aggregates of local CoPs may result in wider and more broadly based Networks of Practice (NoPs) (Brown & Duguid, 2000; Brown & Duguid, 2001).

Surprisingly, the ways in which CoPs might connect with each other, and how this might lead to the emergence of a wider Network of Practice (NoP), have not been examined in any depth. This chapter will consider the influence that the growing use of Information and Communication Technologies (ICTs) has on daily work and communications. It will examine how members of local CoPs begin to use intranet systems for their own ends. This process is termed "appropriation". These appropriations are specific ways of dealing with the technology that transform both the technical system and the social group. This chapter shows how appropriated intranet systems transform a local Community of Practice (CoP) and can favour the emergence of a NoP. It draws on evidence from four case studies and relates the process through which CoPs gradually become connected to each other and lead to the appearance of a NoP. In order to be able to trace the appropriation of the new system over time, each case is based on a local community whose members have used a specific intranet site for at least two years.

The rest of the chapter is organized as follows. The next section defines the notions of CoP and NoP and questions how the use of ICTs might relate to CoPs and NoPs. The following section briefly describes the four cases. This is then followed by an analysis of how the members of these communities appropriate their intranet sites in order to strengthen their links and how their use contributes to the creation of a set of relations among local CoPs and to the emergence of an overall NoP. Finally, some recommendations on how to implement and manage an intranet system to encourage local appropriation and the emergence of overall NoPs are made.

INTRANETS AND THE DYNAMICS
OF CoPS AND NoPS

What are Communities of Practice?

Communities of Practice are social groupings whose members have a joint history, interact frequently, share knowledge and experience similar concerns (Chanal, 2000; Lave & Wenger, 1991; Wenger, 1998). They work together and achieve activities that are for some similar, and for others complementary. As they share their daily work activities over time, they tend to develop similar ways of doing things, interpreting events and dealing with unexpected issues. They also develop a strong sense of identity in relation to their occupation, workplace and workgroup. Even though members of a CoP might not spontaneously name their work group a community, they usually strongly acknowledge their membership of their occupational group and value its rules and principles. Wenger (1998) identifies mutual engagement, joint enterprise and a common repository as the three key features of a CoP.

- **Mutual engagement:** People join the CoP through shared practices. Members of a CoP are linked to each other through their mutual engagement in work activities.
- **Joint enterprise:** Members of the community work together in order to achieve a common goal, be it explicit or not, be it officially defined or not. Members of a CoP are engaged in the achievement of a shared outcome.
- **Common repository:** Over time, shared practices, repeated interactions and the construction of a common history and culture in the community provide more or less material traces of the community. Written files constitute one official and explicit aspect of a common repository. More intangible aspects include routines, rituals, and specific idioms.

What are Networks of Practice?

Shared practices form the basis of the Community of Practice. However, some people, perhaps because of geographical distance, may not be directly connected to each other but still engage in similar kinds of activities. People who do not necessarily know each other, but still share practices, belong to a Network of Practice (Brown & Duguid, 2001). Because of geographical distance, members of a NoP cannot interact directly. Nevertheless, they share daily activities and a specific occupational identity. The NoP links local communities whose members have similar duties and give a minimal coherence to the network.

The relationships among members of a NoP are much looser than the ones that characterise CoPs. However, members of the same NoP know what their work consists of and so they can easily exchange information on occupational topics. While maintaining a 'local touch' to their work, they share common knowledge, culture and actions with those who are not part of their immediate community. In addition, they can benefit from others' experiences and find answers to locally unanswered issues by consulting other members of the network.

NoPs can be seen as drawing together different CoPs in order to combine knowledge in new ways through the mutual engagement of its members to achieve some shared goal. They provide access points for individuals to engage with the network and establish a local identity within the larger organization. When viewed in this way, it can be seen that there might be substantial business benefits in the construction—or reinforcement—of NoPs. It can also be argued that Intranets can provide the tools that will establish this link between CoPs and NoPs.

Intranet Systems: The Link Between CoPs and NoPs?

As ICTs make it possible for people to exchange and work with each other across geographical distances, could they constitute a potential link between the CoPs of the same NoP? It has been established that ICTs can support CoPs (Hayes, 2001; Hayes & Walsham, 2001). For example, Wenger (2001) described software packages dedicated to CoPs, while Brown (1998) claims that intranet technology can be integrated in "real and local" work practices. However, surprisingly, the link between CoPs and NoPs through ICTs has not been fully explored.

An intranet, an internal network based on IP standards, brings various computing applications such as e-mail, databases, groupware, forum and occupational software together on a single platform. These applications can then be made available to some or all members of an organization. Thus, intranets mark a distinction between insiders and outsiders of the network (Newell, Scarborough & Swan, 2001). The inherent flexibility of intranet technology means that the intranet can be easily adapted to different contexts and can be used to achieve diverse goals. Consequently, members of local CoPs, as this chapter reports, can easily appropriate them.

FOUR CASE STUDIES
Data Collection and Methods

To examine how members of CoPs appropriate intranet systems, one has to observe real world practices. Four cases were studied, where each case represents a set of local CoPs whose members have been using a dedicated intranet for at least two years. The cases were studied through multiple interviews in which respondents evoked their activities and work environment as well as the challenges they and their colleagues faced on a daily basis. They also spoke of their adoption and use of the intranet system. Additionally, as CoPs are fundamentally social, focus groups were used. The focus groups consisted of approximately five members from different local CoPs who discussed their use of the intranet and any associated changes in their work. Repeated visits to sites also allowed for the establishment of good relations with key-informants and for instructive, informal conversations that proved invaluable for achieving a longitudinal perspective. Finally, the intranet sites associated with the CoPs were browsed.

CASE STUDIES: SETS OF LOCAL CoPS USING DEDICATED INTRANETS

Each of the four cases is briefly described; cross-case analyses form the basis of the next section.

Case A: Public Health Specialists

The public health specialists consisted of about 1,000 to 1,500 employees of the Ministry of Health, dispersed throughout the national territory and grouped in regional services of 15 to 20 people. In 1996-1997, these professionals implemented an intranet site dedicated to their activities. The site included a repository of experiences and accounts provided by specialist experts and members of the diverse regional services. The increasing availability and use of the intranet had an impact on employees' awareness of the existence of a wider "public health community" at both the national and the regional level. Moreover, the use of the intranet contributed to the extension of interpersonal contacts beyond the limited frame of the regional services. It allowed geographically distributed agents to get to know each other and to establish links according to their mutual concerns.

Case B: Insurance Company Salespersons

Like the public health specialists, the 3,500 salaried salespersons of an insurance company were also dispersed throughout the national territory and worked in local teams of about 15 people. Salespersons in any one team share many activities with salespersons in other teams, but traditionally, most felt that they were in competition with other teams from the same geographical area. In 1999, the central headquarters of the company introduced an intranet. The intranet was not widely used at first, both because of limited IT competencies of salespersons and because of the perceived competition among teams. Gradually however, newcomers have come to use the intranet more regularly and have

Table 1: Data Collection Methods for the Four Case Studies

What?	How?	Why?
Interviews	• 15 to 30 interviews for each case • Semi-structured, recorded, transcribed • Maximal diversity of respondents (length of service, localization, jobs)	• Understand the perception and use of intranet and the work group for different employees • Observation of the main uses of the intranet • Description of jobs and work environment
Focus groups	• Three-hour meetings with about five respondents (colleagues from different groups but similar tasks) • Informal discussion + semi-structured meeting guide • Entirely recorded and transcribed	• Get a view of the social dimension of use and of CoP's dynamics • Processes experienced by different groups accounted through discussion among different members
Key informants	• Repeated visits to organizational sites • Privileged relations with specific Members of CoP	• Selection of respondents for interviews and focus groups • Lengthy discussions that put processes in perspective
Browsing of intranet	• Browsing of dedicated intranet on site, most of the time in presence of a CoP member	• Knowledge of structure and content of the site • Understanding of the perception of the intranet by members of CoP

transmitted part of their expertise in browsing the intranet to old-timers. This has favoured socialization and collaboration among employees with differing lengths of service and has encouraged a number of new commercial initiatives.

Case C: Buyers for a Railroad Company

In 1997, buyers of the railroad company (about 2,500 employees working in local teams) implemented an intranet site dedicated to their work. The intranet has now been fully integrated in their daily tasks. Buyers use the site to order supplies and to get information about their shipments. Use of the intranet has reinforced a pre-existing trend towards the greater centralization of procurement. It has also deeply affected work processes and tasks: purchasers' practices have become more transparent to the other departments and they have reinforced the buyers' awareness of being part of a joint enterprise. Finally, shared sections of the intranet, such as the tracking of procurements and shipments, have enhanced the buyers' professional image.

Case D: The Computing Department of a Large Organization

In 1998, the new head of a computing department (consisting of about 400 employees working in a single building) decided to improve an existing intranet site that had previously mainly contained administrative forms. The upgrading of the site coincided with a restructuring of the organization. When the revised intranet site was launched, it reflected the new organization of the department and made it possible for members of different teams to identify their new tasks and to accomplish them more efficiently. The intranet is widely used and has encouraged teamwork and facilitated the implementation of various projects. Use of the intranet has lead to a strengthening of professional identity and its shifting use has reflected the changing relationship between salaried and temporary employees.

FROM CoPS TO NoPS

This section will examine the move from disjoint local CoPs to a coherent wider NoP. Firstly, it will examine local CoPs' appropriation of intranets. When members of a CoP appropriate an intranet, its use appears to strengthen the main features of local communities. However, even if local CoPs are reinforced by the use of intranets, specific sub-groups can become isolated from the core community. This topic will form the second strand of this section. Finally, the emergence of NoPs through the situated use of an intranet will be discussed. The use of the technological network favours the appearance of a new organizational network from the increased relationships among local CoPs. It will be argued that the use of intranets favours the emergence of NoPs.

Local CoPs' Appropriation of Intranets

In all four cases, intranet use has supported the three defining features of CoPs. In the case of the computer professionals (Case D), intranet use has reinforced the mutual engagement of the community of computer specialists. Extensively used, the intranet has provided new links to both old-timers and newcomers and has encouraged social processes among them. Furthermore, specific intranet applications were tightly linked to various aspects of mutual engagement. For example, sophisticated repositories containing pictures, detailed organizational and geographical information, when available, were highly praised as they helped employees to locate distant colleagues, which provided them with a sense of proximity, regardless of physical distance.

The intranet also helped members of CoPs become aware of the existence of the joint enterprise. Until the mid-1990s, the public health specialists' (Case A) sense of shared aims was centred mainly on local services and regional offices. The diffusion of the intranet throughout the regional offices and the accounts of "best practices" held in the national inventory gave a concrete and enduring expression to the national character of this occupational network. The use of the intranet eased the connection of local CoPs to a national network.

Over time, mutual engagement in practices brings about resources that allow shared meanings to be developed. These resources constitute a repertoire-in-progress that can usefully be expressed through an intranet. The intranet gathers in a single "virtual space" the elements of a repertoire that were previously disparate. It can be used to localise experts on a topic of particular interest to CoP members, regardless of geographical distance. For example, before the implementation of the intranet, the public health professionals (Case A) who needed solutions to unusual problems simply took advice from peers they already knew (i.e., that were geographically close to them). With the intranet, they have increasingly relied on the "specific experiences" section of the site, which has allowed them to contact experts on a national basis.

As intranet use gradually penetrates CoPs, it can also contribute to their transformation. For example, it can contribute to the emergence of new practices and lead to the re-negotiation of meaning in a joint enterprise. The railroad company buyers (Case C) illustrate this point. The implementation of the intranet was aimed at reinforcing the centralization of purchases. Thanks to the intranet, it has also become possible for buyers and ordering departments to track and follow up the shipment of an order more precisely. Finally, the intranet has been linked to an extranet that has connected the firm's IS to that of its main suppliers. The intranet and the extranet have also modified the relations between the railroad organization and its main partners. With these new activities, the buyers' community has come to define itself as a service provider for the other departments of the firm and as a powerful group related to external suppliers.

Widening of CoPs and Isolation of Particular Members

In the four cases, intranet use widened the community to which members felt that they belonged. Insurance salespersons (Case B), for example, used to identify themselves with a small team of about fifteen close colleagues working in the same area. With the intranet, they have become more aware of the integration of their team with a wider group whose members may not know each other but who share occupational practices. The intranet has become a showcase for the wider community of geographically dispersed members as well as for other employees throughout the firm. This combination of internal and external images (how people perceive themselves and how they think other people perceive them) has reinforced and enlarged their CoPs. This enlargement makes it possible for a NoP to emerge.

However, the use of intranets also contributes to the exclusion of some of the members of a CoP. The computing department case (Case D) illustrates the intriguing process by which the use of the intranet has reinforced the CoP while also isolating and excluding some of its members. As seen above, the intranet has contributed to the revival of the sense of shared enterprise and to the emergence of new informal cooperative identities after the reorganizing of the department. However, the restructuring also led to changes in occupational roles between temporary and salaried workers. Before the restructuring, temporary workers perceived themselves as full members of the department. Their tasks were similar to salaried workers and their salaried colleagues perceived them to be full members of the department. The reorganization led to a greater differentiation of their activities: salaried employees now deal with strategic design issues while temporary employees are tasked with their implementation.

The intranet eased the coordination between the two kinds of teams, but without direct mutual adjustment. Use of the intranet exacerbated a growing lack of direct communication between salaried and temporary workers. Two distinct directories were implemented: the salaried workers' directory is comprehensive and regularly updated; the temporary employees' directory has never been systematically refreshed. Members of the department—whatever their status—have contested the legitimacy of these two directories. Nevertheless, these distinct sections have forced members of the department to think of their relationship with colleagues in terms of status differential and then to enact the growing isolation of temporary workers.

Emergence of NoPs Through Situated Intranet Use

Use of intranets favours the interweaving of local CoPs and, at a higher level, encourages the emergence of a NoP. However, the emergence of a NoP might be accompanied by tensions.

First, the use of intranet systems encourages an increase in the overlapping of local CoPs. When people use an intranet system, they become more aware that their occupational group is not restricted to the local CoP. Thanks to repositories, the swapping of experiences, forums, and so on, they start to interact electronically with colleagues who do not belong to their local CoP. For example, the railroad buyers (Case C) used to think that they mainly belonged to a regional service isolated from the regional headquarters and distant from other occupational groups. Due to the sharing of experiences in particular, the use of the intranet has made it possible to link all regional services together and to initiate an overall sense of occupational identity. Use of the intranet does not contribute to the overlapping of local CoPs through joint activities, as these communities remain separated and most of their members do not meet directly, but through the greater visibility of shared practices and through increased interaction. Similarly, shared and differentiated knowledge crosses over local communities thanks to the intranet. In the case of the health ministry (Case A), accounts of experiences and best practices have been shared throughout regional services. They indicated which teams had successfully solved any unusual problem, for example, a new and wide pool of infection, and they helped to identify specialised national experts.

Such gradual overlapping of local CoPs gives rise to NoPs. In all three cases in which members of CoPs were dispersed throughout the national territory (cases A, B and C), the intranet has contributed to the emergence and a growing recognition of a NoP. The latter may have always had the potential to exist, but it has only become part of the employees' daily work life thanks to intranet use. A process of change of identity has also accompanied the interleaving of local CoPs and the emergence of the overall NoP. In the case of insurance salespersons (Case B) in particular, the change in work-related identity was striking. Salespersons still felt that they were professional salespersons and hence that their main activities had to do with clients. However, they also developed a sense of belonging to a general network of colleagues with whom it was useful and rewarding to exchange. Besides, identification with the NoP is salient when its members stress that the intranet represents their community in the face of the rest of the organization. The intranet positively contributes to the image members of the NoP think outsiders have of their network. Moreover, identification with the NoP and appropriations of the intranet reinforce each other. Peers use the intranet because they identify with the community. Conversely, using the intranet reinforces their identity and enriches the community. For example, the railroad buyers (Case C) have changed their tasks with the intranet (increased centralization of supplies) and have refreshed their occupational identity (from isolated buyers to a structured national occupation that mediates between functional departments and external suppliers).

Nevertheless, the emergence of a NoP also occasions tensions at different levels, especially among local communities and with the rest of the organization. Among local communities, shared and distributed knowledge and practice do not clear all conflict or competition. Contributions to the intranet oscillate between what one wants to share with a wider audience and what one wants to keep to the more local group. In the case of insurance salespersons (Case B), for example, separated teams used to feel competition with one another as their respective clients' zones could overlap. Because of this local competition, contributions to the site by local salespersons remained scarce during the first eight months of the intranet. However, salespersons balanced a sense of internal competition with the desire to acquire recognition in the whole network and, over time, as a growing number of salespersons published their most successful experiences on the intranet, it became necessary for the others to contribute to the site. Those who had not yet published online tended to be considered as not proficient enough in new technologies or, even worse, as less efficient in their job.

Regarding the rest of the organization, tensions arise from the greater visibility of the NoP in its host organization, which can improve its "legitimacy" and ensure its funding in various resources, and maintain its members' desire to remain among peers. The buyers' case (Case C) illustrates this point. The intranet has favoured the recognition of their occupation in the whole organization by making their business more transparent. However, simultaneously, buyers have implemented sections with passwords. Intranet use gives rise to renewed regulation between what members of the network think they should share with the rest of the organization and what has to remain in the group. This result echoes both Brown and Duguid's (2001, p. 199) assertion that distinct practice constitutes barriers among networks and Van Maanen and Barley's (1984) famous reminder of conflicts between organizational and occupational logic in firms.

Finally, the emergence of the NoP can contribute to the disruption of an established official organizational structure. The NoP emerges beyond, or perhaps in reaction to, the official organization and thus may be a threat it. Even more than CoPs, the NoP, due to its transverse nature, triggers changes in firms and crystallises the disputes that these upheavals can occasion (Wenger, McDermott & Snyder, 2002).

CONCLUSION:
MANAGERIAL CONTRIBUTIONS

The following suggestions about how to implement and manage intranet systems for CoPs and NoPs have been derived from the cases presented in this chapter. In particular, management needs to achieve a delicate and changing balance in three main areas: (1) Initiative vs. Control, (2) Communitarian Principles vs. Competition, and (3) Official vs. Emergent Processes. These three topics form the basis of this last section of the chapter.

Initiative vs. Control: How Much Should be Left to Members of CoPs to Implement and Manage?

Defining the intranet project too tightly and preventing the expression of local initiatives presents obvious drawbacks, as members of CoPs will not appropriate systems that are imposed on them and that they are unable to customise. However, if too much room is left for local initiatives this can lead to the emergence of multiple fragmented intranet sites that do not help with the establishment of links among CoPs. From the case studies, it appears to be useful to alternate phases in the management of the intranet. Initially, light management and relative freedom of use favours the appropriation of the tool. Later, more control encourages expected outcomes at the level of the overall network.

Communitarian Principles vs. Competition: How to Balance Principles with Politics?

The "sense of community" in CoPs and NoPs provides support to their members, but it does not actively favour the searching out of new practices or new knowledge from outside the community and might even inhibit innovation. On the other hand, leaving too much room for competition and for the expression of political struggles impedes the sharing of valuable knowledge throughout the network. It therefore seems important to ensure that a basic level of knowledge, practices and rules are established in order to permit dialogue among local communities, as well as to provide incentives for competition and sharing in the network, notably through different sections of the intranet.

Official vs. Emergent Processes: Should an Intranet be Officially or Informally Managed?

The official management might ignore emergent and improvisational dynamics of change that contribute to the richness of real world practices. However, on the other hand, the lack of official support weakens the legitimacy and visibility of local CoPs or of the overall NoP. 'Coaches' at various levels therefore appear as useful intermediaries. They make it possible to connect CoPs among themselves as well as with the official management of the firm. Finally, intranet systems propose applications that make it possible to simultaneously allow for greater freedom for members of CoPs to appropriate intranets and to establish access rights that preserve CoPs from the rest of the organization.

REFERENCES

Brown, J. S. (1998). Internet technology in support of the concept of "Communities of Practice." *Accounting, Management and Information Technologies, 8*, 227-236.

Brown, J. S., and Duguid, P. (2000). *The social life of information.* Boston, MA: Harvard Business School Press.

Brown, J. S., and Duguid, P. (2001). Knowledge and organization: A social-practice perspective. *Organization Science, 12* (2), 198-213.

Chanal, V. (2000). Communautés de Pratique et management par projet: A propos de l'ouvrage de Wenger (1998): Communities of Practice: Learning, meaning and Iientity. *M@n@gement, 3* (1), 30.

Cohen, M. D., and Levinthal, D. A. (1990). Absorptive capacity: A new perspective on learning and innovation. *Administrative Science Quarterly, 35* (1), 128-152.

Dodgson, M. (1993). Organizational learning: A review of some literatures. *Organization Studies, 14* (3), 375-394.

Fiol, C. M., and Lyles, M. A. (1985). Organizational learning. *Academy of Management Review, 10* (4), 803-813.

Gherardi, S., and Nicolini, D. (2000). The organizational learning of safety in Communities of Practice. *Journal of Management Inquiry, 9* (1), 7-18.

Hayes, N. (2001). Boundless and bounded interactions in the knowledge work process: The role of groupware technologies. *Information and Organization, 11*, 79-101.

Hayes, N., and Walsham, G. (2001). Participation in groupware-mediated Communities of Practice: A socio-political analysis of knowledge working. *Information and Organization, 11*, 263-288.

Lave, J., and Wenger, E. (1991). *Situated learning: Legitimate peripheral participation*. Cambridge University Press.

Liedtka, J. M. (1999). Linking competitive advantage with Communities of Practice. *Journal of Management Inquiry, 8* (1), 5-16.

Newell, S., Scarbrough, H., and Swan, J. (2001). From global Knowledge Management to internal electronic fences: Contradictory outcomes of intranet development. *British Journal of Management, 12* (2), 97-111.

van Maanen, J., and Barley, S. R. (1984). Occupational communities: Culture and control in organizations. *Research in Organizational Behavior, 6*, 287-365.

Virkkunen, J., and Kuutti, K. (2000). Understanding organizational learning by focusing on "activity systems". *Information and Organization, 10* (4), 291-319.

Wenger, E. (1998). *Communities of Practice: Learning, meaning and identity*. Cambridge: Cambridge University Press.

Wenger, E. (2001). *Supporting Communities of Practice: A survey of community-oriented technologies—How to make sense of this emerging market, understand the potential of technology and set up a technology platform*. Version 1.3, March 2001. Available from http://www.ewenger.com/tech/index.htm [July 2003]

Wenger, E., McDermott, R., and Snyder, W. (2002). *Cultivating Communities of Practice*. Harvard Business School Press.

SECTION IV:

MOVING CoPs FORWARD

Chapter XIX

Extending Richness with Reach:
Participation and Knowledge Exchange in Electronic Networks of Practice

Robin Teigland
Stockholm School of Economics, Sweden

Molly McLure Wasko
Florida State University, USA

ABSTRACT

In an effort to replicate Communities of Practice online, organizations are investing in Information Technologies that create intra-organizational electronic networks, or "Electronic Networks of Practice". These networks are designed to enable the creation of electronic "bridging ties" between geographically dispersed organizational members to provide a communication space in which individuals working on similar problems may quickly ask each other for help on task-related problems. This chapter compares the dynamics of knowledge exchange between Electronic Networks of Practice and traditional Communities of Practice. In addition, this chapter examines why people participate and help others in the network, as well as whether participation has an impact on knowledge outcomes and individual performance. In order to investigate these issues, data were collected from a successful electronic network at one of Europe's largest consulting companies. The chapter concludes with a discussion of the results and implications for both managers and researchers interested in the dynamics of electronic knowledge exchange.

INTRODUCTION

Communities of Practice (CoPs) are regarded as essential building blocks of the knowledge economy and are being promoted within organizations as sources of competitive advantage and facilitators of organizational learning. In organizations, CoPs traditionally have emerged through the mutual engagement in work performed by individuals who were either physically co-located or who frequently met each other face-to-face (Orr, 1996; Wenger, 1998). However, due to hyper-competitive conditions in the marketplace and the increasing complexity and diversity of global organizations, knowledge workers engaged in the same practice are increasingly becoming more distributed across an organization's geographical locations. Thus, in an effort to replicate traditional CoPs electronically, management in numerous organizations has invested in computer-mediated communication technologies to facilitate knowledge sharing regardless of time and space constraints. We refer to these emergent virtual communities as electronic networks of practice (ENoPs). We follow Brown and Duguid (2000) in their use of the term "networks of practice", yet we add the term "electronic" to highlight that communication within this network of practice occurs primarily through computer-based communication technologies, such as bulletin boards, listservs, etc.

While traditional, face-to-face CoPs within organizations have received increasing attention, we know much less about the dynamics underlying ENoPs and the electronic knowledge exchange supported by these computer networks. Initial research suggests that participation in these networks provides access to useful sources of technical advice for organizational members (Constant, Sproull & Kiesler, 1996). However, there is ample evidence that simply investing in Information Technologies does not directly enhance knowledge sharing. In fact, researchers estimate that 50-70% of Knowledge Management (KM) projects fail to meet expectations and stated objectives and attribute these failure rates to an over-reliance on Information Technology (Ambrosio, 2000). Thus, a key question for researchers and managers alike is how to turn an empty electronic space into a vital, active forum devoted to knowledge exchange.

In this chapter, the terms electronic networks of practice, networks, and ENoPs are used interchangeably to avoid repetition. The goal of this chapter is to provide guidelines to both researchers and managers interested in studying and supporting ENoPs within and across organizations. In order to do so, we begin by presenting the key characteristics that define an ENoP and compare ENoPs to CoPs. Two questions related to individual participation in an ENoP are then examined: (1) why do people participate and help others? and (2) does participation result in positive knowledge outcomes? Finally, findings from a recent study that investigated the above two questions in a successful ENoP at a global consulting organization are presented and discussed.

ELECTRONIC NETWORKS OF PRACTICE

The concept of a CoP has highlighted the importance of emergent mutual engagement in practice, where mutual engagement typically refers to physical, face-to-face interactions. However, emergent mutual engagement can also occur through text-based communication and discussion fora, such as bulletin boards, listservs and Usenet Newsgroups. Thus, ENoPs are similar to CoPs in that they are a social space where individuals working on similar problems self-organize to help each other and share perspectives about their practice. However, unlike a CoP, in an ENoP mutual engagement occurs through computer-mediated communication, which profoundly affects knowledge exchange in several ways, as discussed below.

First, as mentioned, similar to a CoP, knowledge is exchanged in an ENoP through mutual engagement in practice. Thus, one defining characteristic is that participants in an ENoP interact with one another to help each other solve problems. By posting a message to the network, individuals requiring help with a problem may quickly reach out to other participants who then provide valuable knowledge and insight in response. The network also provides a forum for participants to share stories of personal experiences and to discuss and debate issues relevant to their practice (Wasko & Faraj, 2000). The posting of messages and responses is recorded like a conversation between participants, representing active mutual engagement in problem solving. This characteristic of mutual engagement distinguishes ENoPs from more static forms of electronic knowledge exchange, such as document repositories and other types of databases.

Second, in contrast to a CoP, knowledge in an ENoP is exchanged through asynchronous, text-based computer-mediated communication. In face-to-face interaction, participants perceive a variety of social and visual cues and have access to immediate feedback. However, in electronic communication these cues are filtered out, making it a lean medium of exchange and influencing how knowledge is actually shared between participants (Daft & Lengel, 1986). In addition, the technology creates a weak structural link between like-minded individuals who are physically dispersed, thus eliminating the need for people to know one another personally in order to access knowledge. In an ENoP, the technology supports any number of participants, eliminating constraints due to size. As a result, knowledge seekers are not limited to asking only experts whom they personally know or are able to identify, thus increasing the likelihood of connecting with someone willing and able to help. Additionally, mutual engagement in an ENoP is typically archived and available to all participants in the network. This creates an online repository of questions and answers that can be referred to later by any interested individual, regardless of his or her participation in the original engagement. This contrasts with knowledge exchange in a CoP where access to advice is limited to whom you know, and knowledge is exchanged between seeker and provider without necessarily being made available to other members of the community.

Third, another defining characteristic of an ENoP is that participation is open to anyone with a desire to interact. The electronic links created by Internet and intranet technologies that enable individuals to communicate are practically ubiquitous; thus membership is available to anyone with a connection. In addition, because membership is open, membership is fluid, making it difficult to create and enforce boundaries. This sharply contrasts with the tightly knit relationships between specific members that typify CoP structures. In addition, this characteristic separates an ENoP from a virtual group or team, where members are designated and assigned.

Fourth, participation in an ENoP is voluntary. Individuals choose whether or not they want to participate as well as how often they participate - ranging from simply lurking to becoming an active participant. In addition, individuals have choices about how they participate, deciding whether or not to post questions, replies, or both. Finally, individuals voluntarily determine what they want to contribute, choosing what knowledge they are willing to disclose as well as the length of the messages they contribute, influencing the quality and helpfulness of the knowledge exchanged. This characteristic of discretionary choices regarding voluntary participation and knowledge sharing distinguishes an ENoP from other forms of virtual work, such as virtual teams, where participants are expected to coordinate efforts to deliver a specific outcome.

Finally, participants in an ENoP are typically strangers. Knowledge exchange in an ENoP occurs between people regardless of personal acquaintance, familiarity or location. In addition, because participation is voluntary, knowledge seekers have no control over who responds to their questions. This sharply contrasts with a CoP, where people typically know one another and interact over time, creating expectations of obligation and reciprocity that are enforceable through social sanctions.

We now turn to the two questions we raised above regarding participation in an ENoP: (1) why do people participate and help others in an ENoP? and (2) does participation in an ENoP result in positive knowledge outcomes?

WHY DO PEOPLE PARTICIPATE AND HELP OTHERS IN AN ENoP?

Mutual engagement in an ENoP is open and voluntary and results in the creation of a knowledge repository of archived messages that is available to all individuals regardless of their original participation. Thus, one helpful theoretical lens with which to investigate ENoPs is the theory of collective action and public goods. A public good, for example a public park, is a resource that is created only if a group of individuals or a collective contributes towards its production. However, a public good cannot be withheld from any member of the collective, even if he or she does not participate in the production or maintenance of the good (Olson, 1965; Samuelson, 1954). With public goods, the rational and optimal individual decision is to enjoy the public good without contributing anything to its creation or maintenance and to simply ride free on the efforts of others. However, if everyone were to act rationally and decide not to contribute, then the good would never be created and everyone would be worse off.

ENoPs are a type of collective in which the knowledge exchanged and created is the collective's public good. As discussed above, mutual engagement in an ENoP is open and voluntary. Participation typically results in the creation of a knowledge repository of archived messages that is available to all individuals regardless of their original participation. This begs the question then - why would anyone invest his or her valuable time and effort *helping strangers* in an ENoP if it is in his or her best interest not to do so?

DOES PARTICIPATION IN AN ELECTRONIC NETWORK OF PRACTICE AFFECT KNOWLEDGE OUTCOMES?

Another important issue to investigate is whether ENoPs exhibit the same degree of continuous incremental innovation as CoPs. Previous research has found that individuals participating to a high degree in CoPs were superior performers (Teigland, 2003, 1999). CoPs are generally characterized by rich, face-to-face exchanges through person-to-person interactions. Mutual engagement between individuals in a CoP creates boundaries around the shared practice within which the community's knowledge is embedded. Tacit knowledge is shared relatively easily between individuals within the community, often without ever being made explicit. Furthermore, these tightly knit social structures facilitate the creation of a shared identity through the development of a common language and social capital (such as norms of behaviour, trust, and obligation), resulting in strong social ties between individuals. These characteristics have been argued as essential for the continuous incremental improvements in the community's practice and the reason why CoPs are centres for learning and innovation within organizations (Wenger, 1998; Brown & Duguid, 1991, 1998).

In contrast, as mentioned above, interactions in an ENoP are limited to text-based, asynchronous, computer-mediated communication. As a result, the ability of members to develop a shared identity and common language through narration, collaboration and social construction is hampered. However, ENoPs have a greater reach than CoPs and support the creation of weak electronic "bridging ties" between unlimited numbers of like-minded others from across the globe. Due to the extensive reach of these networks, individuals benefit from ENoPs since they gain access to new information, expertise, and ideas that are often not available locally. As such, these weak tie relationships created in ENoPs potentially increase an individual's access to greater resources and advice than are available in the local community. Thus, one question to ask is whether this extended reach results in positive knowledge outcomes. In other words, are weak electronic links, like their strong tie counterparts, also useful for supporting knowledge sharing and innovation?

EMPIRICAL STUDY AT CAP GEMINI

This study was undertaken in the Nordic operations (Denmark, Finland, Norway, and Sweden) of Cap Gemini and was performed before the merger of Cap Gemini and Ernst & Young Consulting. As a result, the company description considers only the Cap Gemini organization. Cap Gemini is Europe's largest IT services and management consulting company, and within the Nordic region, Cap Gemini has numerous networks designed to enhance the company's Knowledge Management activities. One electronic network was investigated for this study. This ENoP was created by individuals spread across the Nordic countries who were working with applying Microsoft products as part of their task responsibilities with Cap Gemini. In order to communicate with each other, these individuals created the NCN MS Community and developed an electronic network of practice based on listserv technology. This electronic network was nicknamed the L2A2L mailing list, based on the slogan "Learn to Ask to Learn" that was developed to encourage knowledge sharing within this network. Network members primarily used the L2A2L mailing list when they had a question regarding how to perform their tasks at work. Thus, when one person needed help, he or she posted a question to the whole network through the listserv. At the time of data collection, there were 345 members on the mailing list and between five and ten requests for help were posted per day.

Data were collected using a web-based questionnaire that was sent as an email attachment to each of the NCN MS Community mailing list members during January 2000. Of the initial 345 individuals with valid email addresses, we received a total of 83 usable survey responses for a response rate of 24%. On average, these 83 individuals indicated that they had developed personal ties with 2.8 other network members through participation in the listserv. The average age of the respondents was 35.6 years with an average of 4.0 years employed at Cap Gemini and 7.7 years of experience in their competence. The sample was 8% women. Consultation with Cap Gemini's management indicated that the demographic characteristics of the group of respondents were representative of those of the entire NCN MS Community. Specific variables were assessed through survey responses, and participants also provided insights by responding to open-ended questions about their participation.

SURVEY RESULTS

In order to assess why people participate and whether or not participation results in positive knowledge outcomes, we posed four open-ended questions to the participants in the network: (1) why do you participate in the NCN MS Electronic Community? (2) why do you help others with their problems? (3) has your participation in the NCN MS Electronic Community improved your work performance? and (4) how can the NCN MS Electronic Community be improved? The following provides a summary and a discussion of the results.

Why Do You Participate in the NCN MS Electronic Community?

In response to the question "Why do you participate in the NCN MS Electronic Community?", respondents indicated that the ENoP was an excellent means of improving their own level of technical competence. Individuals responded that they learned through their participation by receiving help and information related to their work tasks. Additionally, they felt that participation enabled them to keep current with technical developments as well as to know who was actively working in different areas. One respondent summarized the above in the statement:

"There is so much to know in this field and new applications/methods, etc. are introduced all the time. I never know when I need this new knowledge in my daily work or for a new project. The only thing I know is that I must always learn new things!"

Why Do You Help Others with Their Problems?

There seem to be a variety of reasons why people take time out from solving their own problems to help others in the ENoP. From the answers provided, it appears that a norm of reciprocity developed between the members of the network. In other words, in order to receive help from the network, individuals felt obligated to help others in return. One individual explained:

"It's the way it is! I help them; they help me in return."

In this manner, individuals felt that they ensured that their individual competence level remained competitive, as one respondent wrote:

"Why shouldn't I participate—knowledge devaluates over time. Who likes to sit alone back with yesterday's knowledge?"

In addition, respondents felt that helping others was a part of their job at Cap Gemini. Through their participation, they were able to improve the level of technical competence of the network as a whole and ultimately enhance Cap Gemini's ability to be competitive in the market. One respondent summarized this in the following quotation:

"At the end of the day, we are a knowledge company. My company moves faster the more knowledge can flow freely inside. This knowledge flow will result in happier customers and more business."

Has Your Participation in the NCN MS Electronic Community Improved Your Work Performance?

The third question focused on investigating whether participation in the ENoP had helped improve work performance. Of the 83 respondents, 65% replied that participation in the network had helped them. Two categories of answers were provided. First, participation greatly improved the speed with which participants were able to solve their problems. One individual replied:

"Yes, I get answers to more complicated questions much faster than trying to find the answer by myself."

Second, individuals were able to learn and receive new insights from the network, as one commented:

"Yes. I learn things from every topic. Even when I am not working within the actual topic."

How Can the NCN MS Electronic Community Be Improved?

Finally, participants were asked about how the ENoP could be improved. Suggestions included creating a database of all the postings such that individuals could easily find previously discussed topics as well as a means to educate people on how to use the listserv technology. There also seemed to be a discrepancy in terms of the most effective communication channel for this network. Several individuals indicated that they would prefer a discussion forum to a listserv since they felt that the overall level of emails received daily was too high. We discussed this with the head of the NCN MS Community. However, he felt that one of the reasons that this network did have such a high participation rate was due to the choice of a listserv over a discussion forum. He explained that the listserv led to a higher level of activity since participants automatically received postings in their email inbox, while the use of a forum required that the participant actively enter the discussion forum.

SUMMARY OF SURVEY ITEMS

In addition to the open-ended questions, we also included specific survey items to provide additional quantitative support examining the relationships between participation in the electronic network and knowledge outcomes. Summary statistics and correlations are presented in Table 1. The exact wording of specific items is listed in Appendix 1.

Results indicate that higher levels of participation and tenure in the ENoP are associated with both acquiring knowledge from participation in the network and contributing knowledge to others. In addition, both knowledge acquisition from and knowledge contribution to the network are positively related to individual performance. However, tenure in the ENoP is not associated with higher rates of participation in the ENoP or with individual performance. Finally,

Table 1: Quantitative Results from Survey

	Scale Range	Mean	Std. Dev.	Cronbach Alpha	1	2	3	4	5
1. ENOP Participation Level	1-7	2.3	0.82	n/a					
2. ENOP Tenure	1-50	10.81	11.64	n/a	.06				
3. Knowledge Acquisition	1-7	3.62	1.75	0.95	.52**	.29*			
4. Knowledge Contribution	1-7	2.34	1.57	0.85	.59**	.23*	.52**		
5. Co-located colleagues	0-3.71	2.99	1.05	n/a	.04	.06	.02	.08	
6. Individual Performance	1-7	4.30	1.29	0.82	.41**	.13	.24*	.57**	-.24*

* significant at the $p < .05$ level, two-tailed
* * significant at the $p < .01$ level, two-tailed

respondents were asked about their work-related interactions with co-located colleagues. Results suggest that individuals who rely on their co-located colleagues for help or advice with their work tasks are neither more likely or less likely to participate, acquire knowledge, or contribute knowledge in the ENoP. However, quite interestingly, the survey results indicate that reliance on co-located colleagues is associated with *lower levels* of self-reported individual performance.

DISCUSSION AND IMPLICATIONS

This study indicates that people who participate and help others in the ENoP are not acting irrationally. Rather, they choose to participate in order to gain exposure to critical new ideas and to access help and advice not available locally. In addition, another key dynamic underlying knowledge exchange in this network is a strong norm of reciprocity. Individual participation is sustained by a strong sense of paying back the network by helping others in return. Another key motivation underlying why people participate relates to identification with the Cap Gemini organization, or a strong sense of organizational citizenship. Interestingly, the results suggest that the level of participation in the network is more important for supporting positive knowledge outcomes than the length of time an individual has participated. This implies that newcomers to the network can reap the same benefits of participation as long-standing participants.

Results also indicate that characteristics of the communication technology supporting the network are important. The two major technologies supporting ENoPs are listservs and bulletin board style discussion fora. One advantage to the listserv technology is that it is delivered to participants via e-mail, which people frequently check or are notified automatically when a new message is received. Thus, messages posted to the network are "pushed" to the participants and made visible along with e-mail. However, participants in this ENoP indicate that one disadvantage of this technology is that the messages are not stored in a single repository that can be accessed by newcomers or searched for historical information. Bulletin boards are automatically arranged in discussion threads, making it easier to archive and search prior interactions. However, participants must voluntarily take the time to actually visit and participate in this type of network.

The second research question examined whether the ENoP supports positive knowledge outcomes. Both the quantitative and qualitative results suggest that individual members did improve their individual performance through their network participation. This finding indicates that computer-mediated communication may be sufficient to support the complex interactions necessary for the combination and exchange of knowledge between individuals, thus facilitating their ability to learn. It appears that individuals value accessing new insights and ideas through weak electronic links that transcend their strong tie networks. In addition, there is also evidence to suggest that individuals who participate in ENoPs outperform their colleagues who primarily rely on their co-located colleagues for knowledge and advice.

This finding suggests that knowledge in a tightly knit CoP may be largely redundant, providing little additional information over what an individual may already know, thus impeding the ability to develop new and creative ideas (Granovetter, 1983, 1973). In addition, while CoPs and reliance on face-to face-interactions with co-located colleagues support knowledge exchange, learning and innovation, it has also been suggested that tightly knit CoPs may also lead to the "not invented here" syndrome or the resistance to new ideas not locally developed. Thus, managers concerned with improving knowledge exchange should note that the highly efficient structures that support knowledge integration in a CoP may evolve into core rigidities and competency traps—inappropriate knowledge sets that preserve the status quo and limit new insights (Leonard-Barton, 1992; Leavitt & March, 1988). Our findings suggest that one way to alleviate this concern is to use ENoPs to create electronic bridging links between strong tie communities to enhance the flow of new ideas and innovations.

REFERENCES

Ambrosio, J. (2000). Knowledge Management mistakes. *Computerworld, 34* (27), 44.

Brown, J. S., and Duguid, P. (1991). Organizational learning and Communities of Practice. *Organization Science, 2* (1), 40-57.

Brown, J. S., and Duguid, P. (1998). Organizing knowledge. *California Management Review, 40* (3), 90-111.

Brown, J. S., and Duguid, P. (2000). *The Social Life of Information.* Boston, MA: Harvard Business School Press.

Constant, D., Sproull, L., and Kiesler, S. (1996). The kindness of strangers: The usefulness of electronic weak ties for technical advice. *Organization Science, 7* (2), 119-135.

Daft, R. L., and Lengel, R. H. (1986). Organizational information requirements, media richness and structural design. *Management Science, 32* (5), 355-366.

Granovetter, M. S. (1973). The strength of weak ties. *American Journal of Sociology, 91,* 481-510.

Granovetter, M. (1983). The strength of weak ties: A network theory revisited. *Sociological Theory, 1,* 201-233.

Leonard-Barton, D. (1992). Core capabilities and core rigidities: A paradox in managing new product development. *Strategic Management Journal, 13* (Summer Special Issue), 111-126.

Levitt, B., and March, J. G. (1988). Organizational learning. *Annual Review of Sociology, 14,* 319-340.

Olson, M. (1965). *The Logic of Collective Action*. Cambridge, MA: Harvard University Press.

Orr, J. (1996). *Talking About Machines: An Ethnography of a Modern Job*. Ithaca, NY: ILR Press.

Samuelson, P. A. (1954). The pure theory of public expenditure. *Review of Economics and Statistics*, 36, 387-390.

Teigland, R. (2000). Communities of Practice at an Internet firm: Netovation vs. on-time performance. In E. L. Lesser, M. A. Fontaine, & J. A. Slusher (Eds.), *Knowledge and communities*, (pp. 151-178). Boston, MA: Butterworth-Heineman.

Teigland, R. (2003). *Knowledge Networking: Structure and Performance in Networks of Practice*. Published Ph.D. Dissertation. Stockholm: Institute of International Business, Stockholm School of Economics. Available at: www.teigland.com.

Wasko, M., and Faraj, S. (2000). It is what one does: Why people participate and help others in electronic Communities of Practice. *Journal of Strategic Information Systems*, 9 (2-3), 155-173.

Wenger, E. (1998). *Communities of Practice*. Cambridge, UK: Cambridge University Press.

APPENDIX 1: WORDING OF SURVEY ITEMS
Individual Performance

Please rate the extent of your agreement with each statement using the scale below:

Able to develop creative solutions relative to your colleagues at Cap Gemini	1, strongly disagree, 7, strongly agree
I have a high level of expertise in the technology with which I work	1, strongly disagree, 7, strongly agree
My colleagues at Cap Gemini consider me to be a Guru	1, strongly disagree, 7, strongly agree

ENoP Personal Ties

As a result of participation in the NCN MS electronic community, how many people have you developed personal ties with (i.e., gotten to know well)?

ENoP Participation Rate

How often do you participate in the NCN MS electronic community?

Never, I mostly lurk (reading without posting), 0-5 times per week, 5-10 times per week, 10-20 times per week, More than 20 times per week.

ENoP Tenure

How long have you been a member of the NCN MS electronic community? _____ months

Knowledge Acquisition

From your interaction in the NCN MS electronic community have you:

Acquired knowledge that caused you to develop new insights	1, to a very small extent, 7, to a very great extent
Acquired knowledge that enabled you to perform new tasks	1, strongly disagree, 7, strongly agree

Knowledge Contribution

From your interaction in the NCN MS electronic community have you:

Contributed new knowledge to the NCN MS electronic community	1, to a very small extent, 7, to a very great extent
Contributed knowledge to other NCN MS electronic community members that resulted in their development of new insights	1, strongly disagree, 7, strongly agree

Reliance on Co-Located Colleagues

Co-workers in your location	(1) several times a day, (2) once a day, (3) once every two days, (4) once a week, (5) once every two weeks, (6) once a month, (7) more seldom

Chapter XX

Trusting the Knowledge of Large Online Communities:
Strategies for Leading from Behind

John S. Storck
Boston University School of Management, USA

Lauren E. Storck
Boston University, USA

ABSTRACT

The phrase "leading from behind" is borrowed from group analytic theory, an important branch of group psychology. For some, the phrase may be pejorative: an effective leader is normally in front of group members, not taking a position behind them. However, for large online Communities of Practice, leading from behind and trusting the group is an important strategy. This chapter focuses on how a leader develops the capacity to trust the group. Recognizing that groups of people are powerful and creative organisms that can be trusted is difficult for a leader. For Freud, who thought of groups as unthinking, primitive mobs and for modern managers, who are taught the value of using teams with specific objectives and limited life spans, the idea of unstructured, dispersed collections of people making decisions or taking action is an anathema. Learning to trust the knowledge of a large group takes training, practice and courage. We ground our conclusions in an empirical analysis of the leadership of one large online Community of Practice. Using archives of discussions among community members, we develop leadership principles that support the "leading from behind" approach. We use these data to suggest how managers can lead online communities to form the trusting relationships that are essential for effective knowledge sharing and innovation.

LEADERSHIP AND TRUST IN DISPERSED COMMUNITIES

"The leader ... is perhaps the most important variable determining the prevailing culture and tradition of the group. He must in turn use his ability in the best interest of the group; he is its first servant. He must follow the group ..." (Foulkes, 1975, p. 5).

Much research has dealt with how group members come to trust leaders and other members of a group (Atwater, 1988; Avolio, Kahai & Dodge, 2001; Iacono & Weisband, 1997; Jarvenpaa & Leidner, 1998; Meyerson, Weick & Kramer, 1996). In this chapter, we focus on a relatively unstudied pathway of trust: how the leader of a successful large online professional community develops trust in the group itself. We argue that this focus helps trained leaders harness the power of large dispersed Communities of Practice (CoPs). Our objective is to present a new approach for understanding and applying effective leadership principles to large groups by "leading from behind". If a leader can develop the capacity to trust a group as an entity and trust the group process, we suggest that s/he will be better prepared for the demanding roles required more and more frequently by large, distributed organizations.

The concept of trust is multifaceted, even within the domain of individual behaviors. Different definitions of trust (commonly: A trusts B to do X) refer to levels of confidence, predictability, uncertainty and vulnerability. From an organizational perspective, trust is an important ingredient in the creation of social capital, which is considered by many to be a measure of community development (Bordieu, 1977, 1983; Constant, Sproull & Kiesler, 1996; Putnam, 2000). The relationship between trust and leadership has particular relevance for dispersed communities, yet this relationship has received relatively little attention aside from a more general interest in the concept of trust and its multiple implications for life in the 21st century (Cook, 2001).

Although trust or trustworthiness is often listed as a quality that good leaders exhibit, the concept is far from an easy one to grasp (Bennis, 1989; Dubrin, 2001; Huxham & Vangen, 2000). It is dependent on some form of reliability or constancy and is often discussed in combination with other traits such as honesty, sincerity, vision and virtue.

Figure 1: Leadership and the Development of Trust in Large Groups

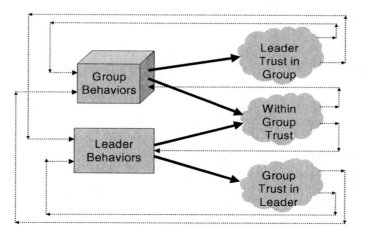

As shown in Figure 1, a group manifests three kinds of trust, all interdependent: (1) trust in the leader by the group—the trustworthiness trait, (2) trust among group members—trust in the group by the group, and (3) trust of the group by the leader. Trust of the group by the leader is (a) having an attitude that the leader's goals will be met by the activities of the group, (b) enacting behaviors that show patience, good judgment on interventions, fairness and predictability, even while challenged by distance and lack of social cues online, and (c) being tolerant of and comfortable with conflicting opinions, new ideas, personal conflict and personal challenges to the leader her/himself. All three kinds of trust are dynamically interrelated with leadership in a large group. Trust enables the creative use of many potential differences among group members (in talents, specific interests, values, goals, communication styles, relationship experience) that is the key to large group innovation and vitality, as well as to the transfer of knowledge and expertise.

Group communication fosters the development of within-group trust. At the same time, the group members' behaviors reinforce the leader's trust in the group. These pathways of trust development depend on members exchanging professional knowledge and social support. Members observe trust developing within the group, which in turn influences group behavior and leader behavior, increasing all three kinds of trust. Leader behaviors act to build trust in her/himself by the group, as well as trust among the group members. As the leader witnesses the development of trust in her/himself and trust among the members, s/he becomes aware of her/his own growing trust in the group process (leader trust in group).

In a perfect world, the different strands of the network of these pathways of trust resonate; reinforcing loyalty to the community and building the sense of identity that is so critical to the development of a CoP. However, community leadership is not typically enacted without anxiety. Leaders often voice three concerns about communities, all indicative of mistrust: (1) communities are too independent of formal organizational structures and can foment rebellion ("let's kill the organization"), (2) freeloaders and slackers can take undeserved benefit or credit from community work, and (3) groupthink potentially biases innovation and knowledge sharing. These concerns are due to insufficient experience in groups with mature and trained leaders and are based on insufficient knowledge about group dynamics, especially the dynamics of large groups.

Very few groups kill an organization or the leader. The group itself is more likely to fall apart than the organization or leader. A highly effective CoP can develop controversial ideas and stimulate creative struggles within any strong organization, yet with knowledgeable leaders, proper time and sufficient re-sources these struggles often result in sharper communications and better solutions. Some of the best organizations in the world are proud to collaborate with former colleagues who become customers or suppliers, extending the reach of the original organization into new regions, both physical and intellectual.

Slacking off is possible, especially in larger dispersed communities. Our leading from behind perspective recognizes that lurkers and listeners are marginal participants who may learn while reading and thinking about group tasks; they participate when the time is comfortable for them (Zhang & Storck, 2001). If a group member slacks off indefinitely, leaders can encourage more participation. Non-participation online should never be the sole reason to purge members. If the group develops and works well with a skilled leader, the slacker will perk up, or remove herself or himself.

The concept of groupthink deals with the unwitting influence of the leader and other high status members of a group to push the group to premature consensus. The notion of leading from behind directly confronts groupthink. The leader diligently protects minority opinion if others do not, as detailed below, and is herself or himself open to new learning. This is not always an easy task, even for a well-trained leader, who, being human, may uncritically enjoy influence and accept praise from the group as a whole.

ANALYSIS OF A LARGE ONLINE COMMUNITY

We view the development of leader trust in the group as particularly problematic for online communities. In order to study this phenomenon, we observed a community of about 400 professionals who have worked together online for over four years. This group—which we call "LG" (Large Group)—

is not a task group, but rather is similar to Communities of Practice in large global organizations that share common professional interests and goals (Storck & Hill, 2000). It is of particular interest because it uses the Internet to bridge many work settings, members are widely distributed and represent different levels of experience and there is significant interaction and activity. At the midpoint of the data collection period, members of LG were dispersed across 29 countries. Their participation in the community helps them become more effective in their work, accomplished across many different organizations. Because of their interests, training and job roles, members of LG tend to be reflective and concerned about personnel issues and human behavior. Their level of experience varies widely (some have international reputations, others are completing professional studies). People join LG to network and learn how to be more effective at their jobs.

Group members develop relationships via the exchange of messages posted to an electronic bulletin board, although some people knew others before LG started or before joining. After LG had been running for about two years, 20 to 30 of the LG members began to meet regularly face-to-face at a major annual international conference of the profession. This informal meeting represents an additional opportunity to develop relationships that were initially formed online. Infrequently, members also exchange e-mail with each other outside of the group.

Using 15,254 messages exchanged by the group during a 45-month period, we read and coded a sample of messages following the general method used by Jarvenpaa and Leidner (1998) and a traditional classification of messages as either instrumental or emotional (McGrath, 1984). A standard, validated instrument was also used—the Trust Scale (Remple, Holmes & Zanna, 1985)— as the basis for operationalizing a behavioral measure of trust based on message content. This measure was augmented with three qualitative analyses of the two longest threads and the leader's e-mails over a 12-month period. Some of the characteristics of the group are shown in Table 1.

Table 1: Composition of LG Membership

Number of people who ever posted during the period analyzed	654
Number of members as of June 2001	372
Number who have ever posted who are still members as of June 2001	237
Number of members as of June 2001 who have never posted	135
Number of people who ever posted who have dropped out	416
Current members who have never posted (lurkers)	36%
Members who have not posted in the past three months (inactive members)	32%
Members who have posted at least once in the past three months (active members)	32%

Figure 2: Message Posting Activity

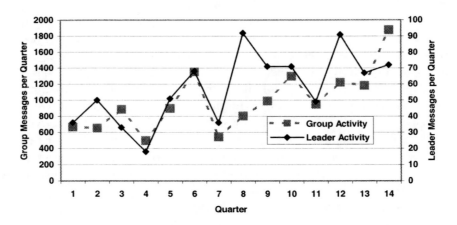

In any quarterly period across all 45 months, between 35 and 45 people typically accounted for 80% of the messages. This subgroup, which changed somewhat as members dropped out and new ones joined, can be considered to be the core membership of LG. On average, if they post more than once, members stay active in the group (based on date of first posting to date of last or most recent posting) for just over one year, with a standard deviation of 13 months. The median length of activity is 7.5 months. In spite of the decline in overall membership, activity during the timeframe of the data, as measured by number of postings per week, increased significantly from roughly 650 to over 1800 messages per quarter (t=3.3; p<.01; see Figure 2).

Using the number of threads and messages dealing with professional issues as a measure of the usefulness of LG for knowledge exchange, it was found that LG is focused on its basic mission: helping people learn more about practices, issues and opportunities in their profession. We found that 61% of the 28 threads with 25 or more messages dealt with professional issues. Also, using a cluster analysis technique to classify 12 randomly selected blocks of messages, it was found that six of the blocks were either dominated by discussion of professional issues or the discussion was balanced between professional issues and what we have identified as relationship development communication. In the remaining blocks, relationship communication dominated the discussion, but in each of these blocks, the discussion also included topics related to professional issues. For many, the essence of a successful community is better communications and relationships. LG is demonstrating a good balance between these two important aspects of group work.

It was also found that there is substantial breadth of participation in any discussion, whether looking at long threads or at random blocks of time (Table 2). The

Table 2: Breadth of Participation

Indicator	10 longest threads	12 random blocks of messages
Average number of messages	60	81
Average number of participants	28	37
Average number of participants per message	0.47	0.46
Percent posted by most active participant	16%	11%
Percent of participants posting more than average	31%	33%

number of different people who participate is roughly equal to half of the number of messages in the thread or the randomly selected block. Also, on average, the most active participant does not dominate the discussion. This broadly based discussion can be viewed as a measure of the success of the group, because it shows willingness on the part of group members to engage with each other.

THE COMMUNITY LEADER

One person has led the community since its inception. He is not a moderator or a censor, nor is he elected by the group or appointed by an outside agency. His leadership role is self-determined and has evolved as the group has matured.

The leader is the most active member of the group, with the number of postings he makes significantly correlated with overall group activity ($r2=.61$, $p<.05$; see Figure 1). On average, he posts a message once every day and a half. However, based on a complete review of his messages, 40% of this activity is administrative or informational in nature. For example, he sometimes relays messages that were inadvertently mailed directly to him, instead of being posted to the group as a whole; he also posts announcements of professional events and provides technical support.

Other major categories of leader behavior also support the knowledge creation and transfer objectives of the group. He makes recommendations, asks specifically for more information and at the same time, is open to objections. For example:

"... here is a wonderful article that I highly recommend ..."

"I did not have time [to do such and such], but you can check this out yourself, in the meantime, on these web pages ..."

"Your excellent e-mail made me think a lot ... about the different ways ... I want to share some of my thoughts with you ... it was not easy for me to get used to ... for those of you ... just try this ... you may be surprised ..."

The leader also considers himself to be a member of the group. In acknowledging his own imperfections, he becomes more human and perhaps more trustworthy. In other examples, he indicates that the discussion will be a learning experience for him as well as others:

"Thanks for pointing out the possibility (that I erred) by ... I agree with you that maybe I was not sensitive enough to the possibility ..."

"An interesting issue came up in ... and ask for your opinion and comments, thoughts and suggestions"

"How do others deal with ...?"

Community members appear to be comfortable dealing with professional issues and relationship development without the leader. We suggest this because of the connection between messages addressed to the leader (in the salutation of the message) and other group behaviors. We interpret messages addressed to the leader as attempts to get the leader involved in the discussion. Regression analysis shows that the group tries to get the leader involved when there is discussion of the values and goals of the group. However, the regression also shows that the leader is less likely to be the target when there are more participants in the discussion (adjusted r^2=.728; F=10.8; p<.01). In other words, the members of LG seem to trust the leader to be observing what is going on (being confident of this because of his regular postings), but involve him less as more people participate. We view this result as not only an indicator of group members trusting each other, but also as an indicator of group trust in the leader.

MEASURES OF LEADER TRUST IN THE COMMUNITY

Leader trust in the community was analysed by considering leader activity in relation to overall posting behavior. Using regression analysis to predict overall leader activity, including administrative and informational messages, it was found that his activity appears to be a result of being addressed in the salutation of the message (p<.001) and to messages related to developing membership (p<.01). However, discussion related to values and goals of the group (p<.01) and to relationship development (p<.05) appear to reduce leader activity (overall regression F=7.4; p<.05). Interestingly, professional issues are not a significant predictor of leader activity. Thus, the leader is willing to leave the community to its discussions of the values and goals of the community itself and of professional issues, the latter being the primary purpose for member participation in the community.

Leader activity for non-administration and non-informational messages is, as one would expect, positively related to the number of days that a block of time covers (longer blocks of time give him more opportunity to post) and to the leader being specifically addressed in the salutation of the message (he answers when message is directed to him). Leader activity is negatively related to the leader's appearing in the body of a message (he seems to wait, feeling that no response is required to an indirect reference to him) and to the number of messages sent by emergent leaders (a statistically weaker result: t=2.2, p<.10). The overall F for this regression analysis is significant (F=6.2, p<.05). Again, this suggests that the leader trusts the community because he tends not to get involved except when addressed by name in the salutation of the message. The timing of the first leader message in the ten longest threads supports these conclusions about leader activity - or, what we are calling "leading from behind". On average, the leader does not enter the discussion until 58% of the thread has occurred. In other words, the leader is "behind" the group for more than half of the time that the community is working together in a thread.

We used the behavioral measure of trust, based on the use of trust words in a message, to identify the factors that predict leader trust. For each of the 15 quarters in the data set (n=500, mean messages per quarter=33.3, s.d.=15.4), we used concordance software to count the number of trust words used by the leader in his messages. This count became the dependent variable—leader trust—in a regression analysis. Leader activity during each quarter, group activity and group trust (calculated in a similar way to leader trust) entered the regression as independent variables. The analysis showed that leader trust is a function of total activity (standardized beta coefficient=.889, t=3.939, p=.003) and leader activity (standardized beta coefficient=-1.292, t=-4.568, p=.001) with an overall regression F=7.831, p=.006. In other words, leader trust increases as community activity increases and as the leader's own activity decreases.

DISCUSSION

"What are the essential functions of a leader of an on-line group? Most of the leader's interventions are administrative - to maintain the list and help smooth it's functioning. In the boundless online environment, this function seems to be the most important characteristic" (Posting from the leader of LG, 2001).

The leader of LG thus describes one aspect of leading from behind. Although he says that the leadership role is largely administrative, we know from the data that he does more than that. He is an active leader in the sense that he posts regularly, yet never active in the sense of dominating or proposing new issues too frequently. He is authoritative and even assertive, yet not authoritarian. He is open in the sense that he shares professional and brief personal information with the community, yet he is cautious to observe boundaries. He is sensitive to human dilemmas and takes the mentor role as well as the leader role, able to offer support to the person who disagrees, thus keeping the community open to new ideas and further discussion.

The personality of the leader we studied, albeit as examined in only one context and in a single case study, illustrates his integrity and openness as well as his consistency, humility and creativity—all aspects of good leaders and, hopefully, all good citizens in any community, commercial or societal. This leader enjoys the community. He can be trusted for advice, guidance, administration and sensitivity to personal situations. He seems emotionally involved in the community and perhaps overidealizes it (this, in our view, will be an issue for the LG's survival or future effectiveness). He has a basic belief in the value of group process. He can be philosophical when required (e.g., when someone leaves the community, he says he has appreciated the fact that they have "travelled" together along "part of the journey"). He is a good leader from behind.

It is also useful to consider what this leader does not do:

- He rarely sets the agenda by starting a thread.
- He rarely crosses boundaries by bringing issues from other groups into LG.
- His postings are not critical and do not interpret anyone's behavior.
- He does not reply to every topic, nor to every person who asks a general question.
- He does not stimulate discussion about the community, although he will enter such a discussion at times.
- He seems to have no plans for the future of the community other than building a global network to learn together.

As indicated in our research model, there are also group behaviors that promote trust of the leader in the community. These include:

- Discussion of values and goals of the community itself
- Long-term membership
- Active newcomers
- Messages from members welcoming newcomers
- Long, intense threads

- The large number of supportive messages responding to messages indicating serious personal crisis (death, illness, job problems)

We emphasize that effective leadership and trust are mutually sustaining. Although trust is inevitably mixed with mistrust, the feedback loops shown in our research model nurture the development of all three kinds of trust. The group trusts the leader; members trust the group; the leader trusts the group; and the cycle repeats and reinforces itself. The important point about our model of leadership and trust is that leadership behavior is part and parcel of important large group dynamics that should not be ignored.

The concept of leading from behind requires that the cycle of trust is kept alive and that it is far from passive. In practice, leading from behind demands much from the leader. It emphasizes that the leader is always a member of the community with an additional role that is unique and demanding. The leader must be there to "contain" many amorphous "human" feelings, thoughts and behaviors that shape the community, over and above its concrete administrative details and strategic goals. Thus, we add another aphorism to the literature on leadership: there is no leader without the group.

CONCLUSION

For some experienced leaders, the notion of leading from behind is one that is both instinctive and sensible. These leaders understand the importance of building trust—within the community and in them as leaders. Some also intuitively understand the value of trusting the community. When these leaders move into the online world, their intuition and experience are challenged.

First and foremost, the counter-intuitive finding that "leading from behind" requires an active leader deserves attention and further study. To be an effective leader of large dispersed communities demands multiple skills, including working with a natural tension between leading from behind and being an active and respected leader. We offer six principles for successful online leadership:

1) Do not set the agenda, other than to be clear about the mission of the community overall. Do state a few clear guidelines about membership and expectations about behavior. Listen and follow the community's communication and issues. In general, do not start discussions and do not post near the beginning of every discussion.

2) Be consistent and participate regularly, not with 'good morning all', but when you have something to say that will inform and contribute. You are a mentor and a leader, a manager and administrator, as well as a servant of the community. If the community has genuine interest for you, you will

frequently have something to say, participating more when activity is higher and participating less when activity is lower.

3) "Walk the talk". Become a member of the community as much as the leader of the community. As a member, you share some of your own mistakes, your questions and your humor, always in service of the community, not to promote your own fame or fortune.

4) At the same time, be authoritative with respect to professional issues.

5) Protect members from scapegoating.

6) Welcome new members and just as importantly, say an appropriate goodbye to departing members who have contributed significantly to the community overall.

Behind these six principles is the overriding need to know what it means for the leader to trust the group. This is more than using skills and experience to be an administrative manager and knowledgeable authority. It means listening and providing input to a community that you respect, enjoy and know you will learn from. It means that trust is more than a two way street—between members and between the leader and each member. Trust is more like a roundabout with the community, including the leader, as the circular trusting and trusted entity in itself (viewing the community cum community). As trust in the leader builds among the community members, the leader also becomes increasingly aware of his/her trust in the group process. Members build trust among themselves and the leadership role is reinforced. Trusting the community also means that the leader has the ability to recognize pieces of mistrust that inevitably surface. With diligent attention to the large group process, the leader can facilitate, repair and renew relationships, as well as support improved knowledge building.

With many organizations espousing increased openness of relationships and seeking new ideas, the need for leaders who can build trusting communities is widely accepted. This will remain a complex task, because "leading from behind" requires continual attention to interpersonal communication, including one's own behavior as leader. The model of leadership and trust derived from this study provides a framework for the development of informed leaders of knowledge-sharing communities in many diverse applications.

REFERENCES

Atwater, L. E. (1988). The relative importance of situational and individual variables in predicting leader behavior: The surprising impact of subordinate trust. *Group and Organizational Studies, 13* (3), 290-311.

Avolio, B. J., Kahai, S., and Dodge, G. E. (2001). E-leadership: Implications for theory, research and practice. *Leadership Quarterly, 11* (4), 615-668.

Bennis, W. (1989). *Why leaders can't lead*. San Francisco, CA: Jossey-Bass Publishers.

Bourdieu, P. (1977). Outline of a theory of practice. Cambridge, UK: Cambridge University Press. Translation by N. Rice, In Studies. In *Social and cultural anthropology*.

Bourdieu, P. (1983). Forms of capital. In J. G. Richardson (Ed.), *Handbook of theory and research for the sociology of education*. (1986). New York: Greenwood Press.

Constant, D., Sproull, L., and Kiesler, S. (1996). The kindness of strangers: The usefulness of electronic weak ties for technical advice. *Organization Science, 7* (2), 119-135.

Cook, K. S. (ed.). (2001). *Trust in society*. New York: Russell Sage Foundation.

Dubrin, A. J. (2001). *Leadership. Research findings, practice and skills*. 3rd edition. Boston, MA: Houghton Mifflin Company.

Foulkes, S. H. (1975). *Group analytic psychotherapy: Methods and principles*. London: Maresfield Library. Reprinted by Karnac Books, 1986.

Huxham, C., and Vangen, S. (2000). Leadership in the shaping and implementation of collaboration agendas: How things happen in a (not quite) joined-up world. *Academy of Management Journal, 43* (6), 1159-1175.

Iacono, S., and Weisband, S. (1997). Developing trust in virtual teams. *Proceedings of the Hawaii International Conference on Systems Sciences*, Hawaii. (CD-ROM).

Jarvenpaa, S. L., and Leidner, D. E. (1998, June). Communication and trust in global virtual teams. *JCMC, 3* (4). On the World Wide Web: www.ascusc.org/jcmc/vol3/issue4/jarvenpaa.html [May 21, 2003]

McGrath, J. E. (1984). *Groups: Interaction and performance*. Englewood Cliffs, NJ: Prentice-Hall.

Meyerson, D., Weic, K. E., and Kramer, R. M. (1996). Swift trust and temporary groups. In R. M. Kramer and T. R. Tyler. *Trust in organizations: Frontiers of theory and research*. Thousand Oaks, CA: Sage Publications.

Putnam, R. D. (2000). *Bowling alone: The collapse and revival of American community*. New York: Simon and Schuster.

Rempel, J. K., Holmes, J. G., and Zanna, M. P. (1985). Trust in close relationships. *Journal of Personality and Social Psychology, 49* (1), 95-112.

Storck, J., and Hill, P. (2000). Knowledge diffusion through strategic communities. *Sloan Management Review*, (41) 2, 63-74.

Zhang, W., and Storck, J. (2001). Peripheral members in on-line communities. In *Proceedings of the Americas Conference on Information Systems*, Boston, 3-5. August 2001.

Chapter XXI

Double Agents:
Visible and Invisible Work in an
Online Community of Practice

Elisabeth Davenport
Napier University, United Kingdom

ABSTRACT

This chapter reflects on work to create computer-supported Communities of Practice among small enterprises in the tourism sector and to establish a knowledge network for destination management. The work was undertaken as part of a project funded by the European Community. The author draws on recent work by Dourish in which he makes a case for an approach to design that takes account of both 'embodiment' and 'embeddedness'. An online knowledge network is embedded in a given domain, but it is also embodied in physical interactors working with machines. Novices who interact in this environment by means of ICTs are thus double agents, working in a domain but also working with artefacts. Where the 'workings' of a device are not fully understood, expectations of what may be achieved in an interaction are likely to be unrealistic; this may affect the reach and richness of a knowledge network.

INTRODUCTION

What do agents or actors in an online Community of Practice (CoP) need to know to participate? The chapter that follows addresses this question by means of a case study that involved a group of novice computer users, loosely affiliated in a small traders association, who took part in an EC funded project over a six month period in 2000-2001. One of the aims of the project was to transform such associations into more substantial learning communities. The case is of interest because it addresses the issue of agency in online communities: the identification and negotiation of aims, tasks, resource allocations, alignments and alliances. In doing this, the case raises questions about what needs to be done at different stages of community activity. The overall aim of the project consortium was to develop learning and support platforms for small firms in the tourism sector and encourage them to aggregate into larger 'virtual enterprises' with stronger competitive presence in the global market. Such an aggregate enterprise might, for example, contribute to regional economic development by managing a group of tourist sites as a consolidated attraction, thus providing a richer (more diverse) and more streamlined (better co-ordinated) experience for visitors. Different learning environments (face-to-face, hybrid, 'pure-play' online) were explored, though all shared a common concept of the workplace as a series of co-ordinated, structured interactions.

The author was a member of a development team in Edinburgh that chose to work with a 'pure play' online scenario, and a prototype set of modules was designed to support and validate learning in this context. The first challenge was to find an appropriate framework to prepare small traders for collaboration in an extended virtual enterprise. The design team shaped the learning platform as an online CoP, a social form that is appropriate to knowledge network activity. Malone and Laubacher (1998), for example, reflecting on what they call the 'e-lance economy', describe a world where the traditional hierarchical corporation has been replaced as the exemplar of organizational work by a new organizational order of networked small organizations, which must be able to rapidly configure resources and tactics in the interests of both change (when required) and consolidation. Others have corroborated this vision in reviews of 'drivers' of the virtual and knowledge economies (Igbaria, 1999; Castells, 2001). In such an environment, expertise may best be acquired and nurtured in CoPs that persist across space and time and are independent of fixed-term teams or projects. Online interaction may strengthen traditional community in different ways. It may make interactions more visible, for example, and thus extend the reach of individual community members (Davenport, Connolly, Spence, Buckner, Whyte & Barr, 1999), or it may sustain interaction when individuals are separated by circumstances or location and provide an archive, or trace of interaction, that contributes to reflective practice (Hara & Kling, 2002).

However, a CoP that is predominately online involves distinctive hazards. Firstly, there is no face-to-face interaction, and participants thus lack one of the 'multiple media' that characterise traditional CoPs. Secondly, an online CoP may be ephemeral and the knowledge created may be lost where innovative local practice is uncoupled from an organization that might use it, unless infrastructure is in place that can sustain what may be learned. Not all online communities are CoPs. As Lutters and Ackerman (1997) point out: 'It is assuredly premature to attribute community to the full range of Net life.' They proffer the term 'collectivity' to describe the 'full range of communities, clubs, groups, gangs, church associations, building societies, skid row hotels and so on that will exist in the Net' (p. 41). Before embarking on the construction of the application in the case study, the design team agreed on a specification for 'community of practice' that is presented below.

Though a number of online platforms are available to support CoPs, the team did not adopt any single one of these. The approach taken was a form of pragmatic bricolage, or building with what was on hand. Construction was thus based on a loose configuration of interaction spaces and resources to support a 'learning template' designed by the overall project consortium. Considerable attention was paid to 'usability' by providing participants with clear instructions to undertake a set of exemplary tasks, with clear and simple screen displays to support navigation across resources. Design and validation were based on standard prescriptions (e.g., Nielsen, 1999). These have been traditionally targeted at understanding individual cognition at the level of the tool, not at understanding agency at the level of co-operative interaction. The importance of this distinction was made clear in the validation of the first prototype. Learners in the project (the participants from SMEs) were novices in terms of collaborative social interaction. They were also novices in terms of cooperative online work. The criteria that shaped the first prototype emphasised simple presentation and navigation, and minimal functionality. In attempting to follow these, the design team made assumptions about what should be made visible, and what should be invisible. These were misplaced.

THE CASE STUDY BACKGROUND

The case, then, involved a development team and a number of learners in the shape of small traders from an Edinburgh neighbourhood with a distinctive historical and geographical profile. The project group (learners and developers) thus faced a number of challenges:

1)   How to convert a loosely affiliated association of traders into a Community of Practice?

2)   How to support this transformation with technology?
3)   How to sustain the emerging configuration?

The CoP proved to be a pragmatic unit for research and development, as it allowed the team to work with an entity whose role in organizational learning has been extensively researched. Brown and Duguid, for example, (1993, p. 187) observe, 'The community of practice, as we understand it, denotes the level of the social world at which a particular practice is common and co-ordinated, at which generic understandings are created and shared, and negotiation is conducted. This is the locus at which it is possible to explore the social and physical context in which artefacts are used, to understand the roles objects play internally and across boundaries.' The project was funded under a track that focused on learning and SMEs, and involved an international and interdisciplinary consortium. The group agreed early on to work with a common learning template consisting of five phases that led participants through a series of group activities of increasing complexity. Each phase provided experience of documentary and interaction genres. The genre portfolio was diverse and was, as the text above explains, a bricolage: it embraced standard office applications (the staples of the world of small business) and freeware (Yahoo!groups) but could be hospitable to genres that might emerge as participants worked on common problems. The templates were intended to help participants learn what and when moves must be made and how to read the moves of others in what may be seen as a form of organizational 'ethology'.

To address the challenge of transforming a loosely affiliated group to a working CoP, the team exploited a framework developed by the author and one of her colleagues (Davenport & Hall, 2001). The framework attempts to identify critical or characteristic components that distinguish CoPs from other types of 'community', an over-used and unspecific term. It draws on a body of work in the last two decades that considers the role of CoPs in knowledge creation. One strand of this is concerned with apprenticeship, or situated learning (Lave & Wenger, 1991), which schools members of a community in how to comport themselves. A second pertinent set of studies discusses micro-level innovations in practice, or situated action (Suchman, 1987) and shows how solutions to local problems are found and appropriated in communities. A further strand is concerned with distributed cognition (Hutchins, 1991) or the collective accomplishment of tasks in groups mediated by artefacts. These elements were combined with work by Star and Ruhleder (1994) that demonstrates that infrastructure for CoPs is a complex technology, shaped in different ways by social interaction. Each of these is labelled as an element in the framework which may be used to explore the following proposition: CoPs, supported by appropriate 'social infrastructure' (SI), are sites for three types of learning: situated learning (SL), situated action (SA) and distributed cognition (DC).

The CoP template was mapped on to the learning shell in the case study in the following way. Phase one of each unit established an 'SL' environment, by capturing the expectations and motivations of participants, and introducing them to the 'ways' of the unit: the tools, processes and the etiquette that shape the online learning space. Participants were required to use narratives of their own experience ('SA') as a starting point in answering the questions. The role of the 'broker' or tutor ('SI') was carefully constructed. Tutors are responsible for managing distributed cognition ('DC') by synthesizing, shaping, and archiving the insights that emerge as learners work first in pairs, then in larger groups that provide suggestions and insights on the problem areas using appropriate artefacts (such as discussion lists and news groups). At each stage, the output from groups was to be archived for 'social learning' ('SL') purposes.

Trust is a critical factor here, as there can be little social learning where sources are not recognized as credible or legitimate. It is important to know who you are working with at any stage of the 'learning process'. The design team were aware of the importance of a sense of presence in online communities (Erickson, Smith, Kellogg, Laff & Richards, 1999), and, within the resource constraints of the project, attempted to provide components of the learning platform that gave at least simple indications of who was online with any individual (when groups are working in synchronous mode) or who had been online (in asynchronous mode). In addition to contributing to a sense of solidarity among learners, such features are invaluable tracking aids for tutors (Hardless & Nulden, 1999).

THE PILOT STUDY AND ITS FINDINGS

Three modules of the learning platform were tested in May 2001 with a small cohort of ten novice distance learners, either involved in the local trader association or intending to start up in business in the near future. The initial findings revealed problems in three areas:

1) The strangeness of the online medium as a co-operative workspace for those who have no prior experience.
2) The significance of the migration from working in pairs to working as a group in a pure play online medium.
3) The characterization of the tutor or broker.

A CoP depends on common perception of cause and effect and on the observation of norms of reciprocity as work is undertaken. Neither of these conditions was easy to achieve in the learners who were the project target group. Though the design team had experience of constructing effective platforms for individual online learning, and of constructing real-time group exercises, the platform as initially designed was perceived as intractable. It inhibited rather than supported learners' understanding of social practice. They were perplexed by a number of incidents and actions. These ranged from unexpected screen loss in response to a keystroke, to fear of submitting a photograph for scanning, as they did not know 'where it might end up being used'. The learners, as was explained above, were relatively inexperienced (many of them were comparative novices to Internet-based work, and one of them was a total computing naïf). They were in no position to work with the off-the-peg systems that had been combined to form the platform (such as Microsoft Office and Yahoo!Groups), though the designers had selected these on the assumption that they would be perceived as 'user-friendly'.

Problems arising from user naiveté were compounded by local system incompatibilities, and much of the early part of the project involved 'repair' (social and technical) work by designers and tutors. These remedial activities were, in effect, attempts to make the internal activities of the system more visible to users. In reflecting on what to repair, the development team initially decided that too much emphasis had been given to 'domain practice' at the expense of 'technology interaction'. Intensive one-to-one evaluation and help sessions were arranged to explain what happens behind the screen when different moves are made, and where information is held and processed across an assembly of local and remote servers. Some learners, however, still failed to become competent in any but the most basic functions. Simple 'computer' or 'information' literacy was thus not the issue. We noted that the more serious difficulties for these learners arose when they were asked to work across groups with multiple modalities.

Working at a distance in pairs did not appear to be a problem for the learners. Even total novices can quickly grasp the basic elements of an e-mail interface, as the concept of sending and receiving mail is familiar. Many learners ran into difficulties, however, when asked to work across an extended group with a broader range of interactive genres (discussion list, archive, dialogue box). A complex set of problems emerged. Some of these were functional, such as the intricacies of posting to discussion lists or how to exploit back-channels (a phenomenon that has been observed in learning communities in other contexts). Others were less tangible: concerns over privacy, discomfort due to uncertainty about what could be seen by what kinds of others and what could not, fear of what might happen in a space whose architecture and limits were unknown. At this stage, we shifted our focus away from the three 'learning' modes (SA, SL, DC) to the social infrastructure (SI) that supports the formation of CoPs, specifically to understanding online interactions and their consequences.

MAKING INFRASTRUCTURE VISIBLE

In face-to-face CoPs, (described in classic studies of physical actors such as midwives, butchers or apprentice steelworkers) understanding of collective interaction is gained by observation. Where members of groups are dispersed (across a site or where they are members of different work shifts), representation of collective interaction may be a critical issue. It is critical where transdomain understanding is at stake (the case of the small traders in this study). Representation may be formal: a relational schema, for example, that models individual and group knowledge may be an important bridge within and across local knowledge regimes. Such schemas are often described as 'boundary objects' (Star & Griesemer, 1989). This class of objects provides common ground for different social actors to work together that includes artefacts, texts, prescriptions, classification systems, and indexes. Understanding of collective interaction may also be conveyed by means of 'soft' representations (narratives, accounts of practice) that are conveyed by individuals (such as gatekeepers and brokers) who are part of boundary infrastructures. This role within corporate CoPs is treated in-depth by Wenger (1998, pp. 235-236), who classifies brokers into three types: 'boundary spanners', 'roamers' and 'outposts'.

Though the project started with a strong focus on the 'learner', the consortium quickly recognized that the tutor role needed equal attention, as the profile that is required is very different from the IT 'trainers' that have characterized investment in interactive training to date. In writing a specification for the tutor role, the team adapted work by Tsoukas (1996) on managerial discourse. A good manager helps those 'lower down' to find more and more ways of getting connected and inter-relating the knowledge that each one has (Tsoukas, 1996, p. 22). In our proposed revision of the learning platform, the tutor/broker, by analogy, takes learners through a process of 'interaction literacy' with explanations of inputs and outputs and pathways that mirror the social learning process as individuals progress from interacting with a tutor, to working as pairs, to participating in group problem solving. At each stage, the tutor encourages learners to expand their experience (by showing individuals, pairs and groups what lies beyond their current understanding), and to make their thoughts visible on the public discussion spaces available in the course platform.

DOUBLE AGENT LEARNING

The findings of this case study of online learners from SMEs are comparable with those of other studies by the Edinburgh group of novice ICT users, notably in the area of the design of online consultation platforms to support e-democracy (Whyte & Macintosh, 2001). These suggest that interaction literacy should be addressed by educators of both users and HCI designers. The concept of exploring the 'black box', invoked in many HCI discussions, may be of help here. By attempting to 'black box', or hide the deep details of technology, the team committed an error that Dourish (2001) suggests is committed by many professional suppliers of infrastructure who ignore the need for sense-making and provide 'one step solutions' that confuse local practitioners. Dourish makes the case for 'reflective' computing, or interfaces that 'account' for the systems that support them. This complements 'reflective practice', and fully fledged members of such communities may be seen as 'double agents', at ease in both online and domain worlds and confident of causes and effects in both. To attain this level of competence, interactive users will require both educational and infrastructural support. The latter involves designers who need to be trained to see their clients in a different way. Rather than patronizing users by 'hiding' detail that might act as a scaffold, they can work with them on extensible infrastructure that takes a user to whatever level he or she requires. Such an approach would entail a different pedagogy, premised on complexity rather than simplicity, which builds on direct observation to transmit an understanding of consequences. Fleming, for example, states that situated learning draws on the 'ordinary, everyday, finely detailed methodic practices of participants to an activity in specific settings' (Fleming, 1994, p. 525). Learning, in this context, means being able to participate appropriately in the settings ... 'where the subject or discipline is being done' (op cit, p. 526). Fleming suggests that situated learning can be engineered by de-constructing the process into a number of analytic steps. The first is to identify how sequences of activities are assembled and constructed in the specific settings in which they are used ('structural anatomy'). Then try to understand how methodic practices are used on a given occasion ('functional' anatomy). Follow this with an exploration of the 'machinery' that supports these activities and practices, by asking how descriptions, facts and processes work together to produce what participants in the learning dialogue recognise as an explanation of the phenomenon in question.

Comparable issues have been discussed by a number of analysts of societal computing and computer ethics in recent years (Johnson & Nissenbaum, 1995; Lessig, 1999; Castells, 2001) who have expressed concern that users, or consumers or citizens have little or no access to the pathways and 'internal' interfaces that shape the transformations and transitions of personal data in human computer interactions. The problem is both structural and political. Transparency is difficult to achieve in this complex situation (what Nissenbaum calls the 'many hands' problem), but it may also not be in the interests of providers of services and applications to reveal how valuable in terms of property rights personal and interpersonal data are. This tendency to opacity may be an intrinsic feature of interaction in the network society. 'Double agent learning' with a focus on visible infrastructure may counteract such a trend.

LESSONS LEARNED

The design team has thus learned a number of lessons from the case study project that have more general implications for design and literacy in CoPs. The first finding is that there is a need for hybrid moderators or tutors who can solve problems that require expertise in both technical interaction and domain interaction. The second finding relates to emphasis in design. In attempting to design a learning platform that was innovative in its focus on social learning, and that would thus compensate for the narrow individualistic approach of much existing 'ICT' training, the team over-emphasized the more abstract context of the learning domain ('embedding'), and neglected the ('embodied') context at hand - the computer mediated workspace. A third finding involves the nature of the interaction problems experienced by learners. These were not merely ergonomic. When learners express concern that they do not understand the consequences of a 'physical' move (such as key-strokes or scanning an image), they are addressing a set of complicated issues about transparency, accountability, privacy and control.

We concluded that participants in online communities are double agents who operate in and need to understand both domain and infrastructure. In attempting to simplify an environment for online learners, we, like many designers, attempted to hide many aspects of infrastructure. However, complex infrastructure (like that of the case study) is not best managed by this tactic, as Mynatt, Adler, Ito and O'Day (1997) suggest. Design for online communities, a space where the social and the technical are coupled, is intricate. Even within a focused and small group, differences will arise over issues like privacy or connection management (Dourish, 1997). In addition to supporting the domain work of socialisation and co-operation to realise goals, online learning platforms need to support understanding of technology configuration and its effects. It is clear that technological trust (Baier, 1986) or trust in the system that supports interaction at any level (participating in community, undertaking a task) is a key factor, and that an overly parsimonious approach to usability that hides what should be visible will undermine participation.

ACKNOWLEDGMENTS

Net Quality was funded by DGXXIII of the EC (DGXXIII 98006361/IT-9). This chapter presents the views of the author, not the overall consortium.

REFERENCES

Baier, A. (1986). Trust and antitrust. *Ethics, 96*, 231-260.
Brown, J., and Duguid, P. (1993). Rethinking the border in design: An exploration of central and peripheral relations in practice. In S. Yelavich (Ed.), *The*

edge of the millennium: An international critique of architecture, urban planning, product and communication design, (pp. 174-189). New York: Whitney Library of Design.

Castells, M. (2001). *The Internet galaxy.* Oxford: Oxford University Press.

Davenport, E., and Hall, H. (2001). New knowledge and micro-level online organization: 'Communities of Practice' as a development framework. *Proceedings of HICSS-34.* Los Alamitos: IEEE (CD ROM).

Davenport, E., Connolly, R., Spence, R., Buckner, K., Whyte, A., and Barr, K. (1999). Making interactions visible: Tools for social browsing. In *CHI 99 Extended Abstracts.* New York: ACM, 35-36.

Dourish, P. (1997). Different strokes for different folks: Privacy norms in three media spaces. *SIGGROUP Bulletin, 18* (1), 36-38.

Dourish, P. (2001). *Where the action is: The foundations of embodied interaction.* Cambridge, MA: MIT Press.

Erickson, T., Smith, D., Kellogg, W., Laff, M., and Richards, J. (1999). Socially translucent systems: Social proxies, persistent conversation and the design of 'babble'. In M. G. Williams, M. W. Altown., K. Ehrlich and W. Newman (Eds.), *Proceedings of CHI99: The CHI is the limit; Human factors in computing systems,* (pp. 72-79). New York: ACM.

Fleming, W. G. (1994). Methodography: The study of student learning as situated action. In G. Gibbs (Ed.), *Learning approaches evaluation and strategy: Improving student learning through assessment and evaluation,* (pp. 525-544). Oxford: Oxford Brookes University.

Hara, N., and Kling, R. (2002). Communities of Practice with and without Information Technology. In E. Toms (Ed.), *ASIST 2002. Proceedings of the 65th ASIST Annual Meeting.* Vol. 39, (pp. 338-349). Medford, NJ: Information Today.

Hardless, C., and Nulden, U. (1999). Visualizing learning activities to support tutors. In *Proceedings of CHI 99, Extended abstracts* (pp. 312-131). New York: ACM.

Hutchins, E. (1991). The social organization of distributed cognition. In L. R. Resnick, J. Levine and S. D. Teasley (Eds.), (pp. 284-307). *Perspectives on socially shared cognition.* Washington, DC: American Psychological Association.

Igbaria, M. (1999). The driving forces in the virtual society. *Communications of the ACM, 42* (12), 64-69.

Johnson, D. G., and Nissenbaum, H. (1995). *Computers, ethics and human values.* Upper Saddle River, NJ: Prentice-Hall.

Lave, J., and Wenger, E. (1991). *Situated learning: Legitimate peripheral participation.* Cambridge: Cambridge University Press.

Lessig, L. (1999). *Code and other laws of cyberspace.* New York: Basic Books.

Lutters, W., and Ackerman, M. (1997). A collectivity in electronic social space. *SIGGROUP Bulletin*, *18* (1), 41-43.

Malone, T., and Laubacher, R. J. (1998). The dawn of the e-lance economy. *Harvard Business Review*, September - October, 145-152.

Mynatt, E. D., Adler, A., Ito, M., and O'Day, V. (1997). Design for network communities. In *Proceedings of CHI 97*, (pp. 210-217).New York: ACM.

Nielsen, J. (1999). *Designing web usability: The practice of simplicity*. New Rider Publishing.

Star, S. L., and Griesemer, J. R. (1989). 'Institutional ecology,' translations' and boundary objects: Amateurs and professionals in Berkeley's Museum of Vertebrate Zoology, 1907-1939. *Social Studies of Science*, *19*, 387-420.

Star, S. L., and Ruhlehder, K. (1994). Steps towards an ecology of infrastructure: Complex problems in design and access for large-scale collaborative systems. In R. Furuta and C. Neuwirth (Eds.), *CSCW '94: Proceedings of the Conference on Computer-Supported Cooperative Work*, (pp. 253-264). 1994 October 22-26.Chapel Hill, NC. New York: ACM.

Suchman, L. (1987). *Plans and situated actions: The problem of human-machine communication*. Cambridge: Cambridge University Press.

Tsoukas, H. (1996). The firm as a distributed knowledge system: A constructionist approach. *Strategic Management Journal,* (17), 11-25.

Wenger, E. (1998). *Communities of Practice: Learning, meaning and identity*. New York: Cambridge University Press.

Whyte, A., and Macintosh, A. (2001). Transparency and teledemocracy: Issues from an E-consultation. *Journal of Information Science*, *27* (4), 187-198.

Chapter XXII

Cultivating a Public Sector Knowledge Management Community of Practice

Shawn Callahan
IBM Cynefin Centre for Organizational Complexity, Australia

ABSTRACT

ActKM is a Community of Practice for people interested in public sector Knowledge Management. Having begun in 1998, the community now numbers more than 550 members and is nurtured and maintained predominantly, but not exclusively, online. Utilising the Cynefin sense-making framework (Snowden, 2002a), this chapter analyses the ActKM community and provides a practical account of its history, purpose, guiding principles, goals, characteristics and dynamics. The chapter concludes with a summary of the lessons learned from the ActKM experience that others might find useful in cultivating a vibrant Community of Practice of this type.

INTRODUCTION

In 1998, a handful of people interested in the topic of public sector Knowledge Management (KM) met to discuss how they might learn from one another. By 2003, this group had grown to become a community of more than 550 people. On a daily basis, members of this community participate in an online discussion forum, with some members meeting face-to-face on the first Tuesday of each month in Canberra, Australia. Now called ActKM (pronounced 'act KM'), this Community of Practice (CoP) continues to thrive and enhance its members.

This chapter describes the factors that have led to the success of ActKM. To ensure that a variety of perspectives is considered, the characteristics and dynamics of ActKM are examined in terms of Snowden's (2002a) Cynefin sense-making framework. The chapter: (i) provides a brief history and account of the purpose of ActKM, (ii) describes its characteristics and dynamics and (iii) concludes with generalised lessons learned from the ActKM experience that others might find useful in cultivating a medium-sized (primarily online) CoP.

HISTORY AND PURPOSE

The idea of developing ActKM arose in response to the burgeoning KM literature, including numerous case studies, that focused entirely on private sector companies. At this time, research rarely addressed the question of how public sector organizations were dealing with KM. Indeed, the literature of the time seemed to assume that the experiences, problems and solutions of the private sector could be directly transposed to the public sector.

Some practitioners in the field, including the present author, were sceptical that this was the case. In search of expertise from the public sector, a meeting was held with Kate Muir of Centrelink (Australia's social security agency) in late 1998. The idea was to build a CoP focused on KM in the public sector. Kate was the perfect person to act as co-founder of such a community. She was a senior and respected manager in the Australian public service and was a prominent and effective proponent of KM. Indeed, she was one of the few people in the Australian public service to include the term 'Knowledge Management' in her title. Kate's background and expertise complemented the interests and background of the author, a KM consultant with IBM who has spent most of his career consulting with public sector agencies.

In the summer of 1999, the first meeting of the Australian Capital Territory (ACT) Knowledge Management Forum was convened (this name later being changed, in 2001, to 'ActKM' to remove the reference to a single geographical location). In attendance were eight people from the following public sector agencies: Australian Federal Police, ACTEW (a local government utility), Department of Health, Department of Finance and Administration, Department of Immigration and Centrelink. The first two decisions of the group were that meetings would be rotated among the members' various organizations and that it would be useful to establish an online discussion forum. Through word of mouth, ActKM grew to 60 members by December 1999.

GOALS AND GUIDING PRINCIPLES

After about a year of informal monthly discussions, during which time a better understanding evolved of what ActKM wanted to achieve, a simple goal and a set of guiding principles emerged. The goal and principles are included in ActKM's Frequently Asked Questions (FAQs) document and are posted to every new member.

The purpose and goal of ActKM is:

- ActKM is a learning community dedicated to building knowledge about public sector Knowledge Management. Our ultimate aim is to be a key source of knowledge regarding public sector Knowledge Management.

In pursuit of this purpose and goal, the members of ActKM support the following guiding principles:

- **Primacy of Knowledge:** Knowledge is the essential resource that an organization must harness to achieve its objectives.
- **Drive to Learn:** People are born with an innate, lifelong desire and ability to learn, which should be enhanced by all organizations.
- **Learning is Social:** People learn best from and with one another; participation in learning communities is vital to the effectiveness, well-being and happiness of people in any work setting.

CHARACTERISTICS AND DYNAMICS

The characteristics and dynamics of ActKM are examined in this chapter through the Cynefin sense-making framework (Snowden, 2002a). This framework recognises multiple domains in a system whereby each domain is understood as a result of a unique constitution of characteristics and dynamics requiring its own set of models, tools and decision-making approaches. George Box (1979, p. 202) made the observation that: 'All models are wrong but some are useful.' The Cynefin framework is useful because it expands the possible perspectives from which an issue can be investigated.

The Cynefin framework defines four domains:

- **Known:** knowledge in this domain is explicit and understandable by the widest possible audience. Everything is known and explicable to those who share a common context (such as working in the same organization). This domain is the legitimate home of best practice, documented lessons learned, the corporate intranet and training programs.

- **Knowable:** knowledge in this domain is knowable to those who have the time, energy and intellect to understand specialised topics. The language is abstracted, thus providing efficiencies for those who understand the specialist terminology, but excluding those who do not and who are therefore unable to converse with these experts.
- **Complex:** people in this domain operate in a complex network of mutual obligations, trust and close relationships. Knowledge, beliefs and values are shared through stories and mutual experiences. This domain of the organization has been referred to as the 'shadow side' (Egan, 1994), indicating that many of the activities in this domain remain unseen by the formal organization and paradoxically would not exist if they were made visible.
- **Chaos:** in this domain people lack any experience to guide their actions. The situations they face are entirely novel and confronting; people will do whatever they can to get out of this space. This space provides huge opportunities for the creation of new knowledge.

The purpose of the Cynefin framework is to enable better sense-making by increasing an awareness of borders and by triggering, through a border transition, different models of decision-making, leadership and community (Snowden, 2002a).

A description of the key characteristics and dynamics of ActKM, from the perspective of the Cynefin framework, is presented below.

KNOWN—THE BUREAUCRATIC AND STRUCTURED DOMAIN

The features of ActKM associated with this domain are: (i) community roles, (ii) the online discussion forum and (iii) community demographics and growth.

Community Roles

A significant aspect of ActKM, in terms of providing a support structure, was the evolution of a core team composed of members who were passionate about KM. These people kept the community moving forward. The concept of the core team gained clarity early in ActKM's development, but its development did not occur because of shrewd planning. Rather, it occurred through an incidental activity that was primarily aimed at developing credibility.

In mid-1999, when ActKM consisted of about 50 members, the founding members thought it would be beneficial to be associated with an already established Knowledge Management association. The intention was to increase our credibility with a view to attracting more members and increasing the 'buzz' in the community. After some searching, the Knowledge Management Consortium International (KMCI) was identified and it was decided that ActKM should become a chapter of KMCI. This required ActKM members to elect an executive board consisting of a president, vice-president, secretary, treasurer and two executive board members. Elections were organized and all the positions were filled. This elected group became known as the 'executive' (now known as the 'core team'). Shortly after the elections, the relationship with KMCI disintegrated and ActKM ceased to be a chapter. The official titles of office-bearers never sat well with the executive and the roles were therefore renamed with everyone in the core team being known as a 'convenor'.

By 2002, the title of 'executive' had been removed because members held a perception that this group exercised executive powers. This perception is understandable in view of the fact that the majority of members had come from public sector agencies and such organizations traditionally have powerful executive bodies. Many members thus felt that they needed to seek permission from the 'executive' to post some messages, initiate special interest groups and make announcements. In fact, the 'executive' had never intended to exercise such powers and had never done so. Terminology definitely affects behaviour, especially terminology that carries certain implications of perceived roles, and the original label of 'the executive' undoubtedly inhibited the flow of information and curtailed members' initiative.

The main function of the core team is to decide the events and activities to be developed for the members. The core team meets approximately once every two months, usually over lunch. Originally voted as the Secretary, Amanda Lee has been vital to ActKM's success. Amanda ensures that there are speakers for the monthly meetings, organizes catering (wine, cheese and biscuits), moderates messages on the online discussion forum and schedules meetings of the core team. The 'community advocates' and 'thought leaders' are also vital. These people pose questions, suggest speakers, promote the forum and provide ideas, references and links among people and organizations.

Online Discussion Forum

An online discussion forum has been a feature of ActKM from the beginning and provides ActKM's rhythm of activity—its heartbeat. A significant proportion of ActKM's codified knowledge resides here and there is now a member initiative under way to create a useful resource by editing and indexing the messages on the forum.

The online discussion operates using 'Yahoo Groups'. This web-based collaboration service provides the technology needed for a community that is international and not for profit. Yahoo Groups is free, members sign up themselves, they decide how much email they want to receive and there is also a group calendar that notifies members of events. The core team can also invite members to join ActKM. This feature has been used to invite thought leaders to join the community with a view to increasing the quality of the online conversation. This has been an effective strategy and ActKM now has pre-eminent KM thought leaders from around the world participating in the online discussion.

The online discussion forum was difficult to establish and sustain. In fact, in the first twelve months, the online conversation was contrived by rostering members of the core team to post messages to ensure that there was at least one message going out to members every week. This activity became less contrived over time and eventually became unnecessary once the community reached about a hundred people. Message volume also increased as relationships grew and became established among the members. Face-to-face meetings seemed to accelerate the development of these relationships—a fact observed in other research (Hildreth, Kimble & Wright, 2000). After personally meeting an online colleague, a member could then visualise that person posting a message and therefore felt more at ease in responding.

Traffic volume on the online discussion forum is variable (see Figure 1). Key events, such as the annual conferences, significantly affect the number of messages posted in any given month. There also appears to be a relationship between the number of messages and the occurrence of vigorous online debate—such as the intellectual tussle between Dave Snowden and Edward Swanstrom in February 2002 (see 'A vigorous debate'). Although many of the

Figure 1: ActKM Online Discussion Traffic Volume

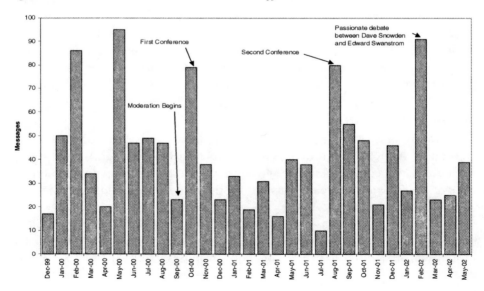

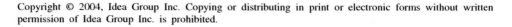

messages in February 2002 were directly related to the Snowden-Swanstrom debate, many others were introducing new unrelated topics. The excitement generated by the debate seemed to inspire other members to contribute to the online forum.

In the beginning, the online discussion was unmoderated. This was a mistake. In August 2000 a member's auto respond feature ('I'm out of the office') malfunctioned and generated more than a hundred messages within a minute. Many members left ActKM that day, particularly those who download their email over a telephone line. Each message is now moderated. In addition to avoiding problems of the type described above, moderation has provided an additional benefit in allowing us to capture emails designed as a personal response or those that are blatant advertisements. After moderation, the traffic volume diminished, but quality increased.

Community Demographics and Growth

Based on email addresses, it is apparent that ActKM has a mix of public, private and academic representation (see Figure 2). The 'unknown' component reflects the significant number of anonymous Yahoo and similar web-based email addresses in the membership.

It is important for ActKM membership to be predominantly from the public sector to ensure that the community achieves its stated purpose. Although members have not been screened or selected, the membership is principally derived from the public sector. This results from: (i) the focus of discussions held in the forum, (ii) the stated intention of the community and (iii) the prescribed composition of the core team (which has always had at least 50% of its members

Figure 2: ActKM Demographics

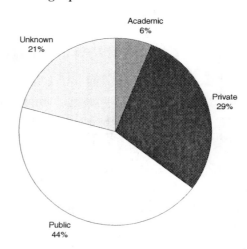

Figure 3: ActKM Growth

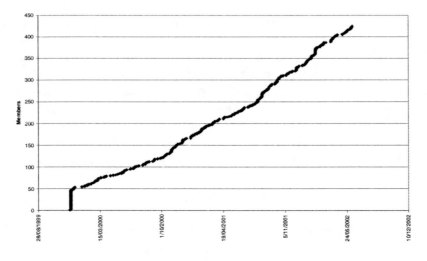

from the public sector). There are few rules that govern the operation of ActKM, but this prescribed composition of the core team is one of them.

The size of ActKM has consistently increased. The data illustrated in Figure 3 starts at the point when the online forum began. The first 50 members were loaded on the first day of using the system, thus producing the vertical growth to be seen in Figure 3.

When people leave ActKM, an automatic message is sent to them asking the departing members to describe, in brief, their reasons for leaving. The responses are usually of two types: their interests have changed or they are feeling overwhelmed with email and are getting rid of some of their listserver memberships.

KNOWABLE—THE PROFESSIONAL AND LOGICAL DOMAIN

Within the second domain of the Cynefin framework—the knowable domain—there are three components of ActKM to consider: (i) face-to-face meetings, (ii) annual conferences and (iii) expert discussions.

Face-to-Face Meetings

The core team understood, based on the available literature on communities (for example, McDermott, 1999 and Lesser & Prusak, 1999), that it was vital to hold face-to-face meetings on a frequent and regular basis. The core team was determined to create an environment, both online and face-to-face, in which people created relationships in order to enhance the knowledge flows throughout the community. With this objective of improving the personal relationships among people in the community, monthly meetings were initially rotated among various government agencies. However, after the first six months, the core team felt that this approach had a considerable management overhead in finding venues and in notifying people of the time and location of the next meeting.

From the beginning of 1999, meetings have been held on the first Tuesday of each month, starting at 5:30 pm and usually finishing at 7:30 pm. The predictable scheduling of the monthly meeting is deliberate. The objective is to ensure that at the same place, day and time each month there will be a gathering of people with common interests and that a member can be fairly certain that the discussions will be relevant and interesting. This form of routine helps to create and maintain ActKM's identity and assists new members to understand ActKM's patterns of behaviour. Experienced members thus know what to expect and new members quickly become comfortable with the workings of the community.

There are always refreshments at a monthly meeting, for which members pay $4. The meetings are usually informal—sometimes the participants merely gather around a table for a discussion with wine and cheese at hand. The average attendance is 20-30 people and the composition of the meeting varies from month to month.

Whenever possible, KM practitioners from the public sector are scheduled to speak about the tangible initiatives that they have implemented, followed by a discussion among the attendees of the lessons learned. Less frequently, a vendor is invited to describe his or her offerings. This focus on public sector practitioners ensures that the community maintains credibility and relevance.

The relationships developed at the meetings definitely affect the conversation that occurs online. When people get to know one another offline, a more relaxed and less adversarial interchange occurs online as trust begins to develop. Members comment on the friendly and welcoming culture that is evident online. Linking face-to-face meetings and the online discussion is a critical success factor in nurturing ActKM.

Annual Conferences

ActKM held its first conference in October 2000. Attendees were charged $220, which covered the room hire and catering costs and left a modest profit for the community to use for other events. The first annual conference attracted 70 people. The topics covered were mainly definitional, with various techniques and sub-branches of KM being discussed. These included knowledge mapping, business intelligence, knowledge strategy and learning histories. The content discussed at this conference reflected the community's relatively immature understanding of KM. The second annual conference was held in August 2001 and attracted more than a hundred delegates. At this conference, the conversation changed. Whereas the 2000 conference had been about definitions, 2001 focused on case studies of practical initiatives and their results. The 2002 conference was another resounding success, with more than a hundred delegates participating in a multi-stream program.

The annual conferences provide another opportunity for face-to-face interactions. In many cases, attendance at a conference is the first opportunity for members from interstate to meet one another and meet people from the core team. There have been instances of members from the same geographical area meeting one another for the first time and deciding to create a chapter of the community in their home state, thus extending and integrating the social network.

Expert Discussion

Dialogue among KM experts is one of the key features of ActKM and is one of the main reasons for members signing up for the online discussion forum. To draw experts out on issues, the author and other core team members post controversial and current topics and then watch the experts swarm around these ideas. The number of regular contributors to the forum can be as low as 5% of the total membership. Based on personal anecdotal evidence, it appears that many members relish watching a debate unfold and then continue these debates with their colleagues in the workplace.

Successful online debates require trust and mutual respect. The contributors must trust the forum not to misuse posted information—for example, by quoting the conversation out of context. The expert contributors must also trust one another to behave courteously in a robust discussion and to seek understanding of alternative points of view. Finally, the rest of the forum must trust the expert participants to convey their thoughts and the ideas of others with accuracy. As Charles Handy (1995) has pointed out: 'virtuality requires trust to make it work'.

COMPLEX—THE INFORMAL
AND INTERDEPENDENT DOMAIN

The features of ActKM associated with the complex domain include: (i) informal meetings and discussion held outside the forum and (ii) the development of the core team.

Informal Meetings and Discussions Outside the Forum

The least visible, but probably the most valuable aspect of ActKM, is the formation of new working relationships through face-to-face meetings outside the discussion forum or formal ActKM events. This aspect of the community is fostered through a value that permeates ActKM—that the only thing we ask of members is that they make themselves available to other members.

The culture of the public sector—with its emphasis on hierarchy and accountability—is conducive to these informal offline face-to-face discussions because many members are unwilling to recount, publicly, what has happened in their agency, especially if the story has negative connotations. For example, one government agency had designed and implemented a program to manage tacit knowledge more effectively. This program was in direct response to a series of failures within the agency that could be traced to a poor use of this type of knowledge. The program designers were asked whether they would like to present their experiences to an ActKM meeting, but they respectfully declined the invitation because they were concerned about revealing the agency's earlier failings. They were, however, quite happy to talk privately with other public sector colleagues and share what they had learned. An open discussion of this innovative program never appeared online, nor at any other public event. People became familiar with it through informal channels, with subsequent benefit for the overall ActKM community.

These informal meetings can take on a range of other forms:

*   A member might see a posting and then organize to meet the posting's author with a view to discussing a specific topic (such as records management or collaboration).
*   People might meet to get a better understanding of what is happening in KM in the public sector.
*   Joint projects between agencies might be developed.
*   Meetings might occur on a regular basis with members meeting for coffee and a chat about the philosophy and practical aspects of KM.

Whatever form they take, all of these informal meetings benefit the community as a whole by strengthening the social networks.

Developing and Sustaining the Core Team

The development of the core team can also be viewed from the perspective of the complex domain in that it displays emergent characteristics and is continually evolving. The core team emerged, as discussed above, from a discussion between Kate Muir and the author. Others joined the group. These were drawn from trusted colleagues and associates who shared a passion for the topic and with whom we enjoyed working. Members are able to join the core team at any time—simply by attending meetings of the core team and becoming involved in fostering the community. New members of the core team, however, do not appear from nowhere. These people usually become increasingly prominent in the online forum and monthly meetings, get to know the core team and then decide whether they want to become more involved.

Chaos—The Uncharted and Innovative Domain

There are many activities that can be viewed from the perspective of the unpredictable and uncharted chaotic domain, but two stand out: (i) the debate between Dave Snowden and Edward Swantrom and (ii) running the first ActKM conference.

A Vigorous Debate

In 2002, between 9 February and 14 February, ActKM witnessed a passionate and sometimes personal debate between Dave Snowden (Director of IBM's Cynefin Centre) and Edward Swanstrom (Secretary General of Global Knowledge Economics Council). A misunderstanding sparked the debate. Swanstrom had thought Snowden was attacking scientific method while arguing for the use of complex adaptive systems, whereas in fact, Snowden's sights were aimed squarely at scientific management. This initial confusion resulted in a series of detailed and informative posts that enthralled the online membership but also left people feeling uneasy regarding the personal nature of some of the comments.

For the first time, ActKM members observed an interchange that was both passionate and at times personal. As Hubert Saint-Onge (2002) pointed out to Snowden during the debate:

"Changing mindsets is a worthwhile cause that requires some level of 'bloody-mindedness': it is not always pretty but it is certainly edifying."

Members posted numerous messages to one or other of the protagonists (on and off the listserver), variously supporting their views and encouraging the forthright nature of the discussion. It was the personal nature of some of the comments, however, that made the core team uneasy. This was uncharted territory for the forum. In one of the more personal interchanges, Swanstrom (2002) commented:

"You also seem to believe that scientists would not jump at the chance of developing 'better' science if it was made available to them. I do not think you have been in a scientific lab for a while."

To which Snowden (2002b) replied:

"I'll happily go back to the lab if you read some history."

The coordinators of the discussion list thought that they might have to intervene. However, before it became necessary to make this decision, the debate was over. The system self-organized and the protagonists sensed that they were in danger of alienating the discussion forum with their strong interchanges and therefore closed down the discussion by agreeing to disagree.

It was interesting to note that, as the debate became personal, Snowden and Swanstrom each exerted additional effort to persuade the other and the wider forum of his point of view. As a result, more detailed posts were made, replete with references to books, articles and other researchers' work. For the interested onlookers, these posts provided a wealth of background material on the topics of complexity, economics, management theory and standards.

This initially chaotic event quickly moved to the knowable domain as the core team came to understand how these types of debates could stimulate the community. A similar debate ensued in October 2002 between Steve Denning and Chris Kimble - again sparked by a misunderstanding. On this occasion, the core team knew that this was a good thing, in that it would help to create the excitement that helps sustain such a community.

The First Conference

The first ActKM conference is another example of activities that began in the chaotic domain and moved relatively quickly to knowable and known space. The core team had never organized a conference. The members of the organizing committee volunteered their services and one of them had very clear ideas of how things should be run. Unfortunately, these ideas were at odds with the rest of the organizing committee and, two weeks into preparing for the conference, this person resigned in displeasure when others did not agree with her.

The team got back on track but two weeks before the conference faced a second crisis when it was discovered that only 25 people had registered for the conference. Because we needed 50 to break even, the organizing committee was on the verge of cancelling the conference. However, in the next couple of days registrations then began to roll in.

As noted above, this first conference turned out to be successful and the organizing committee thus learned that members wait until the last minute to register. The same pattern was repeated in the following year but, by then, we had moved to the known domain and therefore handled the situation without stress.

CONCLUSION

The Cynefin framework is helpful in analysing ActKM. Its domains encourage an understanding of certain aspects of the ActKM CoP that might otherwise have been overlooked. It is apparent that all four domains of the

Cynefin framework are represented in various characteristics of the ActKM community. Conversely, each characteristic of ActKM can be described in terms of the known, knowable, complex and chaotic domains of the framework.

This account of ActKM has demonstrated that an online community does not evolve without encouragement and nurturing. Success relies on the members developing trust based on relationships. If members can meet face-to-face, this accelerates the development of trust. However, in a dispersed international forum such as ActKM, such face-to-face meetings are difficult to organize. In the absence of such personal meetings, the tone and thoughtfulness of messages determines the extent to which people build trust in those whom they have not met.

The online discussion forum thus bonds the community and provides a rhythm of activities that defines its identity. It is prudent to moderate the posts to ensure that unwanted messages (for example, advertisements and personal responses) do not appear. The online discussion forum is the locus of the community's expertise and serves to alert members to the presence of people they might wish to engage—either by posing a question or by meeting face-to-face. From the experience of ActKM, it is apparent that such an online discussion becomes self-sustaining once it reaches a certain critical mass, but that it requires pump priming to reach this point.

The core team orchestrates and influences the environment in which the community operates. The members of this team volunteer their time and knowledge because they are passionate about the concept and dedicated to its success. It is apparent that the provision of opportunities for members to meet and discuss KM in a public sector context fosters the emergence of new patterns of thought and enhances the sense of excitement within the community.

The technology that supports the community is simple, but effective. An international community such as ActKM requires an infrastructure of collaborative technologies that enable on-line discussion, facilitate the storage of documents and provide an accessible group calendar.

The regular schedule of face-to-face meetings provides certainty and an opportunity to build relationships. A variety of novel and relevant topics attracts healthy attendances. The importance of these meetings should not be underestimated - even for a community that is predominantly on-line. The relationships developed at these meetings are later reflected in the quality of online discussions and this, in turn, influences and encourages the wider community.

The future of ActKM appears to be bright. Membership is growing and the conversations are becoming more sophisticated. For those who are interested in learning more about ActKM, the web address is: <http://groups.yahoo.com/group/act-km>.

REFERENCES

Box, G. E. P. (1979). Robustness in the strategy of scientific model building. In R. L. Launer and G. N. Wilkinson (Eds.), *Robustness in statistics*. New York: Academic Press.

Egan, G. (1994). *Working the shadow side: A guide to positive behind-the-scenes management*. San Francisco, CA: Jossey-Bass Publishers.

Handy, C. (1995). Trust and the virtual organization. *Harvard Business Review*, (May/June), 40-50.

Hildreth, P., Kimble, C., and Wright, P. (2000). Communities of Practice in the distributed international environment. *Journal of Knowledge Management, 4* (1), 27-37.

Lesser, E., and Prusak, L. (1999). Communities of Practice, social capital and organizational knowledge, Information Systems review. *The Korean Society of Management Information Systems, 1* (1), 3-10.

McDermott, R. (1999). Why Information Technology inspired but cannot deliver Knowledge Management. *California Management Review, 41* (4), 103-117.

Saint-Onge, H. (2002). <Hubert.Saint-Onge@clarica.com> RE: [act-km] Knowledge Management for Emergency Management [on-line posting] <http://groups.yahoo.com/group/act-km/message/1264> [February 13, 2002]

Snowden, D. (2002a). Complex acts of knowledge: Paradox and descriptive self awareness. *Journal of Knowledge Management, 6* (2), 110-11.

Snowden, D. (2002b). <snowded@uk.ibm.com> RE: [act-km] nth Generation KM [on-line posting] <http://groups.yahoo.com/group/act-km/message/1239> [February 11, 2002]

Swanstrom, E. (2002). <edward-swanstrom@gkec.org> RE: [act-km] nth Generation KM [on-line posting] <http://groups.yahoo.com/group/act-km/message/1238> [February 10, 2002]

Wenger, E., McDermott, R., and Snyder, W. M. (2002). *Cultivating Communities of Practice: A guide to managing knowledge*. Boston, MA: Harvard Business School Press.

Chapter XXIII

Click Connect and Coalesce for NGOs:
Exploring the Intersection Between Online Networks, CoPs, and Events

Nancy White
Full Circle Associates, USA

ABSTRACT

This chapter notes the shift of focus from "online communities" to more purposeful and focused online groups, including distributed Communities of Practice (CoPs). The author identifies the value of CoPs for Non-Governmental and Non-Profit organizations, and suggests that CoPs are formed, stimulated and supported by catalysts, and are richer when contained within larger, more diffuse networks of people.

INTRODUCTION

In the late 90s, there was much energy around Virtual Communities. They were touted as the ultimate web deployment, the key to online commerce and to online education. Early adopters swarmed and websites racked up hits in the millions. Then there was a deafening silence. Commerce and media sites began closing down their discussion boards. Even busy boards like those at CNN were shuttered. Was the online community movement dead? No, it was just transforming itself, settling down and maturing into a space where it had value and applicability.

The bottom line is that online community or online interaction is not the goal. It is one means for helping groups achieve their goals. It is not necessarily about online community but about the conditions and process needed to enable communities to use the online environment. Now networks, groups and Communities of Practice (CoPs) are realizing the promise of the late 90s. This is not just a trend or tool for business; there are particular opportunities for Non-Governmental Organizations (NGOs) and Non-Profit Organizations (NPOs). For NPOs and NGOs, online interaction offers a way to support a distributed community by widening their depth and potentially enriching their learning.

CONNECTION: THE OPPORTUNITY

It can start with a single email. Someone wants to know something and they click on Google, search for a keyword, find a person and draft an email. They send out a little beacon hoping they can connect with someone who can help. The email hits the mark and connects — a response comes back with some links, a few more names. Soon that first email has multiplied and tapped into a network. Questions and answers are exchanged, background shared and connections established. Has a community been born? Maybe. Perhaps just a quickened pulse, a single fleeting burst of activity within a network but the knowledge was shared — and it started with a single email. At once, we have a compelling manifestation that online interaction can support networks, groups and communities. In a catalytic email connection, the power of a network is realized. In the continuation of that relationship, the birth or growth of a group or a CoP may be stimulated.

A group is a collection of individuals with some shared interest. CoPs are particular types of groups where the members share a concern, a set of problems or a passion about a topic and who deepen their knowledge and expertise in this area by interaction on an ongoing basis (Wenger, McDermott & Snyder, 2002). Networks in this context are social networks: people and organizations connected by some common thread or interest. The connection may be geographic, but with the spread of Information and Communication Technologies (ICTs), networks have become global, dispersed and online. Rheingold and Kimball (2000) coined the term Online Social Networks to describe networks that emerge wholly online rather than springing from an existing offline network.

The business world has recognized that both knowledge and the network of people that hold the knowledge are key assets, particularly in an information economy. Dyson, Gilder, Keyworth and Toffler (1994) wrote:

"As humankind explores this new electronic frontier of knowledge, it must confront again the most profound questions of how to organize itself for the common good" (Dyson et al., 1994).

Businesses are well past the first phase of Knowledge Management (KM) that confined knowledge to databases and are focusing on the knowledge networks created and used by people. NGOs are now also rapidly moving in this direction. The World Bank, through the World Bank Institute (2003), has embraced KM and internal CoPs. The EDC Global Learning Group has been exploring the role of communities and CoPs in continued learning for over a decade. The United Nations Development Program has reorganized a significant amount of its work around CoPs. BOND (2002) (a network of more than 270 United Kingdom based voluntary organizations working in international development and development education) in the UK has also recognized the role of CoPs in its work.

Thematic Groups and Special Interest Groups (SIGs) are mentioned more and more in organizational plans, as noted in the 2002 ICT Network notes of the UN, the web pages of the International Water and Sanitation Center and many others. They are particularly useful for tapping into the often under-utilized knowledge of the "Southern" or "Two-Thirds World" countries where knowledge has historically been seen as the domain of donors and developed nations. Governments are thinking about how networks, communities and CoPs can enhance civic participation. This is evidenced by workshops and websites such as those by Unicom, the World Bank, CommunityBuilders in New South Wales and the Canadian Government's emerging CoP initiatives.

CoPs can be effective tools for learning and working in and across organizations. The focus on learning together is of great importance. One can point to cases that show the value of sharing ideas that reduce "wheel reinvention" in a time of scarce resources. Envision people working on similar projects within NGOs or across organizations: AIDS educators sharing tips for reaching target populations, Information Technology managers working through software problems or agricultural researchers sharing data on field trials. These are learning communities and CoPs, which, even though they may be distributed, support specific local community goals like preventing AIDS in a village or ending hunger in a country. They support current concrete learning needs for people who do not have opportunities to come face-to-face in CoPs.

Currently many of these efforts are internal to organizations. What about the potential of connections across and between organizations? What kinds of networks are needed to make and sustain those connections? Consider people in NGOs and isolated communities who have no internal peers with whom to interact and whose local networks may lack diversity, knowledge and experience.

Networks can connect users to experts. The UN (2002) has noted:

"Numerous examples of expert groups exist throughout the UN system especially in programmatic areas where such groups extend beyond the borders of the system (and sometimes are primarily composed of world-wide experts). These groups follow the more flexible concepts of CoPs rather than SIGs, namely flexible groups with strong expert facilitation meeting to develop community and using electronic tools to work together with the membership changing as needed" (UN, 2002).

There is great potential for supporting NGOs to achieve their goals. Online interaction, defined as the creation of persistent communication paths between groups of individuals using ICT, is an important opportunity. Online interaction tools can help realize the potential, yet technology itself is not the answer. If we assume online interaction can be of value, what is the role of these networks in the birth and growth process of more defined subgroups and communities? What are the roles of the catalysts of people and events? How can these elements support knowledge growth and flow in NGOs to help them achieve their goals?

THE CRITICAL QUESTIONS

In moving from theory to practice, how can we maximize the power of online networks to leverage groups and communities of all types? What do we need to know and do? Here are some questions to consider:

1) **The Network Container:** What are the key attributes and relationships between networks, groups, CoPs and other types of communities? Why are the connections between this ecosystem of entities so important? How do we nurture the ecosystem both at an organizational and inter-organizational level?
2) **The Catalysts:** Who and what does it take to keep CoPs robust in the distributed online environment?
3) **The Practices:** What does it take to amplify and sustain these opportunities from a design and process perspective?

THE NETWORK CONTAINER

Existing formal and informal networks, groups and learning communities offer a container to allow the emergence and growth of more focused groups such as CoPs. They provide a basic level of connection and awareness between people with a common interest. In the Internet age, we are not limited by geographic location: connections can be global even when the action is local. One of the core attributes of these global connections is conversation. The Internet allows us more than the exchange of information. By allowing the interactive sharing and building of knowledge within the context of human conversation it allows us to qualify information based on the source, place it in context to see if it has application to our needs and amplify it through the contributions of a group rather than just an individual.

Manifestations of networks might include topical or professional email lists, associations, alumni groups, online bulletin boards or other informal groups. They may be geographically defined or global and without boundaries. They may be defined by language, culture or simply topic. They may have formal organizational support or be networks that grow through grassroots efforts. The critical point is that the network is made up of people, not the tools that support the connections between the people. An email list itself is not a network: the members of the list are the network. Some networks offer more fertile grounds than others; for example, networks that have both a strong core that supports relationships and a wide periphery that supports diversity and offers greater resources to emergent groups. So-called "Old Boy Networks" (networks with unchanging long term members) may be less supportive of emergent groups and often lack the rich diversity that is helpful to new groups.

Finding Others

There are three main ways that people find each other or connect in a network: formal listings, open inquiries and working through an intermediary.

- **Formal Listings:** Networks with formal membership listings may be perceived as easier to access, as a person can look up someone with specific expertise, but the access to these lists and issues of privacy and permissions may limit their usefulness. Wider, looser networks may not have complete membership lists. The lists may be as simple as an email contact together with professional and personal interests and biographies. There are some emerging software tools (e.g., http://www.netdeva.com) that may facilitate identity and relationship building, but at this time, tapping into a network still requires a good search query and an element of chance.
- **Open Inquiries:** During the peak of USENET, a worldwide online distributed discussion system (Internet FAQ Archives, 2002), individuals could post an inquiry to a specific USENET group and expect a response— often a very high quality response. Today, focused online communities and email lists can still offer this opportunity although two factors, volume (which list and where?) and Spam (unsolicited email), may have diluted the effectiveness of this approach. The essential element is finding the right

group, list or community for one's query. However, few utilities identify and categorize these groups despite repeated efforts. The best efforts so far are the Open Directory Project (Publicus, n.d.) and ForumOne's Online Community Report Listings.

- **Working through an Intermediary:** In the now famous Six Degrees of Separation approach, Milgram (1967) suggests that we have close relationships that might be able to open information and knowledge doors better than we can ourselves. "Do you know someone who knows something about ...?" This approach supports the idea that networks are critical in the knowledge arena.

Nurturing and Supporting Networks

There are also different ways that networks are nurtured and supported. Depending on the formality of the network it may be supported by core members or organizations or it may exist simply on the traffic generated by the members. Historically, strong networks reflect a certain degree of shared trust, member reputation and an ongoing interest in the sustenance of the network.

- **Trust and Reputation:** Trust and reputation play very diverse roles in online networks and groups. The manifestation and importance of trust depends on the setting, culture, purpose and circumstance. There is no easy way to assign a uniform value to the role of trust across different networks. In some, trust is not an issue, in others, it is central. As people start coalescing into more defined groups and communities, the role of trust regularly becomes more apparent. Trust can gain significance as more information is shared and more knowledge created together. Breach of trust can also have a more damaging effect.

  Reputation is manifest on a variety of levels. Biographical listings and yellow pages may give a formal indication of someone's experience, education and past accomplishments that provides a springboard to reputation, but the participation of a member in a network may do more to enhance their reputation than an impressive biography. Responsiveness to requests, quality of contributions and reliability when taking on tasks can increase a participant's reputation or social capital.

- **Shared Interest in Networks Nurturing Networks:** Implicit in the interest in networks is the fact that they need support, nurturing, and at times, protection. Members of a network may guard their contacts, shielding them from elements seen as external or threatening. They may volunteer time to support the network formally or informally. Networks live or die by the support they receive and reputation is the main reward for offering support. This is one key attribute of network fitness.

THE CATALYSTS

Networks are by nature open and diffuse. This is particularly true for electronic networks where people may never meet face-to-face. They are great containers for exchanging information but are rarely organized enough to accomplish tasks or to support more in-depth, ongoing, learning experiences. There needs to be a focus on action and specific context of the place or geography of the action: a kernel around which more focused groups can form is needed to mobilize people and resources. If networks are the container, the next element needed for formation of the groups is a catalyst. Here are two: Events and Individuals.

Events

Online communication happens effortlessly across time. The net effect is that it can range from urgent to very unimportant. Messages can be left for later, "when I have time". Attention can be scattered. Action can dissipate with little awareness. When the element of deadlines, beginnings and endings is added; there is a need for urgency and attention. Events can spark a connection. The intersection between people and networks can revitalize the networks themselves by drawing in new people. They can punctuate the rather flat time experience of a network into a here and now, "let's connect" experience.

Events can be time-delimited online conferences, teleconferences, scheduled thematic chats, polls and focused dialogs. The critical factor here is that there is a defined start and end time. They have a high enough value to capture participants' attention and enough interaction to strengthen the relationships between participants.

People

The second catalytic force is that of individuals who both nurture networks and/or decide they want to increase connection and catalyse general networking into a more defined group interaction. They are the people connectors in the network. They have the power to move groups from talk to action.

Neither networks nor groups collectively leverage online technologies for their use unless an individual takes the first step. At the network level, individuals often are stewards of the technology used to support the network. They make software choices, do maintenance and often facilitate the online interaction. Without these services, many networks would disappear.

Individuals also catalyse interaction by connecting people, nurturing relationships, asking stimulating questions and facilitating interaction. When they notice a lull, they add a spark. When there is too much activity or conflict, they mediate the situation. The skills associated with this work come naturally to some but need to be acquired by others and can be supported through CoPs of online facilitators (White, 2002). The individuals are not always sponsored or compensated for the work. Many are motivated volunteers. People as catalysts are an immense resource and community recognition of these people is very important.

Some Examples of Catalysts

KM for Development

A network that spawned a CoP that feeds a network. Bellanet is a Canadian NGO working with the development community to increase collaboration by providing advice and assistance on making more effective use of ICTs. Bellanet recognized the need for a focus on KM within the international development community. On July 19, 2000, they created an email list, KM for Dev (Knowledge Management for International Development Organizations). Today that list has 233 members and as of November 2002 over 1,000 posted messages. The interchanges focus upon the understanding of KM and its role in development as well as the cultural context most of the members experience working across the globe. Those who ask questions on the list are frequently answered. There are spikes in discussions and generation of new knowledge, but the ongoing traffic tends towards information exchange.

KM for Dev is not just an email list with 233 members. Within this larger loosely affiliated network are a series of more tightly bound relationships and vibrant communities which have sprung, in part, out of the KM workshops organized by Bellanet in Washington DC and Brighton in 2000, in Chennai and Maputo in 2001 and The Hague in 2002. These small, highly interactive workshops have not only provided a venue for knowledge sharing and collaborative work but the nurturing of relationships between individuals and their organizations.

The walls of this CoP are quite permeable, as members from the larger network enter and exit via either workshop participation or the deeper discussions that emerge on the list. Song (email communication, December 12, 2002) noted:

"I think that the network members get as much as the CoP members get out of it but in a different way. A colleague of mine was telling me about a group in Central/South America where a group of people lurked on a list for two years saying absolutely nothing but (in) two months created their own network/CoP and were able to mimic the positive behaviour/facilitation from the other network very successfully."

Both Song and fellow member Marc Steinlin of Helvetas, the Swiss Association for International Cooperation, cite the face-to-face gatherings as essential to the community. Steinlin talks of the experience of the first workshop as a galvanizing event that was then affirmed in the newly created email list.

"I knew almost everybody personally, I had this sacred fire from the Brighton Workshop" (personal communication, December 2002).

Steinlin noted, however, as the membership of the list grew and the participating groups at the events varied, that he sensed some dilution of the original community. Steinlin suggests that meeting at least every 18 months and limiting the size of the community is key for a CoP.

In 2002, Bellanet added an Internet Portal for the community to allow greater sharing of resources. It is still primarily populated by staff members and a few frequent contributors; it does not yet appear to be a core element of either the network or the CoP. Yet, it exists and may see more uptake over time. In addition, Bellanet has been a working experiment on open source portal development: an issue of practical interest to the group.

Again, a large network (the international development community) feeds into a more defined network (community of interest) that is primarily supported by the KM for Dev email list. Within the network, a rich connected community exists and supports the members in their work to apply KM to development. The community is punctuated and glued more tightly together through the intermittent face-to-face meetings and catalytic moments on the email list. In turn, that CoP is a strong contributing element to the network. The flow goes in both directions, keeping both stronger than they would be on their own.

South African Online Communications Network

In the fall of 2001, a member of an online facilitation email hosted by the author emailed and asked for leads on potential speakers for a conference on Communities of Practice in Johannesburg. The author recommended Etienne Wenger, who was invited to present. Subsequently the conference organizing committee decided to add a component on online interaction and invited the author.

Since the author was going all the way to South Africa, it seemed logical to tap into her network of online facilitators and see what else might be organized while she was there. Her passion is the NGO sectors and she was concerned the conference might be attended only by the business community. A colleague in that online facilitation network, Tony Carr of the University of Cape Town, arranged for two community based meetings in Johannesburg and Cape Town. Folks working with online interaction in a variety of settings, mostly from academia or NGOs, were invited. Tony tapped into both his education and NGO sector networks.

At both meetings, people expressed surprise and delight to connect with each other. Many had been working in isolation and they were happy to share stories and swap tips. There had not been a locus of attention or energy before the gathering, so there was not enough awareness of each other. The first critical mass was created through connections and initial relationships developed through face-to-face meetings. There was a sense that people could move towards becoming a group with more distinct boundaries and commitments. Tony took the initiative to get things organized. He again reached into his network to generate invitations to participate in an online group.

Initially there was a flurry of activity by a small number of members feeling out and defining the group's domain, community and practice. The Online Learning and Collaboration Network took its first steps. Within three months, the interaction faded out. Tony, as the de facto leader, realized the need for a larger critical mass and is now planning a more focused re-launch. Carr (personal communication, November 25, 2002) wrote:

"I would agree that I act as a catalyst in a lot of situations, but at some point in this process it became lonely being the only other person ... who was thinking consistently about the network as a whole."

He noted that the potential members of the network are typically:

"... busy professionals facing information overload who have limited unstructured time available for reflection and collaboration outside of their immediate work context." (Carr, personal communication, November 25, 2002).

Some in the private sector also have confidentiality issues and some question the value of the time invested in such a network. Tony continues:

"There is also a very limited culture of online discussion in Southern Africa" (personal communication, November 25, 2002).

When he re-launches he will probably again cast the net widely to bring new energy to the group and consider what events and focal points he can offer to nurture the community. His plans include special events to focus attention and draw in new participation. Catalyzed by a series of events and efforts of a catalyst, what began as a connection in a dispersed global network became a more defined South African network with a shared interest in online interaction.

Project Harmony Internet Community Development Project

Project Harmony, a small international NGO based in Vermont, received a grant to develop online communities for NGOs and Small and Medium Enterprises (SMEs) in the former Soviet Republics of Azerbaijan, Armenia and

Georgia. The goal was to look at application of online interaction rather than connectivity. The agency had little previous online community experience. The lead staff person, Paul Lawrence, working in isolation in Baku in Azerbaijan, went on the web to seek advice and information. A web search led him to an existing international network of people working in online interaction. He emailed three who quickly responded with knowledge and support. The author was one of the three. Out of that initial email interaction, he connected and eventually contracted the author to help his project. Right from the start, Internet connections were a key to this project. It truly started with one email!

Paul began to bring in his Project Harmony counterparts in Georgia and Armenia. They in turn brought in local and regional knowledge that informed the work. A network began to emerge that grew beyond the scope of the formal grant project to become a community. This identification of the wider network and the smaller group of key players was critical. In the process of developing tasks associated with the grant, an informal CoP began influencing the organization and shaping this and other projects. Ideas were generated, tossed around and shared. Perceptions about communication, collaboration and the practice of international development within the network shifted. Distributed and isolated field staff grew stronger as they supported each other online rather than relying on headquarters. Through electronic communications, they were increasing their capacity daily. It was not just the small group but the larger network as well. The group started contributing and adding to the larger network, reciprocating the initial support provided.

So, from the international online interaction a seed was planted within a project that supported the development of a multi-country community for field staff of a small international NGO, which in turned spawned a boundary-spanning multi-country community on online interaction for education and community development. Subsequently this community and its larger network have allowed the small NGO to launch a very successful online interaction project on preventing domestic violence and another on school connectivity in the Caucasus. Small seeds ... large trees.

The Practices

Networks connect and catalysts, in the form of events and people, trigger the formation of a distinct group of willing and interested people. This may be a core of geographically co-located people or a wider distributed network of resource folk. What does it take to realize the potential of the online tools to the group and its purpose? Using online space, how can we design, facilitate and amplify these natural network effects?

When approached as a tool for community development, online interaction provides a way to bridge time and distance to bring people together to do something. The key factors in the successful deployment of online interaction are a clear purpose and the appropriate match or blend of tools and processes. Just as you would plan the best use of meeting time, how to use a newsletter or a conference call, online interactions can be strategically deployed. Not because they are there and are "cool". The subsequent factors are the design of the online interaction space and the processes put in play to use the space.

- **Exploration:** What is the group's goal and how might it be enhanced with online interaction? Establish an initial statement of purpose - what are we doing and why? Who else has done something similar? What can we learn from them?
- **Assessment:** What are the conditions at play? Assess the target audience and the environmental conditions to inform further planning and design. Who are the potential players or stakeholders? Consider the relationship between the target group and larger networks that might inform and support the group's goals. Remember that the Internet is bounded by our imaginations, not by who is in the room!
- **Analysis:** Based on the assessment, explore which tools and methodologies can help this particular group of people reach their desired goal within the parameters of their access skills and resources.
- **Design:** Design the online space and processes to reflect all that has been learned so far. Processes such as facilitation, norms and agreements are just as important as the software you choose. Think about timing, punctuation and other factors that can create and hold engagement. Test and refine.
- **Deploy:** Market, launch and deploy the effort with multiple points of ongoing feedback. Listen. Refine. Improve. Report back.
- **Assess:** Glean the lessons learned and share them with the group and more widely as appropriate. Increase the community's capacity to engage online by learning these lessons—not leaving them behind.
- **Cycle:** Do it again, only better this time!

CONCLUSION

The richness of human knowledge is now available globally as well as locally, allowing us to learn, work and be together using online interaction tools and processes. To tap into this richness not only do we need to form groups and CoPs but we need to situate them in larger networks where new ideas and diversity can challenge and enrich the communities, providing both an inflow of members and an outflow of knowledge and information. Catalysts, people and time-delimited events both stimulate the formation and growth of these communities and help to capture and focus attention and resources.

REFERENCES

BOND. (2002). *Knowledge Management.* http://www.bond.org.uk/lte/km.htm [November 23, 2002]

Dyson, E., Gilder, G., Keyworth, G., and Toffler, A. (1994). *Cyberspace and the American dream: A agna Carta for the knowledge age.* Release 1.2. [August 22, 1994] http://www.pff.org/position.html [March 25, 2003]

EDC Global Learning Group. (No date). *EDC Global Learning Group.* http://www.edc.org/GLG/ [March 26, 2003]

Internet FAQ Archives. (2002). *What is Usenet?* http://isc.faqs.org/faqs/usenet/what-is/part1/ [March 25 2003]

Keeble, L., and Loader, B. D. (Eds.) (2001). *Community informatics: Shaping computer-mediated social relations.* London: Routledge.

Milgram, S. (1967). The small world problem. *Psychology Today, 1* (61), 60-67.

Publicus. (No date). *Open groups.* http://www.publicus.net/opengroups//about.html and http://www.publicus.net/opengroups//resources.html [November 23, 2002]

Rheingold, H., and Kimball, L. (2000). *How online social networks benefit organizations.* http://www.rheingold.com/Associates/onlinenetworks.html [March 26, 2003]

Swaak, J., Verwijs, C., and Mulder, I. (2000). *Task groups and communities compared.*https://doc.telin.nl/dscgi/ds.py/GetRepr/File-10580/html [March 25, 2003]

United Nations. (2002). UN System staff discussion forums: Improving information sharing through Special Interest Groups. Note by the CEB Secretariat 14 May 2002. Documentation for the *First Session of the UN System ICT Network.* http://www.unsystem.org/ICTNetwork/Documents/FirstSession/r6sigs.pdf [March 26, 2003]

Wenger, E.C. (1998). *Communities of Practice: Learning, meaning and identity.* Cambridge: University Press.

Wenger, E. C., McDermott, R., and Snyder, W. M.(2002). *Cultivating Communities of Practice: A guide to managing knowledge.* Harvard Business School Press.

White, N. (2002). *Online community manual.* http://www.fullcirc.com/community/communitymanual.htm

World Bank. (2003). *Knowledge sharing.* http://www.worldbank.org/ks/k-practice_qa2.html [March 26, 2003]

Chapter XXIV

Where Did That Community Go? - Communities of Practice That "Disappear"

Patricia Gongla
IBM Global Services, USA

Christine R. Rizzuto
NY Software Industry Association and
Project Management Institute, USA

ABSTRACT

Experience has been gained and a body of literature is building about how Communities of Practice (CoPs) within organizations are formed. We are learning about the progression of communities over time, how they evolve and mature, and about the factors that contribute to their sustainability. However, communities, being "living systems", do not live forever, or even very long. That said, exactly why and how does any particular Community of Practice (CoP) disappear? This chapter will discuss the factors related to the ending of individual communities. Specifically, it will address three basic questions:

1)   *In what ways do CoPs disappear; what are the different paths and patterns?*
2)   *Why do communities disappear?*
3)   *What are ways to help a community transition?*

The material for this chapter is drawn primarily from observations of and experiences with CoPs in IBM Global Services. A number of these communities over the past years have "disappeared", but they have not all "disappeared" in the same way. The authors will discuss patterns and variations that have emerged as these communities vanished from the organizational scene. In working with these communities, they have also developed a general guide to aid in the communities' transitioning. The authors will very briefly describe the steps in this guide.

INTRODUCTION

A Community of Practice (CoP) is an organizational model with deep roots and a long history. From hunting and gathering tribes through modern project management professionals, human beings who share common work goals need to hone their talents and pool their resources and expertise, and have formed community groups. Now called Communities of Practice (CoPs), they vary widely in form and content and can range from stand-alone study groups to professional guilds to corporate or association-sponsored communities.

The concept of a CoP used in this chapter comes from the work of Wenger and Snyder (2000), who define it as "a group of people informally bound together by shared expertise and passion for a joint enterprise", or similarly, as a collection of individuals bound by informal relationships that share similar work roles and a common context (Snyder, 1997).

Recently, recognition has grown of the importance of CoPs to the overall knowledge economy and to the goals of organizations grappling with rapid change. Many organizations have started programs to help support communities. As a result, much knowledge about how CoPs form and develop within organizations has been gained and shared. However, less knowledge is available about what actually happens to CoPs as they mature, evolve, decline or vanish. Yet, it is no secret that communities appear and disappear, divide and merge, grow more active and less active and in general show discernable patterns in their progress over time.

The focus in this chapter is on one particular aspect of community life within organizations: the phenomenon of communities' disappearance. Communities, even those with strong beginnings and of much value to a sponsoring organization, do not exist forever. Thus, our starting question is: What happens to these CoPs? Specifically, how do they disappear, what paths do they take and why do they disappear?

Obviously, CoPs that disappear can become an issue for an organization that depends on their bodies of knowledge and support for competency development, learning, training and market leadership. In these cases, it is important to see how and why communities disappear so that possible interventions may be implemented. Other times, however, the organization is pleased to see communities disappear that it thinks no longer serve the organization's goals. In these cases it may be just as valuable to understand the "hows and whys" of community disappearance to help both the community members and the organization, even when the organization may not realize the value.

Our starting point with regard to community disappearance is, in a sense, neutral. Disappearance is not viewed as a good thing or a bad thing. In some cases the disappearance of a community may be a normal event and important to the overall health of an organizationally-sponsored CoP program. In other situations where communities just disappear, it may be symptomatic of a non-supportive, or even hostile, environment. What we have learned from working with and observing CoPs that disappear may help organizations and community leaders navigate through situations where a CoP is experiencing an undesirable decline or may help a CoP go out of existence in a way that is valuable to its members and to the organization alike.

The objectives here are to describe different patterns of how communities disappear and to discuss a few of the predominant factors that seem to precipitate their departure. We end with a brief description of ways of dealing with communities that may transition out of existence. Designing interventions to help prevent communities from going out of existence is an important area but is beyond the scope of this chapter.

OVERALL APPROACH AND BACKGROUND

The observations about communities are drawn from work over six years in a Knowledge Management (KM) program dealing with almost seventy CoPs within IBM Global Services. The limitations of observations drawn from a single organization are recognised and so one cannot speculate how far these observations can be generalized. However, it is worth noting that IBM Global Services is a very large and complex organization, spanning the globe and having many subdivisions and distinct lines of business. The CoPs within the organization show wide variability in how they look, work, communicate and organize. Like the organization, the communities span the globe and so include geographical and cultural differences as well.

The whole gamut of community formation and evolution provided an initial interest, and observations led to the development of a community evolution model which details potential changes as communities mature and develop their capabilities (Gongla & Rizzuto, 2001). However, for the discussion of "disappearance", communities at the earlier stages of evolution are avoided, since it is difficult to say then if a community had really formed. It would not be clear if this were a community disappearing or just never forming in the first place.

When we say that a community "disappears", what we mean is that the community is no longer recognized as a separate, functioning system with a known, ongoing identity. We do not mean that the existence of the community and all knowledge of it disappear without a trace. So the key questions are: Does the community maintain a coherent, ongoing identity known both to itself and to the larger organization, and does it function as a goal-directed, self-managing system? If the answer to either of these questions is "no", then we define that community as having "disappeared".

About 25 CoPs that disappeared some time during a six-year period were observed. This sample of communities spanned the various lines of business, industries and competencies within IBM Global Services.

PATHS TO DISAPPEARANCE

There are some common ways that communities disappear or go "out of business". Four general patterns emerged, although each also had some variations. Specifically, we saw communities that:

- Drift into non-existence
- Redefine themselves
- Merge with other communities
- Become organizational units

Although there are other paths to disappearance, the four listed above were the primary ones observed. We will now look at each of these patterns in turn.

Communities that Drift Into Non-Existence

In this mode of disappearing, the community usually takes quite some time to fade. It is a long period before it is recognized that the community is no longer really there. Members gradually leave the community, slowly decreasing their participation in community activities until finally there is minimal or no participation at all. The problem is compounded in that, during this drift phase, new members rarely join the community since there is little outreach to them and little response to any overtures from them. Many core members of the community—those who are at the centre in terms of participation and knowledge—leave and are not replaced. Connections and interaction among members may continue, but they cease to be about community matters or the body of knowledge that was the focus of the community. As participation decreases, members stop identifying with the community. Less and less knowledge is shared and developed by the community. Organizational sponsorship and resources dwindle and usually stop altogether at some point. This drifting into non-existence usually takes time because no one specifically is trying to dissolve the community and there is no pressure to end it. At some point, however, the community finally goes out of existence completely, but no one usually knows when that point actually occurs.

Communities that Redefine Themselves

In this mode, the community does not dissolve, but it does disappear, in that the original identity disappears and some new identity is crafted to take its place. This redefinition process takes one of two forms.

1) The members of the community have an "identity crisis". They realize that they do not know who they are any longer as a community. The identity that the members had originally developed no longer fits them, even though they find value in interacting with each other. Usually something significant has changed in the community's environment—for example, a new major business area emerging - that affects how the community perceives itself. At some point, the members start the process of asking themselves again (as they had when they first formed): "Who are we?" "What is this community about?" "What is our common identity?" If the members come up with good answers—ones that the members can agree on—then they become a new community with a new name, even though they may incorporate many of the same members, implement the same processes that they had previously developed and use the same technology for their work. The key difference is that the core identity has changed. It is no longer the same community. The members re-focus on a new area of knowledge and a different practice. They make their new identity known to the larger organization and seek resources for their new area of focus.

2) The community does not form a new identity internally, but it changes its external identity vis-à-vis the larger organization. The community may do some things as simple as changing its name and using different terminology to describe itself to the organization. Other times, the community may remove itself completely from the organizational radar screen, "going underground" and becoming virtually invisible to the organization. The community usually makes an external identity change in response to the organization valuing the community either too much or too little. When the organization values it too much, it may spotlight the community and try to manage more and more of what the community is and does. This becomes distasteful to the community members and so they may remove the community from the organizational spotlight, "pretending" to disperse, but in reality continuing to function outside of the organization's purview. If necessary, they show themselves to the organization but do so as though they were a different community with a new name and identity. In the other

case, when the organization values the community too little, it may withhold resources from the community and even try to actively disband the community. In this situation, just as when the organization values the community too much, the community, by going underground, appears to the organization to have dispersed. The community is then free to pursue its interests and may even re-approach the organization for support under a new name.

In either case, from the outside perspective, the original community has disappeared. If it reappears, the organization perceives it as being a new community. The community, in effect, has redefined itself in relationship to the larger environment even though it is the same community internally.

Communities that Merge

Mergers are a typical way for communities to disappear. As with organizations, communities tend to follow one of two paths to disappearance.

1) **A merger of equals:** Two communities recognize that they have a great deal in common - individuals find themselves joining both communities, the knowledge domain of each community is similar and complementary to the other community, and technology and processes may be similar. Someone finally instigates the idea of joining forces and discussions between the groups ensue. In a sense, the two communities look at each other closely and ask: "Who are you?" "What are you about?" and if the answer that comes back is: "You are pretty much like me", then they often decide to merge. They recognize the benefits of joining forces—benefits such as sharing resources and reducing confusion in the larger organization that stems from having two separate, but similar, communities. A new community, with a combined identity, forms and the members give themselves a new name. The result is that the two original communities disappear and in their place the one, new, combined entity takes over.

2) **A merger of un-equals:** This "merger" appears as an acquisition. What typically occurs is that one community has a distinctive, specialized body of knowledge that can be considered a sub-domain of the body of knowledge within another community. This specialized community joins the broader community, either because it wants to or because it is pressured to do so. In the process, the specialized community disappears as a separate, distinct identity; it takes on the identity of the broader community even though it may maintain its own specialized body of knowledge.

Communities that Become Organizational Units

In this last pattern of disappearance, we see a community stop functioning as a community and become instead an organizational unit—perhaps a program, a project or a practice. The community is taken over by the organization: its mission becomes specifically and concretely defined by the organization; the members are directed as to what they should work on; results are expected and measured; management intervenes to direct and redirect members and processes to meet its objectives. When this metamorphosis occurs, it often does so because the community's knowledge and influence have become very important to the organization. The organization wants more control and finds the community structure too informal. Therefore, while the members of the community may still interact and the body of knowledge may still be enhanced and shared among the members, the reality is that the community has ceased to be a separate, self-managing entity, making decisions for itself. The community has disappeared and been replaced by the organizational unit.

WHY DO COMMUNITIES DISAPPEAR?

Communities, being living entities, are not expected to live forever. However, the intriguing question is: Why should a particular community disappear at a particular time? We recognize that, as with any complex system living in a dynamic, complex environment, the reasons for a particular community's demise will also be complex. Indeed, sometimes it seems that a scenario approach focusing on the myriad forces at play is the only approach that makes sense when trying to describe why a community disappears. However, at the same time we did also notice that certain factors emerged as frequent precipitants to disappearance. These are not "explanations" for the disappearance, but rather they are major changes that occurred which seemed to be prime motivators or catalysts for the community's eventual disappearance.

Specifically, three factors most commonly acted as stimuli or triggers to disappearance. These are:

- Organizational Change
- Knowledge Domain Change
- Community Leadership Change

Organizational Change

Generally, within IBM Global Services, a specific organizational unit or line of business sponsored a particular CoP. The community's mission had some alignment with that particular organizational unit's objectives and some level of organizational support. The CoP was embedded in a larger organization. How that organization related to the community deeply affected how well and even if the community functioned. Communities, of course, dealt with changes in the organization all the time. However, when there was a significant change in the sponsoring organization, then a community almost automatically becomes at risk of its own demise.

The particular key changes in the organizational unit that we saw having most impact on a community were:

- A redefinition or reorientation of the organizational unit that included new mission, new goals and objectives, and new measurements
- A change in the organizational unit's leadership often leading to a setting of new priorities by the new leader and an accompanying redeployment of resources

Whenever any of these organizational changes occurred, one of two things generally happened. Firstly, the sponsored CoPs reacted, sometimes desperately, to figure out how to match their own missions to the needs of the organization and how to re-gain some degree of support, or secondly, the communities acknowledged the major organizational change, decided that they no longer fit or had a role in the organization and chose to disappear. Even when the community took the first path and was successful in realigning with the larger organization, it often disappeared anyway because it redefined itself into being another, different community with a different domain of knowledge, a changed membership and a new identity.

Knowledge Domain Change

The knowledge domain of a CoP is not static. The community constantly refreshes "what it knows", adding to, modifying and deleting from its base of knowledge and expertise. However, what happens if the knowledge domain shifts radically or if the core knowledge becomes dated or obsolete? Consider, for example, the Y2K phenomenon. Many practitioners developed methods and a large body of knowledge about changes to information systems that were needed at that time. CoPs devoted to Y2K were formed. Now, however, that knowledge is itself "obsolete". Not that knowledge gained via Y2K experience is not valuable and used elsewhere, but is there any longer an active, dynamically modified Y2K domain of knowledge or a thriving Y2K CoP?

Sometimes the community's knowledge expands significantly and "bumps up against" other, previously distinct knowledge domains. A community, for example, devoted to a particular method of business process analysis decides that its domain of knowledge is really "business process analysis" and not just one particular method. It begins expanding its membership and knowledge boundaries to reflect this decision. What happens then to other communities in the organization that had formed around other specific business process methods? Mergers and acquisitions are likely possibilities. A similar pattern can occur when a new area of knowledge, with a dedicated community, transforms over time from "innovative" to "mainstream", becoming one sub-area within the mainstream domain. This is what happened, for example, when "innovative" object-oriented methods became mainstream application development methods and mainstream application development communities "absorbed" object-oriented ones. The distinctive identity disappeared.

Other times the knowledge domain is directly impacted by the community's sponsoring organization. The organization may decide to stop investing in or to de-prioritise a particular area of expertise that it had previously considered important. When this occurs, there is a series of follow-up actions: resources diverted from the community, community leaders given no support, disenchantment of community members and members leaving the organization to seek other environments where their knowledge is valued. The community generally disappears.

Community Leadership Change

A CoP has a core—some dynamic centre where there is more energy, more direction setting, decision-making, sharing, interaction, as well as more assumed and expected responsibility for the community as a whole, than in the rest of the community. If the members who are at the centre leave that centre, then major changes are likely, including a strong potential for the community's disappearance.

We have noted two particular patterns that spell trouble for the community's continued existence. In the first instance, the community has been led (often from its inception) by energetic, passionate, savvy leaders who encourage and stimulate lots of activity and attention for and within the community. If these leaders leave and if their replacements not only lack the fire and dynamism but also assume solely a caretaker role, then the community has a strong potential for disappearing.

In the second instance, the leadership change triggering community disappearance is related to a decrease in the size of the core leadership and its ability to commit to the community. If the number of core members decreases significantly, the result is less interaction and stimulation at the community's centre and thus for the community overall. A similar effect is seen if the number of core members remains the same but their ability or desire to commit time and energy to the community decreases. In either case, the community has difficulty sustaining itself.

HELPING A COMMUNITY TRANSITION

Overall, our approach for working with communities who may be disappearance candidates—and virtually all communities are—involves a four-step process: Investigate, Decide, Plan and Implement. These generic steps should not be surprising to any one involved in program management, yet they sometimes are surprising when applied to communities. There is a tendency to simply ignore the issue of transitioning communities out of existence both on the organization's part and on the part of the community members themselves. A similar effect is seen when the transitioning has some degree of recognition, but virtually no time or resources are devoted to it; somehow, things should just take care of themselves. Since a CoP has value to its members and to the organization, it seems more prudent to invest in the community, not just as it forms, but also as it transitions out of existence.

The Investigation Step

The Investigation step consists of three activities: performing a Community Health Check, reviewing it with the community and developing a set of options.

Performing a Community Health Check

As experience was gained through working with CoPs, it became clear that all communities are candidates for disappearing. Consequently, the importance of periodically assessing the working of a community became clear, even if there were no indication of problems, but especially if any of the precipitating factors occurred. The chief method employed was called a Community Health Check, which was conducted at regular intervals and at least once a year.

In a Health Check, evaluation criteria are defined covering the elements of the transformation framework: vision and value system, community strategy linked with business strategy, incentives, measurements, processes, organization, technology and leadership. Each community defines the specifics of how to address the framework elements, so the evaluation criteria reflect how well the community is meeting its own objectives vis-à-vis the elements, as well as fitting in with an overall KM program. Then information is gathered from the community using questions tailored from a master set to reflect the chosen evaluation criteria and the community's profile and needs.

Reviewing the Health Check with the Community

Two things are key when preparing the results of a community assessment for review. First, since CoPs behave as complex systems, close attention should be paid to the context of the community and the myriad internal and external factors that influence the community. Second, because of the uncertainty surrounding these factors, it is important to suspend judgment and forego making conclusions from the findings until the stakeholders have reviewed them and can discuss options. When reviewing the findings with the community, there should be a focus on both the insights into problems and suggestions for improvement offered during the assessment.

Developing a Set of Options

One place to start in developing a set of options for the community is to review the community's performance against the evaluation criteria originally set up for the Health Check assessment. The members can then see the relative strengths and areas for improvement for the community. The community evolution model, referred to earlier, is useful for positioning the community's data within the context of its stage of development or maturity. This helps the leadership understand what characteristics are expected or normal as well as provides guidelines for selecting areas to improve. The information gathered during the assessment should provide a good indication as to which disappearance path the community has already started down or whether the community is a candidate for disappearing. In either case, it is important to talk through this situation and clearly consider the various possibilities. Since there are a number of ways to disappear and often very good reasons for the transition, considering the options here should not be approached as a negative.

The Decision Step

The Decision Step consists of reviewing the options, coordinating with the organization's strategy and making a decision.

With the information learned from the community assessment and the various options developed, the community can proceed with a review of what to do. Generally, a cost-benefit approach is helpful, considering the costs and benefits not only from the point of view of reinvigorating the community but also from the view of transitioning the community out of existence. Using scenarios to consider the potential impacts of the main options can further stimulate a comprehensive understanding of the possibilities. In addition, it is helpful to draw upon the experience of other community leaders who guided community transitions.

If an organizational unit sponsors the CoP, it is important to involve the organization stakeholders in the review. How does the community fit within the organization's strategy? What is its mission vis-à-vis the organization's goal? If the community goes out of existence, how will the organization "cope" without it? It is important to check that the role of the community fits (again) into the organization's strategy and plans, or that the strategy is developed for what to do when the community disappears. At this point, a decision should be made among the options. When making the decision, the focus needs to be on the relative value of the community to the members and to the organization and how best to serve the needs of both.

The Planning Step

In the Planning step, plans are made to handle the major elements of the community in light of the decision made.

In general, the key plans needed are ones for managing the body of explicit knowledge, the membership, the interdependent processes and communications. These are similar to the activities that McDermott (2000) notes for community end-of-life. The activities he details include: capturing history, transferring knowledge, introducing members to a new community and acknowledging contributions. Throughout the planning step, it is important to coordinate with the sponsoring organization. It is also important to be realistic about what can be accomplished with available resources. If the decision had been to redefine or merge the community, then it is important to have a combination of short term actions or "quick hits" that will energize the newly redefined or merged community and longer term actions that will ensure sustainability. If the decision was to dissolve the community and if there still was an identified, active membership, then plans should be made to find alternate places where those members might go for continued community participation.

The Implementation Step

In the Implementation step, the plans are put into action.

Of course, execution is usually "easier said than done". Throughout the implementation, attention must be paid to the changing environment, and plans must be adjusted accordingly. Of particular concern is the preservation of resources allocated for the transition. It is not uncommon for resources to be withdrawn or redirected and to have to be re-secured, perhaps more than once. It helps to have a clear value statement for the transition so that those working on the implementation can easily justify the importance of their work. Throughout the transition the sponsor of the original community should be kept informed and, where appropriate, involved in activities like communication. Finally, the organizational strategy must be updated to incorporate the changes if the communities had been contributing to the overall business objectives.

CONCLUSION

CoPs are fluid, constantly changing, living systems. They do not, and should not, be expected to continue indefinitely. At the same time, CoPs have become an important part of many organizations' business strategies and should not end prematurely. Understanding the paths by which communities may transition or disappear and the possible precipitating factors for these changes will help the community members and sponsoring organizations to recognize when communities are threatened, to transition the communities into new forms, or to help communities more gracefully and effectively cease functioning.

REFERENCES

Gongla, P., and Rizzuto, C. R. (2001). Evolving Communities of Practice: IBM Global Services experience. *IBM Systems Journal, 40* (4), 842-862.

McDermott, R. (2000). Community development as a natural step: Five stages of community development. KM Review, 3 (5), (November/December).

Snyder, W. M. (1997). Communities of Practice: Combining organizational learning and strategy insights to create a bridge to the 21st Century. *Academy of Management Conference,* Boston, MA (August).

Wenger, E. C., and Snyder, W. M. (2000). Communities of Practice: The organizational frontier. Harvard Business Review, 78(1), (January), 139-145.

Glossary

Bulletin Boards

A Bulletin Board is an electronic message centre for exchanging messages on a network. Bulletin Board Systems (BBS) became the main online community in the 1980s and early 1990s before the advent of the World Wide Web (WWW). Users could dial in via modem or telnet and could read and post simple messages. Early BBS were operated through a text-based command line; however, most current versions have an interactive graphical interface. Some BBS are general but most are dedicated to a specific subject. Despite the advent of the WWW, BBS remain popular.

Champion

Product champions have been identified as playing a key role in bringing about change and innovation. The role was first identified by Schon (1963, p. 84):

"Essentially the champion must be a man willing to put himself on the line for an idea of doubtful success. He is willing to fail. But he is capable of using any and every means of informal sales and pressure in order to succeed."

The champion is the person in an organisation who is a committed and passionate advocate of change (Ginsberg & Abrahamson, 1991) who will 'sell' a new technology or a project by providing the energy and enthusiasm to help it overcome organisational inertia. (See also *sponsor*.)

Collaborative Tools

Collaborative tools are software tools that allow a group of users to collaborate on a project or task. The software can have a range of functionality; for example: it can act as a central repository for documents and offer the facility to jointly work on documents - both in real time and at different times. There may be functionality to connect people, e.g., discussion forums, chat rooms. An example of a collaborative tool is Microsoft's NetMeeting. This application was developed by Microsoft Corporation to help users work collaboratively. It is incorporated into Internet Explorer (Microsoft's web browser) and supports chat sessions, whiteboard, application sharing and document sharing.

Engagement

Wenger (1998) describes engagement as a source of identity, which becomes a mode of belonging in a community. He described (p. 174) it as:

"A threefold process, which includes the conjunction of: 1) The ongoing negotiation of meaning, 2) The formation of trajectories, 3) The unfolding histories of practice. It is in the conjunction of all three processes—as they take place through each other—that engagement becomes a mode of belonging and a source of identity."

He further explains (p. 175) the character of engagement, thus:

"... there are obvious physical limits in time and space: we can be only in one place at a time and dispose of only a finite number of hours per day. In addition, there are physiological limits to the complexity that each of us can handle, to the scope of activities we can be directly involved in, and to the number of people and artefacts with which we can sustain substantial relationships of engagement."

Equivocality

The term equivocality refers to the existence of ambiguity, i.e., a situation where a particular stimulus is capable of having multiple, and possibly conflicting, interpretations. Because of this, in highly equivocal situations, people may not even know what questions to ask in order to begin to resolve the situation. Although equivocality and uncertainty are often used interchangeably, they are subtly different. Acquiring and processing more information can reduce uncertainty while discussions and face-to-face meetings are usually seen as the means to reduce equivocality. (See also *Media Richness*.)

Explicit Knowledge

Explicit knowledge is knowledge that is easily expressed, captured, codified, stored, and reused. It is easily transmitted as data and is therefore found in databases, books, manuals, reports, and messages.

Homophily

The theory of homophily, credited to Lazarsfeld and Merton (1954), is that human communication is most likely to occur between people who are alike (i.e., homophilous; having a common frame of reference). Homophily is the degree to which individuals share similar attributes, such as values, beliefs, occupations or education. The phrase 'birds of a feather flock together' is a good example of homophily (McPherson, Smith-Lovin & Cook, 2001).

Knowledge Repositories

A repository in this context is basically a database. A number of types of information can be held and all can be loosely called Knowledge Repositories. In this book a number of examples are listed:

1) A database of best practice
2) A repository of work done in a community of software developers. If a developer produces some good work it can be put into the repository and made available to other developers in the community
3) In one chapter, a database of documents is termed a knowledge repository as it is used in electronic knowledge exchange
4) An archive of messages in an online community
5) A store of tools and discussions that have been used by the community members

Media Richness

Media richness theory was originally proposed by Daft and Lengel (1984). It views media choice as a rational process in which individuals match the objective characteristics of the communication medium with the content of the message. Communication media are seen as varying in their capacity to handle message complexity. High levels of message complexity are termed 'richness' and low levels of complexity are termed 'leanness'. Communication media are seen as having a hierarchy of richness from face-to-face as the highest, through to telephone, electronic mail, personal written text, formal written text, formal numeric text and computerised data as the lowest. Rich messages require rich media, that is, media that are capable of communicating complexity and equivocality. Media low in richness are appropriate for resolving uncertainty through the processing of standard, objective data that defies inconsistent interpretation.

Narration

Narration takes the form of story telling and is a key means by which CoP members share knowledge. This was shown as a central part of the transition from newcomer to old-timer in Lave and Wenger's (1991) community of non-drinking alcoholics. Orr (1997) also showed that the qualities of the stories bestowed members of his copier repair engineers with a form of legitimation and confirmed their status in and membership of the community.

People Finders

This is another term for an Expert Locator, i.e., a system set up within a community or an organisation to help people find an expert in a specific field. (See also *Yellow Pages*.)

Portal

A Portal is a website that offers access to a wide range of services (e.g., e-mail, forums, search engines, online shopping). Some of the larger search engines have made themselves into portals to try to obtain a larger audience. A portal might exist to serve a single market sector; for example a website might be set up with a lot of content but it might also serve as a gateway to other sites and services serving that particular market.

Pure-Play

This refers to interaction that is entirely online.

Routers

A router is a networking device connected to at least two networks. It forwards data packets and communicates with other routers to determine the best route between the sending computer and the receiving computer.

Skunkworks

"A skunkworks is a group of people who, in order to achieve unusual results, work on a project in a way that is outside the usual rules. A skunkworks is often a small team that assumes or is given responsibility for developing something in a short time with minimal management constraints. Typically, a skunkworks has a small number of members in order to reduce communications overhead. A skunkworks is sometimes used to spearhead

a product design that thereafter will be developed according to the usual process. A skunkworks project may be secret."

(From SearchCIO.com http://searchcio.techtarget.com/sDefinition/ 0,,sid19_gci214112,00.html [July 7th, 2003])

Sponsor

A sponsor is essentially the client. The sponsor is usually a member of senior management who has overall responsibility for a project and who will work to convince other senior managers of the potential or viability of the project. (See also *Champion.*)

Tacit Knowledge

Tacit knowledge, according to Nonaka (1991, p. 98) is:

"... highly personal. It is hard to formalize and therefore, difficult to communicate to others ... Tacit knowledge is also deeply rooted in action and in an individual's commitment to a specific context—a craft or profession, a particular technology or products market, or the activities of a work group or team. Tacit knowledge consists partly of technical skills - the kind of informal, hard-to-pin-down skills captured in the term 'know-how' ... tacit knowledge has an important cognitive dimension. It consists of mental models, beliefs, and perspectives so ingrained that we take them for granted and therefore cannot easily articulate them."

An important aspect of tacit knowledge is that it is extremely difficult to articulate. In fact, there are different opinions about whether tacit knowledge can be articulated at all. Some people feel that tacit knowledge can be captured (Huang, 1997). Some feel it cannot be codified without being invalidated (Buckingham Shum, 1998) whereas others feel it cannot be captured or codified at all (Star, 1995; Chao, 1997; Leonard & Sensiper, 1998).

Threaded Discussion

Earlier discussion forums were bulletin board systems where users posted messages that could be read by other users. Threaded discussions differ from the earlier systems in that postings are stored and made visible only within the topic (or thread) to which they refer. This means that when a user wants to read the discussion about a specific topic (s)he can read all the postings in order. (See *Bulletin Boards.*)

War Stories

These are stories told based on the teller's experience and which are told to illustrate a point, perhaps as a contribution to problem solving. The teller's colleagues may learn something from the story. It may even make them think of something else, or lead them to come up with something new and innovative. It can be part of a creative process. (See also *Narration*.)

Yellow Pages

These take their name from the telephone directories with listings according to service. In terms of Knowledge Management, Yellow Pages are directories of experts within the organisation.

REFERENCES

Buckingham Shum, S. (1998). Negotiating the construction of organisational memories. In U. M. Borghoff and R. Pareschi R. (Eds.), *Information Technology for Knowledge Management*, (pp. 55-78). Berlin: Springer. (Reprinted from: Negotiating the construction and reconstruction of organisational memories. *Journal of Universal Computer Science, 3* (8), 1997, 899-928).

Chao, G. T. (1997). Organizational socialization in multinational corporations: The role of implicit learning. In C. L. Cooper and S. E. Jackson (Eds.), *Creating tomorrow's organisations*, (pp. 43-57). John Wiley and Sons.

Daft, R. L., and Lengel, R. H. (1984). Information richness: A new approach to managerial behavior and organizational design. *Research in Organizational Behavior, 6*, 191-233.

Ginsberg, A., and Abrahamson, E. (1991). Champions of change and strategic shifts: The role of internal and external change advocates. *Journal of Management Studies, 28* (2), 173-90.

Huang, K. (1997). Capitalizing collective knowledge for winning execution and teamwork. *Journal of Knowledge Management, 1* (2), 149-156.

Lave, J., and Wenger, E. (1991). *Situated learning. Legitimate peripheral participation.* Cambridge University Press.

Lazarsfeld, P., and Merton, R. (1954). Friendship as social process. In M. Berger, T. Abel and C. Page (Eds.), *Freedom and control in modern society.* New York: Octagon.

Leonard, D., and Sensiper, S. (1998). The role of tacit knowledge in group innovation. *California Management Review, 40*(3), 112-132.

McPherson, M., Smith-Lovin, L., and Cook, J. M. (2001). Birds of a feather: Homophily in social networks. *Annual Review of Psychology, 27*, 415-444.

Nonaka, I. (1991). The knowledge creating company. *Harvard Business Review*, *69*, Nov-Dec, 96-104.

Orr, J. (1997). *Talking about machines: An ethnography of a modern job.* NY: Cornell University Press.

Schon, D.A. (1963). Champions for radical new inventions. *Harvard Business Review*, *41* (2), 77-86.

Star, S. L. (1995). The politics of formal representations: Wizards, gurus, and organizational complexity. In S. L. Star (Ed.), *Ecologies of knowledge. Work and politics in science and technology,* (pp. 88-118). Albany, NY: SUNY Press.

Wenger, E. (1998). *Communities of Practice. Learning, meaning and identity.* CUP.

About the Editors

After 11 years teaching modern languages, **Paul Hildreth** went back to university, in York (United Kingdom), to "convert" to IT. Having completed his MSc, he stayed on to do a DPhil exploring the field of Knowledge Management. This work convinced him that Knowledge Management is not about technology but about people and led him to explore the emerging and fascinating field of Communities of Practice (CoP). Recognizing the pressures imposed on organizations by globalization, he concentrated on researching how CoPs can function in a distributed international environment. The work produced a number of well-received journal and conference papers. Having completed his DPhil, Hildreth now runs his own independent Knowledge Management and computer consultancies. He lives in rural North Yorkshire with Maggie, Tom, and Buzz the cat. When he manages to find a little spare time, he likes to indulge in his hobbies of kit and classic cars, and guitar.

Chris Kimble is a lecturer in Information Systems and Management in the Department of Computer Science at the University of York, United Kingdom. Before moving to York, he was lecturer in Information Technology at the University of Newcastle's Business School, and a researcher in both the Business School and the Department of Computer Science at the University of Northumbria. His broad area of research is Knowledge Management. His areas of particular interests are Communities of Practice and the problems associated with supporting distributed working in cross-cultural or trans-national contexts. He is the leader of the Management and Information Research Group at York and a co-founder of the Northern Interest Group on Information Systems and Organisations. He has supervised several PhD students and has published more than 40 articles in journals, conferences, reports and books. Kimble has also acted as a consultant for information systems textbooks and as a reviewer for numerous academic journals. He is the academic contact for Knowledge Management for the WUN (Worldwide Universities Network) at the University of York and has organised conferences, seminars and workshops at York and elsewhere.

About the Authors

Pete Bradshaw is a researcher at Ultralab. He works on online learning projects for the National College of School Leadership (NCSL), for the Qualifications and Curriculum Authority (QCA) and for Anglia Polytechnic University (APU), United Kingdom. In particular, he has worked on the implementation of nationwide communities for the National Professional Qualification for Headship (NPQH) in England, which has cohorts of some 3,000 enrolling every six months. He has worked in a range of educational contexts for 24 years including head of faculty, advisory teacher and chief examiner. He has co-authored works on the use of ICT in education.

Wim Broer is police commissioner and director of the Police Knowledge Net Institute at the LSOP and he is program manager of the European Police Knowledge Net. During his career he worked in different police forces in The Netherlands and in between as a researcher in the field of policing. He has published numerous articles and reports about police science, neighborhood policing, change management, strategic policy development, information management and knowledge management.

Shawn Callahan is the Australian and New Zealand leader of IBM's Cynefin Centre for Organizational Complexity. He has been designing and implementing knowledge management projects for the past decade and is a hands-on practitioner who has extensive practical experience in implementing a range of tangible KM initiatives. Recent projects include knowledge strategy, lessons learned, communities of practice, narrative, knowledge mapping and intellectual capital management. Shawn was the co-founder of the ActKM, a Community of Practice for public sector knowledge managers.

Elisabeth Davenport is professor of Information Management at Napier University, United Kingdom. She leads the Social Informatics Research Group in the School of Computing, is an associate of the School's International Teledemocracy Centre and is a visiting scholar in the School of Library and Information Science in Indiana University. She has undertaken a number of EC funded projects that have explored technology and communities. Her current research interests include organizational and social computing, management of tacit knowledge and social capital, digital genres, and ethnomethodology in the workplace.

Michael A. Fontaine is a managing consultant and research manager with IBM's Institute for Business Value, USA, where he leads research and consulting projects that support and foster communities and collaboration. Over the past three years, Fontaine has helped many private and public organizations share and exchange knowledge and increase organizational performance by developing effective strategies for Communities of Practice and collaborative technologies. By conducting survey and field research into how communities function, Fontaine has developed methods for understanding the costs and benefits of communities, nurturing the roles needed to sustain communities, and harnessing external knowledge via customer communities. Currently, Fontaine is studying how knowledge work is increasingly taking place in shared virtual environments and how the global economic crisis, a potential world health epidemic, and the reduction in travel and discretionary budgets is influencing the ways in which organizations collaborate.

Benjamin Frost graduated in Business Administration at the University of Mannheim, Germany. Since then, he has gained long-term experience within the field of knowledge management in several international conglomerates. He currently works as a knowledge management consultant at Siemens AG (Germany), providing consulting services and professional support for communities of practice within the Siemens group. Over the past years, he has managed different CoP projects covering a range from research issues to the practical implementation of international communities.

Patricia Gongla is a program manager within the Worldwide Market Intelligence organization for IBM Global Services, USA. Previously, also within IBM Global Services, she focused on collaboration processes and technologies for the Business Transformation Organization and worked for six years in the advanced knowledge management (KM) solutions area with a worldwide team responsible for implementing multifaceted KM programs. Prior to that, she held various consulting and staff positions in IBM related to business process and I/S method development, business and information modelling, strategic information management, organizational innovation, and knowledge-based and expert systems. Before joining IBM, she was a researcher and consultant for various academic and governmental agencies in the areas of stress-related illnesses and program evaluation. She was on the faculties of the University of California, Los Angeles (UCLA) and the University of Southern California. She received a PhD in Sociology from Case Western Reserve University and was a Postdoctoral Fellow in psychiatric epidemiology and evaluation methods at UCLA.

Tally Hatzakis holds a BSc in Marketing Management (The American College of Greece), an MBA, awarded with distinction (Aston Business School), and is completing her PhD research in Information Systems (Brunel University, United Kingdom). Before returning to education, Hatzakis has worked as an account manager managing national and international corporate projects. Her research concentrates on all aspects of people management issues triggered by IT-related organizational change. She is currently engaged in ongoing research with a number of organizations regarding collaboration issues between business and IT during information systems development, change and maintenance.

Donald Hislop is a lecturer at Sheffield University Management School, United Kingdom. His research interests broadly encompass the area of technological change in organizations, with specific interests in the nature of knowledge and the role of IT systems in organizations. Hislop has published in a range of technology, innovation and management journals, including *Journal of Management Studies*, *Research Policy*, *Technology Analysis and Strategic Management* and the *International Journal of Innovation Management*.

Susanne Justesen holds a master's in Business Administration (MBA) with a specialization in Intercultural Management from Copenhagen Business School in Denmark. Besides running her company, Innoversity, with offices in Copenhagen and New York, she facilitates Innoversity Network, Denmark, as well as being actively involved in a range of activities in both academic, business and entrepreneurial settings. Justesen holds board positions in the Danish Association for Entrepreneurs as well as the Danish Initiative for Creativity and Innovation and is furthermore the Danish representative in the international organization, Creativity and Innovation Day (all organizations working to enhance overall innovation and entrepreneurship). She also holds a mentor position for a Danish Masters Program titled, Gender and Culture. She is actively involved in the Master of Knowledge Management (MKM) program, which is a new executive master program offered by Copenhagen Business School and Learning Lab Denmark. In all of these settings, her role has been centered on breaking, crossing, and spanning the boundaries between academics and practitioners in the fields of diversity, innovation and communities of practice.

Lisa Kimball is the founder and lead consultant in Group Jazz, USA, a company that specializes in working with virtual teams and communities. Her background includes 20 years of producing virtual events and communities for global organizations, including IBM, Merck, Hewlett Packard and others. She has trained hundreds of community managers and facilitators. She combines her extensive knowledge of organization design, executive development and learning with experience using the latest media and technology to leverage key processes. Recent virtual CoPs and events designed and facilitated by Group Jazz include the Fannie Mae Foundation's KnowledgePlex community PBS Teacher line, and the US Department of Agriculture's New American Communities Initiative.

Roger Kolbotn works as an advisor at the Norwegian Directorate for Civil Defence and Emergency Planning, Norway. In 2001-2003, he attended Bournemouth University, United Kingdom. His MA dissertation in information systems management examines the role and management of communities of practice for volunteers in the Royal National Lifeboat Institution. His chapter is based on this study.

Maarten de Laat is working on his PhD in the Department of Education at the University of Nijmegen, The Netherlands, where he researches how ICT can support learning in communities of practice (CoPs). He works for the Centre for ICT in Education at IVLOS, University of Utrecht. He is co-founder of KnowledgeWorks, a software company that designs software to support learning and knowledge management and he facilitates a Dutch online workshop on the foundations of CoP in collaboration with Cpsquare.

Amy Ladd specializes in facilitation of virtual teams and communities of practice (CoPs). Her experience includes design and facilitation of virtual interactive communities and collaborative meeting design process. Ladd has served on planning committees for national and regional conferences, co-designed and facilitated organizational retreats and workshops, and taught courses on virtual teams and Sustaining CoPs with Lisa Kimball. As a community facilitator at Caucus Systems and Metasystems Design Group, Ladd helped to evolve and support some of the first online social networks. Ladd was a special projects coordinator at Appalachian Center for Economic Networks where she convened a training program linking businesses in the manufacturing sector, and facilitated the first online CoP for microenterprise training providers in the Specialty Foods Industry.

Laurence Lock Lee is a principal knowledge management consultant with Computer Sciences Corporation in Australia. He has consulted widely to both private and public sector clients on most aspects of KM, but with a specialization around communities of practice, knowledge audits and social network analysis processes. Before joining CSC in 2000, he was employed by BHP, a major global resources company, where he was the enterprise KM practice lead for their IT company. Lee has been working in the knowledge systems field for nearly 20 years, having previously led BHP's corporate research in the areas of artificial intelligence, knowledge based expert systems and human computer interaction from the early 1980s. He holds degrees in Metallurgy (Hons), Computer Science and Business Administration. He has published and presented more than 25 papers in conferences, books and journals on the above topics.

Eric L. Lesser is an associate partner with IBM's Institute for Business Value, USA. He leads the Knowledge and Organizational Performance Forum, a multi-company consortium focused on knowledge and human capital issues. Lesser oversees the Forum's research initiatives and has led multi-client studies on knowledge strategy, CoP, knowledge retention and customer knowledge issues. As a consultant, he has worked with customers in the financial services, legal, technology and government sectors on developing knowledge strategies, en-abling communities and implementing knowledge management solutions. Lesser has spoken frequently on the topic of knowledge in organizations and has edited *Knowledge and Social Capital* and co-edited *Knowledge and Communities*, both published by Butterworth-Heinemann (2000). Before joining IBM, Lesser was a consultant with Mercer Consulting Group. While at Mercer, he served as a project manager and lead consultant on a number of assignments, including reengineering, new product development, organization strategy and design, and change management efforts. Before joining Mercer, Lesser worked as a consultant for Andersen Consulting in its Change Management practice.

Kimberly Lopez is a senior KM consultant for the KM practice area at APQC's (American Productivity & Quality Center) International Benchmarking Clearinghouse, USA. In her role over the last five years, Kimberly has worked extensively in designing knowledge management strategy, methodologies and approaches for organizations such as Dow Corning, Compaq, Hewlett-Packard and Lockheed Martin. She is also responsible for APQC's global partnership with Knowledge Dynamics Initiative, a subsidiary of Fuji-Xerox providing KM consulting services to the Asia-Pacific region. Recently, Lopez served as Subject Matter expert for APQC's Using KM to Drive Innovation consortium benchmarking study. In addition to being a contributing author to APQC's Knowledge Management publications, she authored *How to Measure the Value of Knowledge Management* and *Communicating Success at Compaq* for KM Review.

Anders Lundkvist, PhD, is researcher and assistant professor at Stockholm University School of Business, Sweden. He started his professional career within financial services and has more than 20 years of experience with the use of computer technology in businesses. He has published several books, articles, conference papers, and reports. *The Interactive Company* was in 1999 awarded Marketing Book of the Year in Sweden. Anders Lundkvist is a recognized consultant on customer relationships and innovation issues in Europe.

Mark Lycett holds a BSc in Computing and Business Management (Oxford Brookes), an MSc in Information Systems (Brunel University) and a PhD in Information Systems (Brunel University, United Kingdom). Before returning to education, Dr. Lycett spent a number of years in industry and he has managed a number of national and international business development projects. His research concentrates on all aspects of organizational and information systems development and he is currently engaged in ongoing research with a number of organizations. Dr. Lycett has published a number of works in these areas in a number of leading journals and international conferences.

Brook Manville is chief learning officer and customer evangelist of Saba, a California-based company that is the leading provider of "e-learning infrastructure" and human capital management solutions. At Saba, Manville has responsibility for Saba's thought leadership, customer communities, advisory groups, organizational development and several external strategic initiatives. Prior to coming to Saba, Manville held various positions at McKinsey and Co. from 1987 to 1999; he was elected partner in 1994, specializing in organizational development and knowledge-related strategy. At McKinsey, Manville consulted to several Fortune 500 companies in these areas. In the earlier part of his McKinsey career, he helped lead McKinsey's original knowledge management program and went on to become McKinsey's first director of knowledge management, as well as their CIO between 1991 and 1994. Brook's earlier professional career was a mix of technology, communications and education. Trained as a historian, Brook was originally on the Faculty of Arts and Sciences at Northwestern University (Chicago) and later entered business as a freelance journalist and then a business/technology analyst at CBS, Inc. Brook holds a PhD in History from Yale (1979) and undergraduate degrees in Classics from Oxford (1975) and Yale (1972).

Valerie A. Martin has an established research track record in information management, organizational culture, knowledge management and change. With an MSc in Information Management (Strathclyde University), and a PhD in Computer Integrated Manufacturing (Cranfield University), Dr. Martin has had substantial research and consulting experience in the areas of manufacturing, supply chain management with small companies, and information and knowledge management in IT consultancies, the university sector and the financial services sector. She is currently a research fellow in the Department of Information

Systems and Computing at Brunel University (United Kingdom) and has published in a number of international conferences and journals.

David R. Millen joined IBM Research in 2000 to work on online communities. Millen's current research interests include understanding how individuals and small groups use the Internet and other emerging communications technologies: especially usage patterns, the various roles people play and social networks in computer-mediated communication. For example, in a recent study he examined how an online community of journalists used the archive created from their online conversations as an information resource. To better grasp the rhythms and patterns of the archived discourse, Millen developed a new mode of displaying data called a "conversation map". Before coming to IBM (USA), David worked at AT&T Labs Research, where he explored how new technologies change employee work activities, organizational roles, and patterns of communication. He has also directed a User Interface Design Group, which was responsible for the user interface of business telephones and telephone features as well as conducting exploratory development of advanced speech technologies. Millen holds a BA from Columbia University, an MS in Management from Purdue University and a PhD in Cognitive Psychology from Rutgers University.

John Moran is the founder of Global Gateways, Inc. (USA), and a co-facilitator of two CoPs. Blending more than 30 years experience in industry as an executive, product developer and project manager and in academia as a course developer/instructor, Moran has achieved recognition as a bridge between the academic communities and industry. In all his work, John advocates the importance of learning and systems thinking. Systems thinking is the capability to research and understand the relationships and connections between people, organizations and their environments. Moran's educational background includes a BA in Computer Science from UC Berkeley and an MBA from Golden Gate University.

Mark Neff is a knowledge management specialist within the CSC (Computer Sciences Corporation) Knowledge Program (Australia) and is currently focusing on collaboration processes and technologies in support of project teams. Previously, he worked for three years in the development of and support of communities within CSC. Before that, he was responsible for the development and deployment of computer-based training and a learning management system for CSC. His experience includes system engineering, quality assurance, program management and proposal management on various government programs. Today he consults on KM strategy, helps project teams learn how to work virtually and provides specific recommendations on how to improve productivity and leverage global assets. He has a BS in Marine Engineering from the US

Naval Academy and an MA in Organizational Design and Effectiveness from the Fielding Institute.

Stephen Powell is a researcher at Ultralab, and developer of formal and non-formal online learning communities. He has worked extensively on ground-breaking initiatives working with school leaders for the Department for Education and Skills, and the National College for School Leadership. A feature of this work has been the large-scale nature of the projects and their focus of professional learning. This work has also involved developing a CoP for researchers and facilitators who work remotely across the United Kingdom in a project focussed team supporting the school leader's communities, and it is this work that informs the basis of this chapter.

Christine R. Rizzuto is a PMI certified project management professional with international experience in marketing, sales, IT application development and process management. Her current passion is the application of peer-to-peer, wireless technology to facilitate asynchronous, non-co-located collaboration. She is accomplished at end-to-end system and software design, development and implementation. Her recent major projects include a digital reference for traditional Chinese medicine practitioners and students; managing IBM's world-wide knowledge program that was awarded international recognition by GIGA for excellence in workflow; supporting community development with process, technologies and organization change techniques; creating a worldwide operational data system and warehouse for all business competencies with an inventory of skill proficiencies for more than 200,000 service professionals to support operational, tactical and strategic management decision making; and managing a national customer satisfaction program.

Andrew Schenkel is an assistant professor at the Stockholm School of Economics, Sweden, and a frequent lecturer in their Executive Education programs. Dr. Schenkel is a graduate of the University of Wisconsin, Madison, and Imperial College, London. He received his doctorate from the Stockholm School of Economics. His dissertation focused on learning in the construction of the bridge between Sweden and Denmark. His chapter is based upon that study. His research interests include the study of social networks and their relationship to knowledge management and social capital. In addition, he conducts action research in the pharmaceutical industry at FENIX, the centre for research on knowledge and business creation.

Stefan Schoen graduated in Mechanical Engineering from the University of Stuttgart, Germany, and completed the master's program, Engineering Management, at the School of Business/College of Engineering at the University of

Wisconsin, Madison (USA). He then studied for and was awarded a Doctorate in Engineering from the Technical University in Munich (Germany). Since November 1996, he has been working for Siemens AG in Munich. First, he worked as in-house process and IT consultant with a focus on knowledge management and e-business. Since 2001, he has been department head of the Siemens Competence Centre, User Interface Design, with global locations in Munich, Princeton and Beijing.

John D. Smith received a BA from St. John's College and an MArch from the University of New Mexico. He was a planner, administrator and technologist at the University of Colorado for many years. He has been organizing and supporting CoPs informally for his entire professional life and formally since 1997. He has been instrumental in the development and organization of the Foundations of Community of Practice workshop and in CPsquare. He is an independent consultant working out of Portland, Oregon, speaking and working internationally since 1999.

John S. Storck is an assistant professor of Management Information Systems, teaching in the MBA and executive MBA programs at Boston University's School of Management, USA. Dr. Storck is currently involved in a broadly based research program dealing with knowledge economy issues. His research activities focus on the nature of individual and group work in globally dispersed organizations, with a particular emphasis on how CoPs enhance knowledge diffusion and learning. His prior work has been published in journals such as the *Sloan Management Review*, *Human Communication Research* and the *IBM Systems Journal*.

Lauren E. Storck is a clinical instructor in the Department of Psychiatry, Harvard Medical School, and senior research associate at the Gerontology Center of Boston University, USA. She specializes in consultation services for individuals, teams and larger groups working with issues ranging from career and management strategies to aging (caregiving) and Internet dialogues. Her research on groups helps people maximize collaborative efforts and understand interpersonal communications and relationships in any setting. Dr. Storck is a member of the editorial board of the *Journal for Specialists in Group Work* and was guest editor of the special issue on Class and Inequality for the journal, *Group Analysis*.

Bronwyn Stuckey has been a lecturer of Information and Communication Technology in the Education faculty and launched her PhD research work in Online CoPs for Professional Development. For six years before that she was an educational technologist and instructional designer, developing multimedia teaching and training solutions for a number of leading educational institutions. Her doctoral research has been to explore communities and networks of practice as options for online professional development. She has for the past three years coached and facilitated in the Etienne Wenger Foundations of Community of Practice workshop and has developed a series of case studies of CoPs across many domains and practices including education communities in all sectors (school, tertiary and vocational education).

Robin Teigland of the Stockholm School of Economics (Sweden), received her BA with distinction in Economics at Stanford University. After obtaining an MBA at Wharton and an MA in International Studies at the University of Pennsylvania and working as a consultant at McKinsey & Co., she now researches the organization and management of knowledge work. While her interests include the strategic use of IT, her primary focus is on informal extra-organizational boundary spanning activities and their relationship with a firm's competitive advantage. She has taught numerous courses in strategy, KM and social capital at the undergraduate, graduate, and executive levels as well as consulted within these areas. Fore more information, go to www.teigland.com.

Ian Terrell works at Ultralab researching the use of new technology and learning. He was formerly head of CPD at Anglia Polytechnic University, United Kingdom. In his 27-year career, Dr. Terrell has worked in three universities, for an LEA advisory team and in three schools. He has co-authored a number of works including, *Raising Achievement at GCSE*, *Development Planning and School Improvement for Middle Managers*, and *Learning to Lead*.

Emmanuelle Vaast gained her PhD in Information Systems from the Ecole Polytechnique, Paris. She is an assistant professor in Information Systems at the School of Business, Public Administration and Information Sciences at Long Island University, USA. Her research interests concern the construction of intra-organizational boundaries with practices of IS and the transformation of the relationships between CoPs and the formal organization through the appropriation of new technologies. She has presented her work at the Academy of Management Conference and has published in Information Research.

Wesley C. Vestal is a senior KM consultant for the KM practice area at the American Productivity & Quality Center, USA. In his role over the last five years, Vestal has worked extensively in designing and implementing KM strategies, solutions, training courses, and systems for organizations such as Exxon-Mobil Chemical, Best Buy, Schlumberger, Army Medical Division, the American Red Cross, and the American Cancer Society. Wesley speaks at KM conferences across the US, South America, and Europe, and is an APQC-certified trainer on Knowledge Management and benchmarking skills. Currently, he is serving as Subject Matter Expert for APQC's Replicating the Gains from Six Sigma and Lean consortium benchmarking study. He recently published an article, "Ten Traits of Successful Communities of Practice," in the January/February 2003 edition of the *KM Journal* and has written several articles on KM in APQCs *CenterView*.

Molly McLure Wasko is an assistant professor in the Department of Management Information Systems in the College of Business at Florida State University, USA. She received her BBA in Management at James Madison University, her MBA at Averett University, and her PhD in MIS with an emphasis in Organization Strategy from the University of Maryland, College Park. Her research interests include strategic management of IT, electronic cooperation and collaboration, and leveraging IT to create competitive advantage. She has taught a variety of IT courses at the undergraduate and graduate levels as well as consulted within the above areas.

Lee Weimer brings more than 20 years of experience working closely with business, education and community leaders throughout the world through chambers of commerce and not-for-profit associations. She has been a manager in a local US chamber, and has conducted organization development and grassroots management training through 10 years with the United States Chamber of Commerce and the Center for International Private Enterprise. She is an accomplished speaker, trainer and facilitator. Weimer currently works to co-facilitate the CIO Community of Practice with founder John Moran and consults through her own consulting firm, The Weimer Collaborative, USA.

Nancy White has utilized her facilitation, marketing, communications and management abilities for more than 23 years in broadcast media, not-for-profit and the high-tech community. As founder and president of Full Circle Associates (USA), a communications consultancy, she helps non-profits and businesses connect through online and offline strategies. She has a particular interest in the application of online interaction tools and techniques to non-profit virtual teams and international community development. White is a skilled online host and facilitator who hones her craft on social conversational sites and with distributed CoPs and virtual teams. She is an active chronicler and collector of online facilitation resources, constantly seeking to understand "what works and why" in this evolving world of online interaction. She teaches Online Facilitation and hosts the respected "Online Facilitation" email list. White writes and maintains a large collection of "how to" resources on online communication at: http://www.fullcirc.com/community/communitymanual.htm.

Index

A

altruism 75

B

best practices 19
boundaries 25, 51, 101, 107
building communities 110, 151, 197

C

case studies 25, 47, 99,
    107, 151, 167, 217, 252, 268
chief information officers 126
collaboration 144, 289
collective knowledge 72
common focus 138
communication 48, 157, 186, 208
Communities of Practice 2, 15, 25,
    37, 48, 59, 70, 79, 126,
    134, 143, 150,
    166, 185, 203, 217, 231,
    257, 244, 268, 283, 296
community building 110, 126, 151,
    204, 197

consensual knowledge 39
core members 162, 187
core team 127, 270
corporate context 171
customer communities of practice 107

D

decision-making 303
diversity 79

E

electronic networks of practice 231
ethnographies 2
expert locators 147
explicit knowledge 2, 26

F

face-to-face gatherings 289
face-to-face interaction 232, 258
face-to-face meeting 49, 63, 115,
    136, 154, 174, 190, 204
facilitation 29, 127, 136, 154, 186
financial benefits 3
finding "the expert" 16

G

guidelines 195

H

homophily 51, 80
human resource 5

I

identity 194, 217, 298
innovation 61, 80, 97, 107
innoversity 80
interaction 257
interfaces 263
invisible work 256
IT industry 126
IT platform 134

K

knowledge 76
knowledge base 60, 176
knowledge creation 249
knowledge exchange 109, 231, 248
Knowledge Management
    3, 21, 38, 59, 134, 144, 166, 231, 267
knowledge network 81, 257
knowledge outcomes 232
knowledge processes 38
knowledge repository 234
knowledge seekers 16
knowledge sharing
    17, 25, 37, 59, 143, 166, 231, 246
knowledge source 17

L

leadership 127, 244, 303
learning community 127, 152
learning organizations 59
legitimate peripheral participation
    18, 59, 187
literacy 261

M

make decisions 71
marketing 109

N

media richness 48
meeting face-to-face 268
mutual engagement 231

N

Networks of Practice 217
non-governmental organizations 283
non-profit organizations 283

O

online communities 185, 205, 246,
    257, 283
online international network community
    154
organizational benefits 3
organizational context 139
organizational dynamics 108
organizational effectiveness 25
ownership 186

P

participation 25, 231
peripheral participation 99
platform 261
public sector 267

R

reciprocity 41, 77, 233
relationship management (RM) 25

S

series of suggested guidelines 118
share 76
sharing of knowledge 217
situated 82
situated learning 259
social capital 2, 244
social interaction 2
social network 276
social network analysis 3, 91, 99, 171
social networks 10, 60, 101, 283

T

tacit 40, 62, 176, 234

tacit knowledge 6, 27, 114, 129
trust 21, 38, 71, 126, 244, 260, 270,
     287

V

values 135, 194
viability 135
virtual communities 231, 282
virtual communities of practice 203
virtual teams 233
volunteers 71, 289

NEW from Idea Group Publishing

- **The Enterprise Resource Planning Decade: Lessons Learned and Issues for the Future**, Frederic Adam and David Sammon/ ISBN:1-59140-188-7; eISBN 1-59140-189-5, © 2004
- **Electronic Commerce in Small to Medium-Sized Enterprises**, Nabeel A. Y. Al-Qirim/ ISBN: 1-59140-146-1; eISBN 1-59140-147-X, © 2004
- **e-Business, e-Government & Small and Medium-Size Enterprises: Opportunities & Challenges**, Brian J. Corbitt & Nabeel A. Y. Al-Qirim/ ISBN: 1-59140-202-6; eISBN 1-59140-203-4, © 2004
- **Multimedia Systems and Content-Based Image Retrieval**, Sagarmay Deb ISBN: 1-59140-156-9; eISBN 1-59140-157-7, © 2004
- **Computer Graphics and Multimedia: Applications, Problems and Solutions**, John DiMarco/ ISBN: 1-59140-196-86; eISBN 1-59140-197-6, © 2004
- **Social and Economic Transformation in the Digital Era**, Georgios Doukidis, Nikolaos Mylonopoulos & Nancy Pouloudi/ ISBN: 1-59140-158-5; eISBN 1-59140-159-3, © 2004
- **Information Security Policies and Actions in Modern Integrated Systems**, Mariagrazia Fugini & Carlo Bellettini/ ISBN: 1-59140-186-0; eISBN 1-59140-187-9, © 2004
- **Digital Government: Principles and Best Practices**, Alexei Pavlichev & G. David Garson/ISBN: 1-59140-122-4; eISBN 1-59140-123-2, © 2004
- **Virtual and Collaborative Teams: Process, Technologies and Practice**, Susan H. Godar & Sharmila Pixy Ferris/ ISBN: 1-59140-204-2; eISBN 1-59140-205-0, © 2004
- **Intelligent Enterprises of the 21st Century**, Jatinder Gupta & Sushil Sharma/ ISBN: 1-59140-160-7; eISBN 1-59140-161-5, © 2004
- **Creating Knowledge Based Organizations**, Jatinder Gupta & Sushil Sharma/ ISBN: 1-59140-162-3; eISBN 1-59140-163-1, © 2004
- **Knowledge Networks: Innovation through Communities of Practice**, Paul Hildreth & Chris Kimble/ISBN: 1-59140-200-X; eISBN 1-59140-201-8, © 2004
- **Going Virtual: Distributed Communities of Practice**, Paul Hildreth/ISBN: 1-59140-164-X; eISBN 1-59140-165-8, © 2004
- **Trust in Knowledge Management and Systems in Organizations**, Maija-Leena Huotari & Mirja Iivonen/ ISBN: 1-59140-126-7; eISBN 1-59140-127-5, © 2004
- **Strategies for Managing IS/IT Personnel**, Magid Igbaria & Conrad Shayo/ISBN: 1-59140-128-3; eISBN 1-59140-129-1, © 2004
- **Beyond Knowledge Management**, Brian Lehaney, Steve Clarke, Elayne Coakes & Gillian Jack/ ISBN: 1-59140-180-1; eISBN 1-59140-181-X, © 2004
- **eTransformation in Governance: New Directions in Government and Politics**, Matti Mälkiä, Ari Veikko Anttiroiko & Reijo Savolainen/ISBN: 1-59140-130-5; eISBN 1-59140-131-3, © 2004
- **Intelligent Agents for Data Mining and Information Retrieval**, Masoud Mohammadian/ISBN: 1-59140-194-1; eISBN 1-59140-195-X, © 2004
- **Using Community Informatics to Transform Regions**, Stewart Marshall, Wal Taylor & Xinghuo Yu/ISBN: 1-59140-132-1; eISBN 1-59140-133-X, © 2004
- **Wireless Communications and Mobile Commerce**, Nan Si Shi/ ISBN: 1-59140-184-4; eISBN 1-59140-185-2, © 2004
- **Organizational Data Mining: Leveraging Enterprise Data Resources for Optimal Performance**, Hamid R. Nemati & Christopher D. Barko/ ISBN: 1-59140-134-8; eISBN 1-59140-135-6, © 2004
- **Virtual Teams: Projects, Protocols and Processes**, David J. Pauleen/ISBN: 1-59140-166-6; eISBN 1-59140-167-4, © 2004
- **Business Intelligence in the Digital Economy: Opportunities, Limitations and Risks**, Mahesh Raisinghani/ ISBN: 1-59140-206-9; eISBN 1-59140-207-7, © 2004
- **E-Business Innovation and Change Management**, Mohini Singh & Di Waddell/ISBN: 1-59140-138-0; eISBN 1-59140-139-9, © 2004
- **Responsible Management of Information Systems**, Bernd Stahl/ISBN: 1-59140-172-0; eISBN 1-59140-173-9, © 2004
- **Web Information Systems**, David Taniar/ISBN: 1-59140-208-5; eISBN 1-59140-209-3, © 2004
- **Strategies for Information Technology Governance**, Wim van Grembergen/ISBN: 1-59140-140-2; eISBN 1-59140-141-0, © 2004
- **Information and Communication Technology for Competitive Intelligence**, Dirk Vriens/ISBN: 1-59140-142-9; eISBN 1-59140-143-7, © 2004
- **The Handbook of Information Systems Research**, Michael E. Whitman & Amy B. Woszczynski/ISBN: 1-59140-144-5; eISBN 1-59140-145-3, © 2004
- **Neural Networks in Business Forecasting**, G. Peter Zhang/ISBN: 1-59140-176-3; eISBN 1-59140-177-1, © 2004